GW01336073

ALFRED O'RAHILLY
III: CONTROVERSIALIST
Part 2: Catholic Apologist

1. Monsignor Alfred O'Rahilly at Blackrock College, August 1960

J. ANTHONY GAUGHAN

Alfred O'Rahilly

III: CONTROVERSIALIST
Part 2: Catholic Apologist

KINGDOM BOOKS

Printed in the Republic of Ireland
at the Leinster Leader, Naas, County Kildare,
for
KINGDOM BOOKS
56 Newtownpark Avenue, Blackrock, County Dublin.

First published 1993

BRITISH LIBRARY CATALOGUING IN PUBLICATION DATA

Gaughan, J. Anthony (John Anthony)
  Alfred O'Rahilly
    III: Controversialist
    Part 2: Catholic Apologist
  I. Title
378.41956

ISBN 0 – 9506015 – 9 – 4

Copyright under the Berne Convention, all rights reserved. Apart from fair dealing for study or review, no part of this publication may be reproduced, stored in a retrieval system or transmitted, in any form or by any means, electronic, mechanical, photocopying, recording, or otherwise, without the prior permission of Kingdom Books.

© J. Anthony Gaughan 1993

ACKNOWLEDGEMENTS

In connection with the preparation of this book I wish to thank the library staffs of the Central Catholic Library, Dublin Public Library, the library of the Jesuit House of Studies, Milltown Park, the National Library of Ireland, the Royal Irish Academy, University College, Cork, University College and Trinity College, Dublin, for their courtesy and help; the archivists, librarians and custodians of the various institutions and the private individuals mentioned on pp. 317 and 322 for allowing me to consult papers and records in their charge; and all who gave me information, especially those whose names appear on pp. 320-22.

I am indebted to Fr Michael F. McCarthy, C.S.Sp., Walter McGrath, Cornelius Murphy, Rev. Dr Michael O'Carroll, C.S.Sp., Tadhg Ó Cearbhaill and Professor Kathleen O'Flaherty for much helpful criticism.

I am grateful to Dónal J. Counihan, Pádraig de Bháldraithe, Enda Delaney, Patrick Maume, Cornelius Murphy, Fr Fergus O'Donoghue, S.J., and Dónal Ó Luanaigh for drawing my attention to important source material.

As with regard to Volumes I, II and III, Pt 1, I am particularly indebted to Pádraig Ó Snodaigh, Dr C. J. Woods and especially Maurice O'Connell for their continuing, exceptional and practical interest in the progress of this work.

I am grateful to Helen Murray for typing the manuscript and to Mrs Eileen Francis for assistance in this regard.

An acknowledgement is due to the late Liam Miller for the design and layout of the book.

I feel honoured in having this book launched by Monsignor Patrick J. Corish, historian and former president of St Patrick's College, Maynooth, and in having the foreword to it written by Senator J. J. Lee, professor of modern history, University College, Cork.

J. ANTHONY GAUGHAN
56 Newtownpark Avenue
Blackrock
County Dublin
1 May 1993

To the memory of
Kevin McNamara, archbishop of Dublin (1984-1987),
ecce sacerdos magnus

CONTENTS

Acknowledgements 5

List of Illustrations 9

Foreword 11

Introduction 12

Part 2: Catholic Apologist

Religious Writing and Lecturing 13

Defender of Religion, Christianity and Irish Catholicism 53

Upholder of Catholic Social Theory 85

A Priest at last 128

The Final Years 170

Epilogue 213

Appendices	217
1 Radio Talk by Alfred O'Rahilly on Thérèse Neumann	217
2 Alfred O'Rahilly's Reply to H. G. Wells in the *Standard*	224
3 Cork Corporation and the Proposal for a New Maternity Hospital in the City	284
4 Editorial drafted by Alfred O'Rahilly in *Standard* of 20 April 1951	290
5 'The Doctor, the State and the Community' by Alfred O'Rahilly	293
6 Psychological Profile of Alfred O'Rahilly	305
Addendum	309
Corrections	314
Sources	317
Index	328

LIST OF ILLUSTRATIONS

1. Monsignor Alfred O'Rahilly at Blackrock College, August 1960 (photo. Fr Seán Farragher, C.S.Sp.) *frontispiece*

2. The O'Rahilly family in the garden of their home at Listowel, 1890 *between* pp. 128-9

3. Third year philosophers, including Alfred, St Mary's Hall, Stonyhurst, summer 1911

4. Alfred with Joseph Downey and Professor Arthur Pennington at the National Institute of Dairy Research, Reading, August 1924

5. Alfred with Professor William Magennis, Séamus Caomhánach and Professor Joseph Reilly at Konigshof Hotel, Bonn, August 1935

6. Alfred with Timothy O'Mahony and Fr Thomas F. Duggan in Hamburg, August 1939

7. Alfred addressing a session of the Summer School of the Catholic Social Guild at Stonyhurst, July 1947 (photo. Ronan O'Rahilly)

8. Alfred with Joseph P. Walshe, the Irish ambassador to the Holy See, in Rome, June 1950 (photo. Ronan O'Rahilly)

9. Group, including Alfred, at U.C.C. on conferring day, October 1942 (photo. *Cork Examiner*) *between* pp. 160-1

10. Alfred with Professor Denis Gwynn and John Pius Boland at U.C.C. on conferring day, 18 July 1950 (photo. *Cork Examiner*)

11. Cartoon of Alfred and College F.C.A. guard of honour at public reception and garden party, hosted by U.C.C. for Cardinal John D'Alton, 17 June 1953 (*Quarryman* 1953)

12. Alfred addressing Catholic University Students' Congress at U.C.C., 1 July 1953 (photo. *Cork Examiner*)

13. Group, including Alfred, after his ordination at Blackrock College, 18 December 1955 (*Standard* 23 December 1955) *between* pp. 192-3

14. Alfred with Archbishop John J. McCarthy and Fr Vincent J. Dinan, C.S.Sp., at Blackrock College, August 1960 (photo. Fr Seán Farragher, C.S.Sp.)

15. Group, including Alfred, at Clonliffe College centenary celebration on 12 October 1960 (photo. Lafayette)

16. Alfred with General Seán Mac Eoin and Frank Duff at Booterstown church, 7 July 1965

FOREWORD

Alfred O'Rahilly III: Controversialist, Part 2: Catholic Apologist brings to a conclusion a remarkable study of a remarkable man. The sub-titles of Fr J. Anthony Gaughan's four volumes on O'Rahilly, Academic, Public Figure, Social Reformer, and now Catholic Apologist, are an indication of the variety of roles played by O'Rahilly over half a century of frenetic activity. And how he played those roles! Given the vigour of his commitment, any one of them would have sufficed to exhaust an ordinary mortal. But he brought extraordinary energy and ability to all of them. A prodigious worker, and formidably learned, he ranged widely over numerous fields. His thinking, an intriguing mixture of the traditional and the innovative, defies facile labelling by those who like to slot their subjects into convenient pigeon holes.

Fr Gaughan never makes that mistake. Only an accomplished biographer could have struck the right balance in dealing with so myriad minded a man, and so controversial a subject, in a manner that is fair both to O'Rahilly and to his numerous critics. Fr Gaughan's previous studies of neglected biographical subjects like Austin Stack, Tom O'Donnell, Constable Jeremiah Mee, R.I.C., and Thomas Johnson, which were themselves notable contributions to historical understanding, have equipped him to approach even so formidable a subject as O'Rahilly with insight and sensitivity.

The material that Fr Gaughan has so assiduously assembled, and his judicious assessment of that material, must be taken into account by anyone concerned not only with the life of O'Rahilly, but with arriving at a balanced perspective on the Ireland of his generation. That Ireland is rapidly disappearing, for better or for worse – probably for better and for worse. Although O'Rahilly died as recently as 1969, he seems to belong to a different age. That makes Fr Gaughan's study even more valuable, as a record of an epoch unfamiliar to a younger generation, and one which is in danger of being treated dismissively by an uncomprehending, if not actually hostile, later public.

O'Rahilly has been fortunate in his biographer. By achieving the right tone between engagement and detachment, by his respect for the evidence, and by his sureness of touch on so many controversial topics, Fr Gaughan has put all students of modern Ireland deeply in his debt.

J. J. LEE
Department of Modern History
University College, Cork (15 July 1993)

INTRODUCTION

Alfred O'Rahilly I: Academic dealt with Alfred O'Rahilly's remarkable career as an academic and a scholar. *Alfred O'Rahilly II: Public Figure* treated of Alfred as a public figure and as a leader and moulder of public opinion from 1915 to 1954. *Alfred O'Rahilly III: Controversialist, Part 1: Social Reformer* traced his career as a controversialist in his role as a social reformer.

This second part of volume III considers Alfred as a Catholic apologist. It also describes his final years, from his wife's death in September 1953 to his own in August 1969.

RELIGIOUS WRITING AND LECTURING

Alfred's output of religious writing and lecturing was varied and considerable. The pamphlet *Faith and facts*, his first work in apologetics, was published by the Catholic Evidence Guild in London in 1917. This compendium of Catholic doctrine proved to be a popular *vade mecum* and was reissued in Dublin in 1928.[1]

The Eucharist

Alfred had an exceptional reverence for the Eucharist and throughout his life attended Mass daily. When the opportunity arose he took peculiar delight in standing in for the altar servers. He continued to attend Mass daily even when he was abroad, as when he represented the Irish Free State at the I.L.O. conferences at Geneva in 1924, 1925 and 1932. He frequently recalled that after the day's deliberations almost invariably he and some of the other distinguished representatives discussed religion well into the night. Quite a few of them were staunch defenders of Catholicism. Yet, each morning Alfred would find himself to be the only visitor at the local *abbé*'s Mass.

Owing to his wife's illness, Alfred was unable to attend the Mass in the Phoenix Park, Dublin, which was the climax of the Eucharistic Congress at the end of June 1932. In an article written on the following day and published in the *Catholic Mind* of July 1932 he recorded his impressions of the Mass which he heard broadcast by Radio Éireann. He described how he had participated in the Mass, and in the recitation of the Rosary during the procession preceding it, in the diningroom of an hotel. And he continued in what must have come very close to capturing the mood of the Irish Catholic psyche:

1. While upholding the value of a *vade mecum* and even the 'penny catechism', Alfred was acutely aware of the importance of continuing religious education. In the *Standard* of 24 September 1948 there was a criticism that the religious knowledge then taught in the primary schools was not relevant, particularly as it did not mention communism. Alfred replied in the same issue that he was opposed to lessening the time devoted to the religious instruction of young children in order to deal with subjects, such as communism, which would be neither intelligible nor tempting to them until many years later. For him the real dangers to be avoided in religious education were: (1) formalism in religion and abstractness in its teaching and (2) want of further education at a later period when problems, such as communism, had become real and pressing.

Alfred O'Rahilly III: Controversialist

> For a brief space our land was a vast cathedral, vibrant with the prayer of millions. We were all at that great Mass in the Park, we all knelt for the Benediction. Not only we, but our forbears. It was as if the pent-up religion of our persecuted ancestors had been waiting for this glorious day of triumphant expression. The Mass-rocks in the hills must have leapt for joy, and the spirits of those who once gathered in little thatched Mass-houses must have been hovering near. One felt one's individuality merged in a great racial resurrection; today each of us was but the representative of those to whose heroic sacrifices we owe our faith. And when at the Elevation we heard the tinkle of Patrick's bell, we knew that that sound has gone forth to the ends of the earth. *Exivit sonus eorum.* In a simpler world men of our race carried the gospel to them that sat in darkness. So today we thank God for our spiritual heritage, we join with our faithful departed in an act of national homage to Christ our King, and we pledge ourselves to take up in a neo-pagan world the God-given mission of our race.

Alfred then declared that, while the Irish treasured the faith, a great deal remained to be done to carry out its imperatives. He highlighted the social ills of the country, including the 'hideous slums' in Dublin and elsewhere, and asked 'Is Dublin a city of Catholic culture because a million people congregated there for Mass?'

Alfred was invited to make the Irish contribution to the Eucharistic Congress in Budapest in the last week of May 1938. He prepared a paper entitled 'The social implications of the Eucharist'. However, owing to academic commitments, he was not able to travel to the Congress and the paper was read by his friend, Francis O'Reilly, secretary of the C.T.S.I. Alfred began with a remarkably detailed description of the social co-operation and organisation of the early Christian community. Since then, he noted, the social problem had become infinitely more complex. One saw in the *Acts of the Apostles* the close association of the social fellowship with the breaking of the bread, the sacred meal instituted by Christ after he had washed the feet of the apostles. He urged his co-religionists to find in the Eucharist the simple freshness of fellowship which first blossomed in the cenacle.

Religious Writing and Lecturing
Papal infallibility

Alfred was a doughty defender of the doctrine of papal infallibility. In a review of René Fülöp Miller's *The power and secret of the papacy* (London 1937) in the *Irish Independent* of 23 November 1937 he acknowledged that the author, a non-Catholic, had dealt sympathetically with the First Vatican Council, Pius IX, Leo XIII and to a lesser extent his three successors. However, he pointed out that the author had failed to distinguish between (1) the infallible magisterium and (2) the fallible administrative and diplomatic acts of the pope. He was dismissive of the author's comment that the *Syllabus or collection of modern errors* of 1864 'summarised and denounced the whole thinking of the new age'. With justification he claimed to have 'demolished' this 'stupid view' in his comprehensive article 'The Syllabus' in the *Irish Ecclesiastical Record* of January 1933.

'Why I am a Catholic'

On 27 November 1938 in the Gresham Hotel in Dublin under the auspices of the Legion of Mary Alfred delivered a lecture entitled 'Why I am a Catholic'. He stated that he had consented to speak on the subject because, apart from being proud to be a Catholic, he considered that he should at least be ready to stand up and proclaim the faith that was in him when thousands in Mexico, Spain and Russia had recently died for that faith. Reflection on the subject convinced him that he had so much to say on the subject that he would require to give not one but twelve lectures. At the outset he dealt with the authenticity of the New Testament. Then taking Christ's resurrection, the central fact of the New Testament, he asked was any historical event half so much vouched for?

The New Testament, however, Alfred continued, could not be an adequate guide to the full teaching of Christ. He claimed to illustrate this by taking each of the seven sacraments and showing how, relying on the New Testament alone, Martin Luther had to shift his position and admit that he could not arrive at certainty regarding their number. This showed the need for a teaching Church, a guiding Church, which was capable of interpreting and instructing. In a typical sally, he referred to a splendid book written in answer to Luther by Henry VIII, which earned for its author the title of Defender of the Faith – a title still retained by English monarchs, though they now represented a complete denial of much of what Henry VIII defended. He stressed the impossibility of measuring spiritual things by material standards and counselled an attitude of humility in matters of faith. In an explanation of why he had not touched on papal infallibility or the primacy of Peter, he said that apologists no longer dwelt on answering questions on these subjects. Once one proved the necessity for a teaching Church there was no claimant for that position other than the Catholic Church.

Alfred concluded by listing aspects of the Catholic Church which appealed particularly to him. It was a religion in which the essentials were clear, yet in which one had a great sense of freedom. Moreover, it was universal and one. It was the only effective custodian of spiritual and corporate liberty and stood for the noble and decent things in life against licence and sensuality. Above all, it was founded on reason and satisfied all the needs of man.

Critic of political systems and contemporary philosophers

On 8 November 1942 Alfred was at his doughtiest as defender of the faith when delivering a lecture entitled 'To whom shall we go?' in the Aberdeen Hall, Gresham Hotel, Dublin, again under the auspices of the Legion of Mary. He recalled that two thousand years earlier that question was asked and answered by the questioner himself. It had again become particularly relevant with a bewildered world groping through chaos and disorder for a new order. Alfred surveyed the main political philosophies which men had worked out and tried to make the basis of ordered existence. He pointed to the fallacies inherent in them and their invariable tendency to end in dictatorship, the loss of human dignity and personal freedom, the destruction of spiritual values and the deflection of men's activities from their true goal. Any system chosen should stand or fall according as it was informed by the spirit of Christianity. This spirit was to be found pre-eminently in the Catholic Church which was the last bulwark of corporate freedom and the greatest champion of moral truth. The Church had never been assimilated by the State and its greatest victory was the separation of spiritual and secular authority, not a divorcement of one from the other, but a defining of the sphere of authority of each in which each was supreme. The Reformation had in many countries destroyed that scheme of things and religion had become merely a department of the State and they now had the phenomenon of State idolatry, based on bad philosophy and bad religion.

Alfred was severely critical of some contemporary philosophers, including Professor Cyril Edwin Mitchinson Joad and Bertrand Russell. He referred to a British bio-chemist who had inquired into the nature of sin and concluded that it was a chemical product! He was equally dismissive of a trend in educational theory that all the child needed was protection from hostile influences leaving the rest to spontaneous action. Such philosophies and theories could not sustain a 'new order'. The common good, the good of the State, even the material welfare of the individual were not strong enough motives to hold the human being to right action in times of stress. There had to be a supernatural foundation for human conduct and a spiritual end to be attained and a spiritual authority to instruct and direct towards the attainment of that end. All social systems were to be assessed according as they were inspired or not by the spirit of Christianity.

Science and religion

In November 1942 Alfred, with Fr James Bastible, organised a course in Catholic apologetics at U.C.C. As part of the course each year he delivered eight lectures on 'Science and religion'. These and an extra lecture were broadcast from Radio Éireann on Sunday evenings from 23 January 1944 onwards. In the first lecture 'What is science?' he explained that science dealt with the 'how' and not the 'why of things'. It was purely descriptive and had nothing to do with cause or substance. Many modern philosophies had succumbed to the mesmeric ideas of science, but fundamental philosophy, including natural religion, was independent of science. It was not the business of science to deal with fundamentals or values. He warned people to sharpen their critical faculties and to immunise themselves against scientists who exaggerated their own competence and 'wandered off their beat', and suggested that there was no answer to the riddle of life. There was, but it was beyond science.

In his second talk 'Science and God' he declared that the scientist's job was to describe the behaviour of things. Such a procedure was quite incapable of proving or disproving the existence of God. Alfred again warned against 'the blandishments of scientists who, leaving their equations and their laboratories, pontificate irresponsibly on fundamental questions on which ordinary people are just as competent to pronounce'. In his third talk, 'The Catholic Church and science' he put forward the proposition that no doctrine of the Church or teaching of the faith was at variance with established scientific facts. He dismissed the argument that non-Catholic scientists began their investigations without bias and many of them rejected their religion. Everyone, he insisted, had a bias and the loss of religion had nothing to do with science. Alfred's fourth talk was on 'The alleged warfare of science and theology'. He dealt with the condemnation of Galileo. No defence could be made of the condemnation, he conceded, but he pointed out that the churchmen involved had been misled by the science of their day and that opponents of the Church had utterly exaggerated the significance of the incident. He compared modern scientists unfavourably with the Church. They were gradually and pointlessly being absorbed by the great State machine but the Church stood where it always stood – a great peaceful international body without arms, without force, asserting man's spiritual independence.

Alfred's fifth broadcast talk was on 'The Bible and evolution'. The Bible was a spur not an obstacle to scientific investigation and discovery. Christians in general and Catholic priests in particular had ever been in the forefront in archaeology and cultural anthropology. Catholics and especially priests advocated the advancement of scientific knowledge and knew that the deeper one delved the more one had need of God to give meaning and purpose to life. The sixth talk was on evolution. Alfred declared that the fundamental differences about the theory of evolution were not theological but rational and the debate on the subject was in no way a religious issue. In his next talk on 'Science and ethics' he dealt with nineteenth-century agnostics such as Thomas Henry Huxley and Charles Darwin, pointing out that even they retained the moral code of Christianity, the creed of which they had rejected. That old liberal creedlessness was not natural to man, who, if he rejected God, created his own idols, the idol of some being the all-powerful State. He criticised the more extravagant claims of the proponents of psycho-analytic theory and agreed that scientists, on finding life, according to their analysis, to be so 'pauperised' had decided to restore religion 'as an emotion'. The near religion of science, however, would never satisfy man and he challenged scientists to have the honesty to either accept Christianity or reject it.

In his eighth talk, 'Miracles', Alfred maintained that Catholics approached this subject with critical minds and free from extreme prejudices. They differed from many others, for whom the question of the possibility of miracles was foreclosed before ever reaching the examination of facts. Some modern intellectuals were so overladen with specialist prejudices that they were unable to find room for inconvenient facts. One could reject the miracles at Lourdes, but in such a case common honesty should compel one to produce some explanation for happenings, such as the sudden disappearance of tumours. He argued that the evidence of miracles at Lourdes was such as would impress anyone without agnostic blinkers. In a final talk, 'Science and education', Alfred dealt with objections and queries which he had received. The success of education he declared was not to be judged by the diffusion of knowledge of physical and natural science, for this might be made the tool of a false ideology and the totalitarian State. Rather was it to be assessed by how far people were enabled to assert their natural rights against financiers, bureaucrats and technocrats to pursue human ideals. He warned that the tendency of science was to treat men as things and to ignore the sacred rights of human personality, which was alien to the microscope and test tube. Science enabled men to blow Monte Cassino into a shapeless ruin, but only Christ could shape men into the monks who founded it.

Alfred intended to compile a book on religion and science based on his nine radio talks. Pressure of work, however, prevented him from doing so and in *Religion and science* he had the talks published in 1948.

Alfred O'Rahilly III: Controversialist

Doctrine of the Assumption of Mary

The doctrine of the Assumption of Mary was defined as a dogma of faith by Pope Pius XII on 1 November 1950. The announcement that the pope intended to define the dogma signalled the beginning of a great deal of adverse comment by the evangelical Churches. The editor of the *Standard* requested Alfred to prepare some articles on the subject, especially in view of criticisms made by the Anglican archbishops of Canterbury and of York which received wisespread coverage in the press and were broadcast on the B.B.C.

In 'Our Lady's Assumption: Protestants and the pope' in the *Standard* of 1 September 1950 Alfred stated that he had received a five-page article by Victor Bennett on the proposed dogma, reprinted from *Theology* of September 1948. This had been circulated as a pamphlet to him and others as among 'those who are able to bring any influence direct or indirect on the Roman authorities'. He expressed his amazement at the seeming ignorance of Bennett of the immense historical and critical output of Catholic scholars on the subject. The attitude of Bennett and his colleagues, Alfred claimed, was summed up in: 'We are united in holding that the Church of England was right to take the stand which it took in the sixteenth century and is still bound to resist the claims of the contemporary papacy.' He wondered then why they were so exercised that the pope should not say something unacceptable to those outside the Catholic Church. In 'Theology and history' in the *Standard* of 8 September 1950 Alfred addressed Bennett's objections: 'The point of present importance . . . is the ridiculous notion that from a theological argument you can establish a historical fact. The historical data on which to build up a certitude for the Assumption is quite inadequate.' Alfred pointed out that Catholic scholars were in unanimous agreement that the bodily resurrection and assumption of Mary could be no more established by historic proofs than her death and burial. However, this in no way affected belief in the Assumption, as the Catholic Church held that a fact implied in a dogma could become a tenet of the faith, though it lacked historical proof.

In 'The pope and the dogma' in the *Standard* of 15 September Alfred took issue with the contention of adversaries that the pope was intent on forcing the dogma on a reluctant people and particularly on recalcitrant scholars. He illustrated at length how the Holy See was in close touch with bishops, theologians and people and that the pope did not exercise his prerogative positively without long investigation and consultation. In the same issue of the *Standard*, Alfred replied to an article by C. W. Dugmore in the *Manchester Guardian* of 5 August 1950. Dugmore, who was the lecturer in ecclesiastical history in the University of Manchester, claimed that support for the definiton of the dogma was contrived in that 'the mass of the ignorant peasantry in Ireland, Spain and Latin America had been exhorted by the pope to petition for the definition of the new dogma'. This was a very partial explanation of the provenance of the dogma of the Assumption, replied Alfred. The pope had consulted the Catholic bishops of the world in the matter. Moreover, a number of national and international congresses – involving the theologians of some thirty nations, including Belgium, Poland and the United States – had, after study and debate, sent petitions for the doctrine to be defined as had two hundred universities, theological faculties and major seminaries. To Dugmore's contention that there had been Catholic 'protests against the proposal to define' the doctrine, Alfred pointed out that this was not very significant, amounting to only a small number of Catholic theologians who had availed of their undoubted liberty to argue not against the belief but against its definition as a dogma of faith. Alfred declared that Dugmore's charge that the pope's policy of 'setting up a totalitarian Church' indicated an ignorance of the manner in which doctrine developed in the Catholic Church from popular devotion through theological debate to authoritative definition by council or pope. Finally, Dugmore protested against a measure which would injure 'the growth of understanding between Christians'. In reply, Alfred took no prisoners. He asked do not Protestants understand very well what is meant by the Assumption? Did Dugmore mean to imply the misleading idea that Anglicans were slowly swallowing the Council of Trent but would find it difficult to digest this new morsel. In some fundamental ways, he continued, the Thirty-Nine Articles were nearer the Catholic position than *Doctrine in the Church of England*, issued in 1938. In this document the signatories could not agree and therefore Anglicans need not agree on: whether Christ had a human father; whether he worked any miracles; whether he rose corporeally; whether he is present in any real sense in the Blessed Sacrament; whether there are angels and devils; whether there was a Fall; whether there is eternal punishment and so on. This was the outcome, after fifteen years' work, of a commission appointed by the predecessors of the two leading Anglican archbishops who were then waxing indignant at the Catholic Church for consecrating an almost universally-held belief in the Eastern and Western parts of the Christian world.

In 'History of the belief' in the *Standard* of 22 September 1950 Alfred demonstrated that there was explicit literary evidence for belief in the Assumption from the fourth century; that doubts later arose due to a repugnance to accept the irrelevant and exaggerated accounts contained in legends; that those legends, however, testified to a belief in the Assumption in the third or even the second century; and that the festival in honour of the Assumption was celebrated from the latter half of the sixth century onwards. In 'The Catholic rule of faith' in the *Standard* of 29 September he wrote that it was irrelevant for the archbishops of Canterbury and of York to urge against the dogma that 'the Church of England refuses to regard as requisite for a saving faith any doctrines or opinions which are not plainly contained in the scripture'. The history of the Church, he claimed, showed the fundamental fallacy of that position. With gusto he then criticised the treatment of the subject by the British quality journals and newspapers. The *Spectator* denounced the 'incredible indifference to historical science' of Catholics and announced the 'proclamation of a complete divorce of the Christian religion from intellect and reason'. This attitude of intellectual superiority, noted Alfred, was reminiscent of Tacitus and Celsus. He described how Kingsley Martin, editor of the 'near Marxist *New Statesman*', mocked with execrable taste this 'geographical' transfer of 'the body of a middle-aged woman' and suggested that 'the pope appeals to the miraculous to save his flock from Marxist materialism'. To the *New Statesman*'s summing-up of its treatment of the subject: 'We are Protestants or nothing', Alfred retorted 'Chiefly nothing'. The *Daily Worker* employed T. A. Jackson, who for many years was the leader of the League of Militant Atheists in Great Britain, to explain that the new dogma was designed 'to placate the peasants'. Alfred observed that peasants, which was once synonymous with pagans, was now, it seems, accepted as the proper epithet for Catholics. The *Church Times*, noted Alfred, rather wishfully anticipated 'conscientious secessions' of 'educated Roman Catholics'.

At the conclusion of these articles Alfred expressed his regret at having to argue with fellow-Christians. He suggested that it would be much better if Anglicans and Catholics recognised how much they had in common and that there was a general acceptance of the fact that the views of the two denominations on Church dogma differed. However, there was a sting in the tail of his piece. He wrote of the Anglican opponents of the dogma: 'If they would drop their sneering at Rome, we could work together more efficiently against Moscow.'

In a series of thirteen articles in the *Standard* from 1 December 1950 to 23 February 1951 Alfred raked over the embers of opposition to the dogma of the Assumption.[2] In the first three articles he claimed to explain why (1) Protestants and (2) some intellectuals had found the proclamation of the dogma a provocation. The Protestant opposition he ascribed largely to an obsessional phobia of Rome. That of some intellectuals he claimed was due to an out-of-date Voltairian anti-clericalism. They were under the delusion that, if they ousted the Church from public life, they could replace it by a pliable liberal state. This, however, seldom occurred. Rather was the Church replaced by a Church-State, wherein the upholders of a 'liberal ethic' were given short shrift.

The Church of Ireland bishops published a 'pastoral on the new dogma' in the *Irish Times* of 15 December 1950. It was also published in full in the *Derry Journal* and elsewhere. In the *Standard* of 22 December Alfred expressed his disappointment that the appearance of a Church of Ireland pastoral, which was a rare event, was prompted not by the necessity to warn members of the Church of Ireland against agnosticism and communism but to give 'official guidance' on, and to make a 'public protest' against, the Catholic dogma of the Assumption. He pointed out that the Catholic debate on the dogma had not

---

2. By that time Alfred, it seems, had developed almost an obsession with regard to the dogma of the Assumption and the attitude of Anglican divines to it. His enthusiasm for the subject was shared by very few of his colleagues. On at least one occasion John Busteed quickly ended a discussion by remarking that all dogmas could be considered to be assumptions!

contained the smallest piece of polemic against Protestantism and that there never had been any suggestion that Protestants were expected to join Catholics in their belief in it. He ridiculed the charge that the 'Roman Church' by defining the dogma was cutting itself off from 'the rest of Catholic Christendom'. In 'By what authority?' in the *Standard* of 29 December Alfred painted a jaundiced picture of the Church of Ireland. He concluded that 'the prelates of this little man-made Church could only be regarded by their flock as convenient officials under the constitution of 1870'. Their Church's credal statements were bowdlerised and mutilated to suit their Calvinist-minded fellow members. Nor was there any finality about their creed; it could be altered by a suitable majority. Were such men, he asked, in a position 'to throw mud at the world-wide episcopacy in communion with the see of Peter?'

In 'The Church and the book' in the *Standard* of 5 January 1951 Alfred pointed out that common to all Protestant denominations was the replacement of the Church by the Bible as the final deposit of revealed truth. The weakness of this position he illustrated with a quotation from Ronald Knox's *The belief of Catholics* (London 1937):

> The inspiration of the Bible was a doctrine which had been believed, before the Reformation, on the mere authority of the Church; it rested on exactly the same basis as the doctrine of transubstantiation. Protestantism repudiated transubstantiation and in so doing repudiated the authority of the Church; and then, without a shred of logic, calmly went on believing in the inspiration of the Bible, as if nothing had happened! Then Christians – nay even clergymen – began to wonder about Genesis, began to have scruples about the genuineness of II Peter. And then quite suddenly it beame apparent that there was no reason why Protestants should not doubt the inspiration of the Bible . . . For three centuries the inspired Bible had been a handy stick to beat Catholics with; then it broke in the hand that wielded it, and Protestantism flung it languidly aside.

Alfred characterised the authors of the Church of Ireland pastoral as waxing indignant at Catholics for believing a dogma not in the Bible. In so doing they had coolly assumed the very criterion by which they differed from Catholics; in effect, they were criticising Catholics for not being good Protestants.

In 'The pastoral and the pope', 'The mother of God', 'Our Lady in the gospels', 'Protestant prejudices', 'Devotion to Our Lady', and 'An Anthology of Our Lady' (*Standard* 12, 19, 26 January, 2, 9, 16 February 1951), Alfred exhibited a remarkable knowledge of Christology, Mariology, the development of the Roman primacy and the history of the Christian belief in the Assumption. In 'Nailing a lie' in the *Standard* of 23 February he took issue with an editorial in the *Church of Ireland Gazette and Family Newspaper* of 15 December which read:

> The teaching of the Church of Rome since the twelfth century had been to deny religious liberty to those outside her communion; and her practice has been, and is, to use repressive measures wherever she has the power to do so. We could fill this issue of the *Gazette* with proofs of these statements by extracts from the official teaching of the Roman Catholic Church, illustrations from history and reports of present-day happenings.

The editor quoted Louis Veuillot, the French Catholic writer, in support of his charge: 'When we are in a minority, we ask for religious liberty in the name of your Protestant principles. When we are in the majority, we refuse it in the name of ours.' Alfred established with authority the natural history of the quotation as follows: (1) The phrase was never used by Veuillot and was repudiated by him. (2) It was used by Montalembert as a controversial dig at an opponent. (3) He took it from Macaulay, for whom he had a misplaced admiration. (4) Macaulay, in using the phrase, made no specific reference to Catholics; he applied it to 'all bigots of all sects'. Not content on leaving the battleground without a final salvo, Alfred pointed out to the editor of the *Church of Ireland Gazette* that the quotation was particularly applicable to that Church which three centuries earlier had declared that 'the religion of papists is superstition and idolatrous' to tolerate which would be 'a grievous sin' and which at that time – having been stripped of its physical power – was proclaiming the duty of the defamed Catholic majority 'to tolerate truth'.

Alfred O'Rahilly III: Controversialist

Alfred's articles were widely read and discussed. No attempt was made to answer his sharp criticism of the Church of Ireland pastoral. In a letter, published in the *Standard* of 5 January 1951, Harvey Evans of Trinity College, Dublin, challenged the editor to publish the pastoral in full and give his readers a chance to judge for themselves whether it was written in the spirit of an 'attack on our fellow Christians' and whether 'Dr O'Rahilly's many criticisms' were justified or not. In a note in the same issue Alfred expressed his regret to have found it his duty to defend his religion against the Church of Ireland which should be a close ally against agnosticism and communism. He pointed out that the pastoral had been published in full in at least two other Irish newspapers besides the *Irish Times* which had numerous Catholic readers. It was clear that the pastoral, instead of confining itself to the scriptural issue which alone concerned the author's creed, was a deliberate attack on the Catholic belief and dogma of the Assumption of Our Lady. He continued that, if he had misrepresented the views of its authors, he would be glad to have any such instance pointed out to him for rectification. And he concluded: 'I fail to discover in the vague letter of Mr Harvey Evans any proof that I have been inaccurate or unfair. He cannot deny that the legend [concerning the Assumption] has been distorted, that Benedict XIV is wrongly and partially quoted, and that the pope has been declared a heretic and the Catholic Church a sectarian organisation.'

Clash with W. B. Stanford

Alfred had a deep and abiding love for the Catholic Church as an institution and felt obliged to respond to attacks on it from any quarter. In April 1944 W. B. Stanford, regius professor of Greek in T.C.D., published *A recognised Church: the Church of Ireland in Éire*. He complained that unacceptable politico-economic and religious pressures were being exerted on him and his co-religionists in the Church of Ireland. Alfred considered these and other charges in articles in the *Standard* of 21, 28 April and 5 May 1944. With a skilful use of the data provided by the comprehensive census of 1936 he demonstrated that members of the Church of Ireland held a disproportionate number of the better-paid positions in the State. In fact, he

Religious Writing and Lecturing

argued, any reasonable person would conclude from the statistics that Catholics who constituted more than 90% of the population had a genuine grievance of being discriminated against in most of the relatively better jobs.[3] On the issue of religious pressure Stanford wrote: 'There is an energetic spirit of evangelism today. It is everywhere about us, in newspapers, on the radio, in bookshops, on bookstalls in the streets, in public meetings, in private conversation', and he went on to associate this with 'souperism'. Alfred replied by giving a history of that term.

Professor Stanford's reply was published in the *Standard* of 19 May 1944. Alfred responded in the issues of 19 and 26 May. He noted that Stanford was irritated at being referred to as an Anglican. Yet, he pointed out, it was Stanford himself who had adopted the term. Moreover, Alfred continued, this was a strange reaction from one who 'with crude rudeness' had referred to Catholicism as 'Romanism'. He showed that remarks made by Stanford about John Scotus Erigena were lamentably inaccurate. Stanford had objected to Alfred quoting from W. E. H. Lecky, the T.C.D. historian, because he was a rationalist and presumably not a Protestant. Alfred reminded Stanford that Lecky's memorial service was conducted in St Patrick's Cathedral by the dean, one of the latter's 'most valued friends'. To Stanford's expression of shock that 'ancient wrongs done by the churches were quoted in Christian journals', Alfred replied that Stanford, it seemed, had no objection to quoting and distorting them in a Christian pamphlet and reminded him that it was he who had, in effect, begun the controversy. Finally, Stanford jibed that Alfred had shown 'skill in handling phrases isolated from their context'. Alfred pointed out that Stanford gave no illustration or proof for this statement, while he had given extensive quotations from the pamphlet. In the *Standard* of 26 May Alfred rebutted further criticisms by Professor Stanford.[4]

3. Alfred had touched on this issue earlier when he attacked the Cork Savings Bank in the *Catholic Mind* of April 1937. The *Cork Examiner* of 1 March 1937 reported that the Church of Ireland bishop of Cork presided at the annual meeting of the bank's depositors and had declared that he himself was not a depositor. This prompted Alfred to highlight the almost exclusive Church of Ireland membership of the bank's executive committee and the fact that none of its senior employees were Catholics, notwithstanding the fact that the substantial majority of the depositors were the Catholic citizens of Cork.
4. Towards the end of his life Professor W. B. Stanford (1910-1984) recalled this controversy. Having referred to the positive aspect of his pamphlet on the

Alfred O'Rahilly III: Controversialist

Petty exchanges

One of the more petty exchanges between Alfred and Stanford centred on the use of the term Roman Catholic. Stanford insisted on referring to Catholics as Romanists and as Roman Catholics. Alfred objected to both designations. A number of queries on the subject prompted him to write '"Roman Catholics" or just "Catholics"' in the *Standard* of 16 June 1944. Drawing on an article by Fr Herbert Thurston, S.J., in the *Month* of September 1911, he declared that the term Roman Catholic was imposed on British Catholics by the British government and an Established Church. He claimed that, when used in Ireland, those using it, in effect, were seeking to impose an appelation which implied that Catholics were 'a degenerative (Roman) branch of some undefined collective unity (the Catholic Church) and also were a foreign (Roman) body as opposed to the national body (the Church of Ireland)'. He declared that he had no objection to giving to members of the Church of Ireland the name they gave to themselves but demanded a reciprocal courtesy from them.

Some of Alfred's interventions on behalf of the Catholic Church indicated a lack of perspective. In the *Standard* of 13 March 1942 in his 'Pat Murphy' column he took issue with an editorial in *T.C.D.: a college miscellany* of 26 February 1942 which he described as an attack on the Catholic Church. In the *Standard* of 3 April 1942 W. John White, chairman of the T.C.D. publishing company, and B. Waldo Maguire, editor of the magazine, rejected Alfred's allegation. In the same issue of the *Standard* Alfred drew attention to what he had objected to in the editorial, namely: (a) 'the present system of government of Ireland by capitalists and clerics must be changed' and (b) 'Ireland is in a medieval slumber – land of saints and scholars

---

Church of Ireland, he continued: 'On the negative side one could criticise the historical and theological claims of the "other side" in letters to the public press. So I rashly embarked on a controversial correspondence in a Dublin newspaper with a far more experienced and skilful controversialist, Dr Alfred O'Rahilly of Cork. I cannot recall what the subjects of debate were since I kept no record of them, and I certainly would not like now to search through newspapers to find out, since I soon came to regret this negative approach. Except perhaps as a brash gesture of defiance it was futile, like most disputes of this kind, convincing nobody who was not already convinced. And it made enemies among formerly well disposed people' ('Memoirs of Professor W. B. Stanford').

Religious Writing and Lecturing

and priests and tuberculosis and syphilis'. He dismissed what White and Maguire had written in reply as minor and irrelevant and noted that they had expressed no regret for their 'nasty, crude and libellous innuendos and statements'.[5] In that context he took obvious delight in drawing attention to the irony of their reference to his comments as a 'gross breach of good taste'.

Alfred's combativeness was aroused by nonsensical bigotry. In the *Standard* of 1 August 1947, over the pseudonym 'Ollamh', he attacked a review in *John O'London's Weekly* of *The Catholic Church against the twentieth century*, which among other things misrepresented and ridiculed the Catholic Church's attitude to the miracles claimed to have been attested at Lourdes. This prompted a letter detailing the crimes and corruption of some of the more notorious popes, as well as other anti-Catholic polemics. He had little difficulty in replying to it. In the two articles in the *Standard* of 22 and 29 August 1947, in which he did so, he claimed to have read the thirty-four volumes of Ludwig von Pastor's *History of the popes*.

In his exchanges defending Catholicism, Alfred had no equal. Whereas the content of his polemics was soon forgotten the style and vigour were not. He claimed these were justified on the grounds that in all instances he was merely reacting to controversial allegations and statements. In this regard he liked to quote: *'Cet animal est très méchant; quand on l'attaque, il se défend!'*

For some, however, this was not an adequate explanation or justification. These polemics and the coat-trailing associated with them left a cloud over his memory. In *Trinity College, Dublin, 1592-1952: an academic history* (Cambridge 1982) by R. B. McDowell and D. A. Webb, during a discussion on the relationship between Trinity College and the Catholic Church, it is stated that by the late 1930s 'there was no openly-expressed hostility except in the cheaper Catholic press and from a few eccentrics like Alfred O'Rahilly, ostensibly professor of mathematical physics at U.C.C., but in fact a self-appointed

5. Alfred had a special dislike for derogatory references to the Mass and unfair criticism of the Catholic priesthood. His sensitivity in this regard caused him to over-react occasionally, such as when he published a jaundiced review of F. R. Higgins's *The gap of brightness: lyrical poems* in the *Irish Independent* of 7 May 1940. This was resented by Higgins's friends and led to an exchange between Alfred and the Irish correspondent of the *Catholic Herald* soon after Higgins's death on 8 January 1941.

oracle on every aspect of politics, sociology, economics and religion.'

Devotional writing

Much of Alfred's religious writing and lecturing was devotional. He was fascinated by the account of the life of Christ in the four gospels. His intention to publish a comprehensive life of Christ and the extent to which he realised it has been treated elsewhere.[6] Apart from his pamphlets and books on various aspects of the life of Christ,[7] he published a review of Giuseppe Ricciotti's, *The life of Christ* in the *Standard* of 15 August 1947, lectured on 'Christ, the brother of the worker'[8] and contributed seasonal articles to the press during the Holy Weeks of 1938, 1940, 1943, 1945, 1949, 1950, 1951 and 1954, and on occasion at Easter and Christmas.[9]

6. See J. A. Gaughan, *Alfred O'Rahilly I: Academic* (Dublin 1986) 200.
7. See *ibid.*, 200-1, 205-6.
8. See J. A. Gaughan, *Alfred O'Rahilly III: Controversialist, Part I* (Dublin 1992) 46.
9. The Holy Week articles were as follows: 'How Jerusalem spent Good Friday', *Irish Independent* 14 April 1938; 'Under Pontius Pilate', *Irish Press* 19 March 1940; 'The first three words from the cross', *Irish Press* 20 March 1940; 'The last four words from the cross', *Irish Press* 21 March 1940; 'In the high-priest's courtyard', *Standard* 16 April 1943; 'Crucified', *Standard* 23 April 1943; 'Doubting Thomas', *Standard* 30 April 1943; 'The Holy Shroud I', *Standard* 16 February 1945; 'The Holy Shroud II', *Standard* 23 February 1945; 'The Holy Shroud III', *Standard* 2 March 1945; 'The Holy Shroud IV', *Standard* 9 March 1945; 'The Holy Shroud V', *Standard* 16 March 1945; 'The Holy Shroud VI', *Standard* 23 March 1945; 'Gethsemani', *Standard* 11 March 1949; 'Before the Jewish Court', *Standard* 18 March 1949; 'Christ and Pilate', *Standard* 25 March 1949; 'The great refusal', *Standard* 1 April 1949: 'The way of the cross', *Standard* 8 April 1949; 'Pictures of the passion I', *Irish Press* 11 April 1949; 'Pictures of the passion II', *Irish Press* 12 April 1949; 'Pictures of the passion III', *Irish Press* 13 April 1949; 'Pictures of the passion IV', *Irish Press* 14 April 1949; 'Calvary', ', *Standard* 15 April 1949; 'Figures of the passion I', *Standard* 24 February 1950; 'Figures of the passion II', *Standard* 3 March 1950; 'Figures of the passion III', *Standard* 10 March 1950; 'Figures of the passion IV', *Standard* 17 March 1950; 'Figures of the passion V', *Standard* 24 March 1950; 'Figures of the passion VI', *Standard* 31 March 1950; 'St Peter and the passion I', *Standard* 9 March 1951; 'St Peter and the passion II', *Standard* 16 March 1951; 'St Peter and the passion III', *Standard* 23 March 1951; 'Peter and the risen Christ', *Standard* 30 March 1951 and 'Our share in what happened on Calvary', *Irish Press* 15 April 1954. Alfred's articles on Christmas and Easter were as follows: 'Bethlehem', *Standard* 20 December 1946; 'The other cross', Easter Number 1948; and 'The resurrection', *Standard* 11 April 1952.

Religious Writing and Lecturing

Alfred's first major publication was *Father William Doyle, S.J. A spiritual study* (London 1920). The book went to many editions and printings, not least because of its subject. Fr Doyle had been very well-known and liked throughout the country. He was a powerful preacher and much in demand for retreats. During his service as an army chaplain he attracted much love and respect from many kinds of men and was killed while he attended the wounded near the crossroads at Frezenberg in Belgium in August 1917.[10]

Alfred received numerous requests to give public lectures on the life of Fr William Doyle. When he did so, he attracted large audiences. He delivered the first of these in the St Francis Xavier hall at Upper Sherrard Street, Dublin, on 19 February 1923 to raise funds for the Pioneer Total Abstinence Association. Sometimes the lectures were reported in considerable detail as when the *Cork Examiner* of 19 November 1925 covered his lecture on the previous evening to an overflow audience at the Catholic Young Men's Society rooms in Cork. Almost invariably he gave the lecture to help some organisation or society to raise funds. He lectured on 'Fr Willie Doyle, S.J. – patriot, hero, priest' in the Gaiety Theatre, Dublin, on 28 January 1934 in aid of the Extension Fund of the Church of the Sacred Heart, Donnybrook. By that time he was not content with merely recalling the heroic life and death of Fr Doyle. He spoke of the neglect of asceticism and the current 'lust for money, power and pleasure'. In particular, he deprecated the fact that refined luxuries were being provided in a world in which millions of people were starving. He declared that it was a delusion to consider that schemes such as the building of houses and the appointment of commissions were adequate in solving the social question. The retreats for workers, such as those initiated by Fr Doyle, were equally important to that end. The whole organisation of the life of the country was at variance with the spirit of the religion of the people. They had capitalism, urbanisation, machine production, even the arithmetical democracy of modern parliamentary government, but there was no organic Catholic social structure. No social nostrums would be effective without religion and its motivation.

Alfred intended to write a biography of Nano Nagle, foundress of the Presentation Sisters, and collected material over a

10. For more, see J. A. Gaughan, *Alfred O'Rahilly I: Academic*, 164-6.

period of twenty years to this end. However, eventually a book was published in 1959 by Fr Timothy J. Walsh.[11] Alfred delivered lectures on Nano Nagle. These, for the most part, were given to audiences in convents. On at least one occasion, however, the lecture was open to the general public. On 22 April 1951 the Capitol Cinema in Cork was filled to capacity to hear him lecture on Nano Nagle. He began by sketching the background against which she came to Cork in her forty-sixth year to work for the education of the poor Catholic children of the city. In 1666 there was an enactment that every papist schoolmaster was to be captured and transported to the Barbadoes, in 1695 an attempt was made to prevent the Irish people from going abroad to be educated and in 1731 the Charter Schools were founded to wean Catholic children away from the Catholic faith. Five years after her arrival in Cork in 1764, Nano Nagle had established five schools, three for girls and two for boys. In 1775, with three associates, she founded her order and in 1777 her first house was opened in Cork. During her labours in the city until her death in 1784 she sowed good seed, as was evidenced by the order's three hundred convents spread throughout the world.

Mass stipends, indulgences

Alfred concerned himself with practices in Catholic devotional life which caused most perplexity to those outside the Church. He made an exhaustive study of the origin of Mass stipends in general, and the attitude of British civil law to the practice in particular. On at least one occasion he faced the thorny question of indulgences. There were exchanges between George G. Coulton and Arnold Lunn on this in the *Catholic Herald* in September 1945. Alfred considered that more heat than light had been generated by the controversy and in a letter in the *Catholic Herald* of 21 September 1945 he clarified the various issues raised as follows:

> 1. An indulgence, properly so called, is the remission of temporal punishment incurred by sin the eternal guilt of which has already been cancelled. It is usually expressed in days or years of former severe canonical penances for

11. For more on this, see *ibid.*, 166-7.

Religious Writing and Lecturing

which some lesser special condition, for example, prayer or alms, is nowadays substituted. Underlying indulgences is the concept of an authoritative Church which can impose penance, as well as a theology of the sequelae of sin in the soul.

2. Every Catholic I have ever met, no matter how deficient in secular education, knows that the primary condition for availing of an indulgence is to be in a state of grace.

3. After the fall of Constantinople (1453), Callistus III published the *Bulla Cruciatae* to help to save Europe from the Turks. Spanish influence has secured the continuance of this long after the original need has ceased. But a new need, the maintenance of divine worship, arose; and the Spanish government insisted upon a contribution. About 1900 the total annual amount collected was about £100,000. Not a penny of this went into the pockets of the clergy; it was entirely devoted to the repair and equipment of churches, the support of hospitals and orphanages, etc.

4. As far as I know, this is an 'indulgence' only in a popular untheological sense. It is a concession or dispensation, for example, permission to eat meat on days of abstinence, on condition of performing an alternative good work, that is, alms or – in the case of manual workers or the poor – prayers for the pope's intention.

5. There is nothing wrong in principle with such substitution. But anyone is presumably free to hold that the practice is liable to laxity or misinterpretation. Whether the concession still holds in Spain, I am unable to say.

6. The phrase 'you may buy such an indulgence in the open market' is grossly inaccurate and offensive. So also is the statement that 'for five shillings we may buy the spiritual fruits of many Masses' in Liverpool cathedral. This preposterous charge of open simony, publicly advertised in this paper, is unworthy of any decent opponent. Dispensations, indulgences, Masses, are not 'bought'. A critic may, if he chooses, object to prayers being promised to church benefactors. But he should not formulate his objection in language which is scandalous and repudiated by every Catholic theologian as well as by canon law.

Alfred O'Rahilly III: Controversialist

Lourdes

After agreeing to give a talk on Radio Éireann on St Bernadette Soubirous and the Marian shrine at Lourdes Alfred read a number of books by non-Catholics on the subject. In the *Standard* of 13 December 1946 he commented on a number of them. He dismissed *Lourdes* (1939) by Edith Saunders as 'a concoction of virulent anti-clericalism and cheap irreverent rationalism'. Franz Werfel's *The song of Bernadette* (1942) did not receive a very high rating either. In effect, he described it as no more than a work of historical fiction. He found Margaret Gray Blanton's *Bernadette of Lourdes* (1939) interesting and sympathetic. It was, he pointed out, based on the monumental, though turgid, *Histoire de Notre-Dame de Lourdes* I-III (Paris 1926-7) by L. J. M. Cros, S.J. However, he was severely critical of Mrs Blanton's attempted natural explanation of the visions of Bernadette and her evaluation of the saint's religious vocation.

In the *Standard* of 29 April 1949 he wrote that a relative of his – in fact his sister, Sr Mary Antonia, then in Liverpool – had sent him a book which was 'causing a sensation in one of the local Protestant high schools' and 'to which no reference could be found in the Catholic press'. This was Dr George Bancroft's *The conquest of disease: the story of penicillin*, in which the final chapter was headed 'Penicillin and the miracle of Lourdes'. Bancroft argued that the allegedly healing properties of the water at the grotto in Lourdes could be due to penicillin rather than to the intercession of the Virgin Mary. Alfred pointed out that the water at Lourdes had been analysed several times for inorganic and organic matter and each time scientists had concluded that 'there was not a trace of a single product – biological, mineral or pharmacological – which could explain the cures'. He went on to demonstrate the wholly unsatisfactory and inadequate nature of Bancroft's theory in a number of other ways. He concluded with the biting remark that Bancroft simply wished to sell his book by shocking the religious-minded bourgeoisie but all that he had done was to expose his own ignorance.

Thérèse Neumann

Alfred was fascinated by unusual phenomena associated with religion. In *Studies* of June 1938 he discussed the historical

Religious Writing and Lecturing

evidence for the stigmata of St Francis of Assisi. From 1946 onwards when researching the passion and death of Christ he made an intensive study of reported stigmatists since St Francis was found to be such in 1224. He became particularly interested in the case of the contemporary stigmatist, Thérèse Neumann. With the assistance of Fr Naber, parish priest of Konnersreuth, and Rev. Mother Teresa, O.S.B., of St Scholastica's Abbey, Teignmouth, Devon, England, he communicated with Fraulein Neumann. Despite serious travel restrictions within Germany, he visited Konnersreuth two years after world war two and was impressed by what he witnessed. On 23 April 1951 he gave a radio talk in which he was critical of Hilda C. Graef's *The case of Thérèse Neumann* (Cork 1950).[12] In July of that year in a programme on Radio Éireann he and Dr Hilda C. Graef, a native of Berlin, convert to Catholicism and a Cambridge don, discussed the case of Thérèse Neumann. He rejected Dr Graef's attempt to explain the stigmata as due, in effect, to a form of religious hysteria.

Alfred continued to be fascinated by the German stigmatist and visited her again in June 1956. At that time he was conducting a voluminous correspondence with a number of persons on the extraordinary phenomena associated with the person of Thérèse Neumann. At the request of Matthew Feehan, editor of the *Sunday Press*, he contributed twenty-six weekly articles on the 'seer', as he referred to her, between 24 November 1957 and 1 June 1958. The articles constitute a comprehensive account of the life of Thérèse Neumann up to that time and of the phenomena associated with her. Alfred was sympathetic to a praeternatural explanation of the phenomena but no more than that. He was critical of the views of Dr Hilda C. Graef and of Fr Paul Siwek, S.J., who had also published a book on Thérèse.[13] He illustrated the inadequacy of their attempted rational explanation of the phenomena to be witnessed at Konnersreuth and was particularly dismissive of Dr Graef's patronising treatment of the confessor-penitent relationship of Fr Naber and Thérèse Neumann.

---

12. See Appendix 1.
13. P. Siwek, S.J., *The riddle of Konnersreuth, a psychological and religious study* (Dublin 1954).

Alfred O'Rahilly III: Controversialist

Shroud of Turin

Earlier Alfred had taken a deep interest in the Shroud of Turin. He was first made aware of this mystifying artifact at Blackrock College in the autumn of 1898 when he attended a lecture on the photographic study of it by Secondo Pia. In the mid-1930s when the grand design of writing a comprehensive life of Christ was taking shape he studied all the circumstances surrounding the Shroud of Turin with characteristic thoroughness. As a result, he entitled the section of his work on the passion and death of Christ as 'The Crucified: on the Shroud and in art'.[14] From 1937 onwards he lectured on the Shroud. He used numerous illustrations and almost invariably began by announcing: 'This is not intended as a lecture on the Shroud, but as a meditation on the Passion.' He also generally prefaced his lecture by stating that he was concerned with facts not faith and that the authenticity or otherwise of the Shroud depended on the former not the latter. Few of those who heard his lecture were left in doubt as to his own conviction in the matter. When open to the general public, the lecture was immensely popular[15] and he received numerous requests to give it. Between 1937 and 1951 scarcely a year passed without reports of it appearing in the local and national press.[16]

14. This was published as *The Crucified* in 1985. For more on this, see J. A. Gaughan, *Alfred O'Rahilly I: Academic*, 200-1.
15. The *Cork Examiner* of 25 February 1951 reported that more than a thousand persons attended Alfred's lecture on 'the Holy Shroud' in the Town Hall, Killarney, a few days earlier.
16. People from many parts of the country heard Alfred's lecture. On 5 December 1937 he delivered it to the Cork University Graduates' Club and the Academy of St Thomas at U.C.C.; on 27 February 1938 in the Aberdeen Hall, Gresham Hotel, Dublin, under the auspices of the Legion of Mary; on 10 April 1938 in the City Hall, Cork, to raise funds for the local Conference of the Society of St Vincent de Paul; on 25 March 1939 at the Dominican Convent in Galway, at the request of Bishop Michael Browne; on 15 December 1942 at St Angela's College, Cork, under the auspices of the college's Catholic Literature Guild; on 25 March 1943 at the City Hall, Cork, for the lord mayor's fund; on 14 April 1946 at the Savoy Cinema, Cork, to raise funds for a local Legion of Mary hostel; on 23 February 1947 at St John's Theatre, Tralee, under the auspices of the local branch of the C.Y.M.S.; on 30 March 1947 at the Grand Central Cinema, Limerick, under the auspices of the Catholic Library Institute; on 21 March 1948 at the Fr O'Leary Total Abstinence Hall, Cork, under the auspices of the Cork branches of the Pioneer Total Abstinence Association; on 15 February 1949 at St Mary's Hall, Belfast, under the auspices of the Newman

Religious Writing and Lecturing

Foreign missions

Alfred was imbued with the conviction that every follower of Christ was obliged to spread the 'good news'. As a young Jesuit he expressed his preference for a life of service on the foreign missions. Had he remained a Jesuit, there would never have been a likelihood of his seeing such service, because of his outstanding academic ability. At heart, however, he remained a missionary. He was always involved in a crusade of one kind or another. This, at times, caused some of his contemporaries to be edified, some to be amused and some, especially his academic peers, to be infuriated.

Alfred had a great affection and admiration for sisters, brothers and priests who served on the foreign missions. For many years he was particularly friendly with the Missionaries of the Sacred Heart in Cork and delighted in officially opening their annual fund-raising bazaar. In appealing for support for the Sacred Heart Fathers he invariably described Ireland's missionary activity as part of the nation's historic destiny and likened the missionaries of the twentieth century to those of the past. In proposing a vote of thanks to a lecture on the missions of the Holy Ghost Fathers in the Arcadia Theatre, Cork, on 14 March 1938, Alfred was topical. He declared that Ireland should regard the foreign missions as its 'spiritual colonies'. But, he noted, these colonies were radically different from those which the Führer was then coveting. His long-standing interest in, and support for, the foreign missions was acknowledged when he was requested to give the introductory lecture to 'Out of the darkness', the first documentary film on the work of Irish missionary sisters, which had its premiere in the Savoy Cinema in Cork on 24 September 1950.

As president of U.C.C. Alfred was particularly helpful to missionary orders and societies in facilitating the admission to degree courses of Africans, lay and clerical, to train as second-level teachers for mission-schools. He helped to establish in U.C.C. a centre for the Guild of SS Luke, Cosmas and Damian, the international association of Catholic doctors, and in association with it a medical missionary society to prepare students

---

Society; in March and April 1950 at Kanturk and Mallow respectively under the auspices of the Legion of Mary; on 20 February 1951 in the Town Hall, Killarney, at the request of Fr John J. (Bob) Murphy, adm., Killarney parish.

who wished to work for a time as doctors in the Catholic missions overseas. In addition, he welcomed the visits of the superiors and representatives of missionary orders and societies to the College and presided at their addresses. In 1938 on her return from Nigeria, where in the previous year she founded the Medical Missionaries of Mary, Mother Mary Martin spoke to the women students at U.C.C. Alfred was most enthusiastic in his comments on the new society and declared that it was an indication of how the Church could adapt itself to new needs and new situations.

Alfred ensured that the academic community acknowledged the achievements of distinguished missionaries. In June 1932 he was instrumental in having an honorary M.D. conferred on Dr Anna Dengel. Prior to the conferring, as acting dean of the medical faculty, he introduced Dr Dengel. A native of the Tyrol, she graduated from U.C.C. in 1919. From 1920 to 1924 she worked as a doctor in mission stations in the Indian province of Rawalpindi. During the course of a lecture tour of the U.S. in 1925 she founded the Society of Catholic Medical Missionaries.

On 8 July 1952 Fr Francis Griffin, C.S.Sp., at Alfred's prompting, was conferred with an honorary LL.D. As vice-chancellor of the N.U.I., Alfred introduced Fr Griffin. He informed the assembly that Fr Griffin was a native of County Clare, had been educated at Rockwell College and Fribourg University, had lectured on moral theology at Blackrock, had been a missionary in the foothills of Mount Kilimanjaro for seven years and eventually, since 1950, was the superior-general of the world-wide congregation of the Holy Ghost Fathers.

Earlier, on 21 February 1950, Alfred had introduced the apostolic nuncio, the Most Rev. Ettore Felici, titular archbishop of Corinth, when he was admitted to the degree of LL.D. *honoris causa*.

Moral and social principles

Apart from dealing with apologetics, doctrine and devotional subjects, Alfred wrote and lectured a great deal on the moral imperatives of Christianity. In 1948 he published *Social principles* and *Moral principles*.[17] The first was a series of eight talks

17. For more on these, see J. A. Gaughan, *Alfred O'Rahilly I: Academic*, 84, 97, 196, 206.

Religious Writing and Lecturing

on radio which he delivered from February to April 1945, the second a similar series of broadcasts in January and February 1946. A perceptive report in the *Irish Times* of 28 February 1946 captured the tone, content and quality of these broadcasts:

> Dr Alfred O'Rahilly, who on Sunday night gave the last of a series of eight talks on 'Moral principles', has a unique position in Irish broadcasting. He is the only one of our radio talkers whose personality impinges on the listeners with anything like the force of such celebrated radio men as the late Mr Middleton, Mr J. B. Priestley, or the radio doctor. It is true we have other frequently-heard talkers – such as Monsignor Ryan, Monk Gibbon and Brinsley Mac-Namara – whose voices and styles have become known to many listeners, but none of these establishes his identity at the microphone as quickly and unmistakably as does Dr O'Rahilly.
>
> It is partly by his very distinctive voice that Dr O'Rahilly impresses the listeners. It is slightly harsh and aggressive in tone, but always firm, clear and confident; and his accent, like that of the three English broadcasters mentioned, is always sturdily provincial. Matching his voice is a characteristic style of argument which is also slightly harsh, aggressive, clear and confident. From the outset he gives the impression that he knows his own mind, that he knows clearly the reasons for what is in his own mind and the reasons for the wrong ideas in the minds of others. But, in spite of his certainty in his arguments, he never loses sight of the difficulty other people may have in understanding or accepting them. So he is at pains to make everything clear and simple; to help by illustration and analogy those not accustomed to abstract thinking; and, in his arguments, to pile proof upon proof so as to leave the issue far beyond doubt.
>
> Such great and rare gifts make his broadcasts very effective, but they would be even more effective if it were not for two faults. The first is their excess of quotation. Many of his quotations, of course, are apt and illuminating; and are from the works of men whose names carry conviction. Many others, however, are from works by men whose names add little or no weight to the argument, and are in

a form not nearly so persuasive or so striking as that in which Dr O'Rahilly could stress the same argument. In a lesser controversialist I should suspect an attempt to overwhelm the ill-informed by a parade of names, but in Dr O'Rahilly I can only suppose that he is led into this method of argument by his extraordinary facility for remembering what he has read.

A most serious fault is the note of personal animus against the Huxleys (past and present), H. G. Wells, Bertrand Russell and others whose views Dr O'Rahilly regularly attacks. For example, in the last but one of his recent series he referred scathingly to a statement by Bertrand Russell as 'a piece of dogma put forward by an elderly aristocrat'. The effect of that kind of reference is to bring the talk down from the level of scholarly disputation to that of a 'scene' in a county council.

Dr O'Rahilly's great co-religionist, Chesterton, could attack the doctrines of all these people without any loss of urbanity. In particular, he could attack incessantly the teaching of Mr Wells and still remain on friendly terms with him. The advantage of this attitude is that it leaves the reader, or listener, in no doubt that it is an opinion, and not a person, that is being opposed, whereas the O'Rahilly method may leave some people under the mistaken impression that his quarrel with Darwinism or Materialism is the outcome of a personal feud with the Huxleys and their friends.

It also seems to me that there is little profit in Dr O'Rahilly hanging so much of his broadcast and published work on the ideas, whether or not mistaken, of Marx, Huxley and their followers. He goes over this ground so often that I sometimes imagine that there is at the foot of his garden a little colony of hardshell Darwinians who come out and make rude noises at him at nights.

Radio broadcasts

Alfred was well-known as a broadcaster because of the number, variety and quality of his contributions on radio. On 7 March 1936 he broadcast a talk on St Thomas Aquinas (see p. 49). At the end of that year Dr Thomas J. Kiernan, director of

Religious Writing and Lecturing

Radio Éireann, invited him and others to give a series of talks entitled 'If I were director of broadcasting'. In his contribution Alfred purported to speak on behalf of the listeners in rural as well as urban Ireland. He relayed a criticism of the amount of time given to jazz and the suggestion that more time be allotted to céilí music and Irish and Anglo-Irish songs. In addition, he appealed for an occasional broadcast of opera and orchestral music. He called for instructive programmes on all aspects of agriculture and emphasised his conviction of the necessity for propagating moral and social principles, which would ensure that the nation escaped the excesses 'associated with Moscow and Berlin'.[18]

Just over a year later, again at the request of Dr Kiernan, Alfred gave a talk for Radio Éireann on 2 February 1938. It was autobiographical, provoked considerable interest and was published in the *Kerryman* of 12 February. He made radio appeals for charitable organisations, such as one for the International Catholic Girls' Protection Society on 4 May 1940. Beginning on 23 January 1944, he delivered nine weekly talks on religion and science. From 25 February to 15 April 1945 he broadcast the series of eight talks on social principles and from 6 January 1946 onwards the similar series on moral principles. (For more on these, see pp. 17-19, 38-9.) In 1945, 1947, 1948 and 1950 he spoke on the important Christian festivals. In 1948 he participated in book-review programmes. In one of these he reviewed Paul Derrick's *Lost property: proposals for the distribution of property in an industrial age* (London 1947). He was impressed: 'I regard it as a really important book . . . for he is tackling, in terms of the contemporary world, a problem which we who write or lecture on private property and distribution must squarely face . . . Mr Derrick is no dreamer; he has elaborated his scheme with a wealth of practical detail.' In July 1951 he and Miss Hilda C. Graef took part in a radio discussion on Thérèse Neumann and the phenomena associated with her.

18. About the same time Francis O'Reilly, secretary of the C.T.S.I., appealed to Alfred for support in his efforts to have a 'Catholic Hour' broadcast from Radio Éireann (letter, dated 26 October 1936, Francis O'Reilly to Alfred O'Rahilly). On 4 March 1942 in speaking to a paper, delivered to a meeting of the Literary and Philosophical Society of U.C.C. attended by Patrick J. Little, T.D., minister for posts and telegraphs, Alfred deplored 'the over-negative emphasis' in broadcasting and appealed for a more positive expression of the religious and social principles for which Irishmen had died in the past.

Alfred O'Rahilly III: Controversialist

Need to challenge secular world

Throughout his life Alfred crusaded for the implementation of the moral principles of Christianity in public as well as in private affairs. To this end he urged his co-religionists to become involved in Catholic Action which he defined as knowing, loving, practising and standing up for one's faith. He regarded this last as a particularly important duty of the Christian, namely, to face up to the challenge of the secular world with his or her ideals and life-style.

Sometimes Alfred set out the challenge in rather stark terms, as when he addressed the annual conference of the Catholic Truth Society of Ireland in October 1930. Speaking on 'The pagan world into which Christ was born', he compared 'modern paganism' to that at the time of Christ. 'For the cult of Caesar substitute the omnipotence of the State, for servitude read wage-slavery, translate spectacles and gladitorial combat into plays, talkies and war' and, he added, parallel quotations from the philosophers, novelists and poets of both periods. He declared that one gained an insight into the paganism of the first century from the writers of the early Church, many of whose pages were more apposite in their own time than in any of the intervening centuries. Their most scathing denunciations were directed against sexual vice, obscene mythology, open or disguised polygamy, divorce, abortion, child exposure, unnatural vices and indecent plays. It was the duty of Christians to combat such paganism. They would be called bigots and fanatics and would be accused of *odium humani generis*, as were the early Christians. But they need not flinch from the mild martyrdom of intrigue and invective. He regretted that they had not used their new-born freedom to adopt a Christian view of the State or to discard anti-Christian economics. But he warned that social and economic transformation could not save society without high motives, self-sacrifice and goodwill.

Champion of the disadvantaged

Most frequently Alfred referred to the inequalities and injustices which followed from the capitalist system. He urged his fellow-Christians to work towards a radical reformation of

Religious Writing and Lecturing

society and emphasised their duty to care for their most vulnerable 'brothers and sisters'. This was the burden of his lecture 'What is wrong with the world?' at Killarney on 7 January 1932 which was organised to raise funds for the local conference of the St Vincent de Paul Society.

Alfred addressed a large gathering of the unemployed at the Morning Star Hostel, North Brunswick Street, Dublin,[19] on 23 May 1935. He told them that he was neither a capitalist nor a communist and believed that every Catholic should be something better than both. The social conscience of the people of the country needed to be aroused. In restructuring society, they had to begin with the right principles. There had to be social, not State control. This would include the control of prices and production policy, and getting people back on the land. Underlying such control was the realisation that their Christianity had to be social and that they had duties one to another.

On 29 November 1936 Alfred lectured on 'Facing the issues: Christ or chaos' in the Gaiety Theatre, Dublin, to raise funds for Legion of Mary hostels. The Spanish civil war cast its shadow over his address. Communism, he announced, was a new intolerant religion. Atheism, with the emotional outfit of a crusader, had arisen and was threatening the world. He urged his co-religionists, in the face of this new challenge, to assert the natural rights of the individual and the family and the spiritual liberty of the Church. The vindication of the freedom of the Church was of the first importance, since it was the greatest of libertarian institutions in their time, standing alone between the individual and the State. He recalled that in the early Church all persons, even slaves, were regarded as brothers and sisters. They had a tremendous responsibility to ensure social justice. That responsibility could no longer be shifted on to an alien government. There was not much use in studying papal encyclicals if they were not going to see that the principles were applied. They needed a corporate structure in the State and an increasing measure of social control. There was no point in

19. The Morning Star hostel was opened by the Legion of Mary for the homeless in 1927. On a number of occasions, when staying overnight in a hotel in Dublin, Alfred visited it. In one of the first issues of the *Irish Press*, that of 15 September 1931, he described the remarkable generosity of spirit of the young men and women who ran it and referred to other equally altruistic and fraternal activities of the *praesidia* (units of the Legion of Mary) which met there.

Alfred O'Rahilly III: Controversialist

denouncing communism if they did not show that their principles could remedy existing injustices. He appealed for a new spirit which would bring their Christian convictions into play into every facet of their daily lives.

On 9 October 1938 Alfred addressed four thousand Franciscan Tertiaries at their first national congress in the Theatre Royal, Dublin. In his paper 'The Third Order and society', he recalled that St Francis popularised poverty, chastity and obedience and he declared that the primary duty of Tertiaries was not to attend a meeting once a month but to put the teachings of St Francis into operation in their everyday lives. Their solemn pledge raised the use of property to the dignity of a religious act.

St Francis preached chastity. The Church fostered celibacy, not by way of despising or deprecating wedlock but to show that instincts were not invincible. But the Church which chanted the praises of virginity was the only institution which defended the sanctity of married life. The marital bond[20] was held up to obloquy and jest in films and newspapers and it was the duty of Tertiaries unashamedly to carry out the ideals they had undertaken and lead in combating such a trend and the overemphasis on sex. There were thousands of people who,

20. For Alfred the marital bond was indissoluble. He enshrined this in his draft constitution of 1922 (see J. A. Gaughan, *Alfred O'Rahilly II: Public figure*, 465). When the question of divorce was debated in Dáil Éireann in February 1925 he wrote a sharp letter, for publication in the *Irish Independent*, rejecting Deputy William E. Thrift's case for divorce on the plea of religious tolerance. He pointed out that the primary objection of the majority of Irish people to divorce was based on natural ethics. They objected to it because it was subversive of family life and detrimental to the social interests of the community. To Professor Thrift's assertion that the 'free profession and practice of religion' by his co-religionists was interfered with by the non-availability of divorce, he expressed surprise that any of them would divorce and remarry as a religious duty. He continued that, according to Thrift, the Irish people should reduce their social legislation to the minimum which was 'obligatory on any little clique in the country'. So, if Muslims settled in the country, legislative sanction should be given to polygamy. Professor Thrift asserted that 'in a matter of conscience the individual cannot be subject to control from any majority'. 'Quite true,' replied Alfred, 'but also quite irrelevant, if it is meant that the individual conscience is not coerced by other people.' He explained that Professor Thrift and others were welcome to their view that divorce was not a social evil but a healthy system, though they would have to go elsewhere to practise it.

By return of post, on 13 February 1925, T. R. Harrington, editor of the *Irish Independent*, returned Alfred's letter. He regretted not publishing the letter, owing to his not having the time to 'wade through all the letters which would flow in', if he initiated a correspondence on the subject.

through force of economic circumstances, could not afford to marry. Those who were more fortunate were under a tremendous obligation to find a remedy to that situation and no amount of quibbling could shield them from that responsibility.

On the virtue of obedience, Alfred declared that it was important that they should have a proper respect for political and social authority. The alternative was anarchy, chaos and misery. However, he suggested that there should be tolerance towards those who were the victims of poverty and injustice, if sometimes they were a little imprudent or extreme in their protest. Such protests should cause the rest of the country's population to examine their consciences.

Catholic Action

From time to time Alfred sounded a clarion call to Catholic Action. In *Hibernia* of February 1937 he compared the relationship between the Christians of his day to the State to that of the early Christians to the Roman empire. He deprecated the tendency to equate Christianity with Sunday observance and worship and called for an extension of religious influence to the whole of people's lives. On 4 June 1939 in a lecture, 'What can we do?', to the annual social study day of the Catholic Women's Federation of Secondary School Unions Alfred appealed for a crusading spirit to do work for Christ. In this context Catholic Action, he said, was a phrase very often used but also very often not fully understood. In Catholic Action they should not exaggerate organisation. It was not something new. Its roots were in the spiritual training each one of them had got in the catechism, the tremendous stream of spiritual power pouring into the lives of every one of them. All Catholics had a lay vocation or ministry. All were called to Catholic Action. This Action, like their religion, should have a social dimension. On 14 January 1940 at a meeting of the past pupils of Rockwell College, Alfred made a similar appeal for Catholic Action, as well as urging past pupils of Catholic boys' secondary schools to join in a federation as their female counterparts had done.

Alfred delivered the main address at the celebrations marking the twenty-first anniversary of the founding of An Ríoghacht (the League of the Kingship of Christ) on 30 October 1947. He noted that the organisation, which had been established by Fr

Edward Cahill, S.J., aimed at 'the practical realisation of the kingship of Christ in our everyday lives'. He gave a critical summary of the social conditions then prevailing in Ireland and declared that it was the duty of every layman and woman by applying the principles of their religion to their daily tasks to ensure a decent quality of life for the entire body politic. Ireland, he said, was in a dangerous position and he called for concerted action against the rival secularist creeds with which the world was threatened.

Duty of Christian intellectual

Frequently, when presiding at conferring ceremonies at U.C.C., Alfred expressed his conviction that, in effect, it was particularly incumbent on university graduates and intellectuals to concern themselves with Catholic Action. In fact, whenever given an opportunity, he never shirked from telling undergraduates and graduates of the great debt they owed society in this and other regards. That he did so almost from the date of his arrival at U.C.C. is clear from the short pamphlet *The mission of the university man*[21] which he published in 1919. With Professor Mary Ryan, head of the department of Romance languages, he had Père A. D. Sertillanges, O.P., invited to the college. Sertillanges was a member of the academy of moral and political sciences of Paris, a distinguished Thomist and had written on the intellectual life from a Christian point of view.[22]

On 11 May 1933 Sertillanges lectured on 'La mission des intellectuels Chrétiens' at the college. He began by emphasising the powerful influence of ideas on world events and quoted the French Revolution and world war one as examples of the effect of insensate doctrines. It was the duty of every intellectual Christian to fight such ideas and influences and to interest them-

21. For more, see J. A. Gaughan, *Alfred O'Rahilly I: Academic, passim.*
22. A widely known work on this subject by him first appeared in 1920. After this was reprinted many times, he published a revised and extended edition in 1934. It was translated from the French by Professor Mary Ryan and published by Mercier Press, Cork, in 1947 as *The intellectual life: its spirit, conditions, methods*. It was at Alfred's suggestion that Seán Feehan commissioned Professor Mary Ryan to prepare the book for publication. Feehan was subsequently to recall that when he founded Mercier Press and during its early years he frequently sought Alfred's advice which was generously given. He also had the company's early publications printed by Cork University Press.

selves in the problems of the day. Next he stressed the need to pursue the truth, wherever it led, and the importance of revealing that truth. Religious truth, he pointed out, was exacting and imposed a duty on its followers. Finally, he urged a sympathetic fellowship between Christians in their search for the truth and a true *entente cordiale* between lovers of truth throughout the world. In his response to the lecture, delivered in French, Alfred endorsed the call for co-operative work among followers of the truth and spoke of the special duties of university students. These were to become wiser and to become better Christians.

Exponent and populariser of philosophy of St Thomas Aquinas

From the time when as a Jesuit scholastic he was introduced to the work of St Thomas Aquinas, Alfred was an avid admirer of the angelic doctor. While, for the most part, his writing on St Thomas concerned social and political philosophy,[23] his lecturing on the saint tended to have, in effect, a pastoral emphasis. With a view to increasing the awareness of undergraduates of the stature of Aquinas, he was instrumental in introducing a festive lecture at U.C.C. in honour of the saint on 7 March or a day close to it from 1924 onwards.[24]

In the first of these lectures he gave a conspectus of the life and work of St Thomas. He noted St Thomas' distinction as a mystic and as the author of the best known eucharistic hymns. He was also a model university professor, indefatigable in procuring manuscripts, in securing accurate translations of the Church fathers and Aristotle and in his commitment to scholarship and research. Next Alfred outlined St Thomas' role in Christianising Aristotelian philosophy. He recalled that the advent of Aristotle's philosophy in a Latin translation effected one of the greatest mental revolutions in history. It was a new world of thought which burst suddenly on Europe. Many of the best teachers in Paris and elsewhere accepted the new ideas and facts with enthusiasm and made little attempt to reconcile them with their faith. St Thomas, however, undertook the gigantic

23. See J. A. Gaughan, *Alfred O'Rahilly I: Academic, passim*; *Alfred O'Rahilly II: Public figure*, 411-30; *Alfred O'Rahilly III: Controversialist, Part I: Social reformer, passim.*
24. See J. A. Gaughan, *Alfred O'Rahilly I: Academic*, 108.

task of reconciling the new ideas with the Christian faith. Alfred noted that in doing so St Thomas was inspired by Petrus de Hibernia (Peter from Ireland) who taught him for seven years in Naples before he joined the Dominican Order.

Alfred next touched on St Thomas' contribution to scriptural studies. This sprang from the latter's clear view of inspiration which he carefully distinguished from revelation. Alfred acknowledged that St Thomas was not an outstanding man of science like Roger Bacon or Albert the Great. But he had few, if any, equals in the realm of social and political science. He referred to St Thomas' seminal views on private property, democracy and tyranny. Finally he stressed the importance of Catholic or Christian philosophy as a platform for the Christian faith and appealed to students to ensure that their knowledge of such philosophy and their religion kept pace with their growth in secular knowledge.

What St Thomas had done in the thirteenth century had to be done afresh in each generation. Perennial problems had to be posed and attempted solutions to them had to be expressed in the language of the present. To assist in that process he suggested that a new college society, to be known as the Academy of St Thomas, should be established.

Alfred established this society in mid-October 1931[25] and delivered the first festal lecture on St Thomas under its auspices on 7 March 1932. Speaking on 'St Thomas and ourselves', he maintained that the principles outlined in the *Summa Theologica* were as urgently required in modern times as they were in the thirteenth century. Yet the *Summa* and the other writings of St Thomas were largely unknown to the students of the college. While undergraduates in non-Catholic universities read philosophy, those at the colleges of the National University of Ireland did not. This meant, he said, that their graduates were unprepared for life, especially those who would be working and settling in a country whose culture and civilisation was alien to them. He contrasted the knowledge of Thomistic philosophy in French and Belgian intellectual circles to the ignorance of it among the laity in Ireland. A beginning should be made in the universities to rectify this situation. It was essential to train the whole man and not simply to produce engineers, technicians and persons qualified in the professions. A course in philosophy

25. See *ibid.*, 108-9.

Religious Writing and Lecturing

should be an integral part of university training. He indicated that he hoped to provide such a course in the near future. (He also gave the annual public lecture under the auspices of the Academy on 11 April 1934. On that occasion his subject was not St Thomas but Fr Willie Doyle.)

Alfred gave a talk on St Thomas on Radio Éireann on 7 March 1936. He recalled that the discovery of the writings of Aristotle by Europeans in the thirteenth century produced a great intellectual upheaval similar to that effected in their own time by agnostic naturalism. Conservative churchmen in St Thomas' time condemned him as he attempted to adapt Aristotelianism to Christianity and those who boasted of being modern and up to date neglected him. Similarly in modern times some churchmen kept St Thomas wrapped up in theological textbooks, while lay people were left to fetch their theology from Hollywood, with, perhaps, an occasional dose of H. G. Wells and Karl Marx. They had to get rid of this 'compartmentalising'. To cope with bureaucracy, to protect the family and professional autonomy, they would have to train the men and women in their universities in the sociological principles of St Thomas and his followers.

In his festal lecture to the Academy of St Thomas on 28 February 1939 Alfred warned that university students should guard against that smugness of attitude which resulted from confined scientific study. It was the world outside clear-cut scientific proof that really mattered. Speaking on 'spirituality and the layman', he explained that the lay person's spirituality had to be both public and private. The former was a social activity which should be as keen as any other social activity. He pointed out the economic duties of the Christian in the social life of that time. As an instance of social activity he declared that the Catholic layman should agitate for a living wage for workers.

On 7 March 1946 Alfred lectured on 'St Thomas and ourselves' under the auspices of the Academy of St Thomas. He gave an outline of the life of St Thomas and said that the saint was a living influence from whom much could be learned. Had the reformation not swept aside the medieval philosophers, most of the conflicts of the last two centuries would not have developed. He warned against the danger of irrationalism in their religion for many people were inclined to regard it as no more than custom. They should aim at an all-round development, in which religious and secular education went forward *pari passu*.

Alfred O'Rahilly III: Controversialist

On the following 7 March Alfred lectured on 'St Thomas Aquinas and ourselves' at University College, Galway. Showing the influence of the ethos of that time, he declared that there was no room for neutrality in the world of their time. It was a world of clashing creeds in which the people with no creed would be pushed aside.

A university, Alfred maintained, was not merely a place in which to learn certain subjects and to become a doctor or a teacher but more importantly a community wherein people matured and followed in the steps of Christ. One of the most important features of St Thomas' teaching was his rationalism. He stood by human reason in a way that Luther, Rousseau and Kant subsequently did not. Kant, whose philosophy had a major influence in English universities and in Trinity College, Dublin, denied the possibility of proving the existence of God objectively and abandoned all attempts to apply reason even to natural philosophy. Consequently, it was only the followers of St Thomas who could rightly claim to be rationalists.

Alfred acknowledged that as a scientist St Thomas believed a number of things which were later proved wrong, such as that the world was the geometric centre of the universe. Many modern scientists had dessicated life and turned man into a machine. One disadvantage issuing from this was that it was very difficult to insist that two machines should have respect for each other. This was being realised and some scientists were again addressing themselves to fundamental problems. In this regard the study of St Thomas was just as relevant in their time as in the thirteenth century. Thomism would facilitate an appreciation of Christian humanism, which, sadly, was far from being a feature of their universities. There were far too many people in the colleges of the National University of Ireland in a spiritual coma because, while they developed the secular side of life, they allowed their religion to remain at the penny catechism stage.

Alfred developed the theme 'St Thomas and ourselves' in a major article in the *Catholic Times* (of South Africa) of January 1949. He touched on a number of topics which he had dealt with at great length elsewhere. He illustrated St Thomas' advocacy of what, in effect, was a policy of national self-sufficiency and surveyed his views on trade and money. St Thomas, he declared, was a prime example of practical Christianity.

Religious Writing and Lecturing

He carried his principles into the workaday world around him and did not shut up his message in the sacristy and the cloister. Men of that spirit, he concluded, were needed then as never before. Alfred's admiration for St Thomas extended to the Dominican order. He achieved a life-long ambition when he was received into the Third Order of St Dominic by the provincial, Fr Thomas Garde, O.P., at Muckross Park Convent, Donnybrook, on 9 April 1956.

Religious poetry

At different times in his life Alfred wrote religious poetry but very little of it was published. It tended to be an expression of his devotion to Christ. A typical example appeared in the *Golden Hour*[26] of Nov.-Dec. 1929 over 'A.O'R.' as follows:

O Deus, ego amo Te
My God, I love You,
Not thereby to win salvation,
Nor yet because who love You not
Are punished with damnation.

You, my Jesus, on the Tree
Did atone for sinful me.
For me the whipcord's smart,
For me Your lance-pierced Heart.
Weariness and pain and calumny
And death – for me, for sinful me.

Why then not love You, Jesus, Friend,
You Who loved me to the end?
Not to win a place in Heaven,
Not to escape Hell's endless pain,
Not for any hope of gain,
Not from fear of any rod;
But this is why I love You, Jesus:
Because You are my King, my God![27]

26. Alfred's sister, Sister Walburga of the Convent of St Mary of the Isle, Cork, contributed frequently to this and other pious periodicals either anonymously or over pseudonyms.
27. Earlier Alfred had what a former fellow Jesuit scholastic described as 'a soul-stirring poem' published in the *Catholic Review* (New York) of August 1914.

Alfred O'Rahilly III: Controversialist

Liturgical reform

Alfred's religious writing and lecturing indicates that there was scarcely an aspect of the Christian religion which escaped his interest or attention. He was acutely aware that each generation had to make Christianity its own and encouraged that process. In 1953 he gave considerable encouragement to Fr Clifford Howell, S.J., who was then almost alone attempting to popularise radical liturgical reforms.[28] Alfred had a particular interest in one of these, the dialogue Mass, which ensured greater liturgical participation by the laity. This interest was typical. For him religion was not something to be merely thought about or written about or lectured on but to be prayed and put into practice by clergy, religious and laity alike.[29]

28. Alfred initiated a correspondence with Fr Howell (1902-81) in December 1953 after complimenting him on articles on the Dialogue Mass which he had published in the *Catholic Herald*. (For more on this remarkable Jesuit, see *Letters and notices* (published by the English province of the Society of Jesus), Easter 1981, 235-67; 349-61.) Earlier Alfred had favourably reviewed the work of Fr John Fennelly, another protagonist of liturgical reform. In the *Standard* of 31 October 1952 he commended *A children's Mass Book* for encouraging greater participation in the Mass and suggested that it be re-named 'The People's Mass Book'.

29. The above is taken from Herbert Thurston, S.J., 'The history of the name "Roman Catholic"', *Month*, September 1911; *Catholic Herald* 27 May 1938; 10 February 1939; 21 January 1944; 18 January 1946; *Catholic Times* (of South Africa), January 1949 (vol. XIV, no. 1); *Cork Examiner* 15 October 1930; 8 January, 9 March, 20 June 1932; 13 May 1933; 13 April 1934; 6 March, 30 November 1936; 25 January 1937; 15 March, 10 October, 28 November 1938; 27 March, 5 June 1939; 15 January, 4 May 1940; 6 March, 9 November 1942; 24, 31 January, 7, 14, 21, 28 February, 6, 15, 21 March 1944; 26 February, 5, 12, 19, 26 March, 1, 8, 15 April, 21 May 1945; 7, 14, 21, 28 January, 4, 11, 18, 26 February, 8 March, 15 April 1946; 8 March, 31 October 1947; 22 March 1948; 7 April, 25 September 1950; 25 February, 23 April 1951; 9 July 1952; *Irish Catholic* 1 December 1938; *Irish Independent* 15 October 1930; 30 November 1936; 30 May, 10 October, 28 November 1938; 5 June 1939; 6 May 1940; 9 November 1942; *Irish News and Belfast Morning News* 22 January 1949; *Irish Press* 24 May 1935; 7, 9 March, 30 November 1936; 10 October 1938; *Kerryman* 1 March 1947; *Limerick Leader* 31 March 1947; *Standard* 14 March, 24 October 1947; 27 July 1951; *Universe* 17 October 1930; 'Memoirs of Professor W. B. Stanford (1910-84)' (unpublished autobiography in the possession of his daughter, Mrs Melissa Webb, 2 Mount Salus, Knocknacree Road, Dalkey, County Dubin); interviews with An tOllamh Séamus Caomhánach, Captain Seán Feehan, Fr Michael McCarthy, C.S.Sp., and Fr Patrick Sheehan, M.S.C.; papers and writings of Alfred O'Rahilly and the sources already cited.

DEFENDER OF RELIGION, CHRISTIANITY AND IRISH CATHOLICISM

Alfred enjoyed polemics. He was particularly happy challenging those who attacked religion, Christianity or the Irish Catholic Church.

H. G. Wells

This was nowhere more obvious than in his articles on the views of Herbert George Wells, as expressed in *The fate of homo sapiens* (London 1939). The distinguished English novelist, sociologist, historian and utopian published excerpts from his book in the *Picture Post* of 4, 11 November and 9 December 1939. The *Irish Catholic* reacted by calling for the London weekly to be banned in Ireland. The editor of the *Picture Post* then publicly invited the editor of the *Irish Catholic* or a person nominated by him to reply to Wells. This prompted Francis O'Reilly, former secretary of the Catholic Truth Society of Ireland, to telegraph the editor of the *Picture Post* on 16 December as follows:

> Adverting Wells's articles, Professor Alfred O'Rahilly, M.A., D.Litt., D.Sc., Ph.D., University College, Cork, informs me willing if commissioned by you to reply to Wells in your paper. O'Rahilly most eminent publicist in Ireland. Suggest you telegraph offer at once.

O'Reilly confirmed his telegram by letter to the editor and to the publisher of the *Picture Post*. He received no reply, however.[1] Whatever chance there was of having Alfred's reply to Wells published in the *Picture Post* was lost to readers in most of Ireland when on 22 December 1939 the English weekly was

---

1. It is understandable that they would not have been in a hurry to do so. Although never sparing of the sensibilities of others, Wells was notoriously sensitive and tended for no great reason to resort to litigation. The *Freeman's Journal* of 5 August 1921 reported that Henry Arthur Jones, the dramatist, had written a book *My dear Wells* in which he examined the collectivist theories and social philosophy of Wells. According to Jones he added 'some playful coaxings' to his critique. On reading previews of these 'coaxings', Wells had threatened the American publisher with a libel action. For more on this aspect of Wells' character, see Michael Coren's *The invisible man: the life and liberties of H. G. Wells* (London 1993).

53

Alfred O'Rahilly III: Controversialist

formally banned from Éire by the Censorship Board on the grounds that it had been indecent. The English *Catholic Herald* of 29 December 1939 reported that *Picture Post* had been banned in Éire for three months and continued: 'This ban, it appears, is the sequel to the publication of an article, summarising a recent book by H. G. Wells, in which Éire and its Catholicity were grossly and unfairly attacked.' In a letter in the following issue of the *Catholic Herald* Francis O'Reilly recalled his offer to the editor of the *Picture Post* and showed that the London pictorial weekly had been banned not for the reason alleged but, in accordance with the regulations of the Censorship Board, on grounds of indecency and obscenity, which had been catalogued over several months. The editor of *Picture Post* published 'The last word about Mr Wells' in his issue of 30 December. This, however, was not the end of the matter. *Picture Post* of 13 January 1940 carried an article entitled 'We are banned in Éire'. In the *Standard* of 26 January 1940 Francis O'Reilly pointed out that in the *Picture Post* of 30 December 1939 and 13 January 1940 no mention was made of the offer by Alfred O'Rahilly to reply to Wells.

In the meantime, on Christmas Eve and Christmas Day 1939, Alfred had prepared eight articles in reply to Wells. These and an extra article were published in the *Standard* between 12 January and 1 March 1940. The articles aroused considerable interest and were credited with almost doubling the circulation of the paper. They also ushered in Alfred's close association with that weekly over the next twenty years. In a letter published in the *Standard* of 8 March 1940 Alfred thanked those who had written to him from many parts of the world concerning the articles. He indicated that he had a lot more to say about evolution and comparative religion and was eager to examine H. G. Wells's 'latest stunt on *The rights of man*' and so proposed to issue the articles in an extended form as a booklet. The booklet was to be entitled 'A Cockney Voltaire', an epithet, which Alfred pointed out, Wells had selected for himself in his autobiography. Pressure of work, however, prevented Alfred from completing the project.[2]

[2]. For these articles, see Appendix 2. With these articles Alfred was not finished with the *Picture Post*. Towards the end of May 1947 Edward Hulton, the then millionaire owner of *Picture Post* and other newspapers, spent a week in Dublin and its environs. In 'Ireland re-visited' in the *Picture Post* of 7 June

Defender of Religion, Christianity and Irish Catholicism

In the *Standard* of 9 April 1943 Alfred added a postscript to his articles on Wells. *The fate of homo sapiens* and another of Wells's literary pieces were reissued as *The outlook for homo sapiens*. This was selected as the book of the month for members of the Readers' Union. Frank O'Mahony, a Limerick bookseller, and a number of his friends were members of the Union. They indicated their disagreement with the choice and returned copies of the book. This prompted the *Readers' News*, the commercial organ of the Union, to embark on a 'war with O'Mahony'. The selection committee charged that 'fear of books still existed in Ireland'. Alfred ridiculed the charge, noting that it may never have occurred to the selection committee that O'Mahony and his friends might be 'just bored stiff with the nauseating tripe' which came from Wells's pen. To the charge of censorship, Alfred pointed out that the works of Wells were available in Ireland. He quoted from a letter of 23 September 1942 in which the Readers' Union threatened to stop book supplies to O'Mahony. He maintained that, in effect, this meant that an alien clique had decided to browbeat and to victimise any bookseller who refused to force on his customers 'any blasphemous anti-Catholic bilge' they decided to prescribe. In conclusion, he called on Limerick to 'stand up to the bookbullies'.

John Strachey

Towards the end of 1942 Alfred read John Strachey's *A faith to fight for* which had been published a year earlier. His critique of the book appeared in two articles in the *Standard* of 11 and 18 December 1942. To justify participation in the war, Strachey, who professed to be a communist, set out two 'moral

---

1947 he was dismissive of the censorship laws, the influence of the Catholic Church and the State's promotion of the Irish language and culture. Alfred was requested by Peadar O'Curry, editor of the *Standard*, to reply to the comments made by Hulton, some of which were quite offensive. This Alfred did in 'At it again!: *Picture Post* piffle I', *Standard* 27 June 1947 and '*Picture Post* piffle II: a modern priest in mufti', *Standard* 4 July 1947. He recalled his reply years earlier to the article in the *Picture Post* by H. G. Wells. Then, as his two articles were accurately sub-titled, he 'exploded Edward Hulton's fallacies about Ireland'. His concluding remark would have struck a chord with the *Standard*'s readers: he 'objected to Hulton defaming our religion and ridiculing our national ideals'.

Alfred O'Rahilly III: Controversialist

principles' as follows: 'As the world sinks in havoc and the continents are piled with the bodies of dead nations, these two ideals, truth and love, emerge as fixed stars. They emerge as the sole objectives towards which we can even desire to struggle.'

In his first article Alfred showed that Strachey's ideal of truth was applied science. This in the service of human welfare was to replace religion. He complained that Strachey made no attempt to authenticate his concept of truth. What guarantee, he asked, was there that Strachey's truth, namely, a collection of objectively valid assertions, was desirable or beneficial? He urged that, to one who denied the existence of God, it would be difficult to find any certain ground for affirming that the objective world with its laws was good when much of the apparent evidence indicated the opposite. He showed that Strachey was not so much interested in the discovery of truths as in their utilisation. The ultimate product of such truth was the machine, which was capable of being used in the service of good or evil. Where was Strachey's guarantee that science or the machine would not be misused?

Alfred was dismissive of Strachey's theory that Nature, God's successor, would in this life reward the good and punish the wicked for the good of mankind. He described such a view as humanism without a philosophy of humanity or a metaphysic, a code without a creed. If there was no God, no soul, no afterlife, Alfred asked, should man not ally himself with Nature and by mercy-killing, abortion and sterilisation eliminate mental, moral and physical deficients?

Strachey had claimed that in socialism the individual fulfils himself by his unforced identity with the commonweal. In effect, Strachey, said Alfred, requires the individual's interests to be subordinated to the community, namely the State. Moreover, he did not produce a single argument for limiting the absorption of the individual and the family in the modern all-powerful State. Thus logically he was committed to the totalitarianism which he condemned in the Third Reich.

Strachey had purported to put forward his view as the modern scientific substitute for religion. In describing religion in general and Christianity in particular, Alfred pointed out, he exhibited an astonishing ignorance and the result was no more than a sorry caricature. Alfred concluded that it was surprising that the fanatical loyalty to the truth, so strongly preached by the author, did not lead him to read a little more before presenting his 'pawky miserable ersatz' in place of religion.

In his second article Alfred examined Strachey's second moral principle. This was love, about which he had written that 'it was part of a faith by which we may live in our times'. For Strachey love was biological, said Alfred, and necessary to the survival of the race. Alfred illustrated the inadequacy of Strachey's treatment of the concept of love. Then he took up what Strachey regarded as 'the repudiation of love', namely, 'forcibly to restrict women's activities to unpaid domestic work'. He asked: 'Does Mr Strachey think that the capitalist exploitation of women-workers, with its break-up of homes and family life, is a manifestation of "love"? No doubt there are women fitted and called to do intellectual and artistic work. But we are dealing with the mass of women-workers – clerks, typists, factory hands, charwomen. Is it "love" which has brought them into the labour market, especially when many of their fathers and husbands are idle?' He continued: 'Has this alleged freedom any real survival value, is it conducive to motherhood and to family-rearing?' He went on: 'It is a strange idea of "love" to think that all service should be paid for.'

Alfred next dealt with Strachey's Marxist interpretation of history. This he illustrated with the following quotation from *A faith to fight for*:

> The ideal of love received its decisive formulation in the ancient world in the form of the Christian religion . . . Naturally it was not a mere accident that this ideal or religion appeared just then . . . The idea of an all-embracing human love which excluded the possibility of slavery could never have been born – whether in a manger or in the minds of men, whichever way you like to put it – unless men had been approaching the point at which they had sufficient command of natural forces to be able to do without the enslavement of a part of the people and yet to produce that surplus upon which every civilisation must be built.
>
> In the days of the Caesars, society was approaching this point. And sure enough men called Christians appeared, who taught amongst other things that all men (including the slaves) were equal in the above sense that they were all men of the same clay with the same fundamental possibilities in

them. They preached this world-shattering idea in the form of the doctrine that all men were equal in the sight of God, that the slave had an immortal soul as well as the patrician. But they preached it . . . The Christian doctrine of a love embracing all men grew, and Rome fell.

Alfred poked fun at this 'gospel according to Strachey', wherein the technique of production was so sufficiently advanced by A.D. 30 that slavery could be dispensed with and the condition of the food-supply automatically induced a campaign to abolish slavery. The personality of Christ, the resurrection, the teaching of the gospels and everything else which cannot be thrust into the procrustean bed of the economic-materialist interpretation of history were dismissed as trifles. Alfred accused Strachey of a magnificent impertinence in attempting to present Christianity without Christ. To Strachey's comment, 'and Rome fell', Alfred replied that Rome had risen again. Christ and Caesar were again face to face, the spiritual and the temporal striving for mastery. And, in spite of his vague rhetoric about truth and love, Strachey was on the side of Caesar. For his truth was soulless science and his love mere biological cohesion. He had left in man nothing which escaped the jurisdiction of the praetor's forum.

George Bernard Shaw

In a letter, dated 10 February 1946, George Bernard Shaw formally accepted an invitation by Dublin Corporation to become a freeman of the city. In a separate letter he thanked James Larkin who had sponsored the motion to confer the honour on him. Although in his ninetieth year, he could not resist responding with characteristic puckishness. He urged Larkin to use the labour and trade-union movement as a stage towards communism and, in effect, to free the Irish people from 'Catholic agriculture'. He suggested that Irish farmers should give up 'their petty landlordism' and 'look eastward' to the 'visible miracles' of collective farming.

Alfred reacted strongly to Shaw's letter and in an article in the *Standard* of 1 March 1946 charged him with being offensive to Irish Catholics, whose opposition to communism was well-known. He reminded his fellow Catholics that Shaw disagreed

Defender of Religion, Christianity and Irish Catholicism

with their religion. Continuing, he recalled that, according to Shaw himself, at the age of eighteen, while wandering on Torca Hill, near Dalkey, he discovered that prayer was a 'superstitious practice'. Two years later he left Dublin for London and since then he had crusaded against Christianity. In doing so he was full of assurance, although the only religion of which he had inside knowledge was the one his family had rejected before he was ten.

Replying to Shaw's advocacy of communism, Alfred declared that as usual he disdained argument and simply announced his judgements with 'the leer of a jester' rather than 'the fervour of a prophet'. Drawing from Eugene Lyons's *Assignment in Utopia* (New York 1937) he showed that this was typical of Shaw. Lyons, he pointed out, was an Americanised Russian Jew who lived for many years as a newspaper correspondent in Russia. Although a communist, he was disillusioned by the brutal realities of the Soviet Union. In his book he described Shaw's visit to Russia in 1931. The Russians surrounded Shaw with yes men and functionaries. They had an easy job in screening him from inconvenient facts, for he came to be seen, not to see. He exhibited himself at banquets, in a factory or two, on a hand-tooled collective farm, astride the Napoleon cannon in the Kremlin, wherever camera-men could get 'good' pictures. Lyons reported: 'At first Soviet officialdom was uneasy; the incorrigible oldster might play a few pranks on them. He might have pried into their closets for skeletons of forced labour, valuta arrests, concentration camps; or make nasty remarks about the hard-worked and undernourished proletariat. He might have demanded statistics on political prisoners.' Such fears, however, it seems, were quickly allayed, as it became clear that Shaw was determined to praise everything in the Soviet Union.

With further excerpts from Lyons's book, Alfred showed that Shaw judged collectivisation to be good by the model farm to which he was shepherded. At a banquet in his honour Shaw stated that his friends had loaded him with tinned food, but that he had thrown it out of the carriage window in Poland before reaching the Soviet frontier. This was declaimed on a full stomach and with a mischievous laugh in a country of starving people.

Alfred next commented on Shaw's suggestion that Irish farmers should end their 'petty landlordism', 'look eastward'

Alfred O'Rahilly III: Controversialist

and see the 'visible miracles' of collective farming. This system, Alfred recalled, was inaugurated in 1930. A million farmers were dispossessed of their holdings and deported to the frozen north and to the deserts of Central Asia. In terror sixty million agriculturalists rushed for the shelter of hastily organised collective farms. In 1932-3 there followed a man-made famine during which the farmers' grain was taken by force. Although the extent of the famine which in the Ukraine claimed between four and five million lives was known outside Russia, not the slightest allusion to it was allowed to appear in the Soviet press.

Alfred went on to illustrate the extent to which Shaw's friends and close associates in the Fabian Society, Sidney and Beatrice Webb, were blinkered against what was happening in Russia. In the index to their *Soviet communism: dictatorship or democracy?* (London 1936) there was an entry: 'Famine in Russia, alleged, in 1931-3'. In referring to the ejection from their relatively successful holdings of a million families, the Webbs wrote: 'Strong must have been the faith and resolute the will of men who, in the interest of what seemed to them the public good, could take so momentous a decision'! Their comment when Stalin had 50,000 people slaughtered in December 1934 after the assassination of Kirov was that such an action 'could not but excite adverse comment'![3]

3. The uncritical acceptance by sections of the Western press of Shaw's glowing account of his visit to Stalin's Russia is well exemplified in the *Irish Times* of 3 August 1931:

MR SHAW HOME AGAIN

Mr Bernard Shaw arrived home yesterday after a tour in Russia – and he is sorry to be back. Before he set out he stated to a reporter that it was an insane thing to do. Now he believes that it is one of the wisest actions he has ever taken.

'Russia,' he told a reporter who spoke to him at his Codicote (Hertfordshire) home, 'is putting her house in order. All the other nations are playing the fool.'

'No, I cannot speak to you in detail about the great experiment I have seen. What I have to say must be carefully thought out and written. I am making arrangements to do this.'

'Meanwhile, all I can add is this: We had better follow Russia's example as soon as possible.'

'Were you treated well on your visit?' Mr Shaw was asked.

'Treated well,' he repeated, with a chuckle; 'we were treated like kings, and the food we had was very good.'

'Is the cost of living high?'

Defender of Religion, Christianity and Irish Catholicism

Alfred then turned his attention to the system of collective farming and showed that it was the 'old landlordism writ large'. The collective farms were not a whit more 'democratic' than the crown lands or the big ranches in other countries. The farmers on them became labour gangs, were share-croppers for the government which camouflaged its exactions as taxes, hiring costs of machinery or 'purchases', based on a price fixed for the urban consumer. Every detail of management – acreage, disposal of crops, wages paid – was decided in Moscow, Kharkov or Rostov. The collective farms were denied even the right to own tractors or other machinery which remained a State monopoly. This, declared Alfred, was the reality behind 'the alluring picture' which had been held up as a preferable alternative to what Shaw described as 'Catholic agriculture'. He concluded by advising Shaw that, while his compatriots would enjoy his playing the stage Irishman with pen instead of shillelagh, they would continue to refuse to take him seriously as a philosopher or a sociologist.

Peadar O'Donnell

Alfred particularly enjoyed attacking the humbug of home-based left-wing intellectuals. A typical sally is to be found in 'Pat Murphy's jottings' in the *Standard* of 29 November 1946. He noted that the dean of Canterbury had addressed a meeting in the Mansion House, Dublin, organised by the Irish-Soviet Friendship Society. The 'Red Dean' eulogised the economic, religious and political freedom in the Soviet Union. Alfred reported that such was the tight security for the meeting that only 'comrades' and 'innocents' were allowed into the hall. Tongue in cheek he noted from reports that Peadar O'Donnell, who chaired the meeting, had declared that 'stupid Irish taxpayers got their notions of the Soviet Union "from old wives' tales in religious books".' Earlier in his piece Alfred had described George Orwell's *Animal Farm* as a fairy tale about a Communist State and suggested that it would be an appropriate

---

'Well, it is like everywhere else. You can live expensively in Russia if you want to, but you also can live quite cheaply.'
'No,' Mr Shaw added firmly; 'I can say nothing more about my visit. My last word, for the moment at any rate, is this: On the whole, I should advise a young man to go to Russia and settle there.'

Alfred O'Rahilly III: Controversialist

Christmas gift from Santa Claus for O'Donnell, 'chairman of the Friends of Soviet Russia, then re-named the Irish-Soviet Friendship Society, since Stalin had dissolved the Communist Party of Ireland.'

Evelyn Waugh

An article 'The American epoch in the Catholic Church' was published by Evelyn Waugh in the November 1949 issue of the *Month* and was reproduced a month later in the *Catholic Digest*. At the editor's request, Alfred published a critique of it in the *Standard* of 9 December. As the article was lengthy, he indicated his intention of confining his remarks to 'some expressions of anti-Irish prejudice' which he judged it to contain. In contrast to Waugh's short visit to the United States, he recalled that he had spent a year there between the two world wars and stated that since then he had 'kept in touch' through Catholic American periodicals and books. He professed to have been impressed by the tremendous progress made in matters which interested him. There was a more positive, co-operative attitude to labour, a more constructive effort to combat racial bias against coloured people and an increase of intellectual influence, partly due to the frequent visits of foreign scholars.

Alfred regretted that running all through Waugh's article was a streak of antipathy to the Irish at home and abroad. The letter wrote of 'a contumacious Irish priest proclaiming damnation on all heretics' in Boston. But he omitted to report that this priest – Fr Leonard Feeney, S.J. – had been reprehended by his Irish superior and condemned by his Irish archbishop. Waugh's great ambition, continued Alfred, was to de-hibernicise the Church, and this was clear from his complaint: 'The problem with the Irish is to guard them from the huge presumption of treating the Universal Church as a friendly association of their own.' To this, Alfred responded that the Irish had no need of 'Oxford converts' to guard them against that religious nationalism which, since Henry VIII, had been so characteristic of England. He described as insulting Waugh's remarks about the conduct of the Irish in New York on St Patrick's day and his comment that 'in Boston on any day of the year the stranger might well suppose that Catholicism was a tribal cult'.

Waugh did acknowledge the contribution of Irish-Americans to the American Church: 'The Irish with their truculence and

Defender of Religion, Christianity and Irish Catholicism

practical good sense have built and paid for the churches, opening new parishes as fast as the population grew; they have staffed the active religious orders and have created a national system of education.' Even in this commendation, Alfred detected some barbs. One would imagine, he declared, that the Irish shunned the contemplative orders. Moreover, instead of crediting the Irish with a determination to keep the Faith and with co-operating with God's grace, Waugh attributed their zeal to truculence and practical sense. Alfred objected to the 'very superior way' Waugh wrote of what the Irish had done for education in America: 'The Catholic colleges do not set themselves the aims of Harvard or Oxford or the Sorbonne. Their object is to transform a proletariat into a bourgeoisie.' Alfred reminded Waugh that the people he spoke of were the exiles of a race that never had the characteristics of a proletariat. Moreover, teaching philosophy to dentists, sociology to workers, and many other programmes in the Catholic colleges, could scarcely be construed as having a bourgeois objective.

Concerning Irish priests in the United States, Alfred found Waugh offensively patronising in writing: 'They are faithful and chaste and, in youth at any rate, industrious; but . . . they have lost their ancestral simplicity without yet acquiring a modest carriage of their superior learning or, what is more important, delicacy in their human relations or imagination or agility of mind.' The 'ancestral simplicity' of Irish-American bishops and priests, declared Alfred, presumably referred to their 'uncouth ancestors in the ubiquitous "bogs" in Hell or Connacht'. Their real fault, he suggested, was that they were 'not sufficiently obsequious to their intellectual superiors from Oxford.' He charged that Waugh's comment that 'it is one of the functions of an upper class to remind the clergy of the true balance between their spiritual and their temporal positions' camouflaged a regret that British Catholics were not allowed 'to supply an upper class to this long-lost colony'.

Waugh, it seems, did not feel at home in any congregation predominantly Irish. He complained that they had brought with them to America 'all their ancient grudges and the melancholy of the bogs'. He continued: 'At heart they remain the same adroit and joyless race that broke the hearts of all who ever tried to help them'. Alfred expressed his amazement at the suggestion that the Irish were joyless when they were generally supposed 'to be addicted to singing, dancing and racing and had resisted English Puritanism'. As for the British who tried to 'help' the Irish, most recently 'with the Black and Tans, the Irish broke their domination, but surely not their hearts'!

Alfred maintained that Waugh's real objection and that of some of his fellow English Catholic intellectuals to the Irish was that they found it impossible to treat them as friendly equals, as they would Dutch Catholics. They regarded the Irish as apostate Englishmen. To illustrate this, Alfred quoted Waugh's comment: 'When there was a project for a national Catholic University, Newman went to Ireland. Had Ireland remained in the United Kingdom, Dublin would today be one of the great religious capitals of the world, where Catholics from all over the British empire resorted for education and leadership. That splendid hope was defeated by politicians.' Alfred corrected this rather muddled potted history. Newman, he pointed out, was never in favour of a 'national' university. On 7 March 1856 he wrote to Bishop Grant: 'What is Ireland to me, except the university here is a university for England as well as for Ireland? . . . If there is a college for Catholics in Oxford, or anything approaching to it, I am at once loosened from this place.' Moreover, one of Newman's reasons for resigning was 'because the hope of the university being English as well as Irish was quite at an end'. The project, apart from its inherent defects, failed because English Catholics would not attend the university and the British government would not give it a charter. Least of all credible reasons for its failure was the fact that sixty years later the Irish people, not just politicians, left the United Kingdom. Finally, Alfred pointed out, Dublin was one of the great religious capitals of the world, even if it lacked its full complement of Catholics from the British Commonwealth.

Waugh remarked that should Irish-Americans ever visit Ireland they would be shocked by the cynicism of their Dublin cousins. In fact, wrote Alfred, they did visit the country and were not shocked but edified and consoled. 'One of the most moving sights of my tour' was how Waugh described the crowds with ashes on their foreheads on Ash Wednesday in New Orleans. Alfred invited him to visit Dublin, Cork or any Irish town on the next Ash Wednesday to witness this commonplace of religious practice. Apropos of a visit to Notre Dame, Waugh wrote that the number of those receiving Communion

Defender of Religion, Christianity and Irish Catholicism

was startling to a European, and disposed of the charge of Jansenism often loosely preferred against the Irish clergy. Alfred regretted that Waugh did not have the opportunity to visit the churches in Dublin or Cork any morning and witness a similar eucharistic practice. In a final remark Waugh declared: 'To the Europeans it seems that the Irish have been led to betray their manifest historical destiny.' Alfred expressed surprise that Waugh seemed to be under the illusion that Ireland was not in Europe. He continued that it was clear that the destiny which Waugh had in mind was that Ireland should 'be a subordinate part of England'. Such a pronouncement he described as 'nauseating' and 'pontifically pompous' and concluded that, while 'Mr Waugh, the novelist, we appreciate; Mr Waugh, the rabid unionist, we understand and refute; Mr Waugh, "the European", uttering jeremiads over us we refuse to take seriously'.

Voltaire

It was inevitable that Alfred at some stage would come to grips with Voltaire, the outstanding apostle of irreligion. In the *Irish Independent* of 8 August 1939 he reviewed *Voltaire* (London 1938) by Alfred Noyes, a recent convert to Catholicism. When first published this book, in which the author portrayed Voltaire as a sincere theist, an admirer of true religion and one who had a hatred of superstition and corruption, caused a sensation. He attracted further publicity when the archdiocesan authorities in Westminster insisted on some clarification before the book could receive an *imprimatur*. Some of Noyes's co-religionists thought the book was the ebullition of a half-baked convert, some thought it was a subtle attack on the Church, while many felt that their historical sense had been outraged.

Alfred acknowledged that Noyes had done a good service in placing Voltaire's life in its historical context and in requesting that he be judged amid the rather cynical and depraved world in which he lived. However, he cautioned that this could be carried too far, if it resulted, as he implied it did, in the denigration of contemporaries and the whitewashing of hypocrisy. He contended that, while Noyes had shown that the real Voltaire was very different from the traditional portrait and that his beliefs were nearer to Christianity than was usually supposed, the author had succumbed unduly to his own enthusiasm and had become too much of an apologist for his subject. Alfred declared that, as the science and philosophy of Voltaire were 'dead', the investigation of his views concerned the historian, not the religious apologist. He concluded that Noyes, 'by his exaggerated reaction against the perversions of cheap rationalists', had paved the way for some future historian to give a more objective picture.

Already Mary Ryan, professor of romance languages at U.C.C., had rebutted in her pamphlet *Alfred Noyes on Voltaire* (Dublin 1938), some of the claims made by Noyes. Alfred, however, considered that a more detailed response was required. He suggested to Kathleen O'Flaherty, then a promising scholar, that she should do so. She agreed, but first she had to complete her doctoral studies. Eventually Dr O'Flaherty's *Voltaire, myth and reality* was jointly published by Cork University Press and Blackwells of Oxford in August 1945. A second edition appeared in December and a third early in the following year.

Alfred contributed fourteen pages of additional notes to the book. In the first of these notes he rebutted Voltaire's attack on the historicity of the New Testament. The second took issue with Voltaire's charge that St Joan of Arc was a deliberate imposter. In the third he showed that Voltaire's comments on the appalling massacre of St Bartholomew's day were inaccurate and misleading. The fourth note was designed to debunk the extravagant claims made by some rationalists on behalf of Voltaire as a scientific pioneer.

Dr O'Flaherty's book was well received in Britain. It was favourably reviewed in a number of the London quality newspapers, including the *Sunday Times* which made it the book of the month. This was in stark contrast to the reception it received at home from what Alfred was wont to refer to as 'the metropolitan intelligentsia'. They saw the hand of Alfred behind it and reacted accordingly. Typical of their attitude to the book was a review in the *Irish Times* of 29 September 1945, written by Vivian Mercier but published anonymously.

Mercier began by describing the book as 'Dr O'Rahilly's counterblast to Mr Alfred Noyes'. Alfred's description of Voltaire as a 'Prussianised farceur' and H. G. Wells as 'that self-styled Cockney Voltaire', he selected as 'the chief plums from Cork's truest heir to the mantle of Maginn'! Coming to the book

Defender of Religion, Christianity and Irish Catholicism

itself, he acknowledged that it was a conclusive though 'dreary' refutation of Noyes' book. He described O'Flaherty as utilising Voltaire's correspondence to 'persistently nag' at Noyes. Extrapolating an inept syllogism from the book, he suggested, on foot of that, that O'Flaherty was hardly entitled 'to sneer at Voltaire's powers of reasoning'. His final quibble was typical of the entire piece: 'Is it impossible for a university press to find a competent proof reader? "Venemous" (*sic*), a word Dr O'Flaherty finds much occasion to use, is misspelled thus throughout.'

Thomas Hogan[4] reviewed *Voltaire, myth and reality* in the *Bell* of November 1945. He recalled that Mary Ryan had already peppered the fabric of Noyes' book with erudite text and context in a pamphlet. But, he continued, and it would seem with Alfred in mind, 'Cork has not finished with Voltaire'. He stated that Dr O'Flaherty had 'armed herself with an impressive array of quotations, culled from every cranny of the twelve volumes of the Firmin Didot edition of Voltaire's *'Oeuvres'* and had produced 'a literary sawn-off shot-gun'. He concluded that she had used these quotations effectively to show that Voltaire was 'a liar, a coward, a malevolent anti-Christian, a rogue and a scoundrel'.

O'Flaherty, he reported, had criticised Noyes for failing to consult original texts. In her account of a quarrel between Voltaire and President De Brosses she was dependent on a secondary source because of war-time restrictions. This was a relatively insignificant section of the book and O'Flaherty, in a footnote, indicated her inability to consult the primary source. Nonetheless, on foot of this alone Hogan criticised her for 'dogmatising on secondary or even tertiary sources'. In the preface O'Flaherty explained the purpose of her book and the theme to be pursued. Hogan chose to ignore this and described her treatment throughout as 'nagging and querulous' and 'niggling and spiteful'.

Hogan's next criticism, that of O'Flaherty's treatment of the 'Calas case', was acknowledged by the author when in the second edition of her book she extended the treatment of this subject. Hogan made some further valid points complaining that

---

4. This was a pseudonym for Thomas (Tommy) Woods, a civil servant in the department of external affairs, who occasionally wrote a column and reviewed books in the *Irish Times*.

Alfred O'Rahilly III: Controversialist

to abstract Voltaire from the cruel and corrupt age in which he lived was fatal to a just appreciation of him. Voltaire's attitude to the Church should be related to historical facts. In France the Church had become tied to a tyrannical and corrupt State with inevitably evil results. It was against the whole social structure that Voltaire launched his attacks and that structure, 'unfortunately', included the Church. In the violence of the attacks Voltaire went at times, conceded Hogan, far beyond what logic, or even the circumstances of the time, demanded. In the light of the substance of Hogan's critique, there was a delicious, albeit unconscious, irony about his concluding remarks: 'Charity and an awareness of the beam in our own eyes demands that we be not too harsh in our view of all Voltaire's attacks on religion.'

Dr O'Flaherty was aware of the principal motivation behind these reviews. In a note to the second edition of her book she wrote: 'Some critics have considered my treatment one-sided and have accused me of forgetting Voltaire's gifts as a writer; evidently they did not read the preface. No one has queried the accuracy of my quotations and translations or impugned my arguments. Hence I find no reason for altering my views, even though they did not please some reviewers.'

Irish Tribune, a weekly review of affairs

The publication of the *Irish Tribune, a weekly review of affairs* in 1926 gave Alfred another platform for his vigorous Catholicism. This weekly had its roots in a meeting held in Cork on 8 November 1925 to protest against the outcome of the Boundary Commission. Those attending the meeting, who were later described as Irish-Irelanders and readers of the *Leader*, established An Cumann Aontacht, with a view to defeating the proposals of the Commission. Within a few months this organisation had ceased to exist, but not before its members had successfully persuaded Alfred to partially fund and to edit a publication which would give public expression to their views. Laurence P. Byrne was hired to supervise the publication of the newspaper, the first issue of which appeared on 12 March 1926. Byrne, who used the *nom-de-plume* Andrew E. Malone, was a well-known journalist, whose Irish-Ireland credentials were impeccable. His support for Sinn Féin policies was clear from

Defender of Religion, Christianity and Irish Catholicism

his regular contributions to *New Ireland* in 1917 and 1918. In mid-March 1918 he was ousted out of the editorial chair of the Irish Labour Party's *Irish Opinion: a weekly journal of industrial and political democracy* because of his pro-Sinn Féin tendencies. Subsequently he was best known as a theatre critic. After taking up his post Byrne, in a letter, dated 18 February 1926, appealed, on behalf of Alfred, to W. P. Ryan and his son, Desmond, to write for the new publication. He informed Ryan that the *Irish Tribune* was to appear under the editorship of Alfred as an alternative to the *Irish Statesman*. And he added: 'The policy of the paper will be quite definitely Irish with an economic tendency.'

In preparing for the inauguration of the new weekly Alfred was chiefly assisted by Eamon O'Donoghue, lecturer in the Celtic Studies department in U.C.C. At his suggestion, Alfred in early February 1926 sought the advice of William O'Brien, then in retirement in Mallow. On receiving it, he replied, in a letter, dated 17 February 1926:

> I hope to send you a draft of the policy for criticisms and suggestions which I should be very glad to have from one of your experience and eminence.
>
> I may have explained myself badly and hurriedly. In any case I am not dogmatic and am open to help and advice.
>
> A hurried explanation.
>
> (1) I do not want a merely local paper. I want an All-Ireland paper. I think the present Dublin weeklies are too much entrenched in the banks of the Liffey. A recital in Dublin, or a teacup row in the Abbey, assumes national proportions in their eyes.[5] I want to see Ireland in proper perspective. Cork, Kerry, Belfast, everywhere – besides Dublin. (Personally, I am a federalist. That is, I think local autonomy apart from national unity should be developed. I do not see how the North is ever going to come in except on a federal basis.)
>
> So I hope no further 'mangling' is involved in the paper's policy.

5. This was a reference to the widespread coverage of the disturbances in the Abbey Theatre on 11 February during a performance of Seán O'Casey's *The plough and the stars*.

(2) Re 'Catholic'. I quite agree with you. No intolerance or bigotry. I merely meant that we shall hold ourselves free to advocate Catholic social principles.

Alfred concluded by appealing to O'Brien to provide an article for the paper's first issue.

Two days later O'Donoghue wrote to O'Brien. He reminded him that he was 'an old campaigner and colleague of the *Cork Free Press* days'. He indicated the motivation of those launching the new paper as follows: 'Apart from this project, I submit that, at the present juncture, it is essential that young men and old among us, here in Munster, should join together and endeavour to re-adjust the national orientation, which, somehow, seems recently to have drifted from its traditional moorings.' With a view to a 'frank exchange of views' on the matter, he suggested that Alfred and he were eager to call on O'Brien.

In the last week of February Alfred and O'Donoghue visited O'Brien. Alfred felt very honoured at meeting O'Brien and his wife, Sophie. In addition, he was delighted to receive a long article from O'Brien on Tim Healy which he published in the first two issues of the new weekly. Apart from an issue which should have appeared on 9 April, *The Irish Tribune* was published each week until its final issue of 31 December 1926. After Alfred left U.C.C. for a sabbatical at Harvard in September, Daniel Corkery supervised its publication, but by the end of the year no one was willing to continue to take editorial and financial responsibility for it.

Alfred expended much energy in ensuring the initial success of the weekly. He persuaded Frank O'Connor and Seán Ó Faoláin to contribute to it.[6] Subsequently the *Irish Tribune* was disparagingly described as Cork's answer to George Russell's *Irish Statesman*. Its admirers regarded it as complementing the Anglo-Irish, Anglophile, Protestant emphasis in that publication. This was true in the case of economics and politics and especially with regard to topics with which Alfred dealt.

6. Other contributors included: Beirt Fhear (J. J. Doyle), John Busteed, James Carty, Daniel Corkery, Aodh de Blacam, Thomas D. Donovan, J. L. Fawsitt, Hugo V. Flinn, Frank Gallagher, F. R. Higgins, James Hogan, D. M. Lenihan, Patrick J. Little, Criostóir Mac Aonghusa, Andrew E. Malone, Seán MacEntee, Seán Milroy, Monk Gibbon, R. J. P. Mortished, Cormac Ó Cadhlaigh, Shán Ó Cuív, Eoin O'Mahony, T. F. O'Rahilly, Desmond Ryan, W. P. Ryan, W. F. P. Stockley and Tórna (Tadhg Ó Donnchadha).

Defender of Religion, Christianity and Irish Catholicism

Ó Faoláin must have found his association with the *Tribune* useful when he founded *The Bell* in 1940. Although the latter concentrated on fiction and poetry, it also purported to deal with the economic, social and other issues facing the newly independent country and it also published articles on national and international affairs.

At the beginning of June Alfred had Laurence P. Byrne dismissed. On 4 June Byrne informed W. P. Ryan that he had been sacked because of his having objected to the use of the paper as a tool of local protectionist business interests. However, in a letter, dated 14 June, Alfred informed W. P. Ryan that Byrne had been sacked for incompetence and lack of attention to his work. He illustrated this by enclosing the corrected final proofs of a poem 'Romantic Ireland' submitted by Ryan, which had been published by Byrne in a mutilated form.[7] Alfred apologised to Ryan and expressed a hope that he would continue to write for the paper.

Reviewer of plays, books and films

In the issue of 14 May 1926 Alfred published a review of George Bernard Shaw's 'Saint Joan' then being presented in Cork. He acknowledged that he was not 'an up-to-date drama critic'. Yet he complained that the fourth scene in the play was 'intolerably dull', and the speeches of some of the characters were 'tiresome and irritating' and that the last scene was 'fantastic and forced'.

Alfred then donned his historian's hat. He compared the play to a forceful lecture in philosophy and history at which the audience was not allowed to raise difficulties. Shaw had reconstructed history to prove a thesis, namely that organised religion is the enemy of religious genius. When facts were not available to this end, then Shaw invented them. Moreover, his characters were all weighed down with the knowledge of what happened during the intervening centuries and so lacked the

---

7. See *Irish Tribune* 28 May 1926. The last three lines gave the poem its meaning. With no supervision from Byrne, the printer, to Alfred's horror, had omitted them because of lack of space. However, it seems that Byrne's performance was unsatisfactory in other ways also. In his letter to W. P. Ryan, having stated that Byrne 'was not a success', Alfred added: 'We have been trying to disinter correspondence and accounts'.

spontaneity and freshness of living persons from whom the future is hidden. They viewed their own age, continued Alfred, 'with the eyes of post-Victorian cynics'.

Alfred questioned Shaw's contention that the Catholic Church burnt St Joan as a protestant. He rejected Shaw's identification of the Church with 'any little local collection of clerics even when they act illegally'. He complained that Shaw had fraudulently suppressed the fact that Joan had appealed to the reigning pope and professed entire submission to the Church and that Pope Calixtus III declared twenty-five years after the trial that a procedure which was null and void had been followed and an iniquitous sentence had been pronounced.

Shaw's obvious distaste for Catholicism aroused Alfred's pugnacious instincts. Alfred could be generous in his role as a drama critic. In the *Cork Examiner* in the same year Alfred reviewed the presentation of Seán O'Casey's 'Juno and the paycock' by the Abbey players in the Palace Theatre in Cork. He was of an emotional disposition and found the play most moving. In his review he singled out for special commendation Barry Fitzgerald's Jack Boyle and Sara Allgood's Juno. He was also fulsome in his praise of the manner in which O'Casey had developed the character of Juno. Beyond the shrewd and witty sayings scattered through the play uttering home truths in jest or irony, he pointed out, there was no moralising in the play. But there were lessons to be learned and one would be very dull-witted indeed who left the Palace Theatre without an increased conviction that work and sobriety and above all the cessation of unnatural fratricidal strife were the greatest needs in the Ireland of their day.

In reviewing books on controversial topics for the *Irish Tribune* Alfred ensured that the Catholic point of view was heard loud and clear. His opening sentences in a review of Jan Herben's *John Huss and his followers* in the issue of 19 March were typical: 'This is a very biased polemical work full of disputable statements and devoid of references. It seems to be designed as an attempt to curry favour with Protestant England and to portray Huss as the Wycliff of Bohemia.' He went on to illustrate Herben's ignorance of the fundamental doctrine held by Huss and drew attention to a number of historical errors repeated in the book. In concluding he acknowledged that Huss was a pioneer Czech patriot and regretted that the Catholic

Defender of Religion, Christianity and Irish Catholicism

Church under the influence of Germanisation did not identify with the national and linguistic aspirations of the Czech people.

Alfred was even more abrasive in his review of R. H. Murray's *The political consequences of the Reformation* in the issue of 21 May. He emphasised the need for a scholarly work on the subject, but regretted that the present offering was but a collection of 'ridiculous generalisations' and a book 'crammed with *obiter dicta*'. He illustrated the limitations of Murray's knowledge of Catholic political theory and showed that his knowledge of it and of the Schoolmen depended on second-hand 'borrowings'. To Murray's: 'The Sinn Féiners of Ireland exemplify the theory of Suarez and Mariana': Alfred replied: 'The Black and Tans presumabaly exemplified the political consequences of the Reformation.' He highlighted Murray's partial treatment of Melanchton, Calvin and John Knox and examined critically his partisan account of the massacre of St Bartholomew's day. In Murray's opening chapter on Machiavelli Alfred pointed to a lot of irrelevant information, including 'the hoary and oft-repeated lie that the Jesuits taught that the end justifies the means'. He concluded that there was not a fertile or original idea in the book and very little connected with its purported subject.

Alfred wrote 'Senator Yeats as theologian' for the issue of 23 April. This was a response to 'Our need for religious sincerity' by the distinguished poet in a London publication, in which he was abrasively critical of the Irish Christian Brother, who edited *Our Boys*, for alleging that the well-known ancient English carol 'The cherry tree' ridiculed in blasphemous language the Holy Family. In his piece Yeats implied that 'Christian Brothers', 'Catholic ecclesiastics' and the 'Irish religious press' did not believe in the Incarnation and that Irish Catholics were ignorant fools. Alfred had little difficulty in showing that Yeats' version of the Incarnation did not approximate the accepted orthodox version of that doctrine. To the poet's assertion that Ireland had produced but two men of religious genius – Erigena (*sic*) and Bishop Berkeley – Alfred replied: 'Personally I believe that Yeats has never read a single line of Eriugena in the original and I have yet to discover the religious writings of Berkeley.' Showing that he could be as insulting as Yeats, Alfred declared: 'I have never before seen in cold print such offensive stupidity.' To Alfred's disappointment, Yeats chose to ignore this sharp riposte.

Alfred O'Rahilly III: Controversialist

From time to time Alfred reviewed films for the *Standard*. Invariably he did so from an unyielding Catholic perspective. Besides, he had a strong antipathy to the sheer shallowness of films, the absence of any reference to religion in them and the pervasive materialism implicit in Hollywood productions. In the *Standard* of 25 July 1941 as 'Pat Murphy' he 'let off steam', to use his own expression, in regard to *Kitty Foyle*. For Kitty, it seems, marriage was only 'a piece of paper'. Eventually she made the right romantic decision for the wrong reason. The deciding motive was that she would be in a socially awkward position if she did not secure that 'piece of paper'. Alfred complained that the reiterated theme of disrespect for marriage and of completely ousting religion from life was bound to have a deleterious effect on young people.

In the *Standard* of 22 August 1941 Alfred renewed his role as film critic, describing *Mr and Mrs Smith* as 'a vulgar performance ridiculing marriage as cohabitation with or without a legal entry to one of the States of the U.S.A.' In the same issue he was equally dismissive of *Laughing Irish Eyes*. He reported that the Cork audience laughed uproariously at the blacksmith residing in a large cut-stone house, the attempt to present a 'County Cork Fair' and a Blarney stone which could be seen to be about three feet above the ground.

In the *Standard* of 30 January 1942 he reviewed *Blossoms in the dust*. The film described an orphanage in Forth Worth, Texas, which had been founded and was run by an American widow who had lost her only child. Alfred was irritated by the assumption that this excellent institution was a unique and original product of the progressive American spirit. He recalled that while in the U.S.A. he had visited two Catholic orphanages and that there were hundreds of them in that country. Hollywood, he charged, like the B.B.C.'s Brains Trust assumed that the Catholic Church did not exist and chose to ignore the fact that 'for centuries thousands of women had abandoned home for Christ's sake to care for His little ones'. He regretted that the only concession to religion in the film was the sound of *Adeste fideles* in the background as Christmas, in effect, 'the annual recurrence of toys and a tree', was represented.

In the *Standard* of 6 March 1942 he expressed his unstinted admiration for Orson Welles' *Citizen Kane*. He saw it as a sermon in celluloid. For him Kane's appalling preoccupation with

Defender of Religion, Christianity and Irish Catholicism

Kane pointed up the moral that subordination of self was essential to the achievement of human happiness. In the same issue he gave a mixed review of the 'Dr Kildare' films. He cautioned against the simplistic and partial picture they gave of hospital life. Rather harshly he declared that the kind-hearted dedicated Dr Kildare in real life would most probably be either keen on making money or having a good time or would be absorbed in some specialist hobby in which his fellow-humans would be just raw material for experiment. He criticised the absence of any reference to religion. This meant that people had no real motive for living and no consolation when dying. Scientific humanism, he insisted, was not an adequate substitute for religion. He quoted H. L. Mencken that liberals 'have come to realise that the morons whom they sweated to save do not want to be saved and are not worth saving'.

In the *Standard* of 25 June 1943 Alfred reviewed 'Fire over England', an account of the reign of Queen Elizabeth I. He took issue with the pseudo-history it contained, such as Elizabeth bossing Burghley instead of the reverse, the glorification of the exploits of Francis Drake, an international pirate, and an unhistorical hint that the queen had scruples at sharing his loot. All through the film he detected hints that Catholics were naturally murderers and tyrants. He recalled that that was the current Elizabethan version of Irish papists fighting for their country. Of a cameo showing bearded Dominicans hastening to burn an English sea captain, Alfred asserted defensively that England was not then at war with Spain and so the captain merely received the treatment meted out to pirates, in accordance with the law of the sea. All the Spaniards in the film, he complained, were portrayed as Wild West stories depict Mexicans and Indians. Spaniards allegedly were taught to believe that their enemies were not human beings. Alfred found one incident quite familiar. To illustrate Spanish treachery, a hint was dropped to an English prisoner to escape, with secret orders, given at the same time, to shoot him when so attempting. Alfred recalled that a friend of his captured by the Black and Tans was thus murdered when 'attempting to escape' and that a similar hint given to himself when arrested found him quite unreceptive.

Alfred acknowledged that the Spanish Inquisition was 'a rather violent method of cultural defence', which he was not

Alfred O'Rahilly III: Controversialist

prepared to defend, but he called for a sense of historical perspective in regard to it. Even the most prejudiced historian such as Llorente had estimated that in its four centuries of existence the Inquisition had 30,000 persons executed. In the recent Spanish civil war, he noted that ten times that number of innocent men, women and children were murdered in one month! And in December 1934, 50,000 persons were executed as a reprisal for the assassination of Kirov. Alfred wondered aloud how intellectuals who could swallow these atrocities could be so horrified at the Spanish Inquisition.

In the *Standard* of 1 December 1944 Alfred reviewed the film, 'Madame Curie', and a biography of her mother by Eve Curie.[8] Apart from a few caveats concerning a lack of balance in the treatment of some episodes due to the need for dramatisation, he described 'Madame Curie' as a splendid film. He was less impressed by the biography. Showing a remarkable knowledge of the subject, he demonstrated that the achievements of the Curies were exaggerated and isolated from the work of their predecessors and contemporaries. This Curie cult, he speculated, was partly inspired by a rationalist clique at the Sorbonne and partly to atone for the long neglect and tardy recognition on the part of the University of Paris. In the second part of the article he attempted to explain why Marie Curie lost her Catholic faith and died an agnostic. Drawing mainly from Eve Curie's biography, he was at pains to show that this was due not to her involvement in scientific study and research but to other factors. He declared that there was no necessary connnection between eminence in science and a lack of religious faith. Thus other pioneer physicists such as W. C. Roentgen, discoverer of X-rays, was a theist and Henri Becquerel, discoverer of radiation from uranium and co-winner of the Nobel Prize in physics with the Curies, was a practising Catholic.

Erwin Schrödinger

In the *Standard* of 23 February 1945 Alfred reviewed Erwin Schrödinger's *What is life? The physical aspect of the living cell*. Schrödinger was senior professor at the Dublin Institute for Advanced Studies and the book, published by Cambridge University Press in 1944, was based on lectures delivered under the

8. E. Curie, *Madame Curie* (London 1942).

Defender of Religion, Christianity and Irish Catholicism

auspices of the Institute at Trinity College, Dublin, in February 1943. Alfred declared that, while he found a great deal in the book to disagree with, he would have avoided making any comment were it not for 'an unexpected epilogue of five pages in which the "gross superstitions" of "all official Western creeds" are discarded together with "their naïve idea of plurality of souls".' This assertion, he pointed out, was not supported by any argument in the book. In fact, the epilogue, which he described as 'a chant of deterministic pantheism and an extraneous chunk deliberately and provocatively added for some unexplained emotional reason', had no perceptible connection with the rest of the book. However, he felt impelled to deal with the book lest 'this vague and amateurish incursion into philosophy' should acquire an importance from the author's standing as a theoretical physicist.

Alfred pointed out that the author's main thesis was that classical physics could not explain the permanence of the material carriers of heredity, known as genes, which were of molecular dimensions. While he agreed with the thesis, he was scathing about Schrödinger's use of jargon and lack of clarity in presenting it. He was intensely critical of an attempt by Schrödinger to answer the question: 'How can events in space and time which take place within the boundary of a living organism be accounted for by physics and chemistry?' The author's misguided faith in physico-chemistry, he claimed, 'derived its plausibility from his ignoring the really vital phenomena: ontogeny, experimental embryology, regeneration and functional unity'.

Alfred claimed that Schrödinger had been confirmed in his mechanical materialistic outlook by his failure to grasp the Aristotelian-Thomist theory of life. To illustrate this he quoted the latter's comment 'that from the earliest times of human thought some special non-physical or supernatural force (*vis viva* entelechy) was claimed to be operative in the organism and in some quarters is still claimed'. Highlighting the lamentable ignorance implied in this remark, Alfred asked: 'Does he think that Aristotelian entelechy is either an expression of primitive animism or something imposed from outside, as Cartesian ultra-dualism maintained? Is he ignorant of the fact that *vis viva* merely means kinetic energy? Does he think that form (entelechy) is a 'force'? Does he equate non-physical with super-

Alfred O'Rahilly III: Controversialist

natural? He replied to his own questions: 'I am afraid he does.' Schrödinger described as silly, questions asking whether men, or animals or plants had souls and added that even a sillier question was to ask 'whether women or only men had souls'? Here Alfred saw an allusion to the oft-refuted legend that at the Council of Macon there was a serious discussion of the proposition that only the male of the human species had a soul.[9]

Alfred noted that Schrödinger had frequently quoted from the works of Spinoza including the assertion: 'Neither can the body determine the mind to think nor the mind the body to move or to rest nor to do anything else, if such there be.' This, he pointed out, was the theory of psycho-physical parallelism. The body acts as if there were no mind and the mind has no influence on bodily processes. Alfred quoted from a number of leading authorities to the effect that such a theory had long been outdated.[10]

Returning to the epilogue Alfred quoted Schrödinger: 'According to the evidence put forward in the previous pages the space time events in the body of a living being are deterministic.' Alfred replied that the preceding pages did not contain one iota of evidence or worthwhile argument bearing on the psycho-physical problem. And he quoted a number of leading physicists who rejected the kind of 'deterministic dogmatism' proposed by Schrödinger. Alfred continued that the pantheism implicit in the latter's speculation was not new. Had not St Thomas Aquinas written a monograph 'On the unity of the intellect' against such views when proposed by the Averroists? Perhaps the author was hinting that there was no 'I' and that consciousness was not really proper to the individual but part of a great pool which belonged to nobody in particular and had no more influence on events than the whistle on the motion of a steam engine. In that case what Schrödinger had described as our 'incontrovertible direct experience' was an illusion and the external world a collective dream. In the face of such a conclusion, Alfred proposed to cling to the 'gross superstitions' of

9. For a recent treatment of this, see J. M. Nolan, 'The unfortunate affair at Macon', *Intercom*, December 1990.
10. Typical was the following from William McDougall, F.R.S.: 'although in the opening years of the century psycho-physical parallelism was the orthodox creed of psychologists and biologists it has now disappeared from the scene and survives merely as a historical curiosity still hugged by a few intellectual tortoises' (*Modern materialism* (London 1929)).

Defender of Religion, Christianity and Irish Catholicism

his Catholic creed and declared that he had no intention of sinking into a pantheistic bathos which negated both ethics and science.

In a tailpiece to his article Alfred was at pains to justify his severe criticism of the views of Schrödinger. He stated that he had immense respect for 'this distinguished physicist when on his own beat'. However, Schrödinger should not expect to be treated with the same deference when he chose to wander into the fields not only of biology and psychology but also of philosophy and religion in which his deficiencies were so obvious.

Alfred's critique of Schrödinger's work caused a sensation. The Dublin Institute of Advanced Studies, of which he was a senior professor, was then enjoying enormous prestige. It specialised in mathematical science and Celtic studies and provided a platform for some of the leading scholars in these disciplines to give of their best during the war years when speculative science had been driven from the continental and British universities. Schrödinger was a disciple of Einstein and claimed to have achieved a synthesis that had escaped his master's grasp and of which the latter had approved. The sensation was all the greater because of the conclusive manner in which Alfred had challenged Schrödinger's views. As the Dublin correspondent wrote in the *Catholic Herald* of 12 March 1945, Professor O'Rahilly 'demonstrates, with exhaustive documentation, that the work of the senior professor of the Dublin Institute of Advanced Studies culminates in a completely unacceptable doctrine of pantheism'. In the face of the onslaught, Schrödinger preserved a discreet silence.

International reputation

Alfred had an international reputation as a Catholic apologist and polemicist from the 1920s.[11] In fact, it seems, his eminence in this regard was recognised more abroad than it was at

11. He also enjoyed an international reputation as a scholar and an educationalist. The *Catholic Herald* of 26 November 1921 reported: 'Professor O'Rahilly, of the Cork University College, who was released from Berehaven some weeks ago on an indefinite parole, is at present in London where his services are at the disposal of the Irish plenipotentiaries. The professor is a scholar with a European reputation. In no country in the world outside Czarist Russia would a man of his rank as an educationalist be treated as he has been.'

home.[12] In 1926 the editor of the *Leader* bewailed the backwardness of Irish Catholicism in the matter of intellectual propaganda. 'If we had educated Irish Catholic laymen like Belloc or Chesterton,' he wrote, 'how much better things would be . . .' The editor of the London-published *Universe* replied that when he read this he was at a loss and continued: 'We should have thought that Professor Alfred O'Rahilly was pretty nearly Mr Belloc's equal in brilliance of exposition and argument and perhaps his superior in certain fields of learning . . .'

In the first week of June 1929 a supplementary estimate, issued by the minister for external affairs, provided for the appointment of an envoy extraordinary and minister plenipotentiary to the Holy See. It was disclosed in the press that 'Professor Alfred O'Rahilly, Count Gerald O'Kelly and Mr Charles Bewley, K.C.,[13] 'had been short-listed and in that order for the post, but that the last mentioned would most probably be appointed.' In the *Catholic Herald* of 7 June 1929 the paper's Irish correspondent speculated that, apart from his national record, Alfred's reputation as a distinguished apologist and scholar made him a suitable candidate for the prestigious post. The correspondent also implied that an anti-nationalist lobby had been at work to block Alfred's appointment.

Alfred's eminence as a Catholic apologist was invariably acknowledged by those who introduced him to audiences or reported his lectures. Generally speaking he was referred to as a leader of Catholic Action, as in the report of his address to the

12. This is not to suggest that Alfred's contribution in this and other fields went unrecognised in his own country. In a letter in the *Leader* of 28 February 1953 Stephen Rynne invited readers to list 'ten of the most worthwhile people in Ireland'. In the issue of 28 March a 'Dublin Reader' replied with a list headed by Alfred and which included four other professors prominent in public affairs. In Cork Alfred was held in the highest esteem. In particular, there was no lack of appreciation of his contributions to the industrial and social life of the city. When it became known in 1926 that he was about to depart for a year's sabbatical at Harvard University, the lord mayor, Councillor Seán French, presided over what was, in effect, a civic farewell dinner, attended by public representatives, city officials and representatives of the university, the trade unions and the business community. For an account of this remarkable tribute, see *Cork Evening Echo* 13 September 1926. Distinguished contemporaries, such as William O'Brien, M.P., and his wife, Sophie, had a high regard for Alfred. When her husband died in February 1928, Mrs O'Brien sent Alfred a signed photograph of him, with a statement to that effect.

13. For more on Bewley, see W. J. McCormick (ed.), *Memoirs of a wild goose* (Dublin 1990).

inaugural meeting of the Academy of St Thomas at U.C.C. in November 1932. Occasionally he was introduced in more homely terms as when Fr Denis Moynihan, Adm.,[14] on 8 January 1932 described him to a Killarney audience as a man 'whose voice and pen are always at the service of the Church'. Alfred's eminence as a Catholic apologist was appreciated by his colleagues in U.C.C. The *Cork Examiner* of 21 May 1933 reported a lecture in the college on 'The Catholic literary revival'. In proposing a vote of thanks to the lecturer, Professor William F. P. Stockley declared 'that under the influence of Professor Alfred O'Rahilly in U.C.C. it was now possible to think and act like a Catholic, which had not been possible in his day'. In a letter to Alfred, dated 14 June 1948, Bishop Daniel Cohalan, his former antagonist, wrote: 'I realise and bear testimony to the great work you have done for religion and education.' Cohalan's successor, Bishop Cornelius Lucey, also appreciated Alfred's sterling service to the Catholic Church. As part of Cork's civic reception on 16 June 1953 for John Cardinal D'Alton, he arranged a lecture in the city hall. Rev. Professor William J. Philbin of St Patrick's College, Maynooth, spoke on 'Faith and Christianity'. At the bishop's request Alfred seconded the vote of thanks. He stressed the importance of the laity becoming more knowledgeable about their religion, the Mass and above all social principles.

A profile in the *Cork Holly Bough* of Christmas 1932 stressed the social thrust of Alfred's polemical writing and lecturing and declared: 'He has a protective instinct for the underdog and wishes to shield him from the catch-cries and half-baked theories of the insincere agitator. He looks into the future, sees society galloping towards chaos, and would lead it back by the rein of Christian principles to what he considers the golden age of humanity – the thirteenth century.'[15] It was as a champion of the Christian spirit in philosophy and social ethics that Alfred was best known in Catholic circles in Germany.

The *Catholic Times* of South Africa in its issue of 19 January 1940 informed its readers that Alfred had begun his reply to H. G. Wells' allegations against the Catholic Church. It noted

---

14. Administrator of Killarney parish (1927-41), later bishop of Ross (1941-53) and bishop of Kerry (1953-69).
15. By virtue of his *The thirteenth, greatest of centuries* (New York 1913) and other publications, James J. Walsh was probably the best-known protagonist of this thesis at that time.

that on a previous occasion Hilaire Belloc had discredited Wells as a historian and looked forward to Alfred discrediting him as a writer on scientific subjects. It concluded: 'O'Rahilly's reputation in Ireland as a forceful worker in all Catholic and national movements and as a profound scholar is only overshadowed by his standing as a polemical writer of unusual pungency and brilliance.'

Alfred also attracted the attention of his co-religionists in the United States. Some of his admirers there expressed disappointment from time to time that his writing was not as widely known or regarded as authentic a part of the Irish literary and cultural tradition as was the prose and poetry of James Joyce, George Russell (A.E.) and William Butler Yeats. For them this was all the more regrettable for, as David Gordon in the Jesuit weekly *America* of 24 July 1937 mused, Alfred's writing was a vehicle of 'a philosophy, which has come down the centuries in a pure immitigable stream through St Paul the Jew, through St Augustine the African and through St Thomas the Italian'.

Attitude to 'the metropolitan intelligentsia'

Alfred's prowess as a Catholic apologist and polemicist was not regarded with much sympathy by those who did not have his commitment to Catholicism, Christianity or religion. Many fair-minded people found the vigour of his polemics objectionable. The pleasure he took in challenging experts in their own field and particularly in showing that he was at the very least their equal left a residue of resentment. In addition, purporting to be a man of the people, just another 'Pat Murphy', he enjoyed baiting 'the metropolitan intelligentsia'. The result was that those who disagreed with his views did not usually challenge them, but attempted to pretend that he did not exist or that he was so eccentric that it was not necessary to reply.

The attitude of 'the metropolitan intelligentsia' to Alfred was remarkable. It seems they found it difficult even to mention his name. Elsewhere an extraordinary example of this has been noted in the case of Professor George O'Brien.[16] This ignoring of him, however, was by no means unique. A radio broadcast on

16. J. A. Gaughan, *Alfred O'Rahilly I: Academic*, 191-4. Louis McRedmond recalled his amused reaction and that of his fellow-undergraduates when at their first lecture on economics O'Brien, after recommending a reading-list, fairly bristled and warned them against reading Alfred's tome *Money*.

Defender of Religion, Christianity and Irish Catholicism

the B.B.C. by Arland Ussher on 'Contemporary thought in Ireland' was published in the *Listener* of 11 September 1947. It was a fine survey of contemporary Irish letters and thought. He referred with approval to the 'school of Roman Catholic neo-Thomism' as an antidote to the philosophy of idealism which kept the mind closed in on itself.[17] In a further favourable comment on neo-Thomism he noted its influence on the poetry of Robert Farren and Thomas McGreevy, but ignored Alfred's exposition of Thomist thought and his efforts to popularise it for some thirty years. Showing some lack of dispassion, Ussher described Kathleen O'Flaherty's study of Voltaire as 'tight-lipped and censorious' and, in a reference to Alfred's additional notes to it, added that it had appeared with 'the imprimatur of the president of Cork University'. Later, when adverting to trends in social and economic thought, he referred to *Money* as 'interesting and provocative'. Again, although everyone mentioned in the broadcast, some thirty or so persons, were fully named, Ussher could only refer to the author of *Money* as 'the aforementioned president of Cork University'.

Conor Cruise O'Brien, over the pseudonym Donat O'Donnell, published 'The Fourth Estate – 5: The Catholic press' in the *Bell* of April 1945. For him the Catholic press meant, in effect, the *Irish Catholic* and the *Standard*. While he did mention Alfred's name in relation to the *Standard*, he could not resist the temptation to be offensive. He wrote: 'Towards the end of 1938 Mr P. J. O'Curry became editor and a new policy began, consisting largely of Professor Alfred O'Rahilly. The Professor is, among many other things, one of the most remarkable journalists since the German-American terrorist, Johann Most, who used for seven years to write a four-page daily single-handed.' O'Brien continued: 'Professor O'Rahilly probably does not write all of the *Standard* every week, but it would be feeble to say that he has imposed his personality upon it. It is he who has given it a social policy, consisting of his own monetary theories, he who fights its battles with H. G. Wells and others, he who

17. He continued with the following interesting observation: 'But in the main our writers seem to think they can preserve a virginal neutrality in the world of warring ideas, an art for art's sake, without even the courage of that ascetic doctrine [neo-Thomism]. If they show the intellectual pugnacity upon which we used to pride ourselves, it is only to attack censorship or to praise Marxist communism.' And, foregoing a moral judgment on these attitudes, he pointed out that they were, at the least, inconsistent with each other.

orients its attitude to science and philosophy and life.' 'Under his occupation,' he concluded, 'the *Standard* shifted to something that might almost be described as the left and its circulation soared to 50,000.'

In a humorous piece in the *Standard* of 13 April 1945 Peadar O'Curry, over the pseudonym Manus O'Neill, construed O'Brien's remarks as implying that Alfred wrote everything which appeared in the paper. So far from being an effective rebuttal, this served only to underline the accuracy of O'Brien's judgement, which was an admirable example of one redoubtable controversialist recognising another. Although occasionally he showed a lack of judgment,[18] it would be difficult to exaggerate Alfred's importance as an apologist for religion, Christianity and Irish Catholicism. The controversial and even harsh tone of some of his interventions and the regrettable resentment he aroused occasionally arose from his combative temperament. It was also due, however, to his decision to be as iconoclastic as his agnostic and liberal opponents.[19]

18. From time to time his zeal led him to act somewhat in the manner of Don Quixote. The *Cork Examiner*, for example, on 4 March 1937 published a paragraph by its London correspondent on Jack Doyle, whose parental home was near U.C.C. In an unsigned piece in the March issue of the *Quarryman*, the students' magazine, Alfred, in effect, objected to the description of Jack Doyle's much publicised romances as 'a number of indiscretions'. An article by Seán Ó Faoláin in the *Bell* for February 1946 occasioned another over-reaction by Alfred. Ó Faoláin published a light-hearted piece on his son's first confession. In the *Standard* of 15 March 1946, over the pseudonym 'Sagart', Alfred complained that Ó Faoláin in his anxiety to write a short story did not mind providing a subtle mockery of a sacred subject. He charged that the piece was 'a subtly sceptical repudiation of the Catholic evaluation of sin' and he challenged it practically line by line.

19. The above is taken from *Cork Examiner* 8 January 1932, 17 June 1953; *Irish Catholic* 9, 16 November 1939; *Irish Press* 19, 20 February 1946; *Leader* 31 October, 7, 14 November, 5 December 1925; *Standard* 5 January 1940; Papers of Liam de Róiste, diary, vol. 54, 30 April 1926; Papers of William O'Brien, AU.8, letter, dated 17 February 1926, O'Rahilly to O'Brien, AU.9, letter, dated 19 February 1926, Eamon O'Donoghue to O'Brien, AU.16, letter, dated 2 March 1926, O'Rahilly to O'Brien; Papers of W. P. Ryan, LA11/F/70, letter, dated 18 February 1926, L. P. Byrne to Ryan, LA11/F/71, letter, dated 14 May 1926, L. P. Byrne to Ryan, LA11/F/72, letter, dated 7 April 1926, L. P. Byrne to Ryan, LA11/F/73, letter, dated 4 June 1926, L. P. Byrne to Ryan, LA11/F/36, letter, dated 14 June 1926, O'Rahilly to Ryan; interviews with Patrick Maume, Mrs Eilís Mercier (*née* Dillon) and Professor Kathleen O'Flaherty; papers and writings of Alfred O'Rahilly and the sources already cited.

UPHOLDER OF CATHOLIC SOCIAL THEORY

Alfred had few equals as an exponent of Catholic social theory. As a Jesuit scholastic, especially during his time at St Mary's College, Stonyhurst, he became convinced of the importance of the social teaching of *Rerum Novarum*. He regarded it as the only viable alternative to what he later described as the excesses of Berlin, Manchester and Moscow, namely, fascism, capitalism and communism. Throughout his life he expended a great deal of energy in crusading for the practical implementation of Catholic social teaching. To this end, he organised courses at U.C.C. for workers and, after spending a year reading sociology at Harvard, he established a lectureship in the subject at U.C.C. which he personally filled on a voluntary basis for nine years. He initiated a countrywide movement in adult education, served as a member of the Commission on Vocational Organisation, took an active interest in Muintir na Tíre, Macra na Feirme and Bantracht na Tuatha and wrote and lectured extensively on Catholic social theory.

On the one hand, Alfred considered as crucial the teaching of the social encyclicals on the importance of the common good of society and its corollary, the emphasis on the duties and limitations associated with private property. On the other hand, he saw great merit in Catholic social teaching in so far as it discouraged undue encroachment by the State on the rights and independence of the family, the Churches, trade unions, professional organisations, universities, newspapers and other smaller organisations and societies. Very much an individualist, he found this aspect of Catholic social theory particularly congenial. He was given an admirable opportunity to promote it by the controversy which followed the dropping by the first inter-party government of the mother-and-child scheme in April 1951. In explaining in the *Standard* to a wide readership the principles invoked by those who opposed the scheme, he emphasised this aspect of Catholic social theory.

Impasse between department of health and medical school at U.C.C.

By a curious coincidence at the time of the collapse of the mother-and-child scheme an impasse had developed between the department of health in Dublin and the medical school at

Alfred O'Rahilly III: Controversialist

U.C.C. The question at issue concerned the provision of clinical training in obstetrics and midwifery for the students of U.C.C. and the method to be followed in appointing a professor who would also act as master of a maternity hospital or unit. Ultimately there was the question of the appointee's academic independence which Alfred, doubtless with the revelations concerning involvement of doctors in the German concentration camps in mind, pointed out was 'more than ever necessary in the world of today, not least in medicine and in medical education'.

Difficulties with regard to facilities for clinical teaching for U.C.C.'s medical students became acute at the beginning of 1937 when James M. O'Donovan, the professor of medicine, accused the medical staff of the North Infirmary of a lack of co-operation or even of goodwill in the matter. The situation, it seems, was not much better in the other local hospitals. As a result of meetings between the concerned parties, including Alfred as registrar of the College, the more immediate difficulties were resolved amicably. This series of meetings which were attended by representatives of the department of local government and public health also led to the government announcing its intention to build a semi-voluntary maternity hospital to be located in Cork County Borough. In a letter, dated 3 April 1937, the department agreed to a detailed scheme submitted by the U.C.C. Medical School for the new hospital and proposed that 'the professor of midwifery for the time being at U.C.C. shall be a member of the visiting medical staff of the hospital and shall act as master of the hospital'. No further progress, however, was made and further delay was caused by world war two with its attendant stringencies.

With the ending of world war two and no immediate prospect of the promised maternity hospital, Alfred, on behalf of the medical school, set about improving the facilities for clinical training in obstetrics and midwifery. He prepared a detailed memorandum which proposed close co-operation between the U.C.C. faculty of medicine and nearby Erinville private hospital. On 18 June 1945 he forwarded copies of the memorandum to the hospital's board of management and to the department of local government and public health. Less than a year later the hospital board had agreed to the proposals in the memorandum. However, further negotiations on the matter with the depart-

Upholder of Catholic Social Theory

ment dragged on for another year and were not completed before the dissolution of Dáil Éireann in January 1948.

In 1947 the health functions of the department of local government and public health were assigned to a newly-established department of health. The first minister was Dr James Ryan of Fianna Fáil. Following the general election of February 1948 Dr Noel C. Browne took charge of the department of health in the new coalition government, which was officially styled 'inter-party' because of the negative connotations attaching to coalitions at that time. For months Browne was absorbed in the eradication of tuberculosis. Thereafter he set about radically improving the country's general hospital and medical facilities. He planned to have new regional hospitals built in Cork, Limerick and Galway. In a letter, dated 18 October 1948, the department of health informed the South Cork Board of Public Assistance that a new hospital was to be built at Wilton, on the outskirts of the city. A copy of the letter was sent to the faculty of medicine at U.C.C. In the letter the minister pointed out that the new hospital would be the principal maternity hospital in the region, that it would be a teaching hospital for undergraduate students and that it was very desirable that there should be close liaison between the hospital and U.C.C. Such liaison, the minister continued, could best be achieved by arrangement with the university authorities, whereby the senior resident obstetrician and gynaecologist of the hospital should also hold the chair of midwifery and gynaecology in the university. Should the university authorities agree to this proposal, the appointment to the hospital would be made upon the recommendation of the Local Appointments Commissioners, who would be advised that, in view of the fact that the person appointed to the hospital would also hold the university appointment, due regard should be given to the interests of the university in constituting the selection board. The salary attaching to the office would be fixed in consultation with the university and would be payable in agreed proportions.

A special meeting of the South Cork Board of Public Assistance was held in January 1949 to discuss the staffing of the maternity unit of the proposed regional hospital at Wilton. Before the meeting was the letter from the minister for health and a long submission prepared by Alfred on behalf of the

Alfred O'Rahilly III: Controversialist

U.C.C. Medical School.[1] Alfred complained that, apart from a copy of the minister's letter to the Board of Public Assistance, the Medical School had received no further information in the matter. He recalled that for many years all the parties involved had assumed that there was to be a new women's hospital on a central site in the city. Clarification was required, he stated, as to whether that agreed project had been modified or abandoned.

In view of 'the complete absence of information and consultation', it was, continued Alfred, difficult to comment on the proposed arrangements for staffing, managing and running the new hospital. However, 'the minister's unexpected proposal that the resident in charge of the hospital should be appointed as professor of gynaecology and midwifery' raised 'the grave issue of university autonomy'. This was considerably aggravated by the fact that the professor would be a 'whole time' official of an outside independent administrative system. Under such a dual control it was obvious that occasions for conflict and divergence were only too likely. He rejected the minister's proposal for 'a joint appointment' as entirely impracticable, as the Local Appointments Commissioners and the University senate could not act jointly. Next he had little difficulty in dismissing the minister's contention that 'joint appointments' were already in place in University College, Galway. On the question of the filling of an immediate vacancy on the staff of the medical faculty of U.C.C., Alfred illustrated that the minister's proposal was entirely unsatisfactory. He informed the Board of Public Assistance that the medical faculty had recommended that no change be made in the tenure of the professorship of gynaecology and midwifery and that the post would be filled in the usual manner. After a great deal of discussion of details, members of the Board of Public Assistance and the representatives of the Medical School, led by Alfred, reached agreement on the method whereby appointments should be made to the proposed hospital and in their opposition to the minister's proposal regarding the chief appointment.

1. Alfred's submission included a printed memorandum which showed that 'the project to replace Erinville hospital by a women's hospital, quite distinct from the proposed regional hospital at Wilton, was unanimously approved by Cork Corporation, was accepted by the government (at least until 1946), and – with certain modifications subsequently approved by Erinville hospital – advocated by the medical staff of University College, Cork.' For this memorandum, see Appendix 3.

Upholder of Catholic Social Theory

As Alfred indicated to the South Cork Board of Public Assistance, the usual steps had been taken to fill the vacant chair of gynaecology and midwifery and a professor was appointed on 7 April 1949. In the meantime, 'on at least three occasions', Alfred had appealed to the department of health to receive a deputation of U.C.C. representatives to discuss the matter, but to no avail. Then on 27 March 1951 Dr Browne put forward a new proposal. This involved the immediate appointment of a full-time, non-resident obstetrician for the Cork District Hospital. Again the Medical School was not consulted, although the proposal, as Alfred pointed out, contained a clause that this whole-time State official 'may, subject to the consent of the minister for health, be permitted to hold a part-time teaching appointment' in U.C.C.

Dr James Ryan, new minister for health, facilitates settlement

Dr Browne resigned on 11 April 1951. A general election was held on 30 May and a new Fianna Fáil minority government, with Dr James Ryan resuming as minister for health, was installed on 13 June. At a conference between representatives of U.C.C. and members of the South Cork Board of Public Assistance on 18 January 1952 Alfred insisted that the objections to Dr Browne's proposal of 27 March 1951 were serious. Speaking on behalf of his colleagues he declared that Browne's proposal meant that there was to be in Cork a State monopoly of a mother and child service, with a full-time State appointee in complete control of the clinical teaching of medical students and of the training of midwives. He recalled that in 1908 with the establishment of the National University and its constituent colleges Irish Catholics obtained a workable provision for higher education. An essential part of this was that, unlike the case of the Queen's Colleges, the State was not to control appointments. They were then, he charged, faced with an attempt on the part of the State to appoint to the chair of midwifery and later to those of medicine, surgery, etc. He pointed out that the appointee could, at the minister's discretion, hold a teaching post in U.C.C. Conversely the minister could refuse his permission and thereby deprive U.C.C. of clinical facilities for training medical students. Furthermore, no provision was

Alfred O'Rahilly III: Controversialist

made for the control and co-ordination of teaching by the professor. He warned that this latter point was one which would be insisted upon when in the near future their clinical facilities would be investigated and inspected under the new Act. Hence the very survival of the Medical School was at stake.

The chairman, Martin Corry, T.D., pointed out that the Board was bound by a decision which it had taken in accordance with the minister's recommendation. However, most of the members were influenced by Alfred's Job-like prediction concerning the Medical School. They agreed to invite the new minister for health to open officially the new maternity wing of the district hospital and to ask him to meet a deputation on that occasion concerning the matters at issue. There were four representatives from U.C.C., including Alfred, on the deputation which met Dr Ryan, as a result of which the matter was settled to the satisfaction of all the parties concerned.

The importance of the matter at issue was highlighted when at the beginning of 1953 the American Medical Association (A.M.A.) announced that it had withdrawn recognition from the medical faculties of the constituent colleges of the N.U.I. The main criticism of the A.M.A. was that these medical schools were not adequately staffed and did not have satisfactory supervision over clinical teaching. Alfred was empowered by the Medical School to make the improvements which were necessary in anticipation of a future A.M.A. inspection. After intensive negotiations with the Cork teaching hospitals and Erinville hospital he arrived at an acceptable solution to the question of appointments over which until then the College had little influence. He also instituted other reforms. After an inspection at the end of 1953 the Medical School was again recognised by the A.M.A. These were not the only services he rendered to the Medical School. At his prompting and with his assistance, his son, Ronan,[2] published *Benjamin Alcock, the first professor of*

---

2. Ronan O'Rahilly (1921-   ) became a distinguished *alumnus* of the Cork Medical School.
From 1943 to 1945 he worked in the Royal Hospital and the Nether Edge Hospital in Sheffield. Thereafter he held the following academic appointments:
    1946-48 lecturer in anatomy, University of Durham
    1948-50 lecturer in anatomy, University of Sheffield
    1952-55 assistant professor of anatomy, Wayne University
    1955-62 associate professor of anatomy, Wayne State University

anatomy and physiology in Queen's College, Cork and *A history of the Cork Medical School 1849-1949* in 1948 and 1949.

Aftermath of resignation of Dr Noel Browne

The impasse in which Dr Noel Browne had found himself in Cork was as nothing compared to his difficulties in Dublin, where he was at odds with the Catholic bishops, the medical profession, and most seriously of all, his cabinet colleagues and even members of his own party. The circumstances surrounding the controversy about the 'mother and child scheme' have been treated extensively. In recent years Ruth Barrington and first-hand accounts by Noel Browne and James Deeny have provided interesting new insights into the affair.[3] The scheme was part of

---

1961-62 and 1969-72 visiting investigator, department of embryology, Carnegie Institution of Washington, Baltimore
1962-69 professor of anatomy and chairman of the department of anatomy, Saint Louis University
1969-90 director of Carnegie Embryological Collection
1969-74 professor of anatomy, Wayne State University
1974-90 professor of human anatomy, University of California, Davis
1978-90 professor of neurology, University of California, Davis
1991-   Gastprofessor, Institut für Anatomie und spezielle Embryologie, Universität Freiburg, Schweiz.

Apart from some two hundred chapters and articles in medical collections and periodicals, his publications include: *Living anatomy* (Cork 1949), *Anatomy. A regional study of human structure* (E. Gardner, D. J. Gray, R. O'Rahilly, Philadelphia 1960), *An atlas of the anatomy of the ear* (B. Vidic, R. O'Rahilly, Philadelphia 1971), *Developmental stages in human embryos*... (New York 1973), *A colour atlas of human embryology* (Philadelphia 1975), *Developmental stages in human embryos*... (Washington, D.C. 1987), *Human embryology and teratology* (R. O'Rahilly and F. Müller, New York 1992) and *The embryonic human brain: an atlas of developmental stages* (R. O'Rahilly and F. Müller, New York 1993).

From 1978 to 1988 he was editor-in-chief of *Acta anatomica*.

He was the recipient of honorary doctorates from the Université de Montpellier and the National University of Ireland in 1982 and 1989.

For more, see J. A. Gaughan, *Alfred O'Rahilly I: Academic*, 258.

3. See R. Barrington, *Health, medicine and politics in Ireland 1900-1970* (Dublin 1987); N. Browne, *Against the tide* (Dublin 1986); and J. Deeny, *To cure and to care: memoirs of a chief medical officer* (Dublin 1989). See also E. McKee, 'Church-State relations and the development of health policy: the mother-and-child scheme 1944-53', *Irish Historical Studies* xxv (1986-7); A. Sheehy Skeffington, *Skeff* (Dublin 1991) and J. H. Whyte, *Church and State in modern Ireland 1923-1979* (2nd ed., Dublin 1980).

Alfred O'Rahilly III: Controversialist

a Health Act put through the Oireachtas by the Fianna Fáil government at the time of the establishment of the separate department of health in 1947. The implementation of this part of the Act was shelved by de Valera and his colleagues because the Catholic bishops objected to some of its provisions. When Fianna Fáil was replaced by the inter-party government after the general election of 4 February 1948, implementation became the responsibility of the new minister, Dr Noel Browne. He forged ahead with this, despite renewed objections from the medical profession. Because of the objections the government dropped it. Browne resigned from his ministry and from his party Clann na Poblachta.

Browne did not leave the government quietly. To justify his stand he had sixteen letters on the affair from himself, from his party leader and colleague in the cabinet, Seán MacBride, from the Taoiseach, John A. Costello, and from members of the hierarchy delivered to R. M. Smyllie, editor of the *Irish Times*, for publication. They were published by Smyllie on 12 April 1951. Smyllie also wrote a powerful editorial in support of the stand taken by Browne.

Attack on hostile reaction of *Irish Times* to bishops' intervention

Alfred dealt with the controversy in the *Standard* of 20 April 1951. This carried an editorial which he had drafted[4] and an article headed 'Mother-and-child scheme – issues made clear: the bishops and the people'. In the article he recalled that a short time previously Aneurin Bevan had threatened to leave the British government if a charge was made to Health Service patients. Nonetheless, the chancellor, Hugh Gaitskell, imposed such a charge. The result was no more than shouts in the House of Commons 'Where's Bevan?', as he hid behind the Speaker's chair. By contrast, Alfred noted, in Ireland news of the resignation of Dr Browne had overshadowed that of the dismissal of General MacArthur, commander-in-chief of the U.N. forces in Korea. It was also accompanied by a flood of vituperation and an indecent public washing of dirty linen. He indicated that his object was to refute 'hostile misrepresentations' and to vindicate certain important principles which were basic to the incident.

4. For this editorial, see Appendix 3.

Upholder of Catholic Social Theory

In passing Alfred recorded his view that the whole business had been quite unnecessary. There was no doubt as to whom he regarded as the main culprit. He recalled that he had 'considerable dealings' with Dr Browne concerning a proposed teaching hospital. Of the former minister's crusading spirit and genuine idealism there could be no doubt but he stated that he had also become aware of his lack of administrative experience. He remembered that he found it impossible to get Dr Browne to realise that serious social principles were involved in his blueprint scheme. In fact, he added, there was such an 'underground attempt' to turn the principal medical chairs at U.C.C. into full-time civil service appointments that he was preparing to appeal to the bishops in defence of university autonomy, as they had 'unofficially come to our rescue on a former occasion under the late government'. Thus he had 'a small-scale rehearsal of the present crisis'.

Alfred declared that the worst damage done by the incident was the opportunity for criticism it gave to those who were secretly or openly 'the enemies' of the ideals and principles held by both sets of disputants. He charged the *Irish Times*, 'true to its tradition of episcopophagy', with exploiting the occasion to the full. Its editorial under the caption *Contra Mundum* canonised Dr Browne as the modern St Athanasius, the champion of orthodox Christianity, 'against the world'. But, he pointed out, the editorial contradicted its title as it implied that the whole world or at least all Ireland was with Dr Browne against the bishops: 'a gallant fight has ended in defeat . . . It is certain that the goodwill of the people at large follows him in his fall, and that tens of thousands of families will be the sadder for it . . . This is a sad day for Ireland.' An exception, Alfred continued, was made for the medical profession: 'With a united cabinet on his side, Dr Browne might have prevailed against them.'

Alfred next quoted the editorial reference to the Catholic bishops:

> The Church entered the arena. Thus, not for the first or second time in Irish history, progress is thwarted . . . The most serious revelation is that the Roman Catholic Church would seem to be the effective government of this country.

Alfred O'Rahilly III: Controversialist

Thus, declared Alfred, the episcopal enumeration of certain social objections to Dr Browne's views is asserted to be 'the domination of the State by the Church'. Obviously, he continued, when the *Irish Times* makes pontifical pronouncements on sociology, as it constantly does, this is not – nor would it ever be even if it were listened to – domination of the State by the *Irish Times*. Hence the primary objection is to the fact that those who formulated the views are Catholic bishops.

Alfred pointed out that, apart from the bishops, every competent Catholic sociologist in the country upheld the same principles. As a lecturer in sociology he had expressed similar views to medical and other audiences. Thus it would be worthwhile to examine these principles, independently of the personalities who expressed them. This, however, he noted, the editor of the *Irish Times* was not prepared to do. Alfred showed that 'unwilling to derogate from editorial omniscience he adroitly "passes the buck" to the plain people' in writing: "For ourselves, we cannot pretend to follow the reasoning; and we doubt if it will be followed by the puzzled and disappointed people of this country . . . The plain man unversed in subtleties will be at a loss to determine why the Church should take sides in the matter at all." Alfred, in his comment on this, went for the jugular. 'This subtly disguised confession of incompetence – I feel tempted to call it dishonest bluff – leaves me at a loss why the *Irish Times* should take sides in the matter at all. Except, of course, to have a dig at Irish Catholics, particularly our bishops, who are inferentially represented as incapable of relevance or reasoning.'

Alfred declared that it was bad enough to have the editor of the *Irish Times* lecturing Irish Catholics on social principles which he professed not to understand. It was worse to find 'this self-appointed lay archbishop of Dublin' calmly assuming a social principle of his own which principle, if accepted, would lead to the most abominable totalitarian tyranny, namely the suppression of all institutional criticism of government. He recalled that not a long time before the *Irish Times* had praised the late Catholic bishop of Berlin for his courageous criticism of the Nazi regime. It could hardly be said that what is right for a German bishop is wrong for an Irish one. Thus the contention must be that criticism was allowable only when the *Irish Times* agreed with it. He drew attention to the issue of 2 April in which it reported without comment an outburst of the 'Imperial Deputy Grand Chaplain' of the Orange Order in Belfast against grants to Catholic schools 'as a real danger to Northern Ireland and to the Protestant cause'. If, he added, a Catholic bishop or clergyman in the Republic made such an attack on Protestant schools, the editor would rightly raise a shrill protest. But he is silent when the Orange Order claims to dictate to the State.

Alfred asserted that Irish Catholics had never tried to muzzle or browbeat the Protestant synod or the synagogue. He quoted from an account of a recent speech by the Taoiseach, John A. Costello, in Dáil Éireann:

> While they were a government they would receive representations and complaints from any religious group in the country. One of his first duties as Taoiseach, in March 1948, was to receive representations from the Jewish community, to whom he had given undertakings on behalf of the government, and they had been scrupulously kept.

Alfred also quoted a speech by Seán MacBride to the same effect. He urged that the issue raised by the *Irish Times* was quite general. The Catholic bishops did not claim any privilege. Their claim to record ethical criticisms, in public or in private, concerning government measures, was one which was equally applicable to religious minorities; and, indeed, was even a more vital liberty for them. The issue involved was the right of citizens, through their religious associations, to pass moral judgements on the State. To deny this right was 'plain totalitarianism'.

Alfred reminded the readers that in communist countries the State tolerated no independent associations – neither Churches nor trade unions. It claimed immunity from opposition or criticism and liquidated dissidents. Except for those who openly avowed such monopolistic tyranny, it was illogical and even intolerable that 'a small clique of journalists' should deny the right of the Catholic bishops to pass an ethical-social verdict on legislation. What was really absurd was to admit that any pressure-group – political party, trade union, intelligentsia or newspaper – could publicly indulge in criticisms, from the making of which Catholic bishops, representing ninety-five percent of the population, were to be excluded. He emphasised that, in any country in which the Catholic Church lost its freedom, the State had made 'short work' of the counterparts of the *Irish Times*, not to mention other Churches and trade unions. It was playing with fire to urge the State to ignore and to muzzle Churches and professional bodies such as that of medicine.

Alfred accused the editor of the *Irish Times* of playing up to the natural lay prejudice against clerical dictation. But, he declared, no issue of clericalism arose at all. They resided in a mixed State, in whose constitution religious liberty was enshrined. On the constitutional plane, the bishops did not claim the right to legislate or to dictate legislation. They claimed, as did other institutions and even individuals, the right to give an ethical appraisal of impending or existing legislation. Moreover, in their contention in the present case, they were not advocating any privileges for clerics or even for Catholics. The principles they invoked, already enunciated in the constitution, were not specifically Catholic at all. And, inasmuch as they protected the medical profession against regimentation by the State, the principles ought also to be acceptable to trade unionists, especially to those who looked forward to a measure of managerial association and greater responsibility. He regretted that it was necessary for the bishops to intervene. Ignoring the fact that it was as bishops not sociologists that the hierarchy had intervened, Alfred continued that their intervention had been necessary because most lay people, including the legislators, had very little training in sociology.

Alfred quoted from the bishops' letter to the government of 10 October 1950. It stated that 'the powers taken by the State in the proposed mother-and-child health service are in direct opposition to the rights of the family and of the individual and are liable to very great abuse'. In the letter this assertion was explained in detail. It was further elaborated in a letter from the Archbishop of Dublin to the government, dated 5 April 1951. Alfred quoted excerpts from this letter[5] and dismissed as

5. (1) 'In this particular scheme the State arrogates to itself a function and control, on a nationwide basis, in respect of education, more especially in the very intimate matter of chastity, individual and conjugal.' (2) Similarly, 'in respect of health services, which properly ought to be, and actually can be, efficiently secured, for the vast majority of the citizens, by individual initiative and by lawful associations'. (3) 'In this particular scheme, the State must enter unduly and very intimately into the life of patients, both parents and children, and of

scandalous the charge that those who had misgivings about the scheme – the clergy, sociologists, the middle class, the medical practitioners – were not eager to improve the conditions of maternity and childhood. Child mortality was ultimately due to bad housing, malnutrition, insufficient wages, the poor condition of many of the dispensaries, the financial straits of voluntary hospitals. Such a state of affairs could not be remedied merely by a new clinical bureaucracy. Moreover, as was evident in socialist and communist countries, the attempt to produce amelioration by handing the job over to the State not only failed to solve the problem but produced worse evils.

Next Alfred outlined the course of the discussions on the scheme. The tendency of the State to take charge of health, he stated, began with the Health Act, 1947, to some provisions of which the bishops took exception in October 1947. This objection they repeated on 5 April 1951 as follows: 'In sections 21 to 28 the Public Authority were given the right and duty to provide for the health of all children, to treat their ailments, to educate women in regard to motherhood and to provide all women with gynaecological care. To claim such power for the Public Authority, without qualification, is entirely and directly contrary to Catholic teaching on the rights of the family, the rights of the Church in education, the rights of the medical profession and of voluntary institutions.' He rejected an attempt by Dr Browne to justify the scheme by a reference to the provisions of the constitution concerning education. As elsewhere,[6] he argued that national schools were family schools, whose management was mostly entrusted by the parents to their religious organisations, Catholic, Protestant or Jewish. Whereas, if national schools were to be organised in the manner in which it was proposed that guidance concerning family health was to be dealt with in the mother-and-child scheme, 'national

---

doctors.' (4) 'The State must levy a heavy tax on the whole community, by direct or indirect methods, independently of the necessity or desire of the citizens to use the facilities provided.' (5) By this taxation 'the State will in practice morally compel the citizens to avail of the services provided'. (6) The scheme 'must succeed in damaging gravely the self-reliance of parents, whose family wage or income would allow them duly to provide of themselves medical treatment for their dependents'. (7) The scheme will largely involve 'ministerial regulations, as distinct from legislative enactments'.

6. See J. A. Gaughan, *Alfred O'Rahilly III: Controversialist, Part 1: Social reformer*, 203-16, 274-80.

teachers' would be appointees of public authorities and would be under their control.

If the State, continued Alfred, wished to give medical help to families it should proceed as it did in education, where it did not establish State schools or appoint teachers over the heads of the parents. Just as the State subsidised family schools, mostly through the respective religious bodies, so let it subsidise mother and child health through a scheme which would allow the families to become patients of their own doctor who would not be amenable to bureaucratic interference. The primary objection to the proposed scheme was not to its being 'free', but to the substitution of the State for institutions, existing or capable of being created, ultimately responsible to the families concerned. This reluctance to allow the State further power over individuals and families was not mere obstructionism. They had only to survey the world to realise the damage of allowing the State to control family and education.

Alfred set out the arguments for and against a 'means test' with regard to the proposed medical service. The service, he pointed out, would have to be paid for by the community by direct and indirect taxation. He acknowledged that one of the accepted functions of taxation was to produce a more equitable redistribution of income than could be secured by free economic forces. The ideal, as envisaged in the Catholic theory of a just wage, was that the family should itself be able to pay for its requirements – housing, food, education, sickness and old age. But, as there were unsurmountable difficulties in the economic rehabilitation of families, the second best system had to be adopted. This involved the supplementing of wages by family allowances and social services. After making the case for the social services, he asked should the recipient of free services be confined, individually or by class, to those in economic need? In short, he replied, this was a question which required investigation in connection with each proposal. Obviously he realised the strength of the argument in favour of a 'no means test'. A means test did not apply to national schools, public libraries, etc. Nor did he deal directly with the pragmatic approach adopted by the Catholic bishops to the national health services in Northern Ireland, of which Catholics, in effect, were the chief beneficiaries. He concluded by urging that in every case an attempt should be made to ensure a minimum of bureaucracy so

Upholder of Catholic Social Theory

as not to restrict the recipient's choice unduly. Such a scheme he urged the government to devise without delay to help those mothers and children of Ireland who lacked proper medical care.

Further criticism of *Irish Times*

As was customary in the case of a controversial subject, the *Irish Times* published a more than usual number of letters from its readers during the following weeks. For the most part they were in tune with the paper's editorial and hostile to intervention by the Catholic bishops. Alfred returned to the fray in the *Standard* of 27 April with an article entitled 'The political question and the theological issue'. Before treating of his topic, however, he assailed the editor of the *Irish Times* in particular, and the Irish press in general. He compared the tactics of R. M. Smyllie to those 'of a malicious urchin who throws a stone at a church window and then runs away, watching from a safe hiding place the ensuing commotion'. After an editorial 'of shallow bigotry', he declared, space had been given to correspondents to assail their Catholic fellow-citizens with venomous scurrility. Next he noted that here, 'after all our years of studying and lecturing on the social encyclicals', was the first clear chance to protect the rights of the family, to defend 'a good professional organisation' against suppression by the State, and to stand up both for the constitution of the country and the internal authority of the Catholic Church to which the vast majority professed allegiance. Yet, apart from the *Irish Times*, the papers had, in effect, taken refuge in grim silence and had 'carefully avoided dealing with the issue, as if it were a live bomb which might injure the handler'.[7] What a disgraceful mess, he declared, had been made of the whole affair, floods of nasty vituperation on the one hand, and cowardly silence on the other, instead of reasoned discussion. All of which, he declared, convinced him of the wisdom of U.C.C. undertaking widespread and systematic courses in sociology.

Alfred once again distinguished between the political question and the theological issue. The first concerned everyone as legislators, voters, citizens, members of professional bodies or

7. He acknowledged, however, that the 'other papers' had carried 'an excellent letter' on the subject by Father James Kavanagh. The *Irish Times* of 24 April 1951 also published this letter, a fact which he did not mention.

Alfred O'Rahilly III: Controversialist

trade unions. It was the right of individual and corporate criticism of government. That right vitally concerned 'our Protestant fellow-citizens for whom the *Irish Times* professed to cater'. Ignoring the Irish Medical Association's main motivation, namely financial considerations, he continued that the paper had vehemently denied the right of the organised medical profession to express 'conscientious scruples' and 'professional objections'. It had poured derision and abuse on the Catholic hierarchy for pointing out ethical-social objections to a proposed government measure which would probably in any case be invalidated by the supreme court. Then, dismissing the need for ethical estimates of legislative action, the *Irish Times* had effectively adopted a principle which would debar from criticism of the State not only the Church of Ireland, but trade unions and councils, as well as newspapers.

Alfred was critical of a sympathetic report in the *Irish Times* of a speech by E. Warnock, attorney-general of Northern Ireland, who declared: 'The parliament of Éire may sit in Dublin, but the real rulers of the country sit in Maynooth'. 'This stupid slogan, unworthy of a lawyer, was appropriately made in Sandy Row Orange Hall, Belfast, where the bosses of the "Protestant State" sit, just as Mr Smyllie would like their Southern counterparts to sit in the *Irish Times* offices in Westmoreland Street, Dublin.' But, he reminded Smyllie, you cannot proclaim a sweeping general principle of silent acquiescence in State interference and hope that the ban on criticism will not apply to 'your own pals'. He quoted a statement by Einstein, 'an agnostic Jew', deploring the failure of the universities and of the newspapers – and Alfred added that he might have included the workers – to stand up for human dignity and freedom against the Nazis. Einstein had concluded: 'I never had any special interest in the Church before. But now I feel a great affection and admiration for it, because the Church alone has had the courage and persistence to stand for intellectual truth and moral freedom.' Alfred, in addition, recalled that in 1946 Professor Radbruch, a socialist and former minister, opened his course as dean of the law faculty of Heidelberg as follows: 'In the last twelve years we have lived to see all spiritual forces – the universities, science, the courts of justice, political ideologies and parties – collapse under tyranny. Christianity and the Church alone remained master of itself.'

Upholder of Catholic Social Theory

Alfred expressed satisfaction that the current issue of the *Church of Ireland Gazette* 'practically repudiated the *Irish Times*'.[8] He regretted the failure of the *Irish Times* to discuss the social principles put forward by the Catholic hierarchy with the same objectivity as would be expected had they emanated from the Protestant prelates or from lay sociologists. The fact that those proposing them were Irish Catholic bishops was irrelevant, though it surely called for a display of respect and good manners. No one contended that Protestants or Jews were amenable to Catholic episcopal jurisdiction. All Catholic bishops asked 'from outsiders was an educated discussion of the serious issues they had raised'. It was 'deplorable that their arguments have evoked nothing but ill-mannered vituperation'.

Alfred selected a letter by the Rev Frederick R. Mitchell, of the Rectory, Monasterevan, published in the *Irish Times* of 16 April as typical of the 'ignorant ranting', which the controversy had aroused. Mitchell professed great sympathy with 'the patient, long-suffering and law-abiding Roman Catholic laity of our beloved land'. Such 'crocodile tears', asserted Alfred, were a well-known dodge to drive a wedge between clergy and laity, whose relations were none of the reverend gentleman's business. Mitchell then told his Catholic fellow-citizens to remind their bishops that 'their sphere is theology not physiology'. The idea, continued Alfred, that Christianity may be concerned with ethics and politics did not cross Rev Mitchell's mind. He had no use for moral theology. Catholic mothers and girls were to be advised exclusively by State-employed gynaecologists 'unrestricted by sectarian bias'.

Alfred next turned to what he termed 'the ecclesiastical issue' which concerned Catholics alone. One of the channels of the ordinary teaching (*magisterium*) of the Church was through the episcopacy. No one held that an individual bishop, or a local group of such, was infallible. But their decisions should be treated with respect. Against such decisions there was always recourse by way of appeal to the final authority, but this consideration was quite irrelevant in the present case, where the general principles enunciated by the bishops were not only in patent agreement with the papal encyclicals, but also accepted universally by Catholic sociologists and by many outside the Church. Moreover, he claimed, no one in the country had

8. See *Church of Ireland Gazette and Family Newspaper* 20 April 1951.

Alfred O'Rahilly III: Controversialist

produced a simple reasoned argument against the case made by the bishops.

In a passage heavily influenced by contemporary events, Alfred charged that the opposition to the bishops came mainly from a noisy minority. They did not bother much with the loosely-knit Protestant churches, but they strove strenuously to dissuade Catholics from regarding their bishops as guides in faith and morals. The bishops might be right or wrong in a particular case. That did not matter; the main *gravamen* was that bishops were bishops. Thus the present incident had been utilised by certain elements in an attempt to weaken the Church – the great bulwark against communism – just as in the old days the penal laws were concentrated against priests and schoolmasters in order to 'soften up' the ordinary laity. Launching into the rhetoric of the 'Cold War', he continued: 'Let us not be beguiled by this Trojan horse wrapped in the tricolour, nor listen to the bleating of these Stalin-fed sheep in Wolfe Tone's clothing. We can, in the fate of other countries, see the outcome of this dodge of Marxian dialectic. These self-appointed friends of the Catholic laity want to isolate the bishops, so that later on any obstructive Mindszenty, Stepinac or Beran can be dealt with piecemeal.'

Contribution of Deputy Peadar Cowan dismissed

In the debate on the issue in Dáil Éireann on 11 April 1951, Captain Peadar Cowan, T.D., declared that, as a Catholic, he objected to the usurpation of authority by the bishops. If the government accepted the dictation of the bishops in the matter, they were flouting the constitution of the country and acting contrary to their duty as representatives of the public. In a comment on this Alfred declared that Captain Cowan was a lawyer who seemed to have forgotten his jurisprudence. According to him the constitutionality of an act did not depend on its intrinsic content and on the observance of correct procedure, it depended on the motives of the legislators and on the influence experienced in their minds. Such a ruling, Alfred concluded, would invalidate much of the Dáil's legislation which was due to political parties – entities not recognised in the constitution.

Alfred took grave exception to Cowan's implication that the Taoiseach and the cabinet did not really agree with the social principles enunciated by the bishops, but had merely bowed to external compulsion. However, even if that were true, their motive would not be the fear of any spiritual penalties, as they would merely be left to their own consciences. It was obvious that their reason would be the healthy democratic fear of the electorate's reaction. He reminded Captain Cowan that he was not in the Dáil as a Catholic but as a representative of the voters and it was in that capacity that he should have spoken. Did he, Alfred asked, object to the bishops or to the medical profession criticising proposed legislation as an 'usurpation'? Was it only the T.Ds who were entitled to this privilege? He was equally dismissive about Cowan's statement: 'The bishops deal with taxation which is a matter for this House and this House alone.' Did the deputy, he asked, wish to imply that nobody outside the Dáil was permitted to criticise a proposed tax?[9]

Alfred ridiculed an attempt by Deputy Cowan to give the bishops a lesson in theology, when he commented: 'These are matters, as any student of moral theology knows, that are not within the definition of Catholic doctrine on which the bishops may speak with authority to Catholics.' Such a principle, Alfred claimed, would dismiss any authority attaching even to the social encyclicals. Thus Cowan was determined to reduce Catholic teaching and practice to the rigid minimum of what was *de fide*. Cowan quoted the distinguished psychologist, rector of the Catholic University of the Sacred Heart, Milan, and president of the Pontifical Academy of Sciences, Father Agostino Gemelli, O.F.M., who had declared in September 1949: 'Catholic Italy should emulate, and improve upon, the British system of health services.' Alfred commented that there was 'much virtue in that "improve upon"' and that the Irish bishops might have said the same. He also wondered aloud

9. Alfred described Cowan's talk on taxation, without further specification, and of 'no means test' as 'so much hot air'. The taxation involved might be progressive so as to fall mainly on the well-to-do, the 'free' scheme would then be an addition to real wages. Or it might be financed by regressive taxation, for example, by indirect taxes falling chiefly on the articles consumed by the workers; and in that case the working class would be paying for free medical services supplied to the relatively wealthy. Quoting from Paul Crane's 'Who pays for the Welfare State in England' (*Christus Rex*, October 1951), he declared 'in Great Britain the social services have been financed to no small extent by direct taxation levied on special types of individuals within the lower income groups' and 'not by a direct transfer of income from rich to poor'.

Alfred O'Rahilly III: Controversialist

whether Father Gemelli knew in detail what he was talking about. Alfred dismissed as nonsense Cowan's attempt at 'papalising' Gemelli when Cowan alleged of the latter: 'Whatever he says may be safely regarded as expressing the mind of the Vatican.'

Report in *New Statesman* ridiculed

In the *Standard* of 4 May 1951 Alfred attacked a report of the controversy in the current issue of the *New Statesman*. He described Ritchie Calder's account as 'a rehash of an already mouldy dish of the *Irish Times*'. However, there were some new gems of 'typically bigoted misrepresentation'. 'The Irish bishops regarded "unrestricted childbearing as essential to faith and morals".' In which case, noted Alfred, priests and nuns must lack both! The bishops produced 'incredible' arguments against that 'remarkable young man', Dr Browne, 'a medical graduate of Trinity', who had so ably refuted them. '"The prime minister had to appear before the ecclesiastical tribunal"' and, added Alfred, 'apparently just escaped being burnt at the stake'. 'One of the "few courageous deputies" was Captain Cowan who "invoked Father Gemini" [*sic*] whose pronouncements "he recommended Catholic doctors to study".' Alfred could not resist having a further dig at the *Irish Times*. This effort to name the relevant priest was slightly better than the *Irish Times*' boosting of 'Augustina Gemini' 'who might be a woman or twins'.

Reference to letter by Lord Killanin

Alfred referred to a letter by Lord Killanin in the *Irish Times* of 25 April 1951 in which attention was drawn to a passage in the 'London Letter' of 19 April concerning the British Matrimonial Causes Bill: 'The [Anglican] Church's firm and unequivocal oppostion to the bill, as being inimical to the Christian concept of marriage, was expressed by the archbishops of Canterbury and York. After that some of Mrs White's supporters wrote that if she intended defying their lordships they would no longer support her.' As a result the bill was withdrawn and this provoked no comment from the *Irish Times*. Alfred emphasised that this was 'a hefty dig' at the duplicity of the editor of the

Upholder of Catholic Social Theory

Irish Times. Some correspondents, he noted, attempted to parry the blow by pointing out that (1) the bill was not a government measure and (2) the archbishops were in the House of Lords. In effect, this meant that one may criticise Mrs White but not Dr Browne and, because there was no chamber of peers in Ireland, the Catholic bishops had to remain silent. Obviously enjoying the discomfiture of his opponents, Alfred continued: 'At this stage of the proceedings there is little further pretence at argument; there is nothing left but a sedimentary deposit of muddled abuse. In many ways it is a very good thing that this crisis has occurred. It has cleared the air. Our metropolitan bigwigs have been exposed as incompetent and shallow thinkers, whose hitherto half-concealed bigotry has landed them in an impasse. So far from being able to argue against the bishops or against a lay sociologist such as myself, they are incapable of extricating themselves from the totalitarian principle they incautiously invoked.'

Principle of subsidiarity

Alfred next returned to the 'vital issue' at stake. This, he declared, was that the State, though in some respects supreme and supervisory, did not express the total institutional needs of man. It was only one society among many. He quoted from *Quadragesimo Anno* that it was 'an injustice, a grave evil and a disturbance of right order, for a larger or higher association to arrogate to itself functions which could be performed efficiently by smaller and lower societies'. He appealed that this principle, generally referred to as the principle of subsidiarity, in effect, pluralism, be applied to the question at issue. The contention against it, he argued, was that the State should supersede the bishops, the parents and the doctors. The government was 'to be our moral guide, our schoolmaster and our family doctor'. Using quotations from Lord Acton, Cardinal Manning and Jacques Maritain, he argued that the stand of the bishops was, in effect, a stand in defence of religious liberty, the family and the freedom of the professions.

R. M. Smyllie confounded

In the *Standard* of 27 April 1951 Alfred taunted the editor of the *Irish Times* that he was not willing to discuss the issues at stake in the controversy. R. M. Smyllie responded in the *Irish Times* of 28 April. He concluded the column 'An Irishman's Diary' which he wrote over the pseudonym 'Nichevo':

> *Experto Crede*
> The richest joke of the week is to be found in the current issue of the *Standard*. Professor Alfred O'Rahilly, president of University College, Cork, describes the editor of the *Irish Times* as this 'megalomaniac journalist'.

Alfred still hoped that Smyllie would debate the issues and ignored this comment. However, Smyllie did not do so. Realising that his response was generally regarded as being inadequate and irked by Alfred's triumphalism, Smyllie, again in his column 'Irishman's Diary', of 12 May wrote:

> Strolling idly along the southern slopes of one of Dr Alfred O'Rahilly's weekly articles in the *Standard* I happened across a complaint by the learned professor that the editor of the *Irish Times* evidently was afraid to come to grips with him in public controversy. Certainly it is not Dr O'Rahily's fault, for he has written four mountainous screeds in the course of which he has done his utmost to provoke our editor to argue with him. I wonder if Dr O'Rahilly, who, I am told, was once described by one of his own bishops as a lay-theologian ever reads his Bible. Strange as it may appear to the uninitiated I do occasionally and would recommend to the professor the following extract from *Proverbs*: 'Answer not a fool according to his folly, lest thou also be like unto him.' *Verb sap.*, as they say in Cork, – or do they?

Alfred's inevitable reply appeared in the *Standard* of 25 May 1951. It was unsigned and read as follows:

> When 'Irish Times' are Smyling
>
> Nichevo (whose identity is no secret) declared that 'megalomaniac' was not an adjective – and got the Oxford dictionary thrown at his head. He would like, if he dared, to accept Dr O'Rahilly's challenge to argument. But he again

takes up his trifling. He alludes to the 'mountainous screeds' in the *Standard*, though their bulk is only a fraction of the space devoted by the *Irish Times* to the controversy.

'I wonder,' he says, 'if Dr O'Rahilly ever reads his Bible.' Of course he does not; obviously he writes articles and books on the gospels without ever reading them. So Nichevo quotes the book of *Proverbs*: 'Answer not a fool according to his folly.' Does he really think that an opponent of the calibre of Dr O'Rahilly can be fobbed off by this biblical method of calling him a fool? If his arguments are folly ought it not be easy to show him up? By the way, I thought that Protestants relegated *Proverbs* to the *Apocrypha*. What about this pertinent text from the *gospels*: Render to Caesar what is Caesar's and to God what is God's?

Now that the *Irish Times* is becoming piously exegetical, a comment on this text with reference to the present issue would be welcome. *Verb sap.*, as they say in Westmoreland Street; poor sap is what they are saying in Cork.

I used to think of the editor of the *Irish Times* that, even though vanquished, he could argue still. I was wrong. The *Irish Times* is now publishing a series of personal attacks on Dr O'Rahilly, and has succeeded in reaching a low level in Irish journalism, to which neither of the other two Dublin dailies would descend, and whither I am sure our distinguished contributor will not follow him.

Alfred's articles were immensely popular and according to a spokesman for the *Standard* were responsible for the paper's highest weekly circulation figures of some 83,000.[10]

10. Alfred received many letters arising from his articles. One such he sent to Fr Edward Coyne, S.J. He indicated his intention to cover the points raised in the letter in a forthcoming article in the *Standard* and requested advice to that end. In a lengthy reply, dated 19 May 1951, Fr Coyne dealt with the various points raised in the letter: (1) the distinction between the moral and the social teaching of the Catholic Church, (2) the arguments for and against a 'means test', (3) the question of ministerial regulations, (4) the objection to heavy taxation on the whole community, (5) the importance of self-reliance. In conclusion he informed Alfred that an article by him on these topics would be published in the forthcoming issue of *Studies*. On reading Coyne's article ('Mother and child service', *Studies* XL, Summer 1951) Alfred decided that the subject-matter did not require further treatment in the *Standard*. However, in a reply, dated 7 June 1951, to a congratulatory note from Alfred, Coyne urged: 'But do remember that these things come better from a layman and keep your pen sharpened.'

Alfred O'Rahilly III: Controversialist

Myles na gCopaleen enters the fray

In the meantime Alfred's challenge for a reply from the *Irish Times* had been taken up by Brian O'Nolan. In the popular column 'Cruiskeen Lawn' over his pseudonym Myles na gCopaleen he attempted to defend the honour of the *Irish Times* in a series of articles beginning in the issue of 2 May. The intervention of Myles na gCopaleen merely gave Alfred an opportunity to conduct another onslaught on the editor of the *Irish Times*. In 'No answer' in the *Standard* of 11 May he set out the editor's *Contra Mundum* editorial and rebutted it. He emphasised that he had done so because the editor seemed to have been struck with aphasia when he found himself in the unpleasant predicament of either having to withdraw his offensive leader or else attempting to answer arguments against it. Thus, unwilling to accept either of these alternatives, he nevertheless felt that he must do something about it. So he availed himself of the services of his 'hired humorist'.

Alfred conceded that he had argued vigorously against Smyllie's editorial. He declared that he was not acquainted with the editor, but had reason to believe that he was 'a liberal, fair-minded gentleman'.[11] However, he expressed his disappointment that, instead of replying to him with equal vigour, he had 'got his professional jester to emit a stream of irrelevant and stupid personal invective'. He recorded some 'specimens' of the language used towards him by Myles na gCopaleen: 'insolence, arrogance and ignorance', 'a self-licensed demagogue', 'an authority on pig-rearing', 'you wee Cork nuisance'. To a reference by Myles to the *Standard* as 'a small pious weekly' Alfred reminded him that it had twice the circulation of the *Irish Times*. He went on to describe Myles as the editor's 'phraseological gunman', and expressed surprise that the *Irish Times* should publish 'such ill-mannered abuse', and stated that he was almost sorry that he had noticed 'this incoherent ranter'.

Alfred declared that the evasive tactics of the editor were further exemplified by Myles' excursion into lexicography, as if his grammar invalidated his sociology. He then proceeded to show Myles that he could give him a lesson in lexicography, even though it was his own main speciality. And he concluded: 'How irrational and nonsensical it is that, when great issues are at

11. For more on R. M. Smyllie, see Tony Gray, *Mr Smyllie, Sir* (Dublin 1991).

stake, my critic should be wasting space on these verbal jocosities – especially when his own English includes such choice specimens as 'more betoken', 'dunno', 'beyant', and 'by gob'.

Alfred objected to Myles representing his view as: 'The *Irish Times* must shut up. Shutting up independent newspapers is a commonplace as the first move of the totalitarian. Hi there, *La Prensa*.' Alfred added that even a pretence at humour did not justify such a libellous perversion of his views. It was the *Irish Times* which had tried to silence independent Catholic bishops and in so doing the paper's editor had advocated a principle that logically would demand the similar muzzling of Protestants and the silencing of independent journalists. He protested against Myles attempting to saddle him with the 'very principle of which I have accused the *Irish Times*, which, so far, has been unable to elude my charge'.

Alfred ridiculed Myles' attempt to prove that the editor of the *Irish Times* was 'broadminded' because the Irish Times Ltd. printed the *Standard*. He pointed out that the *Standard* often carried advertisements for the *Irish Times* and 'even for M.C.'s column!' It was 'difficult in all this chaff to discover a grain of relevant argument'. The only one he could find, he continued, was that advanced by Dr Noel Browne who, 'under the delusion that our national schools were "State schools" quoted the parallel of compulsory primary education as justifying his scheme. The fallacy in that argument he claimed to have already pointed out in showing that constitutionally the national schools were family schools, and that the parents could use any other schools, or could themselves educate their children.[12]

Like a literary matador Alfred moved in for the kill at the end of his article. He noted that before concluding his piece Myles suddenly 'doffs his jester's cap and bell and writes "My own real view".' Whose view had he been expressing up to this?, asked Alfred. Myles' view, it seems, was that 'The editor, in writing the leading article in question, lacked prudence.' According to him the bishops made 'a perfectly legitimate intervention on a vital matter'. If so, responded Alfred, 'the editor was not only imprudent, he was wrong!' Myles added that, though the bishops rightly gave their moral verdict, they 'should have done so overtly, if only for the sake of the faithful . . . In failing

12. See p. 97.

therein, they lacked prudence.' So, taunted Alfred 'the final dregs of the "Cruiskeen Lawn" consist of a lesson to their lordships on how to conduct episcopal correspondence with the government, by one who is so adept at conducting a polite discussion with an opponent'. He pointed out to Myles that the answer to that unsolicited advice had already been given by the bishop of Galway in the press of 1 May: 'There was nothing secret or underhand in the way the bishops acted. The letters in which they sent their views to the government were not secret. The government were free to publish them if they wished; and, when the occasion required it, they did publish them. The bishops followed the universal usage of sending letters direct, not through the press; for not even governments liked to see letters addressed to them appear first in the newspapers.'

Alfred concluded in the triumphalist tone for which few of his opponents could bring themselves to forgive him: 'No. My arguments have not been answered. The public will not be deceived by this crude strategy of mud-slinging and cynical bluff. Cocksure of their own omniscience, some members of the Dublin intelligentsia tried to browbreat us into deserting our bishops and to stampede us into running away from our social principles. Well, we have stood up to them and reduced them to impotent silence, broken momentarily by the vulgar cat-calls of the pseudonymous jester of the *Irish Times*.' Myles published five further articles in which he pilloried Alfred[13] but they only

13. He did this mainly by criticising Alfred's syntax, lapses in spelling and tautologies. However, he did not manage this without occasionally tripping himself up. The somewhat subjective recollection in Dublin literary circles of the exchange between Alfred and Myles na gCopaleen is well captured in Anthony Cronin's *No laughing matter* (Dublin 1989), a biography of Myles. Cronin first sets the scene by recalling that in the *Standard* Alfred had 'foolishly' attacked the *Irish Times*, whose editor he had described as 'a megalomaniac journalist' and had referred to the paper itself as 'a Protestant organ which had "a tradition for episcopophagy".' He continued:

> Myles had in some ways, a soft target, since O'Rahilly, although president of University College, Cork, was justly regarded as a member of the lunatic right and had been an intellectual apologist for the now discredited Blueshirts; but he was in any case in dazzling form throughout the exchanges that followed and had easily the best of them.
>
> He began by questioning O'Rahilly's credentials. 'An M.A. by gob? I, too, am an M.A. of the same wretched university and can prove documentarily (by producing the preposterous "thesis") that the degree, like the university, is a fake. There is, however, nothing fake about being president of any of its colleges.' In his second article he seized delightedly on

served to emphasise the latter's competence as a polemicist. Realising this at last, he signed off as follows in the issue of 25 May: 'I think I will rest Mr O'Rahilly today. Lecture us, he may, monopolise us, no.'[14]

In 'Government and the people' in the *Standard* of 25 May 1951 Alfred argued that if the constitution had provided for more extensive opportunities for a referendum, as in Switzerland, the current political crisis would not have occurred.[15] He expressed no doubt about the result 'if the issue of a State-monopoly of a mother-and-child service could have been taken out of the hands of the political parties and submitted to a direct vote of the people'. This led him to discuss the projects

> the fact that O'Rahilly had chosen to sign himself 'Dr Alfred O'Rahilly, M.A., D.Sc': 'Note in passing that the sage is a doctor at both ends, which is a most unusual distinction.' He had great fun with the fact that O'Rahilly had called him a hired humorist. He did not deny that he took money, but, he said, 'I formally deny that hired or otherwise, I am a "humorist". I am a most serious and thoughtful commentator, and a large number of persons and interests have found much of what I have written far from funny.' And O'Rahilly's claim that he was exalting himself into a 'super-bishop' provoked one of his most famous witticisms. 'Really,' he said, 'I have no ecclesiastical ambitions . . . I am merely a spoiled Proust.'
>
> All in all the controversy, which he kept going over seven columns, showed Myles at his agile best. He made full use of his persona and was serious and flippant, playful and vicious just as it pleased him.

A more balanced account of the exchange is to be found in Peter Costello and Peter van de Kamp's, *Flann O'Brien: an illustrated biography* (London 1987). After dealing with the libel action taken by the Dublin Institute for Advanced Studies against Myles and the *Irish Times*, the authors continue:

> The remark that led to that action was at least humorous. That cannot be said of what Myles was writing a decade later. By then he was becoming vindictive and more personal in his attacks. In 1951, arising out of the furore over the government medical scheme of mothers and children which brought down the first inter-party government, a feud began with Alfred O'Rahilly, a brother of the aforementioned Celtic scholar, formerly of Blackrock College, then president of University College, Cork. This had nothing to do with the political row in the country at large. It was a clash of personalities, an exchange between equals, for O'Rahilly was able to give as good as he got . . . Myles was as nothing to him, he was a 'hired humorist' of the alien *Irish Times*. Myles was furious and lashed back. But the exchange showed him at his weakest.

14. See *Irish Times* 16, 17, 18, 19, 21, 25 May 1951.
15. As a preliminary to this he had published in the *Standard* of 18 May 1951 a fine article on religious liberty under the heading 'Catholics and liberty'. Subsequently in the *Standard* of 27 July 1951 he expanded on his views on how best the sovereignty of the people could be enshrined in a constitution.

111

Alfred O'Rahilly III: Controversialist

for federalism and vocationalism and the use of the referendum which he proposed unsuccessfully when a member of the constitution committee of 1922. Since then, he suggested, the country had been too much subject to British political ideas. This aroused considerable public interest as did his analysis in the following issue of the *Standard* of the results of the general election.

An unwelcome lesson for Seán Ó Faoláin

An article 'The Dáil and the bishops' by Seán Ó Faoláin in the *Bell* of June 1951 prompted an immediate reply from Alfred in the *Standard* of 22 June. He confessed that he found it 'exceedingly curious' that he and Ó Faoláin writing as lay Catholics should 'arrive at such utterly different conclusions'. Ó Faoláin, he argued, had ignored the vital distinction between the natural rights of the bishops and their supernatural authority, their constitutional status and their religious standing. He expressed surprise to find educated Catholics suddenly discovering that they belonged to a Church which not only upheld Revelation, but defended the natural rights and liberties of individual and family. Had such people read the social encyclicals? His interest was in *what* the bishops said not in *who* said it. They expressed what was unanimously held by Catholic sociologists and many others. If he were an agnostic, he would still in the interests of liberty, especially of the less well-off, strongly uphold the bishops' defence of conjugal and parental rights against invasion by the State.

Alfred continued that with the validity or content of the bishops' objections Ó Faoláin appeared to have no concern whatever. He had just one *obiter dictum*: 'It is not likely that State socialism – of which Dr Browne's scheme was felt to be the thin end of the wedge – would be madly popular with the North.' Ó Faoláin gave no indication as to his view on this and disdained to argue the point. His exclusive preoccupation, Alfred pointed out, was the fact that the defence of liberties emanated from 'Maynooth'. He made it clear that he would not be at all perturbed if analogous pronouncements had been made by the 'Protestant Synod, the Irish Academy of Letters or the Trade-Union Congress'. This game of 'Maynooth-baiting' was silly and dangerous. 'After our wives and children, the next

Upholder of Catholic Social Theory

object of collectivist solicitude might even be the intelligentsia.' Suppose 'the minister for education decided to take charge of our mental uplift by running the *Bell*?' The bishops might be useful then as they had been when they saved the country from conscription. He regretted that Ó Faoláin's treatment of the issue was not more realistic and relevant to the world of that time.

Alfred noted that Ó Faoláin several times used the word 'democracy' without defining it. It seemed for him it indicated the unitary State, over which no autonomous associations could be permitted to exist. At any rate, never once did he mention the family. Moreover, an outsider reading Ó Faoláin would never suspect that the bishops were aiming not at the aggrandisement of the Church, but at the defence of marital and parental rights. Doubtless Ó Faoláin would be up in arms against any aggression by the State against the literary profession, but he failed even to mention that the medical profession was being coerced. He treated the Church most unrealistically as if it was an alien institution run by Stateless refugees: 'Mr Costello, faced by the clerical opposition to a piece of legislation which he and his cabinet, on behalf of the government, on behalf of the people, were proposing, should have strongly and stubbornly resisted the bishops to the limit.' On the one side there was a handful of clerics, on the other, the cabinet, the government, the legislature and the people. It had never occurred to Ó Faoláin that nearly all those people might have heartily agreed with the bishops – or, if he preferred, in spite of the fact that they were bishops! Though Mr Ó Faoláin never discussed whether the bishops were right or wrong, he should not have attributed 'this inhuman detachment to other people such as the late cabinet'. And, if there was any doubt as to what the majority of the voters thought, let there be a referendum. Better still let the supreme court pronounce on the constitutional validity of the State monopolising health education.

Alfred charged Ó Faoláin with making strenuous efforts to frighten people with the bogey of clericalism in writing that: 'The people must feel that there is a wide gap between theology and humanity. They must feel themselves distrusted by their own clergy, for, if this scheme had gone through, who would have worked it almost wholly but a Catholic government, Catholic doctors, Catholic civil servants, the ordinary Catholic

Alfred O'Rahilly III: Controversialist

laymen?' This, Alfred argued, suggested that theology was an abstruse inhuman abstraction concocted by the clergy against 'humanity', that is, humanitarianism or social services imposed in defiance of rights and liberties'. Alfred further paraphrased Ó Faoláin's comment – and why bother about principles and safeguards, when those entrusted with drastic power, the potential oppressors, are Catholics. This, he declared, was extremely dangerous and grossly unfair to 'our Protestant fellow-citizens'.

Having discussed 'the realities of the situation', Alfred next turned to Ó Faoláin's 'rarified academic treatment': 'The Church will properly but always prudently fight for power, and the State will always try to restrain that power within due limits . . . It is the duty of parliament, as Catholics, as Christians of any denomination, to resist that Church for its own sake. For more and more the Church here is approaching near to this point of undue power without due responsibility.' Alfred pounced on this with obvious delight: 'I rubbed my eyes when I read this . . . and the reference to "the history of the Italian city-states and the whole life-story of Dante". By any chance is this a chunk of some discarded historical essay which has irrelevantly found its way into this article.' He continued: 'We in Ireland have solved the problem of Church and State. There is separation without dissociation. Clerics have no privileged status, no exemptions, no subsidies, no legislative or executive power in civil law. Any incitement of the State to curb the Church in this country simply means internal interference in the spiritual sphere and an aggression which would equally threaten all other associations.' The bishops had spoken out, Alfred told Ó Faoláin, because neither sociologists nor the medical profession had been listened to. He applauded the stand taken by the bishops for liberty against the State and compared it to the stand then being taken by their brethren in Eastern Europe. In such situations, East or West, he concluded: 'When it comes to a show down the intellectuals always cut a very poor figure.'

Alfred pointed out that the bishops, without interfering with technical details, had given their moral verdict. They had claimed no special status in constitutional or civil law. The Protestant hierarchy might have made a similar pronouncement. Disobedience to the bishops involved no civil disabilities. He regretted that Ó Faoláin would be taken seriously by outsiders in ridiculing the country's constitutional liberties which were a

Upholder of Catholic Social Theory

model for many countries. Ó Faoláin wrote: 'That part of the constitution which gives equal liberty to all religions is poppycock.' Thereby he wished to depict Ireland as a Church-ridden State, in which Protestants did not get fair treatment. This, charged Alfred, was 'a shocking calumny'. He instanced the relatively recent school attendance bill which seemed to have been designed chiefly to prevent Protestants from having their children educated in their own country or in England without interference from the government.[16] It was declared unconstitutional by the supreme court. Alfred reminded Ó Faoláin that the bishops in their intervention had made no distinction between Catholic or non-Catholic parents or children. They had protested on behalf of all families. Catholics recognised that the liberties they claimed for themselves were equally the rights of their Protestant fellow-citizens.

To Ó Faoláin's complaint that the Catholic Church was too autonomous and influential, Alfred responded that it was curious that he did not attribute this to the statistical fact that Catholics formed the preponderating majority of the community. He reproduced another of Ó Faoláin's grievances: 'Nobody, so far as I have observed, has denied the right of the Catholic bishops to comment on or give advice on proposed legislation, or to enunciate the official attitude of the Roman Catholic Church to proposed legislation . . . In practice, the hierarchy does much more than comment or advise; it commands.' Alfred declared that it was pleasant to record that Ó Faoláin, who, he noted, apparently had not been reading the *Irish Times*, had no objection to the Catholic bishops making remarks about legislation or enunciating the attitude of the Church. But, he did not grant that that implied any obligation on the part of the Catholic laity. At any rate this would seem to follow from his objection to the bishops 'commanding'. In fact, said Alfred, although the bishops made no claim to pass legislation or to annul it as the supreme court could, they did claim to impose a moral obligation devoid of civil consequences. He reminded Ó Faoláin that every club or society, including, for example, the Protestant Synod, could issue commands to its members.

Another objection by Ó Faoláin to the Catholic Church was that, unlike the other Churches, it had 'power'. Alfred

16. See J. A. Gaughan, *Alfred O'Rahilly III: Controversialist, Part 1: Social reformer*, 279.

Alfred O'Rahilly III: Controversialist

responded that the Baptists in America, the Protestants and the Orange Order 'in the North' and many large trade unions had power. Moreover, most competent observers considered that the chief menace to liberty at that time came from the all-powerful State with its police, guns and increasing monopolies. Ó Faoláin, however, continued Alfred, had 'no fears on that head'. The only power he deprecated was that of the Catholic Church for 'it holds a weapon which none of the other institutions mentioned holds – the weapon of the sacraments'. To this Alfred responded: 'Mr Ó Faoláin evidently wants to "disarm" the Church as a menace to the State. I could understand a Quaker regarding the sacraments as "weapons". But a Catholic? . . . If you believe in the sacraments, then you must accept the Church which administers them. If you do not, then it is none of your business. You can always get on without them and without incurring any temporal penalties or civil disabilities. Protestants, as well as agnostics and ex-Catholics, think they get on very well without our sacraments.' He acknowledged that there had been cases in which ecclesiastical disciplinary powers had been misused. This was not surprising. Every institution was liable to abuse at the hands of its human agents. But the remedy was not to incur the much greater evil of inviting the State to abolish individual and corporate rights. Alfred accused Ó Faoláin of nonsense in writing that, if Irish Catholics disobeyed the bishops 'they may draw on themselves this weapon of the sacraments whose touch means death'. Obviously, replied Alfred, it does not mean physical death, and 'certainly not moral death, for by hypothesis the disobeyers are in good faith'.

Alfred had begun by accusing Ó Faoláin of confusing the natural and the supernatural, the spiritual and the temporal. He concluded with a protest against Ó Faoláin's monstrous misuse of language: 'Here in the Republic, as this crisis has revealed to us, we have two parliaments: a parliament of Maynooth and a parliament in Dublin . . . The Dáil proposes; Maynooth disposes. The Dáil had, when up against the second parliament, only one right of decision, the right to surrender . . . This imprudent intervention of our second parliament has roused feelings of the most agonised dismay.' Alfred replied that it would be correct to say that, when up against the supreme court or a referendum, the Dáil had no option but to surrender. For

Upholder of Catholic Social Theory

then one would be referring to the domain of public law and the interactions of constitutional organs. But to talk of a parliament – an assembly for passing laws – at Maynooth was as inaccurate and inappropriate as to speak of a Church at Leinster House. The choice of such terminology, if not due to malicious ridicule, must have been meant to insinuate the view that the State should take over more and more of the Church's task and that the legislature should become intolerant of all autonomous associations. It indicated a hankering for the unitary, totalitarian State which regarded with 'agonised dismay' all the loyalties and ideals which it did not control. Alfred recalled that this was a view expressed by bygone intellectuals like Tacitus and Pliny. It was one propagated then by many of their successors who bowed down in the 'House of Mammon and Stalin'. But, he reminded Ó Faoláin, there was one institution which, 'while rendering to Caesar what is Caesar's, will always claim for God what is God's.

Thirty-five years later Ó Faoláin had neither forgotten nor forgiven Alfred's onslaught on his article.[17] At the time he had remained uncharacteristically silent in the face of it. This was all the more noticeable when, a few months later, in the *Bell* of September 1951, in a letter to the editor, Peadar O'Donnell, he took Bishop Michael Browne to task neatly for an intemperate remark.[18]

Editor of *Comhar* taken to task

Alfred was prompted to rattle the bones of the mother-and-child controversy once more in the *Standard* of 3 August 1951 by references to it in *Comhar*. This carried an editorial on the subject in its issue of Bealtaine (May), some letters protesting against this editorial in the following issue and a further editorial replying to these in the issue of Iúl (July). He quoted from the initial editorial: 'It is directly opposed to the spirit and to the letter of the constitution to say that Mr Costello was

17. In 1985 he indicated to the present writer that he had no wish to discuss Alfred O'Rahilly because of an attack he had made on him in the *Standard*.
18. Bishop Browne, in an address a short time previously to a congress of university students in Galway, in speaking of hostility to the Catholic Church, had ascribed 'the fury of the Orangemen of Sandy Row, the venom of the *Irish Times* and the rancour of the *Bell*' to 'a refusal to see in her the divine'.

Alfred O'Rahilly III: Controversialist

bound to express the opinions expressed by the bishops.' This and the rest of the editorial, he charged, was 'reproducing in Irish the bigoted misstatements of the *Irish Times* and the woolly-minded misapprehensions of the *Bell*, as if no refutation had been published'. Then he pounced on a final comment in the editorial that mention should be made of Dr Browne's work for Irish, which he had learnt and caused to be widely used in the department. This, declared Alfred, was an indication that there were persons who were prepared to sacrifice principles 'to a linguistic fetish'.

In connection with the subsequent editorial in *Combar* of July a reader sent three queries to Alfred. He was asked: 'Are Catholics bound by the social teaching of the Church?' He replied: 'Of course they are. Otherwise the Church would be merely publishing topics for discussion as in a debating society.' He pointed out that the obligation was different from that with regard to teaching on faith and morals. In addition, he acknowledged that social issues tended to be complex and admitted of widespread debate among Catholics. However, he warned that the onus of justification for circumscribing personal, familial and religious rights lay always on those who alleged the exigence of the common good. To the second query: 'Are T.Ds bound by the pronouncements of the bishops?' He replied in the affirmative. In the course of a detailed discussion of this he said: 'The current attitude of the bishops is not confined to them. Their view [the importance of the principle of pluralism or subsidiarity] is contained in papal encyclicals and in the universal teaching of Catholic theologians and sociologists. We need not take seriously the Browne-Cowan attempt to set up an Italian Franciscan as an anti-pope by garbling and bowdlerising a lecture he gave. Nor need we refute the silly idea that a Catholic is bound only by the infallible decisions of a General Council or pronouncements *ex cathedra*. We are also bound by the ordinary *magisterium* of the Church, concerning which moral certainty prevails.'

In the *Standard* of 10 August 1951 Alfred dealt with the third query, which concerned 'the obligation of T.Ds.' He replied by asking the following rhetorical questions: 'Are they bound to observe the natural law as legislators? Are they bound to avoid violating the constitution in the measures for which they vote? Or, as in the case of communists, is the party line their final criterion?' He added that one did not escape from moral obligations by going inside Leinster House. He translated from the initial editorial in *Combar* as follows: 'The members of the government are not bound to accept the opinions of the bishops, who dealt not with the moral teaching of the Church, but with the social teaching, and no Catholic is bound to accept this.'[19] Alfred declared that he had not read in English 'any such naked avowal of this dereligionising of social and public life, any such secularist attempt to imprison the Church in the sacristies'. He continued: 'This editorial in *Combar* is, in fact, a mild literary version of communist ideology, Joe Stalin masquerading as an tAthair Peadar.'

Pursuit of R. M. Smyllie

In articles in the *Standard* of 17, 24 and 31 August Alfred pursued R. M. Smyllie and the *Irish Times* in a manner not calculated to win him many friends. In the first of these 'Church and State or Church-State?' he wrote that he had to hand a booklet *Southern Ireland – Church or State?* He continued that 'the misnomer "Southern Ireland" (which reaches Malin Head!) showed clearly that this pamphlet emanated from the Six Counties area, which arrogates to itself the name of "Ulster".' Published in Belfast by the Ulster Unionist Council for free distribution, it consisted of a two and a half page introduction with the rest of its ninety-four pages taken up with appendices. Alfred described the introduction as a condensed and venomous misrepresentation. Protestants were decreasing in number. 'It is almost suggested,' expostulated Alfred, 'that we are murdering them.' He asked what can be done if our Protestant fellow-countrymen, who have a disproportionate share of the good jobs, will not reproduce themselves. It reported that the mother-and-child scheme was 'welcomed by the people', but how and when was not stated. The introduction concluded, in the words of 'a Roman Catholic member of the Dáil, Captain Cowan, Éire's real rulers are the Roman Catholic bishops'. The appendices included (1) the Browne correspondence, as printed

---

19. Ní raibh aon cheangal ar aon bhall den rialtas glacadh leis an dearcadh a nocht na hEaspaig, Ar an gcéad dul síos ní treoir ar theagasc mhorálta na hEaglaise ach treoir ar an dteagasc sóisialta a bhí á nochtadh agus ní ceangal ar aon Chaitliceach glacadh leis an dteagasc san.'

Alfred O'Rahilly III: Controversialist

in the *Irish Times*. (2) The *Irish Times* editorial *Contra Mundum*. (3) The relevant Dáil proceedings. (4) Letter, critical of episcopal intervention, of P. J. Kilroy, professing to represent the Anti-Partition of Ireland League, published in the *Irish Times* of 8 May 1951.

Having put down his markers Alfred set about Smyllie. He invited readers to observe 'the sinister role of the *Irish Times* in providing ammunition for these Northern bigots'. The 'notorious editorial' which had been 'pulverised' had been given a new lease of life, without even the smallest indication of the trenchant criticisms to which it had been subjected or of the fact that it had been repudiated even in the *Church of Ireland Gazette*. The editor had since then been 'sticking his head in the sand'. Alfred challenged Smyllie that, if he could not meet his arguments, at least to do something to atone 'for the defamation of what he professes to be his country'. Such a withdrawal, he added, would not, of course, be published by the Ulster Unionist Council just as they had concealed the fact that the Anti-Partition League had at once repudiated the statement of P. J. Kilroy.[20] What really saddened him in the pamphlet, he exclaimed, was not so much the dishonest controversial tactics employed as 'the bigotry-inspired adoption of a position whose logical outcome is sheer totalitarian tyranny'. He concluded with a comprehensive list of reasons why he considered members of the Ulster Unionist Council to be no more than 'sanctimonious humbugs who prate of loyalism and liberty'.

In the second article 'State versus Home' Alfred cited the letter sent by the Irish hierarchy to the government on 10 October 1950. He summarised it as stating: (1) The right to provide for children's health and for their physical education belongs to the parents and (2) The power entrusted to the minister under the Health Act was in direct opposition to the rights of the family, no promises of moderation would justify the legalising of such power which might be a ready-made instrument for totalitarian aggression. He recalled that a similar attack on family rights was embodied in the School Attendance Bill of 1943. On that occasion the supreme court intervened. He reported that he had consulted the editorials of the *Irish Times* in connection with that previous political crisis which raised the identical social principle. He quoted from editorials in the *Irish Times* of 4 and 23

20. See *Irish Times* 11 May 1951.

Upholder of Catholic Social Theory

February and 16 April 1943 to illustrate that in that instance R. M. Smyllie was a vigorous defender of the rights of parents. Using a memorable phrase, which Alfred recommended to the Irish bishops, Smyllie had written: 'The issue is one of State versus Home.' And yet, continued Alfred, the issue was not as grave as the current one. The school-powers of the minister left intact all the Protestant schools in Ireland. The editor was concerned only with the small minority of parents 'who choose to send their children abroad for schooling'. In the current case the State was claiming the power not only to inspect children (up to sixteen years old) in school or in the home or wherever the minister directs, but also to give education in health to the children.

In applauding the decision of the supreme court in declaring the Schools Attendance Act 1943 to be unconstitutional Smyllie wrote: 'This country fought for liberty for seven hundred years; instead of a new liberty, it is threatened with a new slavery. Yesterday liberty was reasserted.' Alfred pointed out that in this instance the editor of the *Irish Times* was solicitous for the handful of children sent to English schools lest they be forced to learn Irish. But in the mother-and-child controversy he decried the intervention of the Catholic bishops in their protest against totalitarian powers and their vindication of the rights of parents, Catholic and Protestant. And he charged Smyllie with 'a piece of journalistic tergiversation, a repudiation of former principles' in order to have 'a dig at the Catholic bishops'.

Alfred was not finished with Smyllie yet. In the third article 'Differential charges' he dealt with the differential-rents scheme applied to corporation houses in Cork and Dublin. He described the considerable difficulties associated with such schemes. However, this was but a preliminary to discussing an editorial on the subject in the *Irish Times* of 27 July 1951, wherein the principle of graded rents was accepted and consequently a means test. The editorial voiced strenuous opposition to free or subsidised houses for everybody. Then, Alfred maintained, the editor, realising that he had expressed a contradictory view in connection with the mother-and-child scheme, concluded: 'There is a world of difference between a means test in medical treatment and a means test in housing.'

Alfred exclaimed, 'What a pity that this "world of difference" remains unexplored and unexplained.' He continued that if

Alfred O'Rahilly III: Controversialist

'a question of principle', the title of the editorial, was to be discussed, the main point was not the gratuity of the service or the means test. The vital issue was that the State (directly or through the municipality) should not become the sole schoolmaster, the sole landlord or the sole doctor, that private builders and private practitioners should not be wiped out or economically strangled, that as many people as possible should be allowed themselves to look after their housing and their health as well as the schooling of their children.

Mgr Montini, Fr Edward Coyne, S.J.

In the *Standard* of 14 September 1951 under the heading 'Does the Church favour socialised medicine?' Alfred discussed a letter from Mgr Montini, under-secretary of State for the Vatican, to the Annual Catholic Social Congress in France. The letter had been widely quoted in the U.S. and elsewhere as showing that the Church favoured socialised medicine. He argued that in the letter there was strong support for improved medical services, including housing for those who were not well off and that in the matter of public health the State had a definite but limited responsibility. The financial aid of the State was necessary for the improvement and the extension of the existing services, but the State had to respect the individual and not supersede the family. Thus the gist of Mgr Montini's message was, in effect, that the chief task of the State was to support and coordinate, as needed, the efforts of voluntary institutions.

In a letter, dated 20 April 1951, Fr Edward Coyne, S.J., congratulated Alfred on his article in the *Standard* of that date. He continued:

> It was high time that we all sat back a moment and considered how far we were being swept out from our moorings into the paternal and totalitarian State. We have all been preaching against the encroachment of the State and bureaucracy in various fields, but until it came down to a live and burning question and received concrete application nobody would have bothered to realise how serious the matter was. In this way even the *Irish Times* has done an excellent service, for very pride itself will force Catholics now to acquaint themselves with the rational arguments

against the *Times* and in favour of their own position. No other incentive would have done this except the feeling that they were being mocked at by the *Irish Times*.

These were sentiments which were echoed by Alfred in one of his articles. His sustained criticism of the *Irish Times* in general and R. M. Smyllie in particular was excessive. But at a time when the *Standard* reached its highest circulation figures his detailed and repetitive discussion of the mother-and-child scheme and of the principles underlying the positions of the various protagonists facilitated a widespread appreciation of the issues involved.

Medical ethics, doctor-patient relationship

After the general election of 30 May 1951 de Valera formed a new Fianna Fáil administration with the support of a small number of independent members. The controversy surrounding the mother-and-child scheme simmered on. The Catholic bishops, the Irish Medical Association and indeed Alfred, apart from his articles in the *Standard*, availed of every opportunity to articulate their continuing opposition to the scheme. On 11 June 1952 Alfred addressed the annual congress of the Irish Nurses' Organisation in Cork. As head of U.C.C. and acting head of its medical school he said that he was proud of the nurses of Ireland. In typical radical fashion he urged that all nurses join the I.N.O. and thus be in a position to insist on their salaries and working conditions being on a par with those of nurses in Britain. Nurses, he stated, were more than mere technicians and readers of thermometers. They did not deal with inorganic material but with human bodies and souls, which could not be dissociated. He referred to the mother-and-child scheme and continued that the Irish people were not sceptical or neutral in matters of the natural law. More and more people, trade unionists and employers, were realising that conditions in the modern world necessitated a knowledge of ethics and sociology. Irish nurses, he suggested, should be trained in these subjects so as to be able to cope with the complex issues they had to face in their work.

On 8 July 1952 about two hundred Irish members of the Guild of SS Luke, Cosmas and Damian – an organisation for Catholic

Alfred O'Rahilly III: Controversialist

medical doctors – were joined by members of the Guild from Britain, the U.S., Argentina and elsewhere in Newman House, in Dublin, to discuss 'The doctor, the family and the State.' Alfred was the principal speaker[21] at the meeting which was attended by Archbishop McQuaid. His paper received extensive coverage in the national press on the following day. Alfred declared that the integrity of the doctor-patient relationship was being gravely menaced. In their time, with the technological accumulation of power, the State had once more begun to monopolise all social relationships under its domination and control.

Quoting from *Quadragesimo Anno* he stated that the larger and higher association called the State was more and more arrogating to itself functions which could be performed more efficiently and humanly by the smaller societies, such as the family, the professions and private enterprise. The individual was losing his institutional liberties and becoming a cog in a vast impersonal machine. This was particularly obvious in countries where communism had triumphed.

That of doctor-patient was one of the oldest and primary of human relationships and it had subsisted through all the changes of social structures. Against the doctrine of social permission he maintained that medical secrecy was primarily personal and not just a working arrangement exacted and limited by public order. It was based on the fundamental rights of the human person to confide integrally and with impunity in another who could supply moral or material aid. A person thus entering into intimate relations with another was subject to a duty which came not from a special contract or from public order, but from the confidential nature of the relationship. This was true of the doctor-patient association which, being a traditional and quasi-natural institution, possessed objective natural rights independent of the political community.

---

21. The other speaker was Very Rev. Conor Martin, professor of ethics and politics at University College, Dublin. His paper was much shorter than Alfred's but his comments were far more incisive. Towards the end of the month Dr Jim Ryan, minister for health, published a white paper outlining his intentions with regard to a health bill (Department of Health: *Proposals for improved and extended health services*, July 1952). It contained little to indicate that those who prepared it had been influenced by the lectures earlier in the month. The editor of the *Sunday Press* requested Alfred to contribute an article on the white paper. This, however, was not published, owing to a newspaper strike.

Upholder of Catholic Social Theory

A doctor's professional autonomy was being filched from him when he was saddled with such incompatible duties as those of a health-policeman or when the State obtruded itself into his relations with patients. In such instances he was also being used as a tool by the State for usurping the natural rights of the family. The latter perversion was unfortunately facilitated by the false philosophy with which so many doctors were imbued. Doctors, who repudiated the inviolability of the natural order with regard to the family and regarded marital relations as subject to arbitrary interference, were really claiming for themselves powers which inconsistently they would deny the State. How, he asked, could such doctors make a stand against the State when it prescribed a limit of permissible births or practised sterilisation on one section of the population or euthanasia on another? With such a philosophy they had also deprived themselves of the strongest argument against their being turned into State employees commissioned to direct and to inspect mother and child. The only solid defence of the family was to uphold the pluralistic view of social life, to deny that the political community was all-inclusive, to maintain that other associations – in particular the family – had independent natural rights and duties, internal and external.

Alfred contended that liberty was endangered and natural family rights violated when the State, in pursuit of a monopoly, aimed at the financial strangulation of voluntary hospitals and sought to make medical practitioners into civil servants. Such a blueprint scheme of centralised control always appealed to a bureaucracy. It would not be tolerated in education; it should be strenuously resisted in regard to the mother-and-child service. He went on: 'We do not want our State to be our schoolmaster or our almoner. No one doubts that our families require assistance for education and for medical treatment. We must take care lest this need be made an excuse for hustling us into accepting a large dose of the unitary State.'

It was vital that a systematic course of medical ethics be an integral part of the education of a doctor. There was little prospect of its introduction into 'the so-called liberal medical schools, where there was no agreement on the fundamentals of ethics'. Alfred proposed that the Guild of SS Luke, Cosmos and Damian extend its work by admitting and providing for medical students, and by arranging systematic courses in medical ethics in connection with British universities. Even in their own country it was important that Irish Catholic doctors should be well grounded in social principles and thus able to explain them to the public in defence of their stand. There was widespread ignorance in these matters and the public were inclined to attribute motives of self-interest alone to any concerted action by the medical profession. In particular, it was necessary, he asserted, to dissipate the idea that Catholic doctors were engaged in a proselytising campaign or design to impose specifically Catholic views on other doctors, who, unfortunately had lost the understanding of what was meant by natural law, as distinct from civil and ecclesiastical legislation.

Alfred held that the philosophy of the 'Order of Natural Law' was not a clerical invention designed for the aggrandisement of Catholic churchmen. It was as applicable to Protestant and Jewish families as to Catholic ones. The doctrine was neither specifically Catholic nor clerical. It would be equally valid, he maintained, were it proclaimed by Protestant bishops or lay persons rather than by Catholic bishops. Although for Catholics it was reinforced by ecclesiastical authority, it was based on reason.

The full text of Alfred's address was published as a supplement in the *Standard* of November 1953.[22] In the meantime, after successful negotiations with various interested parties, de Valera had a health act passed on 29 October 1953. This included almost all the features of the formerly contentious mother-and-child scheme and provided a free mother-and-child service to dependants of those insured under the Social Welfare Act of 14 June 1952. Certain adjustments had had to be made to secure the acquiescence of those who had found difficulty with the original scheme put forward by Dr Browne. These concessions, however, were not that significant, and politically Fianna Fáil could claim that it was they who after all brought in the mother-and-child scheme. In *Hibernia* of 11 March 1960 Alfred gave his verdict on the outcome as follows: 'The last

22. The supplement was sponsored by the I.M.A. and constituted part of its disappointed retort to the Health Act 1953 which had become law on 29 October. For Alfred's address, see Appendix 5. Earlier, when the Health Bill had reached the committee stage, the *Standard* of 6 March 1953 carried an editorial drafted by Alfred in which he was very critical of various provisions in the bill. In a letter, dated 6 March 1953, he drew Archbishop McQuaid's attention to the editorial and expressed his hope that the views therein were in agreement with those of the archbishop.

Upholder of Catholic Social Theory

struggle I had [against what he regarded as undue State interference] resulted in the insertion of Section 62 in the Health Act of 1953. Unsatisfactory as it is, it is a considerable concession and it was secured by the bishops.'

Many persons assert strenuously that the initial failure to implement the mother-and-child scheme was due to a conflict between Church and State. T. Desmond Williams, who rejected this view, wrote that the difficulties surrounding the scheme developed into a crisis because of an improbable series of coincidences. These he listed as follows: 'The conditions of coalition government, the tactics of the most successful trade union of all, the Irish Medical Association, Dr Browne's own misinterpretation of episcopal negotiation, the minister's own peculiar relationship with the leader of his party, Seán MacBride, and the special phraseology of Archbishop McQuaid.' He continued: 'All these gave this particular political crisis a character which it would have lacked under different circumstances and with different personalities involved.' Those who were acquainted with Archbishop McQuaid and Dr Noel Browne and who have read the latter's *Against the tide* (Dublin 1986) would have no reason to dispute this verdict. However, an equally credible explanation would be that Dr Browne and his coalition colleagues were lacking in the political skill and parliamentary and administrative experience needed to translate new ideas into acceptable and workable programmes. Browne himself was first elected to Dáil Éireann in February 1948 and was appointed a minister on his first day there. The Fianna Fáil ministers who handled the revised scheme and who conducted the negotiations with the bishops, the medical profession and other interests were senior members of Dáil Éireann with long records in government. Whatever the reasons for the initial failure to implement the mother-and-child scheme the controversy surrounding it continues with the 'Fall of Parnell' to be one of the most enduring shibboleths of recent Irish history. It may be that by his vigorous polemics Alfred contributed to this.[23]

23. The above is taken from *Cork Examiner* 14 January, 14 July, 27 October 1948; 11, 19 January, 13 July 1949; 19 July 1950; 17 January, 5 March 1951; 19 January, 12 June, 9 July 1952; *Irish Independent* 9 July 1952; *Irish Times* 9 July 1952; interview with Tadhg Ó Cearbhaill; papers and writings of Alfred O'Rahilly and the sources already cited.

A PRIEST AT LAST

Alfred's wife, Agnes, died on 14 September 1953 after a short illness. At his request the funeral was private. However, as well as the academic community, a very large crowd, representative of every aspect of the civil and ecclesiastical life of the city, attended the removal of the remains from the Bon Secours Home to the Honan chapel. There was also a large and representative attendance at the Requiem Mass on the following day which was celebrated by Reverend Dr James Bastible, dean of residence at U.C.C. and lifelong friend of the O'Rahillys, with Bishop Cornelius Lucey presiding. As was reported in the *Cork Examiner* of 16, 17 and 18 September, messages of sympathy poured in from all parts of Ireland from public bodies and individuals, including the French and the U.S. ambassadors.[1]

On 15 September Eamon de Valera, Taoiseach and chancellor of the N.U.I., was the chief guest at a dinner in the N.U.I. club in London. During his address he formally conveyed his sympathy to 'Professor O'Rahilly who occupied such a high place in the world of scholarship and as a leader of thought.' Professor Denis Gwynn, Alfred's colleague, published an obituary in the *Cork Examiner* of 18 September. It dealt largely with the achievements of Alfred and his son, Ronan, and their association with U.C.C. and merely concluded that Mrs Agnes O'Rahilly 'had for years led a retiring life'.

Transfer to Blackrock College

Alfred's grief and depression after his wife's death was such that it caused concern to his close friends. He could not face staying in the president's residence in U.C.C. and for ten days resided in a house shared by Con Murphy and Fr Edward Murray, C.S.C., of Notre Dame, then a post-graduate student at U.C.C. Subsequently he stayed with his sister, Cecil, in Dublin.

---

1. W. H. Taft, the U.S. ambassador, enjoyed recalling his first 'brush' with Alfred. He was at a conferring in U.C.C. during which Alfred warned new graduates, who were bound for the U.S., against the dangers to their Christian faith. Taft was subsequently invited to address the assembly and began by stating that he was glad to be able to speak on behalf of the 'spiritual wasteland' already referred to. Alfred was most apologetic and sent the ambassador a collection of books published by the Cork University Press. However, it seems he had not checked the volumes and when Taft opened them he discovered that they were simply 'printer's dummies'.

2. The O'Rahilly family in the garden of their home at Listowel, 1890. *Left to right*: Thomas Francis (Frank), Richard (Dick), Teresa (Sister M. Walburga), Florence, May (Sister M. Antonia), Mrs Julia Mary O'Rahilly, Sheila (Birdie), **Alfred**, Mr Thomas Francis O'Rahilly, Gretta (Sister M. Anthony)

3. Third year philosophers, St Mary's Hall, Stonyhurst, summer 1911. *Left to right, back row:* Joseph Benoit, Richard Corish, Hubert Chadwick, John Joy, William Baker, Joseph Canavan, Edmund Miller, unidentified, Robert Hall, James Scoles, Bernard Swindells, Leo Hicks. *Middle row:* Daniel Fitzgibbon, Patrick Griffin, Lawrence Murphy, Fr John Rickaby (professor of ethics), Francis Nairne, Robert Colley, Austin Hartigan. *Front row:* John Myerscough, Joseph Riedinger, William Turner, Nicholas Ryan, Edward Dodd, **Alfred O'Rahilly**, Michael Meier

4. Joseph Downey (secretary and bursar, U.C.C.), Professor Arthur Pennington and Alfred (registrar and professor of mathematical physics, U.C.C.) at the National Institute of Dairy Research, Reading, August 1924

5. William Magennis (professor of metaphysics, U.C.D.), Séamus Caomhánach (assistant lecturer in Irish, U.C.C.), Joseph Reilly (professor of chemistry, U.C.C.) and Alfred at Konigshof Hotel, Bonn, August 1935

6. Alfred, Timothy O'Mahony and Fr Thomas F. Duggan in Hamburg, August 1939

7. Alfred addressing a session of the Summer School of the Catholic Social Guild at Stonyhurst, July 1947. *Left to right:* Alfred, Dr Frank Aylward, Bishop Henry Vincent Marshall (Salford) and Fr Bernard Swindells, S.J. (rector of Stonyhurst)

8. Alfred and Joseph P. Walshe (Irish ambassador extraordinary and plenipotentiary to the Holy See), Rome, June 1950 (Holy Year)

A Priest at Last

Dr Michael O'Carroll, C.S.Sp., whom he visited,[2] discovered that among his chief anxieties was where he would reside after retiring from U.C.C. He disclosed to Dr O'Carroll, as he also stated in a letter, dated 5 January 1954, to his sister, Sister M. Antonia, that he had made a vow twenty-five years earlier that, should Agnes predecease him, he would seek to be ordained. References to this vow are to be found in his diary on 1 and 15 August 1928. On being informed of Alfred's wish to be ordained,[3] Fr Vincent J. Dinan, C.S.Sp., president of Blackrock College, offered accommodation to him and promised to prepare a comfortable flat in the 'Castle' where he could reside before and, if he so wished, after his ordination. Alfred accepted the offer and took up residence in Blackrock College in November 1953.

Fr Dinan communicated Alfred's intention to Archbishop John C. McQuaid, who received the news with enthusiasm and invited Alfred to dine with him on 17 December when they discussed the matter. Subsequently Dinan prepared a memorandum for McQuaid concerning requirements in Alfred's case with regard to the various steps to ordination and membership of the Holy Ghost Order. Because of the further delays which would be entailed, it was decided that Alfred would be ordained for the archdiocese of Dublin rather than as a member of the Holy Ghost Order. On 4 January 1954, it seems, Alfred was given to understand that he would be exempted from reading a course in theology and would be ordained during the Marian Year, that is, on or before 8 December 1954. Ten days later, from U.C.C. where he had gone to attend some academic business, Alfred thanked McQuaid for accepting him, informed him that this had given him great peace and concluded: 'I ask for no privileges save to be your last curate completely subject to your wishes and commands.' At the same time, in forwarding documents relevant to his ordination, Alfred indicated to the archbishop

---

2. Dr O'Carroll, who was already a friend of Alfred's for a number of years, was asked by Mrs Cecil O'Shiel to see Alfred and try to help him regain his peace of mind.

3. At this time also Alfred sought advice from Thérèse Neumann about his future. This he did with the assistance of a long-standing pen-friend, Rev Mother Teresa, O.S.B., St Scholastica's Abbey in Devon, and the parish priest of Konnersreuth, Fr Naber. Eventually the following delphic reply came back on 23 November: 'The choice is his; religious life in a monastery could suit him.'

Alfred O'Rahilly III: Controversialist

that he intended to reside permanently in Dublin.[4] After these developments he regained much of his former energy. On 12 March he gave a public lecture on 'The lay vocation' and before the end of Lent he had lectured four times on the Shroud of Turin. He gave one of these lectures in aid of the St Vincent de Paul Society in the Mansion House which was filled to capacity for the occasion. During Easter week he addressed a conference of nuns on 'The nun teacher and the young girl of today'.

By the second week of April 1954 the picture had changed. In the meantime Fr Dinan had discovered that McQuaid was less enthusiastic about having Alfred ordained for Dublin. It seems that when the archbishop announced to his chapter that he intended to ordain Alfred for the archdiocese the canons advised against it. This reaction would have been occasioned by the fact that there was little likelihood that Alfred would serve

---

4. Among the documents forwarded by Alfred was his *curriculum vitae*. It began with his date of birth and concluded with a note on the date of his marriage and his wife's death, and the fact that his son and daughter had been provided for. There were paragraphs on his education, association with the Society of Jesus, his university career, the main features of his public life, his published work and work in progress. Besides there were two paragraphs which were obviously intended to impress and influence the archbishop. In the first under 'Catholic work in University College, Cork', he wrote: 'Founded the Cork University Press, which has published many Catholic books; started the course in Catholic apologetics, under the sanction of the bishop; founded the Medical Missionary Society; introduced the Legion of Mary; added sociology and medical ethics to the university courses; introduced a religious ceremony at conferring of degrees; founded the Adult Education Movement; established a large Catholic library in the college.' The second gave a strong hint of what he wished to do after ordination, as well as an indication of why he considered that he should be dispensed from reading a course in theology in preparation for ordination. Under 'Personal studies' he wrote: 'Well qualified in Latin, which I took as a subject for three years in the university and which I used for philosophy; I have learnt Greek (especially the *Koine*) and to a lesser extent Hebrew and Aramaic; I have been studying the New Testament daily for over fifty years; I was university lecturer in Catholic sociology for six years and I have read extensively in moral theology; I have read the whole of St Thomas, including many of his commentators; I have also read Aristotle; I have read and studied all of the fathers up to Chalcedon (451), mostly (except the Syriac) in the original; I have read many subsequent fathers and councils, also several treatises on dogmatic theology – Suarez, Conimbricenses, Wirceburgenses, Pesch, Pohle-Preuss, etc.' A month later Alfred wrote to Archbishop Gerald P. O'Hara, the papal nuncio, informing him of his hope to be ordained and that he was waiting for a dispensation to do only a very abbreviated course in preparation for it. To Alfred's gratification, O'Hara replied: 'You already know so much theology that you could be ordained tomorrow.'

A Priest at Last

in the archdiocese in a pastoral capacity. Also, no doubt the views of some of the canons would have been in tune with a subsequent unkind remark attributed to Monsignor Pádraig de Brún, namely, that Alfred had sought the priesthood merely as an extra feather in his cap![5] Alfred became aware that some serious obstacle had arisen. On 7 May he enquired from McQuaid if there 'was any word from Rome?' and added: 'I shall have no difficulty in seeking to be a lay-brother.' Nothing was further from the truth than this last comment.[6]

Alfred soon became annoyed with McQuaid, thinking that he was responsible for the delay and lack of information. Although they were on friendly terms, theirs was not an easy relationship. This was mainly due to their personalities. No matter what the circumstances Alfred tended to be as informal as McQuaid tended to be formal. At a meeting of the presidents of the colleges of the N.U.I. with a sub-committee of the Irish bishops in the early 1950s when McQuaid declared somewhat pretentiously 'The buck stops here,' Alfred, to McQuaid's obvious displeasure, chortled: 'I suppose you think you are the chief bucko.'

Obviously with McQuaid in mind, Alfred in a letter, dated 19 June 1954, told his sister, Sister M. Antonia: 'I saw Bishop [Joseph] Byrne [of Moshi, Tanzania]. He is wonderfully simple and kind – so different from our Irish bishops.'[7]

Alfred became so despondent at the seemingly indefinite postponement of his ordination that his friends in Blackrock

---

5. Frank Sheehy, principal of Scoileanna Réalta na Maidne, Listowel, made a similar remark when Alfred visited his old school in 1960. The occasion was the official opening of the modern primary school which replaced the original national school. In introducing Alfred to the school assembly, Sheehy concluded an account of his illustrious career: 'After spending sixty years enjoying the best things in life he gave the tail-end of it to God by being ordained a priest.' Alfred, it seems, was not impressed! This, however, did not prevent him from presenting a set of pictures of events from the New Testament to the school.
6. Alfred wrote the letter after he had completed a novena to St Thérèse of Lisieux seeking her intercession for a positive decision about his ordination.
7. In a letter, dated 21 February 1955, referring to McQuaid, Alfred complained to his sister: 'He is rather difficult in some ways, though very spiritual.' On 5 March he wrote: 'Until I came here I had no idea of how difficult and peculiar he was. Yet he is a holy man, and my own views coincide largely with his. I have always found holy people very difficult.' Alfred did not find his interviews with McQuaid congenial. On his way out from Blackrock College to one of them he remarked cheerily to Dr Michael O'Carroll: 'The condemned man ate a hearty breakfast.'

Alfred O'Rahilly III: Controversialist

College feared for his health. Fr Dinan pleaded with the archbishop to have him ordained. This prompted McQuaid to ask Dr Michael McGrath, archbishop of Cardiff, if he would accept Alfred into his diocese following ordination. McGrath, who had spent some years in the Holy Ghost Order and was a friend of McQuaid, agreed to do so. But he suggested that incardination into an Irish diocese would be more appropriate. McQuaid then asked his closest friend in the Irish hierarchy, Dr Jeremiah Kinane of Cashel, to accept Alfred. Kinane, conscious of Alfred's well-known record in Ireland for being controversial, stated that he would prefer the archbishop of Cardiff to take responsibility for him, as in Cardiff he was 'practically an unknown quantity'. But, he continued, if that was not feasible, he would do so, as McQuaid was so eager to enable Alfred to have the privilege of celebrating Mass.[8]

In the meantime Alfred was winding up his forty-years association with U.C.C. On 12 July 1954 he presided over his final conferring and on the following day held a valedictory garden party. On 19 September, his seventieth birthday, he retired from U.C.C. and, at Bishop Cornelius Lucey's request, was conferred with the pontifical order of the Knighthood of St Gregory the Great. There was considerable and generous press coverage of his retirement and Alfred's relatives and friends rejoiced at the papal honour conferred on him. The euphoria soon subsided and back in his flat in the 'Castle' at the end of the year he was again despondent about the prospect of his ordination.

Alfred's despondency continued into the first months of 1955. There was one happy interlude. He had been on a pilgrimage to the Holy Land during the previous August and on 19 and 20 January he stayed with the Jesuit community at Rathfarnham Castle and gave an illustrated lecture on his trip to a most appreciative audience, which included the provincial, Fr Michael O'Grady, S.J.

With a view to receiving information concerning his proposed ordination, Alfred, on 11 March, formally requested

---

8. In indicating his lack of enthusiasm to incardinate Alfred into the archdiocese of Cashel, Kinane declared that (1) No one who was not at least a resident of the archdiocese for a long time was ordained for it, (2) it was unlikely that Alfred would be able to provide a pastoral service as was required by canon law and (3) he suspected that the clergy would regard Alfred as 'eccentric, unpredictable and likely to cause trouble' and so would be opposed to his incardination.

A Priest at Last

Archbishop McQuaid to accept him into the archdiocese. This prompted an immediate invitation to dinner. But neither then nor in a letter from the archbishop, dated 28 July, was there any hint of when he was to be ordained. Alfred had to wait until the fourth week of September to learn officially the time and place of his ordination and confirmation of an earlier indication that he was to be ordained for the archdiocese of Nairobi. In acknowledging this information, he replied to the archbishop on 23 September, indicating that he would 'love to be ordained in Blackrock College chapel where as a boy I witnessed the ordination of Bishop Shanahan'. He professed to have an inclination for privacy in the matter but added that newspapers, friends and relatives would have to be accommodated. He added: 'Perhaps the "sensation" will do good; it will be a tribute to the priesthood.'

In the meantime in early March McQuaid had requested his close friend John J. McCarthy, C.S.Sp., archbishop of Nairobi, to accept responsibility for Alfred. McCarthy agreed to have him incardinated into his archdiocese 'provided he never sets foot in Nairobi'.[9] Thereafter McQuaid set about acquiring the dimissorial letters necessary for Alfred's ordination. These were declarations by the bishop of each diocese where Alfred resided and from others that there was no obstacle to his being ordained. In his submission, accounting for the years Alfred spent in the Society of Jesus, Fr Michael O'Grady, the Jesuit provincial, wrote a magnificent eulogy of Alfred and his achievements. The testimonial from Cardinal Cushing for the academic year 1926-27, when Alfred was at Harvard University, included a note from his eminence indicating his delight that Alfred was to be ordained.

During his time as registrar and president at U.C.C. Alfred had offended some of his colleagues. This was not forgotten.[10] In

---

9. McQuaid was not forgetful of McCarthy's co-operation. In December 1969 in memory of Alfred he sent him £50 to be spent on charitable work in Nairobi.

10. Professor Louis P. Renouf manifested extraordinary bitterness in attempting to block Alfred's ordination. For more on Renouf, see J. A. Gaughan, *Alfred O'Rahilly I: Academic* (Dublin 1986) 102. It was generally agreed that Renouf was hyper-sensitive. He would not have taken kindly to a public correction in his own subject by Alfred in the *Catholic Herald* of 26 November 1943. In a letter to the editor, Alfred stated that he had already privately protested to Renouf for referring to Mivart as a Darwinian. In spite of that, Alfred declared, Renouf

addition, there was his tendency to be confrontational and controversial. Thus, in forwarding a testimonial letter Bishop Cornelius Lucey included a note which must have given McQuaid a jolt. It read: 'I feel I ought to tell Your Grace of the view taken by a number of responsible persons here who have been in close contact with Dr O'Rahilly in U.C.C. It is that Dr O'Rahilly is likely to prove a most difficult subject for any superior to manage and that his ordination is not desirable. With that view I myself am in concurrence.' On 7 October McQuaid graciously replied to Fr O'Grady and added: 'Dr O'Rahilly will not be ordained for this diocese.' On the same day he acknowledged Bishop Lucey's testimonial letter and declared tartly with regard to Lucey's comments about Alfred: 'For myself I have found him completely docile.'

Ordination

In the last months of the year Alfred was busy preparing for ordination. He dutifully attended two two-hour oral examinations on the various theological subjects. In November Archbishop McQuaid in his private oratory in Archbishop's House conferred the preliminary orders on him. On 1 December Alfred wrote in his diary that, complete with Roman collar, he had had his photograph taken. He recalled that he had made his first communion exactly fifty-nine years earlier at Mount St Joseph's Abbey, Roscrea, and continued: 'I remember . . . the preparation provided by the saintly Fr Hilary O'Sullivan, O.C.S.O. How many careless communions I have made since that day. I must do my very best to celebrate Mass devoutly and in a spirit of faith.'[11] Eventually he was ordained on 18 December in the presence of a large and distinguished congregation which

---

had subsequently confused the issue by soft-pedalling the essential teaching of Darwin as logically proclaimed by Weismann and the neo-Darwinians. That the coincidence of the views of Darwin and of Mivart, insinuated by Renouf, was utterly unhistorical was shown, Alfred argued, by the efforts of Darwin to reply to Mivart and by Huxley's venomous attacks on him. Alfred went on to illustrate his point with copious quotations from the works of Mivart.

11. Alfred's father had a serious drink problem in his later years and on a number of occasions went to Mount St Joseph's, Roscrea, to recuperate. Alfred's brother, Michael Anthony, attended the college at Mount St Joseph's, later became a member of its Cistercian community and was a priest-teacher in the college for many years.

A Priest at Last

included his old friend Eamon de Valera.[12] After the ceremony he recorded the following message for transmission by Radio Éireann:

> Is mór an phribhléid agus an onóir domhsa go bhfuil mé i mo shagart ó indiu amach. Ba mhinic dom i rith mo shaoil ag labhairt go puiblí ach seo é an chéad uair riamh nach fuirist dom labhairt.
> Tá mé anois i mblianta deireanacha chiúine mo shaol ag glacadh páirt Mhuire – an chuid eile dem' shaol do chaitheamh ag cosa ár dTiarna.
> Táim ana bhaoch do na cáirde go léir a chuir a ndeaghghuí chugam; a dúirt paidreacha ar mo shon. Ní maith liom poibliocht ach, má thugann an gníomh seo caoi dom léiriú ar mo chreideamh Catoiliceach, beidh áthas mór orm.
> Tugaim díbh go léir mo bheannacht ó mo chroí amach.[13]

I have very often addressed Irish audiences on national, educational and social issues. This is the first occasion on which my personal life has been involved and I find it rather difficult. My rather chequered career, interpreted

---

12. At the reception which followed in the college diningroom Alfred in the course of his remarks joked that it had given him considerable satisfaction to have de Valera kneeling before him to receive his first blessing. Alfred enjoyed teasing de Valera in public. Some fourteen years earlier, when he had considered that de Valera had reneged on a commitment to make the Irish economy more independent of British fiscal policy, he wrote in his 'Pat Murphy's Jottings' in the *Standard* of 10 April 1942: 'I met Professor Alfred O'Rahilly the other day. He told me he was being confused with his brother – and I suppose *vice versa* – and that a lot of people had been congratulating him on his Trinity College lecture in which he proved there were two Saint Patricks. Apparently it was the kind of thing expected of him. "But," he asked with a twinkle in his eye, "could you imagine Mr de Valera attending a lecture by me? I am not in the habit of stopping at A.D. 460 and I might even suddenly try to prove that there are two Devs!"'

13. It is a great privilege and honour for me to be a priest from today onwards. I have often throughout my life spoken in public, but this is the first time ever that I find it difficult.
I am now in the last calm years of my life choosing Mary's part, spending the rest of my life at the feet of Our Lord.
I am most thankful to all my friends for their good wishes and prayers. I do not like publicity but, if this action of mine illustrates my Catholic faith, I shall be very pleased.
I send to all of you my heart-felt blessing.

Alfred O'Rahilly III: Controversialist

favourably, might be regarded as Martha-like preoccupation with 'much serving'. Now, that I am in the more restful eventide of life, I have chosen Mary's part: to sit at the feet of Our Lord.

Through the gracious welcome of the archbishop of Dublin, I have been admitted not only to Bethany but to the cenacle, to receive from Christ a Eucharist and sacerdotal commission.

I am privileged to celebrate Mass in the chapel where as a schoolboy – more than fifty years ago – I first learned to serve Mass.

From my fellow-Catholics I have received an unexpected bounty of prayers and good wishes. I might almost say that Ireland is re-echoing heaven where, as we know, there is more joy over the rescue of one sinful individual than over the ninety-nine persevering holy ones. Indeed I feel embarrassed by all the publicity in which I have been involved. But I shall be happy if my action is taken as a public profession of faith, a humble tribute to the Catholic priesthood, a confession of Christ before men in union with our devoted and martyred missionaries.

God bless you all.[14]

Alfred received numerous gifts on the occasion of his ordination. The one he cherished most was a chalice with the inscription: 'Rev. Dom. Alfredo O'Rahilly. Dec. 1955 ad sacr. Presbyteratum evecto. Prov. Hib. Soc. Jesu [To Rev. Fr Alfred O'Rahilly. Raised to the priesthood in December 1955. From the Irish province of the Society of Jesus].' He fully realised the part played by Fr Dinan, C.S.Sp., in persuading Dr McQuaid to have him ordained and in a typical gesture presented to the

---

14. Congratulations poured in from all over the country and beyond. A number, which came from the Boston area, were prompted by a broadcast by Cardinal Cushing. Many recalled kindnesses done by Alfred in the past. Bishop Leo Parker, of Northhampton, wrote: 'You may wonder why I write to you. I am still a grateful person for the aid you gave me in 1916 and my brother, Fr Anselm Parker, when you so kindly and generously wrote an Appendix to the cosmology of M. Nys. We had just published our translation of the Louvain philosophy: the war was on: some criticisms were made adversely and M. Nys was locked in Belgium. You came to our rescue until in another edition the author of the original French could reply to critics and emend what he had written.'

A Priest at Last

college chapel a set of stations of the cross by the Sligo artist Bernard McDonagh.[15]

The main reservation bishops had concerning the ordination of Alfred was his tendency to become embroiled in controversy. Alfred was aware of this and during the last phase of his life he was far less controversial than he had been hitherto. Joining the priesthood, however, did not entirely quench his combative ardour.

I.R.A. campaign of 1956-7

The first controversy in which Alfred became enbroiled after his ordination concerned the I.R.A. campaign in Northern Ireland at the end of 1956 and the beginning of 1957. This was the most crucial problem facing the governments of both parts of Ireland. On 1 January 1957, I.R.A. activists, Fergal O'Hanlon and Seán South, were fatally wounded in a raid on the R.U.C. barracks at Brookeborough, County Fermanagh. Despite inclement weather, 50,000 people attended the funeral of Seán South in his native city of Limerick and a wave of pro-I.R.A. sympathy swept over the Republic of Ireland.

At the editor's request Alfred published 'The Problem of North and South' in *Hibernia* of January 1957. He began by acknowledging that his remarks on partition would be unpopular. The term, he pointed out, expressed an assumption made by Irish nationalists, among whom he numbered himself. It implied that the whole population of Ireland formed a natural political unit, from which the North-Eastern section had been unjustifiably separated. A further corollary was that the government of the Republic of Ireland was the morally valid government for the whole of Ireland, the Northern Ireland government being merely in possession of six counties.

Alfred suggested that it was difficult to decide whether this assessment was valid or not. But, even if its validity were accepted, certain practical limitations had to be admitted. A *de*

---

15. McDonagh recalled an amusing incident concerning the stations of the cross. Alfred travelled to Sligo at the end of August 1955 to see the work in progress. He and McDonagh named the titles of the seven yet unpainted titles and discovered that they would have fifteen stations. It took them over a quarter of an hour to discover that for the first station McDonagh had painted two, namely, (1) Jesus is condemned to death and (2) Pilate washes his hands.

facto government had rights as long as it was not an alien oppressive usurpation. It was, at the very least, an alternative to anarchy and so its laws had an interim validity. Any attempt to oust it must not involve greater evils than reluctant submission.

He suggested that within the ambit of the nationalist theory certain initiatives could be taken. Provision could be made for representatives from Northern Ireland to sit in Dáil Éireann. He recalled that he had included this in his draft constitution in 1922. They could financially intervene in cases where the Catholic minority in the North was treated less fairly than the Protestant minority in the South. Thus they could allow the Mater Hospital, Belfast, to benefit from the Irish Hospitals' Sweep Fund.

He stressed that, even in the context of the nationalist viewpoint, it was the majority of the people, acting through their *de jure* government, which alone could decide on practical measures concerning partition. This could not be done by any recalcitrant minority inside the six counties and certainly not, he emphasised, by any self-appointed minority inside the twenty-six counties. The use of physical force might conceivably be justified, if decided upon by the Irish government and parliament. However, there was no evidence that this issue had been submitted to the people or that, if submitted, it would receive anything other than 'an utterly negligible minority-approval'. The claim by a small underground clique to the sovereign function of waging war was morally indefensible and politically intolerable.

Alfred urged people to realise the seriousness of the moral, religious and political issues raised by the recent hit-and-run raids. People were being killed and an attempt was being made to supersede the democratically elected government and to usurp the functions of the only lawful army. He dismissed any attempt to draw a parallel with the actions of the I.R.A. during the war of independence. They had behind them a *de jure* parliament and courts and an actually (though precariously) functioning and accepted government. The modern I.R.A. had repudiated the lawful successor of that government.

Alfred next dwelt on the futility of the hit-and-run raids. In Northern Ireland there was close on a million people, culturally and religiously homogeneous, comprising all classes from successful businessmen to dock labourers, intent on a way of life

A Priest at Last

differing in many ways from that of people in the Republic. They were attracted to their welfare state, economically linked to Great Britain and violently prejudiced against Catholics. The idea that the British or the people of the Republic could coerce that minority into a united Ireland was nonsense. The border incursions would only worsen the conditions of Catholics in 'the North' and merely clamp the border tighter by provoking unionist counter-extremists.

The way forward, Alfred urged, was to reject coercion. This involved taking effective measures against the raiders. In addition, they should adopt an attitude of friendly co-operation with Northern Ireland. A reversal of policy was required. By leaving the Commonwealth – which included the Republic of India – they had cut themselves off from friendly allies. By failing to offer a base to Americans – for a war in which they could not be neutral – they had increased their isolation. The casual references to partition at the United Nations were a waste of time.

There was no substitute for direct dealing with fellow-Irishmen in 'the North', who had to be convinced that religious liberty, pluralistic culture and social justice would not be endangered in an Ireland united on a federal basis. To achieve that unity would require a very long process and even then ultimate success was doubtful. The process had been jeopardised by nationalists demanding what was not foreseeably feasible. He urged them to adjust to present realities and to chart a new course practising co-operation for common interests, giving an example of toleration and liberty, renouncing physical force and abandoning irritating propaganda.

Alfred returned to 'The problems of partition' in the following issue of *Hibernia*. He was prompted to do so by correspondents, some of whom sent him press cuttings of the reaction to his article. 'Several important Irish newspapers', he complained, 'funked the issue altogether, while others indulged in the usual claptrap'.

As is clear from a postscript, he was particularly irritated by the stand taken by the *Kerryman* of 12 January 1957. He did not name the *Kerryman* but referred to it as 'an influential provincial paper which professes to be the spokesman of the "virile, uncompromising section of our people".' He quoted from its editorial: 'The people might very well say to their deputies in

Alfred O'Rahilly III: Controversialist

Leinster House: "You condemn and jail those who are trying their way of ending partition; let us hear how you propose to end it . . ." If the border is to go it will go when the youth on both sides of it take its removal into their own strong hands'. He pointed out that this 'anarchic irresponsibility, which is so widespread', contained two assumptions. The first was that 'youth' not only with their strong hands but with tommy guns and bombs were morally justified in waging war on behalf of 'the people'. No cognisance was taken of the fact that most people, including the Catholic bishops, considered such activity to be grievously sinful. The second assumption was that the hit-and-run raids would frighten the Ulster Protestants into surrender. This he described as a unique 'specimen of journalistic credulity' and he objected to the irresponsibility of advocating that when individuals are dissatisfied with government and parliament they should take up arms and operate on their own account.

In the body of the article Alfred dealt with points in letters appearing in the national press, as well as those raised by his correspondents. The most recurring attitude was: 'Britain maintains partition by force against the will of the majority of the Irish people'. He pointed out that this assumed that the inhabitants of the island formed a single political entity within which the votes of all would be added together to secure a decision on the issue of partition. This was rejected by the majority in Northern Ireland. In addition, it was obvious that the activities of the security forces were not directed against the majority in the six counties, but were carried out with their connivance and co-operation. If the British forces withdrew they would be replaced by 'Northern units' and there was no indication that the I.R.A. raiders would have more success against them than they had heretofore. Alfred acknowledged that British policy in the past was mainly responsible for the present impasse. However, what had to be addressed was not past history but present reality. Northern Ireland gained considerably from the British connection. Most of this was achieved not by governmental subsidy but by business and economic relationships. He noted that the prolonged attempts to make an international issue of partition had ended in failure. It was time to get down to the underlying reality, namely the cleavage between sections of the inhabitants of the island, which was not being imposed by any external power.

A Priest at Last

Another issue which surfaced, especially in letters to the *Irish Times,* was resentment at the intervention of the Catholic bishops. Their unanimous condemnation of the hit-and-run raids on Northern Ireland, Alfred pointed out, merely confirmed what was clear on grounds of natural law. He regretted that, because of confusion on the issue, it was necessary for them, as in the mother-and-child dispute, to intervene at all. Some who were not Catholics had expressed resentment at the issue being made Catholic and even clerical. As in the case of the mother-and-child dispute, the bishops were defending natural rights and reminding their flocks of the natural law which was binding on everyone. Some Catholics, Alfred complained, seemed to regard actions as wrong because they were condemned by the bishops, whereas the case was the reverse. One would have expected, he continued, that the solemn pronouncements of the civil and ecclesiastical authorities would have cleared up all doubt in the matter. However, young practising Catholics had rejected the bishops' statement on the plea that they were interfering in politics. This was but a variation of the claim that Maynooth should be silent when Leinster House speaks. It was tantamount to excluding large areas of human activity from ethical evaluation. Politics was to be outside judgements of right and wrong, and the use of physical force under the slogan of 'nationalism' required no justification. He reminded his readers that the attempt to oust morality from large domains of human activity and to regard religion as merely a matter of private devotion was characteristic of Communism and Nazism.

Next Alfred dealt with the effects of the hit-and-run raids. Apart from the death and destruction north of the border, there was large-scale sympathy indistinguishable from postive approval for I.R.A. activity which was seen as romantic heroism when it was no more than sheer anarchy. Pressure was being exerted by unknown organisations and there were contending armed gangs who, like the Sicilian mafia, recognised no authority beyond themselves. Youthful idealism was diverted into killing and destruction and away from much-needed constructive activity.

Alfred next dealt with the moral position of the northern government. Even accepting the nationalist theory, it was in factual possession of the means of social order. He added that it had even 'a higher moral claim for compliance for anyone' like himself who held that the only justifiable way of unifying Ireland was by virtue of a federal constitution. Most of the powers exercised by that government – such powers as were possessed by a Swiss canton – would continue to be exercised by it in a united Ireland. He argued that once force was rejected as a means of solving partition there would be an increase in understanding and friendliness and an easing of corruption, discrimination and gerrymandering. As to the correct attitude to be adopted to the North, he declared that the right of Belfast and its hinterland to remain outside the Irish jurisdiction should be recognised. However, having conceded that, it should be pointed out that, even on their own principles, unionists had unjustifiably enlarged their own area. What justification had they for drawing a boundary to include areas with nationalist majorities, such as Derry city, Counties Fermanagh and Tyrone and South Armagh and South Down. Clearly Northern Ireland was an artificial entity. It was difficult to see how Northern Ireland could call itself 'Ulster' when it had abandoned three intractable counties of the province. It should be put to the unionists of Northern Ireland that they should join a federal united Ireland or give up their jurisdiction over areas in which there were clear nationalist majorities. This, Alfred concluded, was the proper attitude to the problem of partition.

In the March issue of *Hibernia* Ciarán Mac an Fhailí, a Dublin solicitor and a member of Pax Christi, replied to Alfred. Unlike Alfred who had no experience of Northern Ireland, which it seems he had never visited, Mac an Fhailí, a native of County Donegal, was educated at St Columb's, Derry City, was apprenticed for five years to a law firm in the city and had numerous relations in Counties Antrim and Derry. He charged that Alfred was not able to make up his mind whether or not the Dublin government was the lawful government of the six counties also. This was crucial, as one's conviction on that would determine the morality of the current guerilla campaign in which the I.R.A. was engaged. If, on the one hand, the Dublin government was the *de jure* government of 'the North', it followed that (1) the lawful government of the country was being prevented from exercising its function by force of British arms and the unlawful armed revolt of a pro-British minority armed by Britain; (2) all Irish people were bound to overthrow British rule in Ireland

A Priest at Last

and it was the Dublin government's duty to lead that struggle; (3) In the event of the Dublin government losing its authority, by not leading such a struggle, a right to revolt was exercisable by all Irish people subject to British rule in 'the North' and a right to assist in that revolt was vested in all Irish people. If, on the other hand, the Dublin government was not the lawful government of 'the North', then: (1) it had no jurisdiction in 'the North' and so no usurpation of such powers as possible by guerillas in that area; (2) no lawful government existed in 'the North'; there was *de facto* rule by an alien usurper only; (3) subject to certain conditions the nationalists in 'the North' had a right to revolt in arms against the usurpers; (4) subject to similar conditions, citizens of the Republic had a right to join in such a revolt, if they believed that only by such action international justice could be established in Ireland and provided they acted in good faith.

Mac an Fhailí asserted that, if the Irish people constituted two nations, the border was the natural and lawful boundary between them. Whereas, if Irish people were one nation, the border was indefensible. He accused Alfred of suspending his judgement on this issue, as he did not wish to accept the Republican position. He had little difficulty in pointing to anomalies arising from Alfred's suggestion that Northern Ireland nationalist M.Ps be allowed to sit in 'Leinster House'. This would result in their voting on matters affecting people who did not elect them and being incapable of voting on matters affecting those who did elect them. He rejected Alfred's charge that I.R.A. activists endangered the lives of civilians. On Alfred's complaint that a base had not been given to the Americans 'for a war in which we cannot possibly be neutral', Mac an Fhailí commented that this probably referred to a future war with the Soviet Union in which modern weapons would be used. He expressed his amazement that a Catholic moralist should be in favour of such a war. The consensus of Catholic theological opinion, he claimed, was that the uncontrollable and indiscriminate nature of modern weapons, such as the hydrogen bomb, made modern atomic warfare morally unacceptable.[16]

16. As a member of Pax Christi Mac an Fhailí campaigned for nuclear disarmament. He published 'From arrows to atoms: a Catholic voice on the morality of war' in *Doctrine and Life* of June 1959. This was re-issued as a 'Peace News' pamphlet in 1974.

Alfred O'Rahilly III: Controversialist

Mac an Fhailí objected to the implication by Alfred of a lack of courage on the part of the I.R.A. activists when he described them as 'a handful of invaders' who shoot and then run back across the border to hide 'under the skirts of our government'. He rejected Alfred's contention that the British government did not keep in existence the partition of Ireland. The real cause of the moral dilemma was that there was not an Irish State co-extensive with the Irish nation. By virtue of the 'Supplemental Agreement with Great Britain of 3 December 1925' the Irish Free State bound itself to recognise the border. The 1937 Constitution had provided for this – in article 3 – and as long as that obtained the Dublin government was bound to co-operate with the British and Northern Ireland governments in keeping partition permanent.

In the same issue of *Hibernia* Alfred was given an opportunity to reply to Mac an Fhailí. The courage of the I.R.A. activists, he stated, was irrelevant. The sole issue was whether their actions were morally right or wrong. He clarified the difference between a nation and a State; the first was all those who for reasons of origin, tradition, language, character and culture agree in forming one social community; the second comprised all, who, within a determinate territory, were united under the same political authority. The issue was not whether the inhabitants of the island formed one nation but how – by force or by persuasion – they might be induced to form one State. The difficulty to be addressed was that the territorial theory of natural geographical frontiers was rejected by nearly a million of the inhabitants of the island.

Alfred rejected Mac an Fhailí's claim that the government was prevented from functioning in the north of Ireland 'by force of British arms and the unlawful, armed revolt of a pro-British minority'. He acknowledged that Great Britain was responsible for the origins of Northern Ireland. But he pointed to the Ireland Act of 1949 in which Britain pledged itself not to alter the status of the Northern Ireland parliament without its consent and by implication to acquiesce to such an alteration, were it requested. The nub of the question was the attitude of the Ulster unionists who would replace the British forces, were they withdrawn. They would not be intimidated by the blowing up of a few bridges and even if forced into a united Ireland could not be kept there except by the kind

A Priest at Last

of brutal methods currently used by the Soviet Union in Hungary.

Alfred had little difficulty in pointing to the weakness of Mac an Fhailí's argument that, as 'no lawful governmental authority exists in the North' nationalists there 'have a right to revolt in arms against the usurpers' and could be joined by 'citizens in the South'. This did not fit in easily with Mac an Fhailí's previous claim that all the inhabitants of the island constituted one political entity *de jure*. From that it followed that any decision to use physical force could be made only by a majority of the people throughout Ireland. He dismissed Mac an Fhailí's claim that Catholic moral teaching permitted people to participate in revolts, provided they acted in good faith. He rejected the idea that a *de facto* government had no rights and referred Mac an Fhailí to previous comments he had made on the possible 'cantonal' usefulness of such a government in the context of a united Ireland. He set out the background to the finalising of the border between North and South, which was confirmed in 1925 by the three parliaments concerned. This did not mean that they had to acknoweldge the perpetual moral validity of the border. Granted, the unionists had a strong case in the segregation of Belfast and its hinterland. However, they lost their title to Ulster by rejecting three intractable counties and they had spoiled their case by including nationalist areas and then resorting to gerrymandering in order to retain control of their 'unnaturally included territory'. The border settlement could be undone by war or by friendly persuasion, the latter being the only real option. They should extend the co-operation embodied in the Erne hydroelectric project and in the agreement about the Great Northern Railway. Showing a lack of appreciation of the unionist character, he stated that the Republic of Ireland could also seek to remedy the political disabilities of the nationalist minority and intervene in cases of religious discrimination. Above all, they would have to make the Republic of Ireland attractive to unionists.

Alfred ridiculed Mac an Fhailí's claim that the Irish government had a duty to conduct and lead the armed struggle. He reminded him that in civilised countries there was a recognised method of democratic decision. Members of the I.R.A. were part of the people. Let them submit to the electoral judgement of the people. It was intolerable that they take the law into their

Alfred O'Rahilly III: Controversialist

own hands and refuse to acknowledge any votes against them, however numerous. Mac an Fhailí's claim that by failing to join in the war declared by the I.R.A. the Irish parliament and government had lost their authority was a recipe for anarchy. It substituted the gun for the vote and was a prelude to the police State. Alfred summed up the mentality behind the I.R.A. raids as: 'Despising all democratic procedures, a few gangs of gunmen declare "governmental authority" lost by failure to arm and to abet them'.

An Tóstal

The next controversy in which Alfred became embroiled concerned Archbishop McQuaid and An Tóstal. The council of An Tóstal organised a theatre festival each year from 1953 onwards. The programme in 1957 included a presentation of Tennessee Williams's *Rose Tattoo*. Owing to protests from some members of the public, reminiscent of those made against the Abbey Theatre a generation earlier, the play was taken off. Probably to ensure that there would not be a similar occurrence, the council of An Tóstal requested Archbishop McQuaid to inaugurate the festival the following year with a public religious ceremony. However, he declined to do so. When questioned subsequently on the reason for his refusal, he declared that he considered it inappropriate to open with a votive Mass a festival which was to include *Bloomsday,* an adaptation from James Joyce's *Ulysses,* and Seán O'Casey's *The drums of Father Ned*. The organisers eventually withdrew those plays. This occasioned a sharp attack by the editor of the *Irish Times* on 15 February 1958 on the archbishop for his intervention. There followed in the paper's correspondence columns further severe criticism of the archbishop.[17]

In the *Standard* of 28 February 1958 Alfred began with a savage attack on the *Irish Times*. He then argued that the editor, realising that he could not very well reprimand the archbishop for not celebrating a votive Mass, had resorted to misrepresentation when he wrote: 'Next year's Tóstal council will be well advised to submit its programme to the archbishop of Dublin in advance of publication if it is to avoid a similar wastage of

17. For a more detailed account of this fracas, see G. Fallon, 'The Tóstal Affair', *Hibernia,* March 1958.

A Priest at Last

money and effort'. Thereby, Alfred suggested, the editor had implied that the archbishop had attempted to interfere with the programme to be presented by An Tóstal in some way other than by refusing to inaugurate the festival with a votive Mass. Alfred continued that the concern of the *Irish Times* at the 'thousands of pounds' which had been wasted as a result of the financial failure of An Tóstal was not an issue to worry the archbishop unduly when moral and religious issues were at stake. He questioned the claim that An Tóstal would attract visitors to the country earlier than usual. In any case he pointed out the *Irish Times* 'with typical contradictoriness' professed to be really interested only in a handful of 'distinguished critics'. To get those over to Dublin 'the end justifies the means'. No care needed to be taken that 'the dramas presented do not offend and misrepresent the moral and religious susceptibilities of our own people'.

He concluded by regretting that he had written 'so strongly' against the *Irish Times,* but pleaded that he was only voicing the widespread resentment of his co-religionists at the attitude adopted to the archbishop in the columns of the paper.

In the *Standard* of 14 March 1958 Alfred dealt with a report on the same subject which was published in the *Manchester Guardian* of 24 February. He quoted it at some length and it was far more acerbic than the treatment of the topic in the *Irish Times.* Alfred responded that the article 'betrayed the voice of the Old Lady of Westmoreland Street'. And he showed that it was 'an *Irish Times* product'.

Limerick University Project

In the first quarter of 1960 Alfred became embroiled in a controversy surrounding the campaign for a university for Limerick. The city had lost out when higher education was initiated in Ireland in 1845. When pressure was being brought to bear on the British government in the winter of 1838 by committees in Cork and in Limerick to establish a 'Munster College', controversy arose as to the location of the proposed institution. This was eventually settled in favour of Cork. Later in the Colleges Bill, which was passed through the House of Commons in May-July 1845, three colleges were proposed; one for the south, probably at Cork; one for the west, probably at Galway or Limerick; and one for the north, probably at Belfast. As a result of this bill, which became law on 31 July 1845 as the Colleges (Ireland) Act, colleges were established at Belfast, Cork and Galway.[18]

It was not until about a hundred years later that Limerick people began a determined campaign for a university college. The first stirrings of the campaign can be traced to 1935 when public bodies in the city and local branches of trade unions passed resolutions demanding a university college for Limerick. Nothing practical was undertaken, however, until March 1945 when the matter was taken up by the Limerick Chamber of Commerce. They commissioned a report, copies of which they sent to the minister for education and the senate of the National University of Ireland. After receiving a non-committal reply from the minister, the Chamber of Commerce and others requested the mayor, Alderman James M. (Mossy) Reidy, T.D., to convene a public meeting to rally Limerick citizens behind the campaign.

At the meeting, on 21 May 1945, a representative committee, later known as the Limerick University Project Committee, was set up to lead the campaign for a constituent college of the N.U.I. One of its first initiatives was to write to Alfred at the beginning of July. He replied offering to go to Limerick to meet the committee. Probably, because the rest of the letter was not sympathetic to their aim, the committee did not reply to it. Subsequently, on 1 November 1945, the Chamber of Commerce received a reply from the senate of the N.U.I. after its autumn meeting, stating that it was opposed to any measures which would require a change in the charter of the University or the constituent colleges. It also informed the Chamber of Commerce that it had appointed Alfred, then vice-chancellor of the N.U.I., to give information and advice to the Limerick University Project Committee on the matter. Again, probably mindful that Alfred was not in favour of their project, neither the Chamber of Commerce nor the University Project Committee availed of the offer of Alfred's advice and assistance.

The committee then on a number of occasions sought unsuccessfully to have the Taoiseach, Eamon de Valera, who was also chancellor of the N.U.I., receive a deputation to discuss the

18. For an account of the first campaign for a university at Limerick, see Pat Kearney, 'Limerick's campaign for a university: 1838-1845', *Old Limerick Journal*, No. 26, winter 1989, 26-35.

need for a university in Limerick. In a final letter to the committee, dated 7 May 1946, de Valera recommended that they should approach the governing body of U.C.C. After reporting to a public meeting the committee followed de Valera's advice and on 16 July 1946 wrote to Alfred requesting a meeting with the governing body of U.C.C.

Alfred replied on the following day. At the outset he tartly reminded the committee that they had not even acknowledged his letter of July 1945 and that the Limerick Chamber of Commerce had failed to reply to the N.U.I. senate's proposal that he would assist in the matter. He noted that they had already sent details of their proposal to the minister for education and the Taoiseach. Such information, he stated, the governing body would also require before meeting their deputation. He regretted that he had not had an opportunity to discuss the details of their proposal beforehand, as he had in dealing with a similar matter in Waterford. In the meantime he promised that at the next meeting of the governing body in the autumn he would have a sub-committee appointed to meet a deputation from the Limerick University Project Committee. He concluded by pointing out that the governing body would be opposed to any change in the charter of the N.U.I. and would also be concerned about problems which would arise for U.C.C. and the other colleges from the establishment of a new recognised college or an independent university.

On 27 September after considering the correspondence with de Valera and with Alfred the committee decided to abandon their demand for a constituent college of the N.U.I. and concentrate on trying to obtain a school of technology. This they conveyed to Alfred who replied on 4 October that he regretted that they had given up their aim of acquiring a university institution for Limerick. He protested that he was sympathetic to their efforts in that direction and was prepared to go to Limerick and advise them on what was feasible. He agreed that, at the outset, they should seek a school of technology. This letter was discussed at a public meeting on 11 October 1946, chaired by the mayor, Councillor J. C. Hickey. Those attending the meeting, however, rejected Alfred's advice and urged the committee to continue its efforts to obtain a constituent college of the N.U.I. The committee then decided to invite Alfred to Limerick to discuss the Limerick University Project and to address a public meeting.

Alfred O'Rahilly III: Controversialist

It was disclosed in the press on 11 November 1946 that Mayor Hickey had had a meeting in U.C.C. with Alfred concerning the proposal to set up a constituent college of the N.U.I. in Limerick. Hickey reported that, although Alfred expressed his appreciation of the desire of the citizens of Limerick to acquire a university for their city, he had made it clear that he could not support this project in view of the fact that it would require the charter of the N.U.I. to be recast. The mayor further reported that Alfred had sugested that arrangements could be made for conducting certain faculties in Limerick, such as chemistry, engineering and science, for the first two years, the final lectures to be taken in U.C.C. The reaction of the committee to the mayor's report was to urge that the N.U.I. charter be amended so as to give the children of Limerick an opportunity to secure a degree in the faculty of their choice in their own city. The committee renewed an invitation to Alfred to a conference in Limerick with a view to persuading him to support their proposal.

Eventually Alfred agreed to visit Limerick on 11 December to discuss the matter. On 1 December the committee issued statements to the press indicating that the only serious obstacle to the setting up of a constituent college of the N.U.I. was securing an amendment to the N.U.I. charter and implying that, as a result of the proposed meeting with Alfred, this difficulty could be resolved. Alfred was no neophyte when it came to making his views known to the public. On 4 December he lectured on 'Religion in the university' to the Magnificat Society of U.C.D. and availed of the opportunity to detail his objections to any alteration of the N.U.I. charter. He declared that he was opposed to any alteration of the charter because there was a great change of attitude on the part of the State towards the control of education. If they were to throw the 1908 Act, which established the National University of Ireland, into the melting pot and encourage new acts, they would not be left with anything like the measure of university autonomy they then enjoyed. He acknowledged that there were some defects in the charter of the University but warned it was too dangerous to alter it because 'the State will butt in if we do'.[19]

---

19. Apart from issuing statements to the press, the Limerick University Project Committee put pressure on Alfred in other ways also. The committee urged rural district councils and urban district councils in the catchment area of the proposed university to pass resolutions requesting him to support the proposal

A Priest at Last

Alfred attended a private meeting of the Limerick University Project Committee on 11 December 1946. A statement issued to the press indicated that he had expressed his opposition to the proposal that a constituent college of the N.U.I. be established in the city, because that would have necessitated changing the university charter. He also reminded the committee that their proposal would be strongly opposed by the authorities of U.C.C., U.C.D., U.C.G. and the senate of the N.U.I. The statement disclosed that, in view of this, the committee had decided that it would be impractical to proceed with their demand for a constituent college of the N.U.I. or a separate university. The statement continued that Alfred indicated that, if the finance, equipment and staff could be procured, it would be possible to recognise a school in Limerick for first and second year courses in arts, commerce, engineering and science, as well as courses for diplomas in education, social science and public administration. In such circumstances he promised to return, whenever needed, to advise and help with such a project. The committee, however, did not pursue this option and thus that phase of the campaign for a university petered out.

Alfred returned to the subject when he conferred diplomas in social and economic science from U.C.C. on twenty-six students at the Technical Institute in the city on 22 November 1950. In the early part of his address, as the *Cork Examiner* of 23 November reported, he declared that he was in favour of encouraging good secondary schools to keep their students for an extra year, which would exempt them from the first university year. This would save local parents a good deal of expense and would have a very beneficial effect on the secondary schools and the arrangement could be used to give the students a good training in Catholic philosophy as well as in ordinary subjects. An editorial in the *Irish Times* of 24 November concen-

---

for the establishment of a university at Limerick. In acknowledging one such resolution from Listowel Urban District Council, Alfred replied that it was the first official communication he had received from his native Listowel since he had left it almost a life-span before. He added that he had never objected to the university proposal, but what his college and the other colleges of the N.U.I. objected to was any attempt to interfere or modify their charter. Probably because he was irritated by the pressure being brought to bear on him, he concluded: 'Incidentally, I was expecting that Kerry also would put forward a claim for an institution. In fact, a better case could be made for Kerry than for Limerick'.

trated on his continuing opposition to the establishment of a university in Limerick. It endorsed his arguments against such a project: the cost and the difficulty to find competent staff for proposed new institutions in Limerick and possibly also in Waterford. The editorial added a further objection. It argued that there was too much rather than too little university education in the country and deplored the fact that so many able young men and women graduated with professional qualifications merely to emigrate.

In 1959 public discussion of the expenditure required for the proposed transfer of U.C.D. from Earlsfort Terrace in central Dublin to Belfield on the outskirts prompted a renewal of the demand for a university in Limerick. In August of that year a number of letters on the subject appeared in the *Limerick Leader*. Then on 23 September a new impetus was given to the demand when a new Limerick University Project Committee was set up. This committee consisted of representatives of the past pupils unions of the local colleges and secondary schools and met each week at the Christian Brothers School, Sexton Street, Limerick. With Mrs Margaret Liddy as its dynamic secretary and the full support of the *Limerick Leader,* the committee was most successful in drawing public attention to its claim. For the most part, however, the publicity it engendered was ignored by public representatives associated with the government and by the academic community. Doubtless because of his former involvement, Alfred addressed the claim of the Limerick University Project Committee in *Hibernia* of 29 January 1960. Writing under 'Need for clarification and more information: University College, Limerick – the problems', he acknowledged that for those who believed in decentralisation the committee's claim was admissible in principle. However, he went on to highlight the difficulties and problems facing those making the claim.

He stressed the need for a further clarification of, and more information on, Limerick's demand. The renewed agitation, he stated, could be taken as a demand for a new independent university of Limerick and he set out the difficulties to be faced by those making this demand. Next he stated that the Limerick University Project Committee could be seen as demanding a college which would have in its relationship with the N.U.I., the same status as Maynooth. Such a recognised college would face the difficulties he had already highlighted and he insisted it would

A Priest at Last

involve even further 'snags'. Limerick's demand could be interpreted as one for a new constituent college of the N.U.I. This proposal, he urged, was open to all the administrative difficulties he had outlined. In addition, there was 'the far greater objection' that it would mean 'the disruption of our character'. This would lead to the N.U.I. coming under the direct control of the government and thereby the forfeiture of its autonomy. Moreover, he pointed out that the settlement achieved under the Irish Universities Act of 1908 was not merely political. It had, and continued to have, an important religious significance and so its stability was of interest to the Catholic hierarchy, laity and religious, as well as to the colleges.

Finally Alfred suggested that the Limerick committee should aim at establishing something less than a university. He recalled his meetings thirteen years earlier with the previous committee. He also disclosed that he had held discussions at that time with the Catholic bishop of Limerick, Dr Patrick O'Neill. They had then concluded that there was an immediate and simple alternative more immediately feasible. This involved the pupils of the Limerick Teachers' Training College obtaining remission of the first year at university. This could subsequently be extended to some of the excellent secondary schools in the Limerick area, where an extra post-secondary year in school would be beneficial to teachers and students. These students could then complete their degree courses at U.C.C.

Alfred repeated a suggestion which he had made to the Limerick committee thirteen years earlier. This was the establishment of a new university, with sufficient guarantees and economy, which would examine, and confer degrees upon, students from 'associated' colleges and technical institutes. 'Association' would be granted only to institutions which would satisfy certain requirements. To help these institutions the State would have to abandon its niggardly policy as regards secondary education. He recalled that the old Royal University of Ireland and London University granted such external degrees.

P. M. McCarthy, on behalf of the Limerick University Project Committee, replied to Alfred in *Hibernia* of 12 February 1960. He stated that the Committee did not wish to scrap the N.U.I. charter. It merely asked for an additional charter to be granted by an act of the Oireachtas to establish University College, Limerick, and he declared that they in Limerick would not be satisfied with 'Association' or the truncated facilities as suggested by Alfred. Stung by Alfred's implication that the committee had not done sufficient research to back their proposal, he pointed to 11,000 secondary-school pupils in the catchment area of the proposed university. Alfred replied in the following issue of *Hibernia*. He asserted that in 1946 he had requested his colleague, Professor Michael D. McCarthy, to investigate the domiciliary origin of the students in the three constituent colleges of the N.U.I. for the session 1944-45. He quoted the conclusion to McCarthy's report:

> Students from different areas do not necessarily tend to go to the nearest college. For instance, over three-quarters of the Clare students are in U.C.D., and almost the same proportion of the Tipperary students (north and south ridings) are there also.
> Two-thirds of the Limerick students, over half the Kerry students, and almost half the Waterford and Mayo students, are also in Dublin. And, perhaps most surprising of all, one quarter of the students from Cork County (excluding the city) go to U.C.D.
> This makes it quite clear that the area which any newly established university could hope to serve would be very limited.
> The pull of the metropolis is very strong and the expense of keeping a student at a university in, say, Limerick, for somebody resident outside about a ten-mile radius from that city would be the same as in one of the established colleges.
> Apart altogether from the difficulties of finance, of staffing, of maintaining an adequate standard and so on, it may be said quite definitely that any such college would preponderatingly serve only the city in which it would be established.

P. M. McCarthy's suggestion of a new charter for a university at Limerick prompted Alfred to explain the nature and origin of the N.U.I. charter. He recalled that in January 1952 he had obtained counsel's opinion as to its legal status. He quoted an extract from this which concluded: 'I fully agree that there would be many dangers attendant on the introduction of a bill

A Priest at Last

to amend the university charters. The precedent of amending might be afterwards cited as justification for subsequent amendments'.[20]

To the objection: 'Why not scrap the royal charter and trust their own government?' Alfred replied that after a lifetime spent in university education he was not prepared to take that chance. Owing to specious propaganda, the public's awareness of the importance of guarantees for Catholic higher education had weakened considerably since the time of Newman and the Royal University of Ireland. As for the State, the attitude of the bureaucracy had completely changed. There was much more 'Statism' in the country than was generally realised. Alfred concluded by listing his own experiences of attempts by the State to interfere with what he regarded as university autonomy.[21]

P. M. McCarthy responded to Alfred in *Hibernia* of 4 March 1960. Alfred's inevitable response was published in the issue of 11 March 1960. McCarthy stated that the 11,000 secondary pupils the committee regarded as potential students in the proposed university were from the area comprising 'County Limerick, most of County Clare, North Kerry, North Cork and North Tipperary'. To this clarification Alfred replied (with heavy irony) that he was glad to note that a little bit of Clare had been left to U.C.G. and South Cork to U.C.C. He considered that McCarthy's optimism was not borne out by the statistics he had

20. The rest of the extract leading to the conclusion read: 'I understand that the government has been advised that neither it nor the president of Ireland has the power to amend a royal charter. On any occasion since the foundation of the State, on which the necessity for amendment of a charter has arisen, recourse had been had to an act (sometimes private and sometimes public) of the Oireachtas. For example, Holles Street hospital was founded under a charter: this was amended some years ago by a private act introduced at the request of the hospital. I myself am inclined to think that there should be power in the president, on the advice of the government, to exercise prerogative powers not vested in the State, which were formerly vested in the monarch. But in my opinion there must be a law to give him such authority.'

21. These he listed as follows: 'I have had to resist attempts at inspection and at fixation of salaries (see J. A. Gaughan, *Alfred O'Rahilly I: Academic*, 117-18). A few years ago there was a project to deprive our university of two faculties and to transfer them to a purely secularist institute (see *ibid.* 138-42). Quite recently the government tried to impose a joint faculty on T.C.D. and U.C.D.' (see pp. 181-2). He added that after long experience he was convinced that they in the N.U.I. ultimately owed their autonomy, their immunity from State intervention, to the determination of the Catholic bishops to stand by the 1908 settlement of the university question.

secured in 1946, which he cited once more. He argued that U.C.C. had 'high prestige, great facilities and many first-class departments', yet could not stop the flocking of Munster students to the metropolis. He enquired what new formula had the Limerick committee discovered to be more successful in this matter.

He explained that he had intervened in the public debate on the proposed university only because the official advertisement consisted in a demand for a fourth constituent college of the N.U.I. This he had contested partly on administrative grounds but chiefly because it would infringe on the religious – educational settlement of 1908. He corrected McCarthy's contention that the 'Agriculture and Dairy Science Acts' were 'amending acts'. They were, declared Alfred, acts conferring extra endowments voluntarily accepted by the university. It was the university, not the State, which created the two new faculties.[22] The charter remained untouched. To a question from McCarthy whether he was expressing the views of the Irish Catholic bishops or his own, he replied that he was not the mouthpiece of the hierarchy but speaking from experience acquired as registrar and president of U.C.C. over a period of thirty-four years.

Alfred returned to the agitation for a university for Limerick in *Hibernia* of 15 April 1960. He noted that in its latest advertisement the Limerick University Project Committee had declared that they stood by the N.U.I. charter. So, he declared, he had no further reason for intervening. This, however, did not prevent him from recalling the advice, which, he claimed, he had given fourteen years earlier to the previous Limerick committee. He had urged them to concentrate on a campaign for a School of Technology, considering that this would be far more appropriate and advantageous than a university institution, almost certainly bound to be second-rate. Such an institute or school would cater for a wider public, skilled tradesmen as well as qualified technicians, and would receive wide support from local workers and business people. Moreover, the proposal to substitute a properly equipped School of Technology – of

22. Both McCarthy and Alfred presumably had in mind the University Education (Agriculture and Dairy Science) Act 1926 which provided for the creation of a faculty of dairy science, including a professor of agriculture, at U.C.C. and which transferred the Royal College of Science to U.C.D.

A Priest at Last

the type of Bolton Street and Kevin Street, Dublin – for the Limerick Technical School would arouse no controversy. Its success would not really depend on university recognition, though there would be a strong case for that. The Institutes of Mechanical and Electrical Engineers would provide qualifications for higher technical posts. And Limerick could add aeronautics and meteorology.

He recalled two other suggestions which he had made to the earlier Limerick University Committee. The first was that it should apply to the N.U.I. for authorisation for first-year university courses to be conducted locally. The second was 'the externalisation of the Higher Diploma in Education'. He noted that the N.U.I. was under no obligation to impose internal courses for its diplomas. A de-centralisation of that course, he added, would be a great boon to teachers resident outside Dublin, Cork and Galway.

Because of his widespread influence and his authority as a former vice-chancellor of the N.U.I. and an outstanding president of U.C.C., the Limerick committee regarded Alfred's intervention as a serious setback. They pressed ahead, however, with their campaign and their case was presented to the Commission on Higher Education (1960-67) by their legal adviser, Dermot P. Kinlen. In the interim report of the commission they were promised a third-level institution. Such were the limitations attached to this, however, that they had no choice but to reject it. Eventually the government established a higher education authority and proposed to establish under its aegis – an institute in Dublin and in Limerick. The committee was persuaded to accept the latter as an interim step towards their goal. In 1972 the National Institute of Higher Education was established on the outskirts of the city. In 1975 it became a recognised college of the N.U.I. And in 1989 an international commission recommended that it be established as an independent university. The efforts of the Limerick University Project Committee were crowned when, on 22 June 1989, the University of Limerick Act came into effect.

Alfred did not live to witness the successful outcome of Limerick's long agitation for a university. He would probably have claimed that success crowned the efforts of the committee, when, as he had advised, they agreed, as an interim step, to be satisfied with third-level school of engineering, science and technology, short of full university status. He would certainly have been pleased that the establishment of the new university, as well as Dublin City University, did not require the introduction of a bill to amend the N.U.I. charter.

Transfer of U.C.D. from Earlsfort Terrace to Belfield

The proposal to move University College, Dublin, from Earlsfort Terrace to Belfield gave occasion in Dáil Éireann for a discussion of university education in the last week of March 1960. Alfred commented on the ensuing debate in 'U.C.D., Trinity and Limerick', in *Hibernia* of 15 April 1960. At the outset he replied to a charge by Donogh O'Malley, T.D., of being misquoted. He acknowledged that in a postscript to a previous article he should have made it clear that O'Malley had not advocated an unconditional amalgamation of T.C.D. and U.C.D. And he agreed that the latter's proposal had been made 'subject to the satisfaction of the Catholic bishops and the Protestant heads'. But, he complained, O'Malley had not developed this 'chimerical proposal of "guarantees".'[23]

Next he commented on an article in the *Irish Times* of 31 March under the heading 'Deputy deplores religious apartheid in universities'. This referred to a remark by Patrick Byrne, T.D. Alfred described the remark as unmannerly and outrageous. He pointed out that apartheid had come to mean that a privileged minority had denied the natural rights of the majority. In the Republic of Ireland they had the majority seeking to retain the status they had won after a long struggle. They conceded equal rights to the minority with whom they had no desire to interfere. Alfred suggested that what Byrne was really tilting at was the relevance of religion in higher education. If he was really logical, he should also advocate 'neutral' primary and secondary schools, thus depriving the religious minority of their own schools.

---

23. The misquotation O'Malley complained of read: 'Since I wrote the above I have read an account of a meeting in Dublin at which Mr Donogh O'Malley, T.D., made the following statements: (1) "He proposed to advocate in the Dáil the scrapping of the charter of 1908". (2) "The people in power in the National University should be removed. The administration of this 'junta' was a 'downright disgrace' ". (3) "Would it not be a marvellous thing if T.C.D. and U.C.D. could be amalgamated?"'

A Priest at Last

Dr. Noel Browne, T.D., made a characteristically vitriolic contribution to the debate. He considered that it was 'absurd sectarianism and bigotry' that they should have the N.U.I. as well as T.C.D. Not that he believed Trinity College to be the home of liberal thought and ideals. Its divinity school had first to be got rid of from 'within the college walls'. Instead of regarding T.C.D. as a generous provision for the religious minority, he considered that its separate existence was due to 'wounds' which were not yet healed. By contrast he preferred the 'non-denominational' charter of the N.U.I. Alfred retorted that obviously Browne did not realise that the charter was multi-denominational in the sense of catering for Catholic ideals while providing guarantees for non-Catholics.

Jack McQuillan, T.D., considered that it was 'a poor compliment to the strength of the Catholic faith of our people' to be afraid to send students to Trinity. Alfred interpreted this as: 'That is, we should abandon what we have won so that our students should be tested in a Protestant or agnostic atmosphere'. Like Browne, Alfred continued, McQuillan's underlying thesis was the irrelevance of right philosophy and religion in education. They failed to grasp that it was Catholics who were liberal and pluralist. They fully supported schools and a university acceptable to the religious minority, even if it meant extra expense to the community. All they asked was that they, the overwhelming majority, should be left in possession of similar facilities. They held that religion was as relevant in higher as in primary education and so would prefer T.C.D. to be genuinely Protestant rather than liberal-agnostic.

Alfred complimented Dr Patrick Hillery, the minister for education, on his speech opening the debate. The minister had emphasised that, in accordance with the Constitution, the conscientious and religious rights of parents would be respected as regards university education. He went on to declare his intention to set up a commission, one of whose objects would be to investigate 'the question of the functions of higher technical schools and of the avoidance of needless duplication of public expenditure on professional courses in universities and such schools'. He declared that the question of recognising higher technical schools would arise. But such a recognition, Alfred warned, the government could not force on the N.U.I. without violating its charter.

Alfred O'Rahilly III: Controversialist

The minister also announced that another object of the commission would be 'the question of a further constituent college in the N.U.I.' Alfred doubted if the minister realised the implication of this. He then set out to ensure that he did. The addition of another constituent college to the N.U.I., he pointed out, would involve the legislative alteration of its charter, which, he emphasised, was 'the definite guarantee of Irish Catholic claims in higher education'. Moreover, government policy had hitherto been not to alter a charter, for example, that of a hospital or of an institution – like that of the civil engineers – except at the specific request of the body concerned and after a scrutiny by a special parliamentary committee. A legislative move against the N.U.I. would be the first occasion on which the government would be declaring that it was prepared forcibly to alter the charter without consulting either the hierarchy or the university. The government would not dream of compulsorily adding a new college, in addition to T.C.D., to the University of Dublin. Are Catholics to be subjected to interference from which Protestants were exempt. Furthermore, he reminded Dr Hillery, since the Limerick University Project Committee had declared that it stood by the N.U.I. charter, there was no longer a demand for a new constituent college (apart from a recognised college or a new university).

Criticism of Appointments in U.C.D. and of the Presidency of Michael Tierney

In May and June 1960 Alfred intervened in the controversy then uppermost in the minds of the academics of U.C.D. Its origin can be traced to the mercurial temperament of Professor Michael Tierney who was president of U.C.D. from 1948 onwards. He was a brilliant academic and an outstanding administrator. The splendid campus of U.C.D. at Belfield in the southern suburbs of Dublin is a monument to his presidency. However, he also tended to be autocratic and could at times be extremely insensitive. In addition, he had been a leading member of the Cumann na nGaedheal later Fine Gael Party and served as a deputy and a senator in that party's interests. By the mid-1950s he had alienated a number of his colleagues and such was their antipathy to him that they had become a recognisable anti-Tierney faction.

9. Conferring day at U.C.C., October 1942. *Left to right, back row*: Patrick M. Quinlan (later professor of mathematical physics, U.C.C., and member of Seanad Éireann), James Barry (later principal of Crawford Technical Institute, Cork), Francis Fahy (later professor of experimental physics, U.C.C.), Tadhg Carey (later professor of mathematics and subsequently president, U.C.C.), John Barry (later principal of Institute of Technology, Bolton Street, Dublin, and president of the Institution of Engineers of Ireland). *Front row*: Donal McCarthy (lecturer in mathematics through Irish, later professor of mathematical physics, U.C.C., director of the central statistics office and subsequently president of U.C.C.), **Alfred** (registrar, professor of mathematical physics and professor of sociology, later president, U.C.C.), Henry St J. Atkins (professor of mathematics, later registrar and president, U.C.C.), John McHenry (professor of experimental physics, U.C.C.).

10. Conferring day at U.C.C., 18 July 1950. With Alfred are (*left to right*) Denis Gwynn (research professor of modern history, U.C.C.) and John Pius Boland (former Nationalist M.P. for South Kerry) on whom a short time previously an honorary doctorate had been conferred by the N.U.I., at the request of Alfred and Gwynn

11. Cartoon of Alfred and College F.C.A. guard of honour at public reception and garden party hosted by U.C.C. for Cardinal John D'Alton, 17 June 1953. The cartoon was published in the *Quarryman*, 1953. The two officers in the guard of honour were, *left to right*: Michael A. Mac Conaill (professor of anatomy) and Joseph G. Healy (lecturer in Spanish). Alfred had the cartoon printed as his Christmas card that year

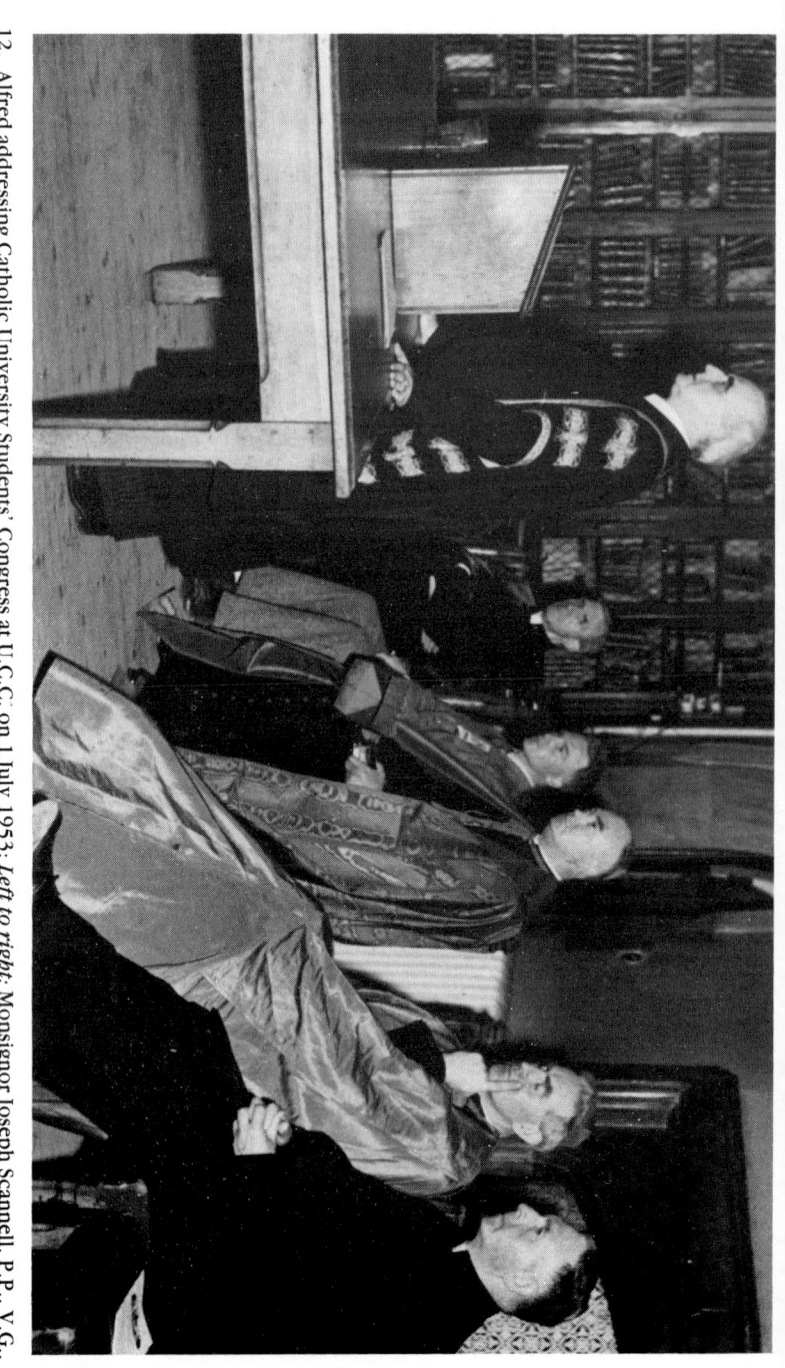

12. Alfred addressing Catholic University Students' Congress at U.C.C. on 1 July 1953: *Left to right*: Monsignor Joseph Scannell, P.P., V.G., dean of Cork; A. M. E. Kennedy, president, S.R.C.; Gerald Patrick O'Hara (papal nuncio), Bishop Cornelius Lucey (Cork and Ross) and Canon James P. Bastible (dean of residence, U.C.C.)

A Priest at Last

In 1960 this group was given an opportunity to embarrass the president seriously. For almost ten years, at the prompting of Tierney, the governing body of U.C.D. had been appointing an unusually large number of assistants on one-year contracts and had given them the title of lecturer or assistant lecturer. The U.C.D. authorities justified the practice in the light of the rapid expansion of the student body and the slow and tortuous procedure involved in having such appointments made by the senate of the N.U.I. Some unease was expressed in U.C.D. circles at the practice and in 1956 a legal opinion on the matter, which was sought anonymously, suggested that such appointments were irregular, as they did not conform to the charter of the N.U.I. In May 1959 John Kenny, an assistant in the faculty of law and a known supporter of Fianna Fáil, took up the matter and requested the governing body to have the legality of these appointments decided. He warned that if they did not do so he would petition the government to appoint Visitors to that end. When his report was rejected, Kenny remained true to his word and the Fianna Fáil government, on 6 November 1959, appointed Mr Justice George Murnaghan, Mr Justice Thomas Teevan and Judge Michael Binchy to act as Visitors to U.C.D. and report on the matter.

Their report was published in February 1960. It disclosed that the practice of the governing body of U.C.D. in appointing assistants as lecturers and assistant lecturers was a breach of the charter of the N.U.I. The government moved to validate such appointments by preparing the 'University College Dublin Bill 1960'. The bill was debated in Dáil Éireann on 28 April and 11, 18 and 19 May 1960. The bulk of the time given for the debate was taken up by contributions from Deputies Noel Browne and Jack McQuillan. In an intervention James Dillon, leader of the Fine Gael opposition, described the debate until then as consisting of three hours of Browne slandering Tierney[24] followed by three and a half hours of McQuillan doing likewise. However, nearly all the deputies on both sides of the chamber were sympathetic to the predicament in which Tierney and the governing body of U.C.D. found themselves and were eager to deal with the difficulty as expeditiously and with as little fuss as possible.

24. Later, on 31 May 1960, Jack Lynch, minister for industry and commerce, expressed a widely held view of some of Browne's contributions on U.C.D. when he interjected on two occasions: 'The fund of filth is inexhaustible.'

Alfred O'Rahilly III: Controversialist

Outside Dáil Éireann the anti- and pro-Tierney forces entered the controversy also. During his contribution to the debate on 28 April Jack McQuillan suggested that the irregular practices in U.C.D. might be duplicated in the other colleges of the N.U.I. This prompted a letter from Henry St Joseph Atkins, president of U.C.C., which was published in the press on 2 May 1960. He stated that there were no college professors or college lecturers in U.C.C. and that all professors and lecturers had been appointed by the senate of the N.U.I. on the recommendation of the academic council and governing body of U.C.C. It was, he stated, the practice to circulate copies of the advertisements of vacant posts to all university colleges in Ireland, including that of the Queen's University of Belfast. In the case of proposed appointments in the faculty of science, advertisements about these were also placed in British scientific and technical journals. He concluded that during the previous forty years two college professors and two college lecturers had been appointed 'on occasions of extreme urgency until the necessary legislation had been enacted'. Although it was generally known that Atkins had an intense dislike of Tierney, this intervention, so unhelpful to the U.C.D. authorities, caused widespread surprise in the academic community. It drew a sharp retort from Professor J. J. Hogan, registrar of U.C.D., and a letter supporting Tierney from Professor Michael Duignan of U.C.G. in the press of 4 May 1960. Both of the factions at U.C.D. were much to the fore at a meeting on 24 May 1960 of the Convocation of the N.U.I. which had been summoned to discuss the U.C.D. dispute.[25]

The dispute was featured in *Hibernia* of 6 May 1960 in a front-page article under the heading 'The bulwark of protection from State intervention has been breached from within'. The article stated:

---

25. At the end of an acrimonious discussion 'Convocation passed the following resolution by a vote of 355 to 55: "Convocation noted with regret the violation of the rule of law in University College, Dublin, revealed by the report of the Board of Visitors, and also noted the failure of the senate of the National University of Ireland to investigate properly the legality of certain appointments when their legality was responsibly questioned . . ."' At this and another Convocation meeting feelings ran high. In a letter to Alfred, dated 3 June 1960, Professor T. E. Nevin wrote: 'The two Convocation meetings were terrible. They were an extraordinary exhibition of hysterical malice and I hope I do not have to attend any similar ones for a long time.'

A Priest at Last

... It is high time, too, for the authorities of U.C.D. to learn that academic freedom cuts both ways. It means freedom for the university to go its own way free from State intervention in ordinary matters, though substantially supported by the State. But within the College it should also mean toleration of divergent views of College policy and freedom for the academic staff from the least hint of penalisation ... For the future this sad story should serve to remind those in authority in the National University that laws and regulations must be either obeyed or amended. A chartered corporation using public funds ought to be scrupulous in respecting its own charter. If, as a result of what has happened, the gates are opened to bureaucratic interference in the life of the university, all parties in it will have much to regret but no one will be so much to blame as the College, which, in the words of the Visitors, 'adopted the course of expediency, and, in doing so, seemed to the Board to overlook the fact that its action might affect not only the university but the other constituent colleges ...'

Support for Michael Tierney

The editorial endorsed this severe criticism of the U.C.D. authorities. However, on the front page of the same edition of *Hibernia* it was stated that inside a different view of the controversy could be found in an article by Dr Alfred O'Rahilly. In this article under the heading 'The U.C.D. fracas' Alfred dealt with the report of the visiting judges. At the outset he protested against the unfair attacks on Tierney in Dáil Éireann. He pointed to 'many irrelevancies and inaccuracies' in the report of the visitors. They confused a faculty with a department. Then they stated that the practice of appointing assistants as college lecturers began in 1953. Alfred stated that it had begun, in fact, twenty years earlier. Indeed, in 1920 there was a college professor of agriculture in U.C.C. To a comment in the report, deploring the number of assistants and demonstrators in U.C.D., Alfred replied that that was a matter of college policy in which no legal question was involved. He described as 'objectionable' the implication that such a policy could lead to 'patronage'. In any case, he pointed out, the relatively high number of assistants at U.C.D. was not unique. There were nearly seventy

Alfred O'Rahilly III: Controversialist

in U.C.C. The report's listing of 'vacancies' in U.C.D., he described as utterly misleading, as it had been published without the explanation for them given by the U.C.D. authorities.

Next Alfred set about explaining the nub of the question. According to the N.U.I. charter university professors and lecturers were to be appointed by the senate, but only on the initiative of the college. Assistants and demonstrators were appointed by the college, which had complete control of number, tenure and salaries. The First Statute, passed by the Commissioners under the 1908 Act, introduced new titles. The college could give the title of 'tutor' to any assistant or demonstrator. It could also confer the title of 'emeritus professor' to a person who had ceased to be a university professor. The Commissioners, Alfred continued, evidently entered into the spirit of the final clause of the charter: 'This charter shall be construed and adjudged in the most favourable and beneficial sense for the best advantage of the college, and the promoting of the objects of this charter, as well as in all courts or elsewhere, notwithstanding any non-recital, mis-recital, uncertainty or imperfection herein.' Bearing in on the decision of the three judges that the titles of college lecturers and assistant lecturers were illegal, Alfred pointed to a parallel case. Statute I gave the president control of 'the servants of the college'. Those 'servants' had been given such various designations as porters, attendants, technicians, typists, secretaries, library assistants, etc. 'Yet the college charter does not mention any of these titles. Presumbly they too are illegal!'

Alfred stated that during his time as registrar and president of U.C.C. there had been a constant effort to classify and to improve conditions for assistants. It was agreed that demonstrators should be appointed annually. The renewal of assistantships was a formality; it was arranged that unless reported to the contrary it was to be assumed that assistants continued in office. The idea that the tenure of assistantships was uncertain, or was dependent on the president was quite false. He recalled that during his forty years at U.C.C. there were only two cases of nonrenewal, both at the instance of the professor concerned. On investigating the matter, he stated, he had been able to discover two such instances at U.C.D. during the previous fifty years. He added that it had always been recognised in all the colleges that if either the academic council or the governing body so decided a vacant assistantship had to be advertised.

A Priest at Last

Alfred explained that the problem of grading assistants and giving higher salaries to senior holders led both in Dublin and in Cork to conferring the title of college lecturers. He continued: 'When I, as president of U.C.C., was authorised to offer the title to certain assistants in the medical faculty, I obtained legal opinion and was advised to proceed. But now comes the peremptory decision of the report on U.C.D.: "that the college lecturers and assistant lecturers are not assistants whom the college is empowered to appoint".' This, Alfred emphasised, was a legal verdict. It had nothing to do with policy – whether or not it might be academically advisable to institute new university lectureships in lieu of those posts.

Alfred questioned the legal verdict because of the assumptions on which it was based. These he listed as follows:

(1) This title constitutes an usurpation of university functions. The report reluctantly admits that the senate does not share this view. Indeed no one could possibly misunderstand the position of such non-statutory teachers. Each is under the control of the professor concerned, and as such takes no part in university examinations, unlike university lecturers.

(2) These people are not assistants. Then what are they? Every assistant lectures in the college. They assist the university staff in teaching and are remunerated for it. It is obvious that the governing body appointed them to the college not the university staff . . .

(3) In spite of the last clause of the charter and of the 1908 commissioners' interpretation, it is assumed that the charter fixed not only the subordinate status but the very vocabulary. (The commissioners said they could be called 'tutors' – a title not contained in the charter.) But, if we accept this new phraseological limitation, the decision of the report will have extended consequences. U.C.D. has other titles for people who have no university status – such as directors of special studies and clinical tutors. Logically all these are also swept away, as are 'recognised teachers' in the Cork hospitals.

Critical of Response of the Government

Next Alfred acknowledged the good intentions of the government in preparing the proposed bill to correct this 'new limitation of vocabulary'. It was necessary because many who came

Alfred O'Rahilly III: Controversialist

temporarily to teach or conduct research in the colleges of the N.U.I. wished to have 'lecturer' in their title, with the need in this regard, as the minister for education had indicated, being particularly acute in the veterinary college. However, he continued, there were serious objections to the bill. It had been drafted and proposed without consulting the university or the college. It purported to validate the existing practice which it assumed to be a breach of the charter. Thus, it was, in effect, a compulsory amendment of the charter. As such it was a dangerous precedent: '. . . such *ad hoc* legislation might next be employed to impose certain positive requirements.'

Alfred urged that U.C.D. had several alternatives to the bill. It could legally appeal against the decision of the Visitors. It could pass a new statute providing that selected assistants might have the additional title of surgical tutor or college lecturer. U.C.D. could ask for an amendment to the N.U.I. charter prescribing how the N.U.I. or one of its colleges could make adjustments to modern conditions. This kind of flexibility was enjoyed by British universities, by the Queen's University of Belfast; and by Trinity College, Dublin, since 1911. This, he suggested, would be the best way U.C.D. could deal with this 'newly imposed straight-jacket of verbiage'.

Alfred published an even more detailed statement on the debate in Dáil Éireann about U.C.D. in the *Irish Independent* of 10 May 1960. One can assume that annoyance at President Atkins's intervention partly motivated his contribution. But his main reason for publishing it was to protest that the debate had 'divagated into such a mass of exaggeration and irelevancies together with a grossly unfair personal onslaught on the president of U.C.D.' He stressed that there were precedents for the appointment of college lecturers and that the practice of doing so in U.C.D. was not a sinister development, as had been suggested. He also emphasised that it was the governing body of each college, advised by its academic council, which appointed college teaching assistants, the university or the college president having no say in the matter. The issue as to whether there should be more university lecturers in lieu of assistants was for the governing body to decide, as was the question of advertising the vacancies for assistantships. He corrected the erroneous view, well ventilated in Dáil Éireann, that the tenure of assistants was uncertain or in some way dependent on the college president. Indeed, he added, he knew from personal experience that any intervention in this area by the latter would be greatly resented. He repeated that in his forty years in U.C.C. there had been only two non-renewals both at the instance of the professors concerned and that he had been able to discover only two similar instances in U.C.D. during the previous fifty years. Alfred decried the intervention of the government, stating that it was only if and when a court decision had upheld 'the narrow Visitors' interpretation' that there would have been an occasion for action by the legislature. The college, with the concurrence of the university, could then ask to be extricated from 'the intolerable strait-jacket of extreme literalness initiated by the Visitors'. This could best be done by granting, preferably by a private bill, to the N.U.I. and its constituent colleges powers, already enjoyed by the British universities and Trinity College. These were powers to adjust university charters to modern conditions by means of a petition, under certain conditions. Such powers would be achieved by seeking an amendment of charters to that end.

Alfred appealed to the government to delay the course of action it proposed because it was 'really the first open breach of the settlement of facilities for higher education which Irish Catholics secured in 1908 after a prolonged struggle'. The government had, probably without realising it, claimed the right to alter that settlement without consulting the Catholic hierarchy, the university or the colleges. From the point of view of the other parties involved this was 'a most dangerous precedent which may lead to further State intervention'.

Debate on the 'University College Dublin Bill 1960' was resumed in Dáil Éireann on 11, 18 and 19 May. Deputy McQuillan quoted the objections to the bill set out by Alfred in *Hibernia* of 6 May. In supporting the bill Deputies James Dillon, Patrick McGilligan and Richard Mulcahy repeated passages from Alfred's statement in the *Irish Independent* of 10 May. The final reading of the bill was passed by Dáil Éireann on 19 May 1960.

In 'The U.C.D. bill' in *Hibernia* of 10 June 1960 Alfred was abrasive in his final comment on it, declaring that the minister for education had, by virtue of it, 'created a mess'. In this article, written before the debate on the bill in Seanad Éireann, he recalled that the government had accepted the finding of the

Alfred O'Rahilly III: Controversialist

Board of Visitors that U.C.D. were not empowered to appoint assistants who are to be designated college or assistant lecturers and, without consulting the university or the college, introduced the bill to validate such appointments. Thus the titles were legitimated not through an amended charter but through parliamentary intervention. He emphasised once again the danger of such a precedent. The bill authorised the governing body of U.C.D. to continue to make those appointments until 31 March 1964. This meant that the college was asked to ignore its charter and to start making appointments to college lectureships under the aegis of legislation and executive order. This Alfred described as a disastrous innovation which he hoped would be rejected. He concluded by pointing to a passage in the bill which, if taken literally, would mean that not only could the college institute college lectureships but the senate could also impose such on the college. This, he emphasised, would not only mean administrative chaos but would upset the recognised division of power between college and university.

The bill was before Seanad Éireann on 1 and 2 June 1960. In a contribution which was severely critical of the report of the Board of Visitors and of the manner in which they prepared it, Senator Michael Hayes (professor of Irish at U.C.D.) quoted Alfred on two occasions. He recalled that Alfred had written in the *Irish Independent* of 10 May 1960 that the report contained irrelevancies, inaccuracies and insinuations. These, claimed Hayes, were mild and charitable words with which to describe the document before them. Hayes also reminded the Seanad of the emphasis Alfred had laid on the fact that the Visitors had 'sorrowfully' to admit that the senate of the N.U.I. had refused to adopt their interpretation in the matter of appointments at U.C.D.

Later Senator Patrick Quinlan (professor of mathematical physics at U.C.C.) referred to Alfred's long-standing opposition to any change being effected in the N.U.I. charter by the government. In so doing he described Alfred as one 'who, perhaps, would rank as the foremost of the university leaders in the past twenty-five years'. After the Seanad debate, in which the spirit of faction was also much in evidence, the bill was returned to Dáil Éireann for its final formal passage.

A Priest at Last

This was the last controversy in which Alfred intervened. It was a minor skirmish compared with many of the conflicts in which he embroiled himself during his career.[26]

26. The above is taken from J. B. Bell, *The secret army* (London 1970); Dáil Éireann: *Díospóireachta parlaiminte, tuairisc oifigiúil: Parliamentary debates, official reports*, vol. 180, 8 March – 7 April 1960, *passim*, vol. 181, 26 April – 19 May 1960, *passim*, vol. 182, 24 May – 16 June 1960, *passim*; Seanad Éireann: *Díospóireachta parlaiminte, tuairisc oifigiúil: Parliamentary debates, official reports*, vol. 52, 20 January – 21 July 1960, *passim*; *University of Limerick, degree programmes 1992-94* (Limerick 1991); *Bulletin of the Catholic Societies Vocational Organisation Conference*, October 1954; *Cork Examiner* 14 October, 11 November, 2, 16 December 1946; 15 September 1953; 14, 15 July, 21 September 1954; *Irish Independent* 13 December 1955; 4, 9, 12, 19, 25 May 1960; *Irish Times* 15 February 1958; 2 May 1960; *Limerick Leader* 23 May 1945; 29 June, 16 October, 14 December 1946; 1, 8 August, 26 September, 10 October, 2, 9, 23, 28, 30 November, 2, 9 December 1959; January-March 1960; *Southern Cross* (Capetown) 20 October 1954; *Standard* 24 September 1954; 23 December 1955; *Sunday Chronicle* 16 October 1955; *Sunday Dispatch* 19 September 1954; *Sunday Express* 19 September 1954; *Sunday Independent* 19 September 1954; *Universe* 24 September 1954; *Waterford Star* 1 October 1954; diaries of Alfred O'Rahilly: 23 December 1953 – 19 January 1954, 8 April – 1 May 1954, 2 May – 23 May 1954, 24 May – 7 July 1954, 11 July – 12 September 1954, 13 September – 26 October 1954, 27 December 1954 – 28 February 1955, 1 March – 9 November 1955, 13 November – 26 December 1955; Dublin Archdiocesan Archives: Alfred O'Rahilly file; University of Limerick, Archives Department: Video recording 'A university for Limerick'; interviews with Dermot P. Kinlen, Fr Michael McCarthy, C.S.Sp., Mgr James McConnell, Bernard McDonagh, Cornelius Murphy, Fr Patrick Murray, Rev Dr Michael O'Carroll, C.S.Sp., Richard O'Flaherty, Pádraig Ó Snodaigh and Mgr Gerard Sheehy; papers and writings of Alfred O'Rahilly and the sources already cited.

THE FINAL YEARS

It was generally understood that after ordination Alfred would be mainly occupied in writing articles and completing his much heralded multi-volume life of Christ. He was also eager to engage in some pastoral work. This he contrived to do chiefly by giving lectures, even before his ordination.

In 1954 and 1955 he was most responsive to those who invited him to give a lecture. He continued to speak on the Holy Shroud of Turin. After a pilgrimage to the Holy Land he gave a number of talks on the Holy Places. And he occasionally prepared addresses on topics given to him. In 1954, before he had retired from U.C.C., he was a much sought-after lecturer. During Lent of that year he spoke on 'The Passion and the Shroud' at Sion Hill Convent, Blackrock College, Milltown Park theologate and finally in the Mansion House, where he had an overflow audience. On 12 March he spoke on 'The lay vocation' at the Gresham Hotel. Archbishop McQuaid wrote on the following day: 'Your lecture was a great success. I am very grateful: but you are only beginning for Dublin.' During Easter week he addressed a conference of 250 nuns, all of them teachers in national schools, on 'The teaching nun and the modern girl.'

Lectures

In 1955 he continued to be a busy lecturer. In January he lectured to the Jesuits at Rathfarnham Castle on the Holy Land. In February he gave this lecture at Sion Hill and on two occasions at Milltown Park. In March he gave a talk to the students in St Catherine's Domestic Science College, Sion Hill. In the same month he lectured on the Holy Land in the Holy Ghost Order's theologate at Kimmage Manor, in Loreto convent school, George's Hill, and Blackrock College. He also visited Tullabeg, where he gave a talk in addition to his lecture on the Holy Land. During the last week of June he delivered fourteen lectures on sociology and his talks on the Holy Shroud and the Holy Land at St Mary's Dominican Convent in Belfast.

The publicity surrounding Alfred's ordination caused him to be in even greater demand in 1956. In March he lectured on the Holy Shroud in Loreto Convent, George's Hill. In April he spoke in the Marian Hall, Milltown, and in the cinema in Arklow. On

The Final Years

1 May he spoke at an outdoor evening Mass on the feast of St Joseph the Worker, in Dundalk. Later in May he was in the Missionary Sisters' convent of Killeshandra, where he gave his lecture on the Holy Shroud and the Holy Land. In this month he also gave a lecture in the St Francis Xavier Hall to raise funds for the Jesuit missions. In June he gave a series of sermons to members of the Third Order in the Franciscan church at Merchant's Quay. Later in the month he lectured at the annual Congress of the Dublin Institute of Catholic Sociology. In July he addressed the St Vincent de Paul Conference of South Dublin and Wicklow. He also gave some talks to non-Christians under the auspices of the Legion of Mary. In the same month he was in Belfast, where he lectured in the Good Shepherd convent and to an annual congress of the Irish Association of Catholic University Students. Later that year he lectured to the Knights of St Columbanus in their premises at Ely Place.

On 25 March 1957 Alfred made his second last broadcast from Radio Éireann. It was a review of Archbishop J. C. McQuaid's *Wellsprings of the faith*.[1] (His last broadcast was on 19 June 1960 when he made a charity appeal for St Joseph's Home for the Aged, Portland Row.) He was the principal speaker (the other two were Fr Robert Nash, S.J., and Rev. Dr Michael O'Carroll, C.S.Sp.) in a symposium on 'Adult Catholicism' at the Shelbourne Hotel on 8 December. More than a thousand people attended; hundreds more were locked out.

He gave his last public lecture at the annual congress of Christus Rex at U.C.C. in April 1963. His paper was 'Catholic social action, the layman's part'.[2]

1. Alfred published an abstract of this review in the *Blackrock College Annual* 1957. In an exchange of letters on 21 and 22 January 1957 between Alfred and Francis McManus arranging the broadcast, Alfred referred to a row which he had with McManus in connection with a review. This, it seems, concerned his exchanges on radio with Dr Hilda Graef (see p. 35). Alfred considered that he had not been treated fairly in the matter and made a vigorous protest privately to MacManus. He charged that, as a result, he had been placed 'in the black book' by Radio Éireann and had been the victim of a boycott by the station. MacManus replied that they in Radio Éireann thought that they were in Alfred's 'black book' and so had refrained from bothering him with invitations to broadcast.
2. See J. A. Gaughan, *Alfred O'Rahilly III: Controversialist, Part I: Social Reformer*, 163. William Declan O'Connell (*Cork Examiner*) and Fr James Good recalled Alfred's opening remarks. He pointed dramatically to a large crucifix in the hall, stated that he had placed it there, had put up other crucifixes throughout the college and was proud to have done so. O'Connell complained

Alfred O'Rahilly III: Controversialist

Apart from lecturing, Alfred conducted one-day retreats.[3] One such retreat was held on 19 July 1959 at Clermont convent in Rathnew, County Wicklow, for members of the Legion of Mary. From 1960 to the end of 1966 he acted as chaplain to a monthly Patrician meeting in the home of Frank Flanagan, at Glenade in Mount Merrion Avenue. Patrician meetings were organised under the auspices of the Legion of Mary and were intended to enable persons to become more knowledgeable and articulate about their Catholic faith. Those who regularly attended these meetings included: William T. Cosgrave, General Michael J. Costello, Frank Duff, John Evans, John Hearne, Patrick J. Little, E. P. McCarron, James McElligott, General Seán Mac Eoin,[4] Edward More O'Ferrall, Maurice Moynihan, Con Murphy, George O'Brien, León Ó Broin, Eoin O'Mahony, William Phillips, Barney Roche and the Earl of Wicklow.

Early in 1962 Alfred received a request for a series of talks on Catholicism from the executive committee of T.C.D.'s Laurentian Society, which catered for Catholic undergraduates. He considered that in the somewhat secularist atmosphere of the college and with the (Protestant) Christian Union and Student Christian Movement engaged in proselytising among Catholic students there was an urgent need for them to receive some advanced instruction. With the approval of Archbishop McQuaid, he arranged to meet members of the Society and their friends on Sunday evenings at 23 Merrion Square, the premises of the St Joseph's Young Priests' Society, to discuss religion. He had hoped that the students would agree to an arrangement, whereby he would deal with a topic proposed by them and that this would be followed by a general discussion. However, the students insisted on one of their number opening each meeting by reading a paper. Alfred found this unsatisfactory, as he found the students more immature and untrained in their religion than

of the less than warm reception given to Alfred by President Atkins and the other members of the staff. According to O'Connell, Alfred was unfazed by this and in an exchange of banter before the lecture 'stole the show' from Atkins, who merely attended to introduce him.

3. As was the case with any priest who was not a priest of the archdiocese, Alfred had to apply to the archbishop for faculties to hear confessions and to preach on each of these occasions.

4. In the first week of June 1964, at the request of Seán Mac Eoin, Alfred consented to act on a national committee to erect a memorial to Michael Collins in Cork city.

The Final Years

he had expected, but he attended the sessions for almost two years during the academic terms. With characteristic generosity he provided coffee and biscuits for each session and presented many of his books on Catholic apologetics to the society.

Alfred eventually became disillusioned with these 'Sunday Conferences'. It seems that members of the Society made little effort to publicise them and attendances never exceeded two dozen. They became more adversarial, with non-Catholic students being invited to read papers in which they attacked Catholicism. Alfred became more and more disenchanted with the meetings, which were not achieving the purpose he intended, namely, the religious formation of Catholic undergraduates. He saw them as merely providing 'a platform for anti-Catholic propaganda by outsiders intent not on understanding our position but on demolishing our creed.' His dissatisfaction culminated on 8 December 1963 when a Presbyterian read a paper making a vitriolic attack on Catholic devotion to Our Lady. He vigorously objected to the tone of the young woman's contribution and tempers became frayed. The outcome was that he wrote an open valedictory letter to members of the Laurentian Society stating that he would be prepared to continue the sessions only if they decided to follow the arrangement which he had originally suggested.

Articles and Books

After taking up residence in Blackrock College Alfred set about publishing articles and completing books on religious subjects. He published 'Our share in what happened on Calvary' in the *Irish Press* of 15 April 1954. Throughout Lent of 1956 he published thirty-nine articles in the *Irish Press*. This he followed with six articles under the heading 'Thoughts on the Easter gospel.' He had a series of thirty-seven articles on 'Passiontide' published in the *Irish Press* in 1957. There followed twenty-eight articles on Thérèse Neumann in the *Sunday Press* between 24 November 1957 and 1 June 1958. He resumed writing for the *Standard* and contributed a weekly topical article from 9 May 1958 to 28 August 1959.

Alfred had not the same success in completing the books which he intended to publish after his retirement from U.C.C. He had *Gospel meditations* published in 1958. This incorporated the series of thirty-seven articles which appeared in the *Irish Press* between 6 March and 18 April 1957. In 1963 he tried to have *The family at Bethany* (Cork 1949) reprinted and in 1964 he was also unsuccessful in an attempt to have *Father William Doyle, S.J. A spiritual study* (London 1920) re-issued in paperback on the occasion of the fiftieth anniversary of world war one. He had a contract for many years with Dover Publications Inc., of New York, for a new edition of *Electro-magnetics. A discussion of fundamentals* (London 1938). However, he could never set about his intended revision of the book and was persuaded by the publishers to allow them to reprint the original work in 1965. Most disappointing to him was his inability to complete his work on 'The Passion and the Shroud', which eventually was published by the present writer in 1985. His age, distractions arising from his readiness to give lectures and his role as adviser to Archbishop McQuaid on educational matters, and an unhelpful attitude which he tended to adopt to publishers militated against his dream of publishing a multi-volume life of Christ. However, the most serious obstacle he referred to in an entry in his diary on 21 January 1955: 'I am cursed with *Gründlichkeit*. I keep on learning and studying, always discovering gaps in my knowledge. After a lifetime devoted to other interests, I am trying to be not only a specialist in the New Testament but also one who has so mastered the details that he can make the gospels living to others.'

Adviser to Archbishop McQuaid on university education for Catholics

During his retirement at Blackrock College Alfred provided advice and information to Archbishop McQuaid on educational matters. Much of this concerned the National University of Ireland and relations between University College, Dublin, and Trinity College, Dublin. However, his role as adviser to McQuaid on university education had begun some years earlier. On his initiative Michael Tierney, Monsignor Pádraig de Brún and himself, the presidents of the three constituent colleges of the N.U.I., met representatives of the Irish Catholic bishops at the archbishop's house to discuss university education in the second or third week of January from 1950 onwards. The Irish

The Final Years

bishops were represented by the archbishop of Dublin, the bishop of Cork, the bishop of Galway and the archbishop of Armagh who, it seems, chaired the meetings. Bishop Lucey acted as secretary from 1953 onwards, when the liaison committee of bishops and university college presidents, as it was then called, was also meeting in the last week of June. It seems that the bishops adopted a listen-and-learn attitude at these rather informal meetings. From the outset Michael Tierney, president of U.C.D., was eager to gain at least the acquiescence of the bishops to a scheme to have U.C.D. transformed into an independent university. This was strenuously opposed by Alfred who considered that the Catholic influence in the colleges of the N.U.I. would be best preserved by retaining the *status quo* and not allowing any tampering with the 1908 charter which established the university. At the request of the bishops, Alfred and Tierney prepared memoranda advocating their respective positions.

Tierney's memorandum was discussed at the meeting in January 1951, but, owing to lack of time, Alfred's counter-memorandum was merely placed before it. Subsequently Tierney continued to advocate a more independent role for U.C.D. The *Irish Independent* of 8 April printed a report of an address by him under the heading 'Case for a new university stressed' and on 17 April it carried a report of another speech by Tierney, headed 'Status of U.C.D. should be raised,' as well as an editorial urging to that end the break-up of the N.U.I. This prompted Alfred to complain to Tierney and to Archbishop McQuaid. There followed a sharp exchange between Tierney and Alfred during which the latter disclosed with regard to his memorandum that de Brún, president of U.C.G., had in a recent letter to him written: 'I am in full agreement with the document you submitted to the committee and would like to have my name publicly associated with you in support of it.' In a reply to Alfred, dated 18 April 1951, McQuaid wrote: '. . . the question of university education for Catholics as a whole, quite apart from the sectional interest of University College, Dublin, is so intricate a problem that much time will have to be directed to the study of the complete position. In the meantime we should not, I believe, give voice to sectional solutions.' He also acknowledged that Alfred's memorandum had not 'even got a fair hearing, much less an answer'.

Alfred O'Rahilly III: Controversialist

In the late autumn of 1951 an agitation was conducted in the *Irish Independent* for an inquiry into the N.U.I. with a view to establishing its constituent colleges as independent universities. In a letter, dated 8 October 1951, Alfred warned McQuaid that the status of the N.U.I. and other issues which had been raised by himself and Tierney at their meetings with the representatives of the bishops 'could very easily be quickly taken in hand by others'. He made a strong appeal that the bishops should reach a decision on those matters and make them known to himself and Tierney.

These issues and the possibility of introducing a Catholic ethos into the colleges of the N.U.I. were discussed by the college presidents and representatives of the hierarchy at their meeting in January 1952. The meeting decided to obtain a legal opinion on the extent to which religious initiatives could be taken in the constituent colleges. This initiative had been taken by Alfred earlier. The result had not been reassuring. In a letter to McQuaid, dated 16 May 1952, he described the advice given to him in 1947 on the matter by Michael Joseph Ryan, S.C., legal adviser to the N.U.I., as tantamount to a recommendation that legally one could not take any initiative which went beyond 'an agnostic neutrality'. A counter-opinion on the matter had subsequently been provided to the hierarchy. However, Alfred admitted that Ryan's view was shared by a number of professors in U.C.C. but, he added: 'I have set out to expel it.'

Alfred referred to a memorandum he had sent to McQuaid the previous week outlining initiatives he had taken in U.C.C. and suggesting that similar steps be taken in U.C.D. He stated that before he retired he was eager to use his influence and standing 'to bring about a forward positive Catholic policy'. He expressed his confidence that with McQuaid's agreement 'we could take important steps for training an elite of integral Catholics not only in U.C.C. but in U.C.D. and U.C.G.' Bishop Cornelius Lucey, he continued, was in agreement with him. He concluded: 'I honestly am convinced that since 1908 we have fallen down on the job and allowed our hard-won colleges to drift largely into a negative liberalism. I think we can provide a remedy.'

Alfred, Tierney and Monsignor Pádraig de Brún met McQuaid and some of his episcopal colleagues in the third week of January 1953. The chief topic on the agenda was the question of the autonomy of clinical teaching in the medical schools of

The Final Years

the constituent colleges. For Alfred the need to ensure this had become acute following the announcement at the beginning of the year by the American Medical Association (A.M.A.) of its refusal to recognise U.C.C. medical school. He had been charged by his colleagues in U.C.C. to reverse this decision. One of the improvements which needed to be made before the A.M.A. would reverse its decision required that the clinical teaching of Cork medical students be under the supervision of the faculty in U.C.C. In a letter to McQuaid, dated 23 January 1953, Alfred reported that he had suggested to his colleagues in Dublin and Galway that a short statement should be drafted by himself or Tierney for the Taoiseach concerning 'the autonomy of clinical teaching in the medical schools'. Initially Tierney made the counter-proposal that the presidents of the constituent colleges should write a letter to the press on 'the autonomy of medical teaching especially as affected by the proposed health bill'.[5] Monsignor de Brún, however, was not eager to do this.

On 27 February McQuaid met Tierney who agreed to arrange a meeting of the three presidents to discuss a joint-approach to the Taoiseach.[6] In a letter, written on the same day, McQuaid informed Alfred of this and urged that, even if de Brún did not agree to the suggestion, he and Tierney should call on the Taoiseach: 'firstly, to assert the principles, secondly, to secure agreement and, lastly, to maintain your link with the bishops'. He indicated his interest in the round of consultations in his concluding remark: 'I can trust you and Dr Tierney, who is most

---

5. This was the bill proposed by Dr James Ryan, minister for health, which on 21 October became the Health Act 1953, providing free mother-and-child service to dependents of all persons insured under the Social Welfare Act 1952. For more, see pp. 126-7.

6. Just prior to his meeting with McQuaid, Tierney had informed Alfred that U.C.D. had sent in 'a financial request to the government for a very large grant for new buildings, etc.' On foot of that he suggested that he alone, representing the N.U.I., should have merely a short informal conversation with the Taoiseach on the matter. In a letter to Alfred, dated 27 January 1953, Monsignor Pádraig de Brún indicated another reason why Tierney's position was somewhat invidious: 'When you bluntly said in archbishop's house that the Dublin professors of surgery and medicine are selected by Reverend Mothers, the archbishop of Dublin merely said: "that is not true", but he did not tell us how they are selected. Of course he himself is in the selection, but I cannot see how that makes things all right for the university.' And I do not believe Dr Tierney will be able to get a full account of all the process of their selection or that, even if he does, it will further the cause of university autonomy.'

Alfred O'Rahilly III: Controversialist

sympathetic to you, to take the integral view.' In the event, the three presidents met at the Shelbourne Hotel on 12 March and later proceeded to a meeting with the Taoiseach. Before returning to Cork on the following day Alfred called on McQuaid and informed him of the outcome of the meetings.

Alfred dominated the annual meeting between the presidents and the representatives of the hierarchy which was held on 20 January 1954. The establishment of a chair of theology at U.C.D. and the relationship between the N.U.I. and T.C.D. were the items on the agenda. The main discussion centred on a memorandum prepared by Alfred at the request of the bishops' representatives on 'Professorship of theology'. The bishops' representatives were in favour of the proposal to establish a chair in theology at U.C.C., and agreed to refer the matter to a full meeting of their colleagues in June and promised a decision on the matter thereafter.[7]

McQuaid was more concerned with the second item on the agenda. This referred to the attitude to be adopted to the attendance of Catholics at T.C.D. and the prospect of a break-up of the N.U.I. At the meeting on 21 January Alfred was most forthright in his demand that Catholics should have available to them a university whose ethos they found congenial. In a note to McQuaid written after the meeting he stated that public opinion was not sufficiently clear on that issue. He suggested the publication of a booklet which would set out and defend the 'minimum Catholic requirements' in a third-level institution. It should include a chapter on T.C.D. giving its history and present status in order to explain the episcopal ban on the attendance of Catholics at T.C.D.

The publication would unofficially represent the view of the bishops. However, he continued that it could not be prepared until they had decided what stand to take on 'the 1908 settlement'. He pointed out that he and Tierney held strongly differing views on this matter. Tierney, he reminded McQuaid, had been requested to prepare a memorandum for the next bi-annual meeting of the bishops on the question by Easter. He complained that they might be over-influenced by this memorandum and forget or not bear in mind the grave dangers involved in a break-up of the N.U.I. which he had outlined at the recent meeting in archbishop's house.

7. For more on this, see J. A. Gaughan, *Alfred O Rahilly I: Academic*, 144-6.

The Final Years

In a reply to Alfred, dated 22 January, McQuaid approved of the suggestion that a booklet on the university question be prepared. He stated that he had in mind something akin to 'the brochure of the late bishop of Clonfert on T.C.D.'[8] He queried Alfred's comment that he and Tierney had strongly differing views on the matter at issue, stating that in conversation with Tierney he found him to be very close to Alfred in 'general attitude'.

Alfred wrote to McQuaid from Blackrock College on 26 January. He informed him that Bishop Lucey who, earlier, had expressed reservations on the subject, had by that time agreed to the proposal about the chair of theology in U.C.C. and had asked what preliminary steps were to be taken while awaiting the June meeting of the bishops. The chair, he suggested, when established could act as a model for U.C.D. He expressed the hope that the meetings of the presidents of the N.U.I. colleges and representatives of the bishops would continue after his retirement. They had been most useful and, in particular, as a result 'Dr Tierney has adopted a very Catholic outlook.'

Alfred reminded McQuaid that there was one fundamental difference between himself and Tierney, as was clear from his replies to memoranda submitted by Tierney. This he set out as follows:

(1) Dr Tierney wants the 1908 act to be amended and our charters withdrawn or drastically modified by parliament. He wants U.C.D. to be made into a separate university in itself.

(2) I maintain that we should make the 1908 settlement for Irish Catholics sacrosanct and intangible. My reasons briefly:

    A If once we put the present system into the melting-pot, we have conceded to parliament the moral right to intervene, to pass university acts. There is in this country no power to issue charters.

    B I am convinced that the result will be much less favourable to us *as Catholics*. I do not trust the politicians, who will be 'undenominational' and will claim further rights for the State.

8. John Dignan, *Catholics and Trinity College* (C.T.S.I., Dublin 1933).

Alfred O'Rahilly III: Controversialist

C   I have challenged Dr Tierney to adduce any Catholic development which we cannot *now* carry out.

D   His arguments, even if administratively valid, are not based on any Catholic issue. For example, he hopes – vainly I think – to get rid of the representatives of the General Council of County Councils from the governing body. I have always sacrificed Cork interests (separate university for Cork) to what I believe to be the Catholic interests (charter-protected autonomy).

Alfred emphasised once more that before they could write in defence of the colleges of the N.U.I. against T.C.D. they must make up their minds as to whether they were going to stick to the 1908 settlement 'or put themselves into the hands of the Dáil'. He repeated that Tierney would be advocating the latter course and hoped that his own counter-arguments would receive due consideration.

From 1950 onwards Alfred opposed a government proposal to establish a centralised agricultural institute. Such an institute would have involved the transfer of the dairy science faculty from U.C.C. to Dublin. On his retirement, his friend and admirer, Professor Patrick M. Quinlan, became U.C.C.'s chief defender. However, Alfred continued to be pre-occupied with the controversy and in 1955 had a number of exchanges on the subject in the press with James Dillon, the minister for agriculture. By August he had decided to align the bishops to his cause. In a letter, dated 3 August, to McQuaid he wrote: 'I am replying to Mr Dillon. We ought to resist his raid on our colleges and the removal of our students to a secularist-technical institute. Behind the scenes – via Protestant farmers, etc. – T.C.D. is making strenuous efforts to get a faculty of agriculture.' In mid-August he submitted a memorandum in which he elaborated on these comments.

In 1955 Alfred was busy preparing other memoranda for McQuaid. In January he submitted two on adult education, in July he provided a further memorandum on the same subject, some weeks later he sent the archbishop a syllabus for a course in sociology. In November he prepared a memorandum which outlined a religious course for the teachers' training colleges. In 1956 he submitted only one memorandum. This was an important one, explaining that Catholic schools were essentially family schools.

The Final Years

In 1958 the government published a proposal to re-furbish the Veterinary College at Ballsbridge. In addition it was to be renamed the Irish Veterinary Hospital and managed by a board of governors which would supervise research and control undergraduate education, involving the admission of students and the appointment of staff. Lecturers from T.C.D. and U.C.D. would continue to give courses at the college and would be under the control of the board. Ninety per cent of the veterinary students were supplied by U.C.D. The U.C.D. authorities pointed this out and issued a counter-proposal. This would have involved reducing the Veterinary College to a purely clinical institution and equipping U.C.D. with a veterinary faculty comparable to its medical faculty. However, in a reference to this a spokesman for the minister for agriculture at a meeting of the Council of the Royal College of Veterinary Surgeons in London on 8 January 1959 declared that the transfer of the Veterinary College to U.C.D. 'would not be acceptable to the government'. Later the government issued a warning that if U.C.D. 'finally declines to agree to the government proposals' it would maintain 'the Veterinary College on the present basis'. This meant, in effect, no funds would be available for much needed reconstruction.

At McQuaid's request Alfred prepared a memorandum on the subject on 12 January 1959. At the outset he described the evolution of the N.U.I. in general and the Veterinary College in particular. He characterised the new proposal as a 'scheme for a secular technical institute which had to be abandoned recently for agriculture'. The new title to be given to the Veterinary College, he described as misleading. He stated that the proposed board of governors was merely a substitute for full State control. Finally, he pointed out that for the first time it was proposed that the N.U.I. and T.C.D. combine to give courses which were assumed to be of university status. Thereby, he argued, the seed was sown for undoing the 1908 settlement and for establishing a mixed secular university. And, he warned, that what was then suggested for veterinary science could equally be proposed for medicine.

McQuaid was not the only one who consulted Alfred on the issue. On 12 January 1959 Tierney called on him to discuss it. In a hurried postscript to his memorandum Alfred informed McQuaid that he had told Tierney that the government's proposal was *ultra vires* in that it violated the N.U.I. charter. He reported that he had advised Tierney to obtain a legal opinion from Patrick McGilligan, S.C., on the validity not only of the proposed arrangement but on the current status of the Veterinary College. There was no authority, he asserted, for university or college to appoint as professors persons, who were civil servants, in an outside institution where they conducted their courses. Professor J. A. Nicholson, who was acting as spokesman for the minister for agriculture, was dean of the faculty in U.C.D. and yet was independent of Tierney and the college. Alfred suggested that if the N.U.I. withdrew from its association with the Veterinary College the government would be 'really up against it', as by agreement with the U.K. Irish veterinary surgeons had to have a university degree. Eventually an arrangement was agreed whereby from 1960 onwards the staff and equipment of the college became the responsibility of the two universities with the department of agriculture continuing to maintain the buildings and to provide the non-technical staff.[9]

Alfred reported that he and Tierney had also discussed the Dental Hospital. They regarded the situation there as unsatisfactory. But at least it was a hospital with lectures being given in U.C.D. They agreed that dental departments attached to St Vincent's and the Mater Hospitals would be much better and in the long run cheaper to construct than a refurbishment of the Dental Hospital.

In the second week of January 1960 Alfred provided two memoranda for McQuaid on refresher courses which had been held in T.C.D. for teachers of science in secondary schools. He warned that such courses could trench more and more on educational, social and humanistic issues and he proposed that alternative courses be held at U.C.D. and other centres. On a more positive note he proposed that an Institute of Catholic Education for the archdiocese of Dublin be established which would encourage and supervise the provision of Catholic education at every level. In a letter, dated 15 January 1960, Fr Liam Martin, the archbishop's secretary responsible for educational matters, informed Alfred that McQuaid agreed with his proposals and was about to put them into effect.

9. For a history of the Veterinary College up to the late 1960s, see E. A. Hirsch, 'Veterinary education in Ireland: a historical review', *Irish Veterinary Journal* 23 (1969) 158-68.

The Final Years

In mid-October 1960 McQuaid sought Alfred's advice on a symposium for secondary schools which had been held by the Dublin branch of the British Biological Institute. At the same time he proposed that a seminar be held for the heads of secondary schools in the archdiocese on university education. In a letter to Alfred, dated 17 October, Fr Martin stated that the seminar suggested by the archbishop could be used to further the establishment of the institute or 'centralising structure' which had been proposed to ensure a united and unifying policy on Catholic education in the archdiocese. Ten days later Martin informed Alfred that already some steps had been taken towards the establishment of the institute. A council of administration for primary schools had been established, as had a committee to supervise adult education. In addition, there was a committee supervising and extending the activities and influence of priest-teachers in vocational schools. In the meantime Martin urged that they press on with organising the seminar for the principals of secondary schools in the archdiocese. He arranged to call on Alfred to discuss a three-fold theme which he proposed as follows:

(1) Is there such a thing as a specifically Catholic university education?
(2) If such exists is it to be had in Ireland?
(3) How can the Catholic secondary schools of this diocese forward the cause of Catholic university education in University College, Dublin?

On 27 October McQuaid wrote to Alfred. He informed him that Captain Peadar Cowan had succeeded in having the Cultural Commission of Dublin Corporation put forward two resolutions for an increase of primary and university scholarships – the latter 'to be held in the University of Dublin or in any constituent college of the N.U.I.' and he asked to be enlightened on 'the true case of the scholarships under the 1908 settlement'. In addition, he requested Alfred to give him the case against a fusion of the N.U.I. with T.C.D. He informed Alfred that some people were advocating 'a system by which either one University of Dublin is recognised with the present N.U.I. as the Catholic counterpart of, and separate from, T.C.D. or one N.U.I. with T.C.D. a college for Protestants'. Alfred met

Alfred O'Rahilly III: Controversialist

McQuaid at his residence in Killiney a week later to discuss submissions he made on these issues.

As the Commission on Higher Education began its proceedings McQuaid became anxious as to what it would recommend. He requested advice from Alfred with regard to a possible break-up of the N.U.I. In a note introducing a memorandum of 21 December 1960 it was clear that Alfred had changed his mind on the subject. He reminded the archbishop that he had hitherto opposed tampering with the N.U.I. charter. But, he warned, they could no longer adopt a *non possumus* attitude. U.C.D. wished to be an independent university. U.C.C. would not object to becoming one. U.C.G. would be left without a choice in the matter. He had always upheld university autonomy and Catholic rights. Yet at that stage, provided they retained their guarantees, he did not consider that the continuance of the N.U.I. should be made 'a Catholic issue'. Even if the break-up of the N.U.I. were not contemplated, there was an overwhelming demand for a modification of the college charters. The Commission would not allow that problem to be shelved.

Alfred set out a preliminary survey of the memorandum which McQuaid would require as follows:

(1) Trinity College
   A critical investigation of its present position to show how utterly unsuitable it is for Catholics. (It is very likely that some members of the Commission will report in favour of 'amalgamation' of the N.U.I. [or at least U.C.D.] with T.C.D.)
(2) A restatement of the minimal claims made in the past by the hierarchy on behalf of the Catholics of Ireland. These were conceded by the British government. It would be monstrous if a native government attempted to whittle them down.
(3) The N.U.I.
   This will show that at present we have the essentials of the Catholic demands conceded.
(4) The conditions under which the N.U.I. could be allowed to be superseded.

Alfred set out the reasons why the break-up of the N.U.I. had to be envisaged. Without advocating this development they had to be prepared for it and be ready to declare how far it was acceptable if carried out. Only if certain legal procedures were practicable and conceded could they agree to the abandonment of the charters. He suggested as minimum requirements (a) the issue of new charters and (b) future modifications thereof by 'letters patent' issued by the president or by the executive council without intervention by the legislature. To ensure these he recommended that the Irish hierarchy should intervene at an opportune time through their two colleagues on the Commission.

On 23 December Alfred reported to McQuaid on a long discussion which he had on the previous day with Tierney about the Commission on Higher Education. They agreed that a committee of the Irish bishops should focus on three main issues from a Catholic standpoint and then intervene. The first issue concerned Trinity College. They agreed that a clear statement should be prepared showing why fusion between the N.U.I. and T.C.D. was to be rejected. This involved a detailed examination of T.C.D., 'especially as regards its "ideological" or cultural-religious education'. Once its pretensions to absorb U.C.D. and propaganda in that regard was checked there was a need for co-operation between the two institutions.

The second issue discussed was the need to modify the N.U.I. charters without an act of parliament. They envied the immunity and autonomy of T.C.D. which had a flexible charter, and even controlled the selection of visitors (the chancellor plus one other). It was most probable that charters could be modified by 'letters patent' issued by the government. However, the practice had been that even a slight change in a charter (for example, of a hospital or the institution of civil engineers) had been made by an act of parliament. They agreed that any doubt in the matter with regard to the N.U.I. charters could be rectified by a general act. Alfred volunteered to obtain the best legal opinion on the matter. On the third issue Alfred and Tierney agreed that if the question of the charters were solved the project of breaking up the N.U.I. need not arise. If by modification of the charters the difficulties in the administration of the N.U.I. and its colleges were eased, the present constitution would be quite workable.

In the second week of January 1961 Alfred provided a memorandum on the relationship between secondary schools and a new apprenticeship scheme introduced by the department of education. Fr Martin on 9 January thanked him for the 'flood of light' which he shed on the subject and continued that his memoranda had 'effects all along the line'. The newly formed Council of Administration for primary schools in the archdiocese, he stated, would have not come into existence were it not for a memorandum on primary schools or family schools which Alfred had submitted five years earlier. He concluded: 'You furnished us with the basis for administrative measures, policies and the necessary impulse.'

Also at the beginning of 1961 Alfred prepared a memorandum in which he was critical of initiatives which had been taken by the Agricultural Institute. It seems that the director, Dr Tom Walsh, had written to Tierney and invited professors in the faculty of agriculture in U.C.D. to act as advisors and research scholars in the Institute. In return Institute research-workers acted as 'demonstrators', in effect, lecturers, in the faculty of agriculture in U.C.D. Dr Walsh had also arranged for some of the Institute's research scholars to provide lectures in T.C.D. On foot of this T.C.D. listed in its prospectus a moderatorship (B.A.) which Tierney subsequently described 'as designed chiefly for our B.Agr.Sc. graduates, enticing them to get a Trinity topdressing and to be more sure of a job in the Institute'. At Alfred's suggestion McQuaid brought the matter to the attention of Tierney, who, in a letter, dated 19 January 1961, replied: 'Should Trinity College persist in its public claim that it has the assistance of the Institute staff for the purposes of its primary degree teaching, I shall be prepared to recommend that we break off all relations with the Institute.'

At that time the increasing number of Catholics who were opting to attend T.C.D. rather than U.C.D. was causing McQuaid some anxiety. He arranged a seminar for the heads of secondary schools in the archdiocese on 6 and 7 May in an attempt to ensure that they would direct their pupils, going on to third level, to U.C.D. rather than T.C.D. On 6 May Alfred gave two lectures; the first was entitled 'The nature of Catholic university education', the second 'Catholic university education in our Irish circumstances'. On the following day he presided at lectures by Tierney and Fr Patrick Tuohy, the senior chaplain at U.C.D. After each of the lectures there was group discussion on two sets of twelve questions prepared by Alfred at the request of the organising committee.

The Final Years

In October Alfred submitted to McQuaid three memoranda on the relationship between the university and Higher Institutes of Technology. At that time he also provided a memorandum on the theological faculty at Queen's University, Belfast. In the following month he submitted his views on how the chaplains could 'Catholicize' U.C.D. He recalled that he had introduced the Legion of Mary into U.C.C. However, he soon realised that it was not very helpful to busy undergraduates. Perhaps he continued, Patrician conferences – meetings sponsored by the Legion of Mary for the discussion of religion – would be more appropriate. He referred to a proposal he had already made, namely, that 'apologetics – call it religion or theology' be made an optional university subject. It would be useful not only to lay people and future teachers but also to nuns. With regard to the supervision of student accommodation he considered this to be a kind of police service and should not be imposed on spiritual guides. For this work 'quasi-proctors' should be employed.

Subsequently McQuaid had Rev Professor Conor Martin, Rev Professor E. F. O'Doherty and Fr Patrick Tuohy call on Alfred on 31 November to discuss his suggestions and learn about initiatives in this area which he had taken at U.C.C. In a note to McQuaid about their discussion he described his visitors as 'fine men; the two professors are keen and scholarly, the chaplain devoted and zealous'. He declared that discussion groups organised by the chaplains were doing excellent work and seemed to be a good substitute for Patrician conferences. The three U.C.D. men, it seems, were far less sympathetic than their archbishop to Alfred's plan to 'Catholicize' U.C.D. They had urged caution and gave him the impression that the general outlook of the staff in U.C.D. was 'non-Catholic to a greater extent than in U.C.C.' According to them this was due largely to fear of clerical control and an exaggeration of the non-sectarian character of the N.U.I. They considered that philosophy courses should not be openly advocated, that medical ethics could not be made a university course and that theology (apologetics) could not be introduced, probably for another generation, when students came better prepared from the secondary schools and the staff-outlook had been changed!

Towards the end of 1961 the government announced that it intended to rationalise courses in Dublin leading to a degree in dentistry. It proposed to amalgamate those provided by the

Alfred O'Rahilly III: Controversialist

College of Surgeons, T.C.D. and U.C.D. into a single faculty of dental science. This meant that the school of dentistry at U.C.D. would be absorbed into a new institution. The alarm bells rang in U.C.D. and in the archbishop's house. At McQuaid's request, Alfred provided a memorandum on the subject. He pointed out that Article 42 of the constitution made it clear that parental rights were paramount in education. And he emphasised that this referred to the education of all students in *statu pupillari* extending from primary school to undergraduate university students. He pointed out with a quotation that the current minister for education, Dr. Patrick Hillery, had endorsed the application of that constitutional principle to university education during a debate in Dail Éireann on 23 March 1960.[10]

Throughout most of 1961 Alfred was engaged in research for the four articles on university education which, at McQuaid's request, he published in *Studies*.[11] The second article which appeared in the journal's 1961 winter edition was well received by Fr Martin. In a letter to Alfred, dated 20 November, he stated that he had already prepared to make offprints available to the heads of the secondary schools and that he intended to ask the Dublin Institute of Sociology, the Catholic Workers' College, the Dublin Adult Education Committee and the Legion of Mary curiae to help in publicising it and in its distribution. He also informed him that 'the T.C.D. circles are very angry and perplexed at your article and find it unanswerable'. A letter from McQuaid on the following day was less partisan in tone. He wrote: 'All your points are valid and are to me very welcome . . . Can't you now see against what a current I have had, and

---

10. Dr Hillery stated: 'I would not be a party to the creation of a position in which the parents of any religious denomination, either that of the majority or the minority, who seek university education for their children, should find themselves with no alternative to the placing of their children, in violation of conscience, in a particular educational institution . . . either directly or indirectly . . . To the letter and spirit of the non-forcing of conscience laid down in the constitution, must be subject any question of a re-apportionment – or redistribution or amalgamation or rationalisation or whatever it may be called – of facilities or courses throughout the four university colleges that may at any time arise.'

11. For more on these, see J. A. Gaughan, *Alfred O'Rahilly III: Controversialist, Part I: Social Reformer* (Dublin 1992) 216-17. In a letter to Fr Martin, dated 3 November 1961, Alfred indicated his intention to develop the four articles in *Studies* into a book of about two hundred pages which would be a comprehensive treatment of third-level education.

still have, to row? We have not a concept of what is a university, Catholic in content and outlook, if not in legal forms!' By return of post Alfred thanked McQuaid for his encouragement and added: 'Sometimes I feel rather isolated.'

Alfred was given an early opportunity to learn how unpopular the unfavourable treatment of T.C.D. in his article was with members of the academic community. He was the principal speaker at a meeting of Pax Romana in U.C.D. on 27 November 1961. Professor John J. O'Meara was in the chair. Alfred made it clear that he did not regard U.C.D. as a Catholic university. In this he claimed that he differed from the archbishop. However, he declared that it was an institution which could be made Catholic in outlook and spirit and which could create a Catholic tradition if its members so resolved and acted on that resolve. He was bitterly attacked from the floor. But, characteristically, he more than matched his critics. This led O'Meara to insist on Alfred retracting some comments he made. The summing-up by O'Meara was later described by a number of Alfred's admirers as 'totally unfair'.[12]

Alfred was hurt by the attacks at the Pax Romana meeting. This he indicated in a letter to Fr Martin, dated 29 November, as well as the fact that at a recent Patrician meeting,[13] which discussed the episcopal ban on T.C.D., the only real supporter he had found was General Michael J. Costello. He told Martin that he had supplied McQuaid with a report of the Pax Romana meeting and continued:

> Something has happened to the 'public relations' of the Church in Dublin. The insidious propaganda of T.C.D. and of the *Irish Times* has had a devastating effect. The students – at least the vocal element – and the good Catholic professional men are all for T.C.D. Even the clergy, I feel, are so bewitched with 'ecumenism' that they think it is wrong

12. In a long letter of complaint, dated 30 November, one of O'Meara's colleagues charged him with adopting a patronising and even insulting attitude to Alfred and concluded: 'The chief purpose of this letter is not to argue about universities but to make the strongest protest against the unworthy treatment of Monsignor O'Rahilly. If he were not a priest, he would not need anyone else to rush to his defence, but because he is muzzled I, for one, resent the fact that in an Irish university his views have been belittled and dismissed on the grounds that he has to act as the spokesman of the archbishop.'
13. See p. 172.

to stand up for our own rights – even if we concede equal rights to Protestants. What I might call the merger mentality is in the ascendant. I have reason to believe that many of the S.Js and of the C.S.Sps[14] are against me. So I feel very isolated and discouraged.

But he concluded defiantly:

Yet I cannot convince myself that I am wrong. I have not adopted my views just to please the archbishop. I have taken this stand all my life. But I think His Grace agrees with me.

In a reply, dated 30 November, Martin alleged that he had evidence that the Pax Romana meeting had been 'rigged'. Alfred had expressed his disappointment that even after his article on T.C.D., the archbishop's pastoral and the seminar at Clonliffe College in the previous May the Catholic position on higher education was little appreciated by so many priests and laypeople. To this Martin replied that it was too much to expect that the trend of a whole period from the death of Archbishop Walsh to the accession of the serving archbishop could be easily reversed. He continued that it was essential to persuade the parish clergy and the religious, who were responsible for secondary schools, of the merit of the bishops' prohibition of the attendance of Catholics at T.C.D. This task would not be easy, he noted, because of the campaign of propaganda in favour of lifting the ban and the denigration by implication of the N.U.I. colleges. He described those who favoured the lifting of the episcopal ban on T.C.D. as 'a small band of active adversaries, who were very disturbed by (a) the advance of U.C.D., (b) the archbishop's pastoral and (c) your articles and speeches'. Martin warned Alfred that he would have to face a very determined opposition. However, he assured him that the archbishop and his staff admired his stand and depended on him to provide material to help educate the Catholic community on the matter.

14. Alfred was aware that there was not much enthusiasm among the priests in Blackrock College for his strong support for the continuance of the episcopal ban on T.C.D. In an earlier letter to Fr Martin, dated 24 November, he had complained that his recently published article in *Studies* had provoked little public debate. In a reply, dated 27 November, Martin suggested that 'supporters of T.C.D.' and an uncharacteristically reticent *Irish Times* were determined 'to kill by silence the effect of this unanswerable indictment.'

The Final Years

By return of post Alfred, as ever delighted with a challenge, informed Martin that he would not shirk taking on their adversaries. On 2 December Martin thanked him for this reassurance. He agreed with Alfred that 'things have been allowed to drift, especially in University College, Dublin'. The reason for this and the strong public opinion among Catholics in favour of T.C.D. he set out as follows: 'I have discovered from the priests still living who were secretaries to Archbishop Walsh that he was quite alone in this matter, amongst both his fellow bishops and clergy of the time, in striving for university rights for Catholics. A small minority of Catholics, lay and cleric, opposed his policy in regard to T.C.D. bitterly.' He explained the antipathy to the archbishop in U.C.D. which Alfred reported as due to a 'fear of clerical domination of appointments in U.C.D.' To Alfred's expression of surprise at the number of members of religious orders who disagreed with the official Catholic attitude to T.C.D., Martin responded mean-spiritedly that such fears harked 'back to the days before 1916 in their prejudices, if not in their memories, when their colleges supplied so much to Trinity College'.

In the first part of 1962 Alfred was busy preparing his two final articles on university education for *Studies*. In early May he provided McQuaid with a memorandum on the teaching of Christian doctrine in primary schools. Later in the month he provided a memorandum proposing that continuation courses be held in those schools.

Memoranda on second-level education

Towards the end of the year there was much criticism in the press of secondary education. It was suggested that the current system should be replaced, that the State should take over secondary education and buy out the existing institutions. The minister for education indicated that he was considering a radical change in the registration of secondary school students. Neither headmasters nor teachers' representatives were consulted or informed about the proposed changes which, it was accepted, were under consideration by the department of education. This prompted a request by McQuaid to Alfred in early December for a memorandum on the situation. Under the heading 'The constitutional position' Alfred pointed out that nearly all schools in the country were family or parental institutions. Thus any alteration in the system should not and need not involve any infringement of parental choice. Under 'Financial Aid' he quoted article 42 of the constitution which prescribes that 'The State shall provide for free primary education, and shall endeavour to supplement and give reasonable aid to private and corporate educational initiative.' He went on to illustrate how the State's contribution to secondary education was 'lamentably deficient'. Under the heading 'Recognised pupils in secondary schools' he noted that only pupils recognised by the department of education counted for a capitation grant made to the school and their total also determined the number of teachers whose incremental salaries were paid by the State. He argued against the suggestion that there should be a national state examination to determine entry to secondary schools. With regard to the basic sciences he admitted that secondary schools, as a whole, were defective. But this arose largely from financial stringency, owing to government neglect. The remedy lay not in deprecating the secondary schools but in equipping them.

In a section on 'Vocational schools' he compared the situation in Ireland to that existing in Holland. Catholic technical or vocational schools in Holland trained 31% of all the technical students while Catholics constituted 40% of the total population. And those Catholic technical schools were '100% supported by public funds'. In Ireland vocational schools were State institutions administered by local committees. However their undenominationalism was partially atoned for by the appointment of chaplains and priest-teachers.

A few weeks later Alfred provided a second memorandum on secondary education. Further information on the government's intentions had been obtained. These envisaged the establishment of a new type of secondary school in any area where second-level education, apart from that in a vocational school, was not already available within a radius of ten miles. Beginning in the west and north-west of Ireland the State was to build, equip and maintain these new schools. Each would be administered by a small committee which would appoint the manager who would have the same status as the chief executive officer in a vocational school. In some undefined way in these schools with a predominantly Catholic student body the Catholic

13. Group after Alfred's ordination at Blackrock College on 18 December 1955. *Left to right*: Professor Cecil O'Rahilly (Dublin Institute for Advanced Studies), Alfred, Archbishop John C. McQuaid (Dublin), Fr Aloysius (Anthony) O'Rahilly, O.C.S.O. (Mount St Joseph's, Roscrea), Sister M. Julie O'Rahilly (Irish Sisters of Charity, Foxford) and Fr Vincent J. Dinan, C.S.Sp. (president, Blackrock College)

14. Archbishop John J. McCarthy (Nairobi), Fr Vincent J. Dinan, C.S.Sp., and Alfre
    Blackrock College, August 1960

15. Group at Clonliffe College centenary celebration on 12 October 1960. *Left to right, back row*: Monsignor Thomas O'Reilly, Michael Tierney (president, U.C.D.), **Alfred**, Monsignor Richard J. Glennon, Monsignor Patrick Boylan. *Front row*: Bishop Daniel Cohalan (Waterford), Bishop Michael J. Browne (Galway), Bishop William MacNeely (Raphoe), Canon Cathal McCarthy (president of Holy Cross College, Clonliffe), Archbishop Thomas Morris (Cashel), Eamon de Valera (president of Ireland), Cardinal John D'Alton (Armagh), Seán Lemass, T.D. (Taoiseach), Archbishop John C. McQuaid (Dublin), Archbishop Joseph Walsh (Tuam), Maurice Dockrell, T.D. (lord mayor of Dublin), Bishop James McNamee (Ardagh and Clonmacnois). For a key to the identification of the other persons in this remarkable picture, see Richard Sherry, *Holy Cross College, Clonliffe, Dublin, 1859–1959* (Dublin 1962) 209

16. Alfred, General Seán Mac Eoin and Frank Duff (co-founder of Legion of Mary) outside Booterstown church on 7 July 1965 after Alfred had officiated at the marriage of Richard M. Humphreys and Deirdre Flanagan

The Final Years

bishop would have some influence, but, like vocational schools, the new schools would be grouped on a county not a diocesan basis.[15] It was desirable to have at least one priest on the staff. The general idea was to confine the new schools to purely literary subjects and to send the students to the nearest vocational school for scientific and practical subjects. The schools would be free or at least the fees would be no more than nominal.

Alfred felt that it was obvious that the new scheme was inspired by the modern or comprehensive schools of England. He regretted this form of Anglicization and the fact that the school-systems in Holland and the Canadian province of Quebec had not been taken as models. In conclusion he stated that the proposed schools and vocational schools were but the first step into a State alternative system to Catholic secondary schools, maintained by preferential provision of public monies. And, as such, this scheme was not only unconstitutional but also in violation of natural rights and distributive justice.

In the first week of 1963 a two-page memorandum prepared by Bishop Vincent Hanly of Elphin on behalf of the Irish bishops as a response to the department's proposal for the new schools was circulated. McQuaid who was in Rome for the Second Vatican Council sent his copy to Alfred and requested his comments on it. After receiving some clarifications from McQuaid on the Hanly memorandum he pointed out that more than a century earlier the bishops had to protest to the British government against a scheme practically the same as that now being contemplated: 'We have the most decided objection to the principle on which such schools are established, inasmuch as they tend to throw into the hands of the State, acting through a body of commissioners, the education of the country . . .'[16]

Alfred suggested that a diocesan committee be established to study the proposals and make recommendations to the depart-

---

15. Eventually it was decided that each comprehensive school would be controlled by an executive consisting of (a) a representative of the bishop (Catholic or Protestant as appropriate), (b) a C.E.O. and (c) a representative of the department of education (an inspector). In the event, soon afterwards comprehensive schools were established at Carraroe, Cootehill, Glenties and Shannon, and a few years later at Ballymun in Dublin and one for Protestants at Raphoe. Subsequently, two Protestant comprehensive schools were provided in Dublin and another in Cork.
16. P. F. Moran (ed.), *The pastoral letters and other writings of Cardinal Cullen, archbishop of Dublin, etc.* II (Dublin 1882) 99-100.

ment. This procedure was followed. After attending the first meeting of the committee Alfred declared himself to be heartened by the exchange of views. He suggested to McQuaid that the bishops should immediately inform the department that the Catholics of the country would show vehement opposition by every constitutional means to (1) the removal of the present mode of decision as to the admission of recognised secondary school students and its replacement by a State country-wide written examination, (2) the establishment of new hybrid secondary schools which, on the analogy of the vocational schools, will be undenominational, co-educational institutions under the control of the department. He added that it was high time that a concerted demand be made for much greater financial aid for Catholic, Jewish and Protestant schools as regards building costs, interest-free loans, extensions, maintenance and equipment. Those responsible for those schools were being blamed for defects which were remediable only if the government did its duty.

On 20 May 1963 Dr Patrick Hillery, minister for education, announced plans for the establishment of comprehensive schools and regional technical colleges. This prompted McQuaid to request Alfred for advice on the matter. As Alfred was not clear what was required, he provided an extended synthesis of various memoranda already submitted. 'Education and the State in Ireland' dealt with (1) primary education, (2) secondary education, (3) vocational schools and (4) university education[17] and the recurring theme was his conviction of the need for his fellow-citizens to insist on their constitutional right

17. He still supported the episcopal ban on T.C.D.: 'The attitude of the hierarchy in prohibiting, except with the permission of the Ordinary, the attendance of Catholic students in T.C.D. is amply justified. We are not a minority here; we are 95% Catholics. And we have an institution of high academic standards, where the faith of Catholics is not endangered . . . Statistics of attendance at U.C.D. show that the vast majority of Irish Catholic parents willingly accept the decision of our hierarchy. The special circumstances of our country justify this attitude. T.C.D. is a much older institution with acquired prestige; it has a splendid site and fine buildings. In comparison, U.C.D. has been hampered and neglected. It will take several years before adequate accommodation is provided on the new site at Belfield. Only when this equality is reached and T.C.D. openly acknowledges that Irish Catholics rightfully have a university of their own might the vigilance of our bishops become more flexible. Meanwhile the present "ban" strengthens the hands of Irish Catholic parents against the enticements of propaganda and snobbery.'

The Final Years

to denominational education at every level. In November he provided a number of memoranda on how much better use could be made of the Catholic School Managers' Association particularly with a view to conducting negotiations with the department of education. The Association, on the initiative of McQuaid, had forged closer links with the Irish bishops and had thereby already become more effective in carrying on a continuous dialogue with the department. The memoranda supplied by Alfred were described by Fr Martin, in a letter dated 20 November, as a much-needed statement of the principles on the basis of which the association should negotiate with the department.

After the general election in April 1965 George Colley succeeded Dr Patrick Hillery as minister for education and set about implementing the plan for establishing comprehensive schools. He also set about amalgamating small country primary schools. He disclosed his department's thinking and policy on this matter at a public meeting in Galway attended by Bishop Michael Browne. The latter objected to the proposals in so far as they would lead to the closure of a great number of small country schools. There followed an exchange between the two and a walk out by a testy Bishop Browne which was reported in the press. To Browne's objection that the wishes of parents had to be a prime concern, Colley claimed that T.Ds. represented parents.

McQuaid, who was again in Rome for the Vatican Council, requested a comment from Alfred on Colley's claim and further advice on the proposed comprehensive schools. Clearly he had been dismayed by the result of inquiries he had already made in the matter. In a letter to Alfred, dated 24 October 1965, he wrote: 'This new minister for education, a cold, forceful lawyer, is examining how "privato" are our schools, if we take a State subsidy. He will sanction no secondary school, unless his survey declares it needful (not because it is the choice of the parents), nor give any help to it at all.' McQuaid's comment on Colley was uncharacteristically partial. Although single-minded, Colley was most genial, engaged in widespread consultation and his promotion out of the department in 1966 was greatly regretted by all who were involved in education.

In a letter, dated 25 October, Alfred stated that if he were still a layman he would have vigorously replied to Colley in the press. The minister's remarks were tantamount to a claim that with regard to the establishment of a school the decisions of the executive were paramount and superseded the managers and the groups of parents concerned. He had no doubt that such a claim was unconstitutional and was rejected by the Supreme Court in 1944. Although he declared himself to be unclear as to what McQuaid required, he proposed to draft a memorandum on the subject. He suggested that in the meantime, with a view to strengthening the position of school-managers, there should be closer contact between them, parents and teachers.

Before drafting his memorandum Alfred requested information from McQuaid concerning Colley's remarks to Bishop Browne and the policy of the minister and his department on secondary schools. McQuaid referred Alfred to Mother M. Jordana, O.P., chairwoman of the Conference of Convent Secondary Schools, and Fr Seán Hughes, S.J., chairman of the Catholic Headmasters' Association, who were then representing the managerial associations of Catholic secondary schools in meetings with the minister and his officials. In this way Alfred was informed of the comments made by Colley to Browne but was not able to obtain the department's detailed policy on existing secondary schools or on the proposed comprehensive schools. Alfred obtained a legal opinion from Patrick McGilligan, S.C., which endorsed his own view of Colley's claim in the exchange with Browne.

On 7 November McQuaid complained to Alfred that the department of education had issued no written statement of policy on comprehensive schools and added: 'There is a policy but it has not been declared and it is being worked out as they move forward experimentally.' He suggested that Alfred compare a report sent to the archbishop's house by Fr Hughes of a meeting between the representatives of the managerial associations and the minister in May with 'the slanted report later issued by the department'. He also suggested that Alfred should arrange a meeting with Mother Jordana and Fr Hughes. On 10 November Alfred replied that, in spite of his best efforts, he was not able from statements published by the department 'to get a clear-cut issue re secondary schools which could be controverted'. He alleged that the minutes of the meeting in May had been so 'skilfully disguised' by the officials of the department that even when circulated to members of the Irish hierarchy they

The Final Years

provoked no objection. In conclusion he warned: 'It would appear that two officials of the department influence the minister and are covertly preparing an invasion of parental rights.'

By 13 November McQuaid had still not acquired a clear grasp of the department's policy on comprehensive schools and he urged Alfred to meet Mother Jordana and Fr Hughes again to try to get some further information on the subject. Even after that meeting Alfred was not able in his report to shed much further light on the government's policy, as, it seems, no detailed policy had been formulated and so the officials in the department could not provide any details about it. Not long afterwards McQuaid's worries about the nature of the proposed comprehensive schools became academic, as the government, ultimately on the advice of the department of finance, moved instead to set up community schools.[18]

Exchange with Provost McConnell

By the end of 1960 Alfred had resigned himself to a break-up of the N.U.I. He had been influenced by Tierney's tireless advocacy of an independent U.C.D. and the likely prospect that the Commission on Higher Education would recommend that development. By the autumn of 1965 he had concluded that the episcopal ban on the attendance of Catholics at T.C.D. had outlived its usefulness. The transfer of U.C.D. from Earlsfort Terrace to Belfield had begun and with it the prospect of a campus which would at the very least match that of T.C.D. He had been greatly impressed by the views of representatives of the Catholic members of the teaching staff of T.C.D. who had invited him to meet them to discuss the matter. More importantly a new ethos had been ushered in by the Second Vatican Council. In letters, in November 1965, to Albert J. McConnell, provost of T.C.D., he suggested that the best arrangement for university education in the metropolis was the inclusion of T.C.D. and U.C.D. inside the University of Dublin.

In a gracious acknowledgement, dated 7 December 1965, McConnell agreed. But he declared that he did not see such a solution working until the ground for its success had been

18. For more on the comprehensive schools and other radical developments in the educational system in the 1960s, see E. Randles, *Post-primary education in Ireland 1957-1970* (Dublin 1975).

Alfred O'Rahilly III: Controversialist

prepared. He regretted that, while there was considerable cooperation and good will between staff and students in particular schools of the two Dublin colleges, there existed none at the highest levels of the two institutions. In spite of efforts by T.C.D. members, he complained, to contact and co-operate with those in U.C.D. there was no encouragement from that quarter. Alfred, he continued, would know from experience the want of co-operation from U.C.D. even towards the Cork and Galway colleges which had made the N.U.I. so ineffective.

McConnell's assessment of who was responsible at the highest level on the U.C.D. side for the negative attitude to T.C.D. was uninformed. Alfred and McQuaid were as responsible as Tierney. Perhaps McConnell's close friendship with both of them partially blinded him to this. On 22 March 1967 the Commission on Higher Education published its recommendations, the principal ones of which were: (1) U.C.D., U.C.C. and U.C.G. to become independent universities replacing the N.U.I. and (2) T.C.D. to remain a separate university. A month later Donogh O'Malley, minister for education, since Colley's transfer to the department of industry and commerce in July 1966, announced the government's intention to combine T.C.D. and U.C.D. in one university of Dublin. Alfred privately welcomed this.

On 5 July 1968 Brian Lenihan, who had succeeded O'Malley, announced that the N.U.I. was to be dissolved; U.C.C. and U.C.G. to become separate universities; and T.C.D. and U.C.D. to be combined in one university of Dublin but each to retain its identity and to have equal representation on the new institution's governing body. Largely because of financial stringency these plans were never implemented. However, they facilitated agreement on 7 April 1970 between representatives of T.C.D. and U.C.D. on a wide range of issues. Three months later with a collective sigh of relief the Catholic bishops announced the removal of their restrictions on Catholics attending T.C.D.

Theories of Fr Denis Fahey, C.S.Sp.

During his stay at Blackrock College Alfred usually took his meals with Fr Michael McCarthy, C.S.Sp., and Dr Michael O'Carroll, C.S.Sp. The three became very close friends. Frs McCarthy and O'Carroll were frequently surprised at how informed and up to date Alfred was on any subject which arose

The Final Years

in conversation. Although Alfred tended to dominate the conversation,[19] his comments were always worth a hearing. There was scarcely a topic which the three did not discuss. One topic, it seems, was never raised. This concerned the theories of Fr Denis Fahey, C.S.Sp., who had been professor of philosophy and church history at the Holy Ghost Missionary College, Kimmage, Dublin. From 1931 onwards Fahey, whom Alfred never met, wrote extensively on Church-State relations and cognate matters in terms of a world-wide struggle between the spiritual and the temporal.[20] His views on 'Judaeo-Masonic subversive activities' in general and the Jewish people in particular caused considerable concern. Many people, including several bishops, a number of priests and Frank Duff, founder of the Legion of Mary, objected to Fahey's more extreme ideas when he first published them. David Goldstein, an American Jewish convert to Catholicism, published an article criticising Fahey's theory that communism was a Jewish invention supported by the Jews worldwide.

By the end of his life it was well-nigh impossible for Fahey to have his books reviewed or given an 'imprimatur'.[21] The appearance of *The kingship of Christ and the conversion of the Jewish nation* with an 'imprimatur' from Dr James Staunton, bishop of Ferns, caused consternation in ecclesiastical

---

19. Dr Michael O'Carroll recalled introducing Alfred to John D. Sheridan. Alfred was delighted to meet the humorist and proceeded to tell him how much he enjoyed his writing. Later Dr O'Carroll informed Sheridan that Alfred had enjoyed the conversation. To which Sheridan replied that probably Alfred assumed it was a conversation but that in fact it had been a monologue.

20. Fahey's works include: *The kingship of Christ according to the principles of St Thomas Aquinas* (Dublin 1931), *The mystical body of Christ in the modern world* (Dublin 1935), *The rulers of Russia* (Dublin 1939), *The kingship of Christ and organised naturalism* (Dublin 1943), *Money manipulation and social order* (Cork 1944), *The mystical body of Christ and the re-organisation of society* (Cork 1945), *The kingship of Christ and the conversion of the Jewish nation* (Dublin 1953) and *The Church and farming* (Cork 1953). He also translated a number of pamphlets on these subjects from the French. For a neat summary of the life and work of Fr Fahey, see *Irish Independent* 22 January 1954.

21. Fahey did receive an 'imprimatur' for his books. However, it should be remembered that the 'imprimatur' does not signify ecclesiastical approval of political ideas or authentication of claimed historical facts, but only a judgement that a work contains no doctrinal or moral error. As time passed, however, the ecclesiastical authorities became alarmed at the moral and doctrinal implications of Fahey's tendency to attribute virtually all evils in modern history to the 'organised naturalism' of the Jews.

circles.[22] Archbishop McQuaid had a meeting with Dr Staunton on the issue and let it be known that he did not consider that any copies of Fr Fahey's latest book should be sold in the Catholic bookstores of the archdiocese. When Fr Fahey died in 1954 Archbishop McQuaid sent a note that he 'must be absent' from the funeral. He also insisted that Maria Duce, an organisation established by Fr Fahey's admirers and supporters, curtail its activities. In 1955 he persuaded its leaders to change its name to Fírinne, which had been the name of Maria Duce's Irish-speaking subsidiary.

Archbishop McQuaid never formally recognised Maria Duce and it seems was deeply concerned that some of its activities and ideals were associated with the name of the Mother of God to whom he had a singular personal devotion. In 1954 he had asked Fr G. Thomas Fehily, director of the Dublin Institute of Catholic Sociology, to report on the organisation. Both were surprised at the size of its membership. With branches in Belfast, Cork and Limerick, as well as Dublin, there were some two hundred members and about a thousand associate members.

Some members of Maria Duce were expelled from the Legion of Mary when they had attempted to infiltrate that organisation. Fr Fahey's former confreres were also embarrassed by his anti-semitic views and those of his followers. After his death they discouraged members of Maria Duce/Fírinne from organising annual demonstrations at his grave, suggesting that people only make private visits to the cemetery. Thereafter the movement dwindled and became extinct.

Alfred's uncharacteristic reticence about the writings and activities of Fr Fahey was almost certainly due to his awareness of the acute embarrassment they caused members of the Holy Ghost Order. Fr Michael O'Carroll could recall only one comment by Alfred on Fahey during his fifteen years in Blackrock

22. It seems that Fahey requested and was refused an 'imprimatur' for *The kingship of Christ and the conversion of the Jewish nation* from those bishops who had been more co-operative with regard to his earlier books. The book was eventually published with the 'imprimatur' of the bishop of Ferns, but it remains unclear as to whether the episcopal approval was actually received. When the question was raised at that time, it was stated, on behalf of Dr Staunton, that the publishers had simply presumed the 'imprimatur'. The editor of the *Irish Ecclesiastical Record* informed Fahey that he could not find anyone to review his book. Eventually a review appeared after Fahey persuaded one of his ex-students to draft it.

The Final Years

College. When someone observed that Fahey quoted a great number of authors in his works, Alfred replied that, while Fahey read widely, he seemed to have digested very little in so doing. The publication in the early spring of 1941 by Alfred of *Money* prompted an exchange of letters between him and Fahey.[23] Alfred indicated that he was not familiar with what Fahey had published up to that time. He warned him to 'beware of the catches of Douglasism' and cautioned him against being too radical, as that would jeopardise any chance of financial reform. Subsequently, in a letter, dated 18 August 1941, he claimed that 'the Portuguese financial system', incorporated 'most of the moderate reforms' for which he was pressing. However, he distanced himself from Fahey's enthusiasm for financial reforms in New Zealand, stating that he was 'no blind admirer' of these, as they involved 'too much State and too much specialisation'.

The only reference in Alfred's huge *corpus* of published work to Fahey was a review of the latter's *Money manipulation and the social order* in the *Standard* of 9 February 1945. This was one of Fahey's shorter works and it did not contain his more outrageous conspiracy theories. Alfred applauded the main thesis in the book which he had already popularised in his *Money* (1941), a book greatly admired by Fahey. The thesis was that unless the monetary mechanism was subordinated to human needs it was futile to be advocating social justice and peace. Alfred commended Fahey's critical treatment of the Gold Standard, but regretted his failure to examine the disadvantages of the country's adoption of, and complete subordination to, sterling. He pointed out that Fahey was aware that hard work and the utilisation of natural resources were as essential to the improvement of the economy as a radical overhaul of the monetary system. He acknowledged that Fahey had many interesting things to say from an environmental point of view about agriculture, fertilisers and bread, but was critical of his seeming acceptance of Major Douglas's then popular economic theories of social credit.

Alfred's attendance at Fahey's funeral on 23 January 1954 was not significant. At that time he was residing in Blackrock College and would have attended from a sense of Christian duty.

Besides, in effect, giving a veneer of respectability to anti-semitic theories, Fahey also had extreme views on freemasonry.

23. Fahey papers, letters, dated 4, 18 March 1941, O'Rahilly to Fahey.

Alfred O'Rahilly III: Controversialist

While never commenting on these, Alfred had a strong antipathy to that organisation. This arose from his awareness of the hostility of the freemasons to Catholicism at different times and different places, not least in France. He wrote about freemasonry on at least one occasion. In a piece under 'Pat Murphy's jottings' in the *Standard* of 14 June 1946 he warned against the danger of secret societies acquiring too much influence. He recalled that in a recent broadcast form Radio Éireann it was stated that an American could not be elected president unless he was a freemason and that President Truman had been the grand master of his own State. He continued that previously he had read of the stranglehold which freemasonry had in France in 1912-13 and still had. In the earlier period in a population of forty million the Grand Orient and the Grand Lodge of France combined claimed a membership of only 36,000. Yet in the chamber 300 deputies out of 580 and in the senate 180 out of 300 were masons. He indicated his suspicion that in Ireland masonry had a strong grip on business, especially on finance.[24] Alfred urged people to be alert about the activities of small subversive minorities. Harking back to the recent turmoil in the Labour Party, occasioned by the fear that it was being infiltrated, he pointed out that in Russia the all-powerful Communist Party numbered only about two million in a population of 170 million.[25]

24. Both Alfred and Fahey would have read Fr Edward Cahill's description of the threat allegedly posed to the Irish Free State by freemasonry in *Freemasonry and the anti-Christian movement* (Dublin 1924) and *The framework of a Christian State* (Dublin 1932). For more on this subject, see T. J. Morrissey, S.J., *A man called Hughes* (Dublin 1991).
25. There is no evidence that while at U.C.C. (1914-54) Alfred ever associated himself with anti-semitic views. Gerald Y. Goldberg, the well-known Cork Jewish solicitor and former lord mayor of the city, in 1983 recalled only one instance of anti-semitism at U.C.C. This occurred in 1934 when the standing committee of the Literary and Philosophical Society, it seems, did not wish to present him with the Alfred O'Rahilly medal which he had won, because he was 'an alien'. However, Goldberg's peers, including Tomás Mac Curtain, son of the famous lord mayor, insisted on justice being done. ('Marian Finucane Show', interview with Gerald Y. Goldberg, 27 July 1983, R.T.É., Sound Archives; 'Gerald Y. Goldberg: A Jew, a Corkman and an Irishman', November 1983, R.T.É., Television Archives). Goldberg expressed his admiration for Alfred, remembered him as a strict disciplinarian at U.C.C. and from his 'first clash' with him in November 1930 concluded that he was resentful of what he regarded as an undue influence being exercised on public life at that time by members of the masonic order (letter, dated 7 September 1983, Gerald Y. Goldberg to J. Anthony Gaughan).

The Final Years

Fr Charles Davis Affair

One topic which was discussed by Alfred and his friends, Fr Michael McCarthy and Rev Dr Michael O'Carroll, was the case of Charles Davis. A priest of the archdiocese of Westminster, he was a former editor of the *Clergy Review*, a well-known theologian and a prolific writer. At a press conference on 21 December 1966 he announced that he had left the Catholic Church and issued the following statement:

> I remain a Christian, but I have come to see that the Church as it exists and works at present is an obstacle in the lives of the committed Christians I know and admire. It is not the source of the values they cherish and promote. On the contrary, they live and work in a constant tension and opposition to it. Many can remain Roman Catholics only because they live their Christian lives on the fringe of the institutional Church and largely ignore it. I respect their position. In the present confused period people will work out their Christian commitment in different ways. But their solution was not open to me; in my position I was too involved. I had to ask bluntly whether I still believed in the Roman Catholic Church as an institution. I found that the answer was no.
>
> For me Christian commitment is inseparable from concern for truth and concern for people. I do not find either of these represented by the official Church. There is concern for authority at the expense of truth, and I am constantly saddened by instances of the damage done to persons by workings of an impersonal and unfree system. Further, I do not think that the claim the Church makes as an institution rests upon any adequate biblical and historical basis. The Church in its existing form seems to me to be a pseudo-political structure from the past. It is now breaking up, and some other form of Christian presence in the world is under formation.
>
> It is my intention to get married. This is not my reason for leaving the Church. To marry it would have been enough to leave the priesthood; for the reasons given I am rejecting the Church. I am marrying to rebuild my life upon a personal love I can recognize as true and real, after a life

surrounded in the Church by so much that is at best irrelevant and at worst an obstacle to genuine human experience.

Davis gave a more detailed and personal description of the reasons which led him to leave the Church in the *Observer* of 1 January 1967. He repeated that he would continue to be a Christian but would not belong to any of the existing Christian denominations. In some press reports it was claimed that his defection from the Catholic Church was as significant as Newman's adherence to it in the previous century. At the beginning of January 1967 Alfred drafted a rebuttal of the claims in the statement issued by Davis. At the outset he expressed his sympathy with Davis on the severe mental struggle which must have preceded his final decision. He excused his intervention on the grounds that Davis had availed of the occasion to give reporters a statement which contained arguments against the cherished beliefs of his erstwhile fellow-Catholics. Alfred noted that Davis claimed that he remained a Christian but the only clue to what he understood by the term was a reference to a churchless 'Christian presence' which was emerging. He next addressed the claim by Davis that the Catholic Church as it existed did not rest 'upon any adequate biblical or historical basis'. This, he declared, would have been less objectionable had Davis stated that certain structural ecclesiastical elements were a later development of what was sufficient for primitive times. Cardinals, canon law, Roman congregations – even the crucifix – while embodying principles latent in the early Church, did not as such exist in apostolic times. But Davis rejected the historical claims of the modern Church to be fundamentally the legitimate continuation and successor of the primitive Church. In not making a distinction between adaptations or contingencies and fundamental beliefs, Davis was logically also bound to repudiate any present-day Christian Church, including the Orthodox and Anglican ones.

Alfred examined the claim by Davis that 'the Church as it exists and works at present is an obstacle in the lives of committed Christians whom I know and admire'. This, declared Alfred, was counter to his own much longer and wider experience and acquaintance with fellow-Catholics. He referred to the hundreds of lay-folk he knew personally, the hundreds of millions of devoted Christians throughout the world, the

The Final Years

thousands of zealous missionaries and the consecrated religious, drawn from all cultures, nations and races. Davis, he suggested, must have been living in a very narrow environment and was probably referring to a small coterie of intellectuals who impatiently demand immediate and premature answers to all problems. He described Davis's charge as 'a monstrous exaggeration' when one considered that, apart from the contribution of the other Christian Churches, the Catholic Church provided the sacraments, fostered personal devotion to Christ and gave a meaning to the lives of countless Christians.

Alfred pointed out that Davis obviously had scant respect for authority. As to authority in the context of dogmatic theology, they were then much more conscious of the reality underlying the terminology of Greek metaphysics. That was what was meant by a revivication of biblical theology. He acknowledged that, as regards disciplinary authority, there was a juridical over-emphasis in the reaction against the Reformation. This was merely an incidental historical fact in the Church, which, after all, had a human side. The recent Vatican Council had corrected that one-sidedness without altering fundamentals. In particular the laity had been given a new status as an integral part of 'the people of God'. Disciplinary authority, he admitted, often involved some tension. This was true not only of the Church but it also occurred in a university, a club, or a trade-union. He noted that a recent British report advocated as a matter of urgency the re-introduction of managerial authority in the ailing motor industry. Authority could be misused, but the other extreme of chaotic anarchy was even worse. He recalled that he had had to submit to disciplinary or legislative enactments with which he personally disagreed. Some form of authority, even in so-called majority rule, was unavoidable. Moreover at that time there was a reassuring proclamation of the natural rights of individuals and of associations.

Alfred returned to the claim by Davis that he was remaining a Christian. In that regard the only explanation he gave was that the Church 'is now breaking up and some other form of Christian presence in the world is under formation'. Such a prediction of utopia, Alfred pointed out, had often been made in the past, especially by various seceding sects. All living religions were institutionalised, they had organic articles. The foretelling of the advent of a romantic anarchy was very unconvincing as a substitute for a church of associated believers. The Church was not 'breaking up', though it might lose some over-rationalised intellectuals. There was certainly vigorous discussion, even controversy, which would last some time. But that was a sign of life, not of apathy or decay. On the horizon he could not descry the 'formation' of an undescribed 'form of Christian presence', whatever that meant.

Alfred concluded: 'Agnosticism I understand, dissident Christian Churches I understand. But this vision of a new form of 'Christian presence' is quite unintelligible to me. I am sceptical of this pipe-dream which Dr Davis proposes to us as his alternative to the Catholic Church, indeed to any Church. Is he serious? Or is he just rationalising a decision he has taken on other grounds?'

Alfred decided not to publish his rebuttal. Davis's former colleagues and friends in England who were shocked and pained by his action and especially by his article in the *Observer* also remained silent. In the autumn of 1967 Davis published *A question of conscience* (London 1967) which was an extended apologia for his action. This prompted some trenchant reviews and a pamphlet by Cornelius Ernst, O.P., entitled *Charles Davis and his book* (London 1967).

There was a further sequel to the publication of Davis's book. The *Times* of 5 January 1968 carried an interview of Monica Baldwin by Neville Braybrooke. Miss Baldwin was the former nun whose renunciation of her vows twenty-five years earlier and the account of it in her best-seller *I leap over the wall* made similar headlines to those prompted by the Davis affair. She declared that he had made a mistake and claimed that there was an analogy between her case and that of Charles Davis.

She expanded on this by commenting on his book as follows:

> What so struck me was that both he and I had failed for similar reasons. We were neither of us sufficiently clamped on to God by prayer. He does not once mention the word prayer in his book. I am convinced that, in his case as in mine, the cause of the trouble was failure to guard the citadel in the early stages. The enemy gets a foothold. When the big attack comes you are swept away.
>
> You have got to have enough faith to hold on and let God lead you to the precipice – or even over it if necessary.

The Final Years

That is what I should have understood twenty-five years ago . . . Prayer is the language that gets you to God . . .
Charles Davis mentions Père Teilhard de Chardin as a man who obeyed unreservedly.
. . . But he takes too narrow a view of the humiliations, misunderstandings and suppressions that Père Teilhard had to contend with . . . It requires a strong will to give up your own will . . . Every time you hold back a bit of yourself the mist between you and God thickens. A darkness comes down and you cannot see what you saw in the beginning. Somehow faith, love and loyalty have to carry you through this period. Do you know the passage where Père Teilhard speaks of a man who sees a light shining through the mist and finds it impossible to reach Christ without plunging into it? Well, perhaps that mist is the crisis through which the Church is passing to-day.

Second Vatican Council

Dr Michael O'Carroll, C.S.Sp., was to recall that Alfred enjoyed discussing the progress of the Vatican Council. Many of the controversies which it reactivated were not as new to him as they were to others. For years he had followed and admired the writings of John Courtney Murray, S.J., on religious freedom. He was also acutely aware of the problem of the competing imperatives of scripture and tradition. His library bore witness to the extent to which he was familiar with the writings and insights of modern theologians. He frequently expressed the view that the new thinking emanating from the Council was a vindication of much of what had been written by John Henry Newman.

Bureaucracy

A subject which continued to prompt Alfred to become voluble was the importance of ensuring that there were no non-essential levels of bureaucracy in any enterprise, public or private. In deprecating bureaucracy in general he made it clear that he was not referring to hard-working civil servants. During his crusade for a radical reform in the country's fiscal policies and banking system he had identified bureaucracy as (1) the domination of the department of finance and (2) the suppression of those technically competent and experienced. The former he described as an

Alfred O'Rahilly III: Controversialist

inheritance from the British regime which resulted in social policy being subordinated to financial considerations, notwithstanding the protests of politicians. The latter he described as the rule of the pen-pushers over the professional and technical people, whether businessmen, manufacturers, engineers, dairy experts, or statisticians. As Alfred mellowed he tended to restrict his critical remarks at this aspect of bureaucracy. However, he continued to argue that, to the detriment of efficiency, the principle that the functioning of technical operations had to be controlled, not by those specially qualified or experienced but by somebody quite unqualified sitting in an office in Dublin, continued to flourish.[26]

Other Priestly Activity

After the publicity surrounding his ordination Alfred received and replied to numerous letters seeking spiritual advice and help. He also continued to exchange letters with scholars who sent him queries on various subjects. He conducted a voluminous correspondence with three of his five surviving sisters.[27] In addition, he frequently wrote to three English women he had met during his pilgrimage to the Holy Land in August 1955, one of whom had been particularly attracted to him and who eventually joined the sisters of the Good Shepherd. Although he complained in his diary of being lonely, he did not enjoy having visitors. When people called to see him at Blackrock College, he did not make himself available except to a few, such as President de Valera, Archbishop George Otto Simms, Dr Henry St Joseph Atkins, his successor at U.C.C., and close friends, such as Timothy and Anna O'Mahony of Cork. For the most part he celebrated his daily Mass in the chapel in

26. For more, see *Standard* 7 May 1943. In April and May 1943 Alfred corresponded on this subject with a like-minded and admiring Dr Thomas A. McLaughlin, architect of the E.S.B.'s Shannon scheme. He pleaded unsuccessfully with the distinguished engineer to publish his strong views on the 'administrative class' in a pamphlet.

27. He wrote only occasionally to his sister Connie (see J. A. Gaughan, *Alfred O'Rahilly I: Academic*, 258). She was a source of annoyance and anxiety to him and his two younger sisters, Cecil and Ena (see *ibid.* 259). Almost always in dire straits financially, owing to bad management, she was over many years in receipt of considerable help from him and Cecil. In the mid-1950s she became particularly tiresome. In a round-robin letter he charged that she had 'for a long time been engaged in a campaign of mendicancy and blackmail . . . writing to bishops, abbots, priests and nuns' and posing as having been 'neglected by hard-hearted relatives'.

The Final Years

Blackrock College. However, he occasionally supplied for the chaplain to the Carmelite monastery in Blackrock. He enjoyed this and became very friendly with the superior and sisters. Because of failing eye-sight he received a rescript from Archbishop McQuaid on 23 December 1965, allowing him to celebrate daily either the Votive Mass of the Blessed Virgin Mary or the Mass for the Dead. And later, on 18 April 1969, owing to the general deterioration of his health, he also sought and was given permission merely to concelebrate Mass.

Alfred dutifully fulfilled another of the duties of his clerical state, namely, the daily recitation of the Divine Office. This he found most onerous. Even before he received the subdiaconate, which imposed this duty, he wrote in his diary that he anticipated finding the obligation difficult. It seems what caused him difficulty was not the praying of the Divine Office but the fact that its daily recitation was imposed as a serious obligation. On 23 December 1965, as well as receiving permission to celebrate daily either of two Masses whose texts he could memorise, he received the faculty from Archbishop McQuaid to say a third of the Rosary or other prayers in lieu of the Divine Office.

At the beginning of July 1960 Alfred attended a reception in connection with the centenary celebrations at Blackrock College. A number of monsignori were present and he complained jocosely in his speech that if he had 'played his cards right' he would now be a monsignor. Within two days it was announced that the pope had acceded to the request of Archbishop McQuaid to create Fr O'Rahilly a domestic prelate. This did not attract much attention, owing to the considerable activity surrounding Blackrock College's centenary. Not that he was entirely ignored. He was given the honour of proposing the toast to the college at the centenary luncheon. Later he was given an opportunity to parade in his purple when he attended the celebration of the centenary of Holy Cross College, Clonliffe, on the following 12 October.[28] As a past pupil, a veteran of the war of independence and a first cousin of The O'Rahilly, he was given a leading role when Blackrock College celebrated the fiftieth anniversary of the Easter Rising. The Proclamation of 1916 was read and he delivered a fiery oration

---
28. He also had an opportunity to wear his pontificals when he officiated at the marriage of Deirdre, daughter of Frank Flanagan (see p. 172).

Alfred O'Rahilly III: Controversialist

which those who heard it vividly recalled almost thirty years later.

Final Illness, Death and Burial

As he advanced into his eighties Alfred remained remarkably vigorous. However, in 1967 he had to spend some weeks in St Michael's Hospital, Dún Laoghaire. In the first week of September 1968 after becoming gravely ill he was rushed to the nursing home in St Michael's where he was cared for by a night nurse as well as a day nurse. He was much shaken by the experience of being so ill and two weeks later, when his condition improved, he legally constituted Fr Michael McCarthy as his attorney to transact his business affairs thereafter.[29] By the end of October Con Murphy had persuaded Alfred to dispense with the services of the night nurse and was able to write to Alfred's son, Ronan, that his father's condition had improved so much that 'he appears to be as good as ever he was'.

Alfred's failing eye-sight left him unable to read. This in no way dampened his spirits or curiosity. He had his sister, Cecil, and his friend, Con Murphy, read the daily newspapers to him. On Easter Sunday 1969 he dined with the community at Blackrock College. In a letter, dated 18 April, to Tim O'Mahony, Con Murphy wrote: 'Alfred continues to improve! We do not know how he is doing it, but he is out every day in the car, visiting people, even going into a hotel for a bottle of beer, and walking as fast as ever he walked. His only complaint is his eye-sight and between you and me we do not think that is so bad

---

29. One of the first actions taken by Fr McCarthy in his new role was to return a large number of books which Alfred had on loan from the library in U.C.C. At this time he also had all of Alfred's book-club, journal and magazine subscriptions cancelled. On retiring from U.C.C., Alfred, partly because of the insensitivity of the library committee, donated his books on philosophy and science to the central Jesuit library at Milltown Park. The rest, with his papers, he gave to the Holy Ghost fathers at Blackrock College and later he appointed Fr Michael McCarthy as his literary executor. After furnishing his daughter's new home, he gave the rest of his property to Blackrock College. The Jesuits showed their appreciation of his generosity by hanging a large photograph of him in the antechamber or reading room of the library at Milltown Park. It hangs beside portraits of Dr Michael Cox and Judge William O'Brien both of whom also donated valuable personal collections to the institution.

The Final Years

either!'[30] At this time Alfred received a visit from Archbishop McQuaid. In recalling that he had much to be thankful for in his life, he told the latter rather perkily: 'I must be one of the few men in Ireland to receive all seven sacraments!'

On 20 July Alfred had lunch at Blackrock College. He was in good spirits but Fr Michael McCarthy sensed from his conduct that he had a premonition that his end was near. A week later he had a massive internal haemorrhage and became very weak but did not lose consciousness. On 1 August he made his last will. The signature indicated an uncharacteristically unsteady hand. That evening Dr J. B. Lyons, who was deputising for Dr P. D. O'Rourke, was called to attend to Alfred. He examined Alfred and then explained what he intended to do for him. Alfred calmly and somewhat magisterially informed him that it was futile, as he was about to die.

Early the following morning Alfred lost consciousness. Fr Michael McCarthy and Alfred's sister, Cecil, were called to his bedside. They remained there until he died just after noon. Alfred's body was laid out in his priestly vestments in the hospital's mortuary chapel. Denis Gwynn was later to describe the scene: 'That strong face, suggestive of a Roman emperor, looked more impressive than it had ever been in his years of strife and achievement. The Roman purple of his robes and biretta seemed a fitting last tribute from the Church which he had served so faithfully.' Obituaries in the press and radio were as generous and fulsome.

On 4 August Alfred's remains were removed to the chapel in Blackrock College. They were received by the college president, Fr Timothy O'Driscoll, C.S.Sp., and the community. Among the distinguished attendance were: President Eamon de Valera, the

30. Alfred's improved condition was due in no small measure to the attention of his nurses, Julia Byrne and Mrs Clare Dixon. They became very attached to him and took him out for drives. He appreciated their kindness and thanked them in little verses, such as the following which he wrote to Mrs Dixon on 14 April 1969:

> To my dear friend Clare
> I send this little prayer.
> May God's blessing be
> On her for all she has done for me.
> She has been wonderfully kind
> To me, now old and blind,
> Who will ever bear in mind
> What I owe her.

Alfred O'Rahilly III: Controversialist

Taoiseach, Jack Lynch; Dr Albert MacConnell, provost of T.C.D., and professors and staff-members of U.C.D. On the following day the Requiem Mass was celebrated by Fr O'Driscoll, with Archbishop McQuaid presiding. De Valera was again in attendance and a strong representation from U.C.C.

In his will Alfred had expressed a wish that his body be laid to rest 'with the Holy Ghost Fathers in their cemetery at Kimmage'. His wish was honoured. The graveside service was conducted by Alfred's close friend, Fr Michael McCarthy, with a large gathering of Holy Ghost Fathers and, once again, de Valera in attendance.

The Holy Ghost Fathers were to be as generous and kind to Alfred in death as they were to him during his years in retirement, making him an honorary member of their institute. The inscription on his small, cross-shaped headstone, identical to all the others in the cemetery, reads:

Msgr. Alfred O'Rahilly, C.S.Sp.
died 2nd August 1969
aged 85 yrs.[31]

---

31. The above is taken from Richard Sherry, *Holy Cross College, Clonliffe, 1859-1959* (Dublin 1962); Denis Gwynn, 'Monsignor Alfred O'Rahilly (1884-1969)', *Studies*, winter 1969; D. H. Manly, 'The Fahey theories', 'Sound history?', 'Fr Fahey and Irish Catholicism', *Ballintrillick Review*, no. 28 (1990); *Cork Examiner* 4, 6 August 1969; *Irish Independent* 25 January 1954, 4, 6, August 1969; *Irish Times* 4 August 1969; *Kerryman* 9 August 1969; *Standard* 7 May 1943, 4 May, 22 June 1956, 6, 13 December 1957, 12, 26 April 1963; Dublin Archdiocesan Archives: Alfred O'Rahilly file; R.T.É. Written Archive: Alfred O'Rahilly file; Papers of Cornelius Murphy: Alfred O'Rahilly file; diaries of Alfred O'Rahilly: 8 April – 1 May 1954; 24 May – 7 July 1954, 11 July – 12 September 1954, 13 September – 26 October 1954, 27 December 1954 – 28 February 1955, 1 March – 9 November 1955, 13 November – 25 December 1955; interviews with John Evans, Mgr G. Thomas Fehily, Peter Hogan, Fr Seán Hughes, S.J., Mrs Deirdre Humphreys (née Flanagan), Mother M. Jordana, O.P., R. D. O'C. Lysaght, Fr Michael McCarthy, C.S.Sp., Cornelius Murphy, Rev. Dr Michael O'Carroll, C.S.Sp., John J. O'Meara, Pádraig Ó Snodaigh, Patrick Joseph Quinn, Fr Patrick Tuohy; papers and writings of Alfred O'Rahilly and the sources already cited.

EPILOGUE

On 12 November 1901 Alfred entered the Jesuit novitiate at Tullabeg with a view to becoming a priest in the Society of Jesus. When on 18 December 1955 he was ordained in the chapel in Blackrock College his life had all-too-soon come full circle.[1] In the meantime he had married and raised a daughter and son. For forty years he had given unmatched service to U.C.C. as assistant lecturer, professor, registrar and president successively. He was one of the most influential persons in the public life of Ireland for a period spanning almost two generations. As a practical social reformer, he had few peers. He had won an international reputation as a scholar in a number of disciplines.

Notwithstanding these achievements, those who were close to Alfred regarded him as first and foremost an outstanding Catholic apologist. It was a role which he filled with considerable enthusiasm in his daily life as well as in lecturing and writing. Fr Donal O'Sullivan, S.J., who gave the annual retreat at U.C.C. at the beginning of the academic year in 1945, wrote to Fr John R. McMahon, S.J., his provincial, on 17 November:

> I thoroughly enjoyed the retreat, though it was at the same time a big strain and the confessions were mission-heavy. O'Rahilly himself and a fair number of the professors attended – the presence of the former does not tend to calm preaching! – and the students packed the chapel. I saw a great deal of Alfred and he was kindness itself to me and at various professorial social gatherings was almost embarrassing in his eagerness to break a lance for the Society. He has done a tremendous amount in his few years of office, even though he has often been *fortiter in modo* as well as *in re*. There is really a wonderful Catholic spirit in the college and the personal example of O'Rahilly is just stupendous. The younger students especially appreciate it.

---

1. In his diary he adverted to this on a number of occasions. On Palm Sunday, 11 April 1954, he wrote: 'Once more I am witnessing the Holy Week liturgy in Blackrock College chapel, where these ceremonies first made such an impression on me as a schoolboy. It seems but yesterday. All the intervening years seem to me almost unreal, like the passing visions of a cinematograph. A little while ago I was a schoolboy; now suddenly I find myself to be an old man.'

Alfred O'Rahilly III: Controversialist

Alfred never concealed his Catholicism nor his strong religious convictions no matter what the surroundings. Douglas Hyde wrote in the *Catholic Herald* of 6 August 1948:

> In London last week I met Professor O'Rahilly, of Cork, and we went for a meal together in a Fleet Street restaurant. The room was crowded, but in five minutes there was to all intents and purposes only one man there – the professor – for his personality is so terrific that, although the most modest of men, he simply dominated the scene.
>
> He told me with pride of the things they are doing in Cork [the course in workers' education at U.C.C.] and was particularly proud of the fact that the men they turn out do not disappear into ivory towers or soft jobs, but take their learning, culture and social teaching with them back to the working-class circles from which they come.
>
> He seemed to me to be one of the most practical and yet most holy people I have met. And I will confess to having got rather a kick out of seeing the looks of blank astonishment and incomprehension on hard-boiled Fleet Street faces when, having finished lunch, he crossed himself and said grace before departing.

Alfred's passionate attachment to his faith was rooted in his family background, his early education and membership of the Society of Jesus during his formative years. Perhaps because he possessed an acute awareness of the inadequacy of human knowledge, science and theology, like Louis Pasteur, he had the simple faith of a Breton peasant. This he sustained by a life-long commitment to prayer. Throughout his life as a layman he attended Mass and recited the Rosary daily.

Alfred's readiness to do battle for the Catholic Church arose in part from his desire to compensate for not persevering with his vocation in his early years. In his diary for 19 April 1954 he wrote: 'In spite of my many faults, I have always stood up for Christ and publicly defended religion. Thus I have made some reparation for my own great tepidity and unfaithfulness.' And on 20 January 1955 he reflected on his departure from the Jesuits: 'I was full of spiritual pride and I was unfaithful to grace. The only consolation I have is that, having been found unworthy to be an officer in Christ's army, I think I have honestly

Epilogue

striven to be a good private.' This was also implicitly recognised by Fr Michael O'Grady, S.J., the provincial, in the dimissorial letter which he provided for Alfred prior to his ordination.[2] By virtue of his temperament and personality, Alfred was attracted to controversy. He was self-opinionated and extraordinarily vain. Nothing gave him more pleasure than an intellectual joust with a person regarded as an expert on some subject or other. For religious controversy he was well-equipped. He possessed a fine mind, was widely read and had extensive and varied experience. Although he gave no quarter in exchanges, he endeavoured not to show any personal animus to his adversaries. Hurts and insults were both forgotten as well as forgiven by him.[3]

Alfred followed the deliberations of the Second Vatican Council (1962-5) with intense interest. He stated that it dealt with a number of issues which had concerned him for many years. Not surprisingly in view of his independent character, he applauded the council's move to correct the juridical over-emphasis on Church discipline which resulted from the Reformation. He welcomed the new vision of the Church as the people of God and its consequent upgrading of the status of lay people within the Church. In particular he was very pleased with the introduction of the vernacular into the liturgy and thereby the restoration of the ideal of corporate worship. He rejoiced at the council's enthusiastic endorsement of ecumenism and the need to respect truths and convictions cherished in other religions and other Christian denominations. But, with regard to ecumenism and the other issues opened up for vigorous debate, he frequently quoted St Augustine: 'In essentials, unity; in doubtful things, liberty; in all things, charity.'

Alfred was more complex and complicated than most people.[4] He tended to beguile his friends and to enrage his adversaries. But he mellowed as he grew older. Dr Kathleen

---

2. Fr O'Grady admired Alfred greatly. In January 1955 in conversation and by letter he informed him that the Society regarded him as a *missionarius excurrens* (an external missionary). He assured him that members of the Irish province were proud of his achievements and felt a great affection for him (see p. 136). In a reference to Alfred's forthcoming ordination, he regretted that the Society had not the privilege 'to have done that crowning' to a 'life so marked with the seal of divine approval'.
3. See J. A. Gaughan, *Alfred O'Rahilly I: Academic*, 193-4; *Alfred O'Rahilly II: Public Figure*, 384.
4. For a psychological profile of Alfred, see Appendix 6.

Alfred O'Rahilly III: Controversialist

O'Flaherty, his colleague for many years when he strode the scene at U.C.C. like a colossus,[5] published an appreciation of him in the *Cork University Record*, summer 1955, and the *University Review*, spring 1955. After mentioning his many achievements in the academic and non-academic worlds, she referred to his capacity for work and for extracting it out of others, his stimulating companionship, and his phenomenal energy, manifested in his quick gestures and rapid flow of talk. Dynamism, she recalled, was his most outstanding characteristic and she continued: 'Those who know him are well acquainted with it; it is the origin of the many emotions to which he gave rise in those with whom he came in contact, for it was impossible to regard him with indifference. It is a source of his brilliance as a polemicist and of the intellectual energy which he continually expended . . . His very manner of walking revealed this trait of his character: it was necessary to run in order to keep up with him . . . His quick glance took in everything . . . When he retired, U.C.C. lost not only an exceptional president but an outstanding personality.'

Fr Michael McCarthy who lived in close contact with Alfred from 1954 to 1969 broadcast an appreciation of his friend from Radio Éireann in August 1969. He described him as magnanimous and forgiving and as possessing a subtle, mischievous but never hurtful humour. In his personal dealings, McCarthy commented, Alfred's generosity and munificence were on the grand scale and his kindness to people about him constant. His pension he spent on books and on charity to the poor. When he died his estate amounted to a mere £1,100. McCarthy concluded that his was 'a kindly heart concealed under a rugged and unpretentious exterior'.

Denis Gwynn compared Alfred in death to a Roman emperor lying in state. Alfred's life reminds one of the advice of the Greek poet, Hesiod (*fl. c.* 800 B.C.): 'In the morning of life, work; in the mid-day, give counsel; in the evening, pray.'[6]

5. Niall Tierney, son of Michael Tierney, recalled that when as a small boy he asked Alfred who he was the latter replied: 'I am the Kaiser of Cork!'
6. The above is taken from Kathleen O'Flaherty, 'Obituary: Right Reverend Dr Alfred O'Rahilly', *Cork University Record*, 1970; diary of Alfred O'Rahilly: 27 December 1954 – 28 February 1955; Dublin Archdiocesan Archives: Alfred O'Rahilly file; interviews with Fr Michael McCarthy, C.S.Sp., and Rev. Dr Michael O'Carroll, C.S.Sp.; papers and writings of Alfred O'Rahilly and the sources already cited.

APPENDIX 1

RADIO TALK BY ALFRED O'RAHILLY ON THÉRÈSE NEUMANN[1]

There is in Bavaria, near the frontier of Czechoslovakia, a village of less than a thousand inhabitants, called Konnersreuth, about five miles from the nearest railway station. This obscure place has achieved world-wide fame and has been visited by thousands of pilgrims, for it is the home of Thérèse Neumann, the daughter of the village tailor, born in 1898 as the eldest of ten children. She is an ordinary peasant woman who finished her schooling at the age of sixteen and then was for four years a servant maid. How curious that the eyes of the world should be drawn to such a person! The reason is that since 1926 she has had the stigmata – wounds on the hands, feet and left side which never suppurate but bleed periodically on Fridays, especially during Lent; she also sheds tears of blood. Thus in a most poignant way she recalls men's minds to the Passion of Our Lord. In a sermon preached on 8 November 1927 the late Cardinal Faulhaber said: 'Today a great message of grace has come out of Konnersreuth: Return to devotion to Christ's Passion.'

There is already an enormous literature on the subject. As I happen to have read extensively in it, I have been asked to speak on it, especially in connection with a recent book, *The case of Thérèse Neumann*. The author, Miss Hilda C. Graef, writes from Oxford. The book is printed in London, has the *imprimatur* of the archbishop of Birmingham, and was published in 1950 by the Mercier Press, Cork. The publisher's blurb states that the work is the 'first critical examination to appear in the English language'. In my view, however, it is an extremely hostile and one-sided production and therefore calls for some critical comments. The author appears to have paid a visit to Konnersreuth but gives no observations of her own. For most of her descriptions she is dependent on the large work of Josef Teodorowicz, archbishop of Lemberg, of which an American translation was published by Herder in 1940: *Mystical phenomena in the life of Thérèse Neumann*.

She uses a highly critical symposium published in the *Etudes Carmélitaines* in 1936 and especially the work of a Polish

1. Broadcast from Radio Éireann on 23 April 1951. The typescript is in the Written Archive of Radio Telefís Éireann.

Alfred O'Rahilly III: Controversialist

physician, Dr Boleslas de Poray Madeyski: *Le cas de la visionnaire stigmatisée Thérèse Neumann de Konnersreuth* (Paris 1940). It is, however, disingenuous to refer to this medical writer as 'the medical expert of the Sacred Congregation of Rites', as he did not write in this capacity and his book is filled with a technical and debatable concept of hysteria. Miss Graef simply accepts his conclusions without reproducing his arguments. She has missed a much better critical work published in French by a Polish Jesuit, Paul Siwek, now a professor in Fordham: *Une stigmatisée de nos jours* (Paris 1950). As to most of the literature favourable to Thérèse Neumann, Miss Graef is unaware of it or at least fails to quote it.

The author's object is to prove that the extraordinary phenomena exhibited by Thérèse Neumann – stigmata, visions, perpetual fast – have a purely natural explanation. Even if she were dealing with a canonised saint, she would be prefectly entitled to do this; Catholics as such are not obliged to regard these phenomena as miraculous. Such a discussion is of great scientific interest but exceedingly difficult in the light of modern psychical research. To be satisfactory the investigation would require a far greater technical apparatus than Miss Graef attempts. But the query I wish to put is this: Is the issue, which can never be decided categorically, of such great religious importance? Even among Catholics in Germany there has been a great difference of opinion; and Miss Graef relies on Fr Waldmann, one of the most vehement opponents of Konnersreuth. Among Catholic scientists and theologians such a dispute is quite intelligible. But does it really affect the ordinary people? Do they consciously raise the question whether God is acting directly or through obscure secondary causes? From my own knowledge of the sturdy Bavarian Catholic rural people, I find it hard to believe that they are obsessed with delusions about miracles. They take the wonderful phenomena as they find them and they thank God for them. In my opinion they are right. As against Miss Graef I hold that a description – still more a sight – of what is happening is of far greater importance than an inconclusive investigation as to whether they are a rather unique manifestation of obscure psychophysical causation. Here, for example, is a quotation from a Jewish physician, who visited Konnersreuth, Dr Wolfgang von Weisl:

Appendix 1

Never could I believe what happens here, had I not seen it with my own eyes: a peasant girl witnesses the Passion of Christ. So strong and fervent is her vision that blood flows in long streams from her eyes down her face; blood from the wounds of her heart and her head crimsons her gown and her head cloth. And as to her eyes – never have I seen such eyes in a hysteric or insane person . . . She weeps bloody tears. In her extended hands of a dull white-like ivory, there shine forth two red marks: the marks of the nails in the hands of the Redeemer.

Presumably this non-Christian doctor does not believe in a miracle; yet he was profoundly affected by this living reproduction of the Passion of Christ.

I myself would much prefer to give my hearers further such descriptions, to try to show them why the thousands who have visited Konnersreuth were so deeply affected. But I must perforce follow Miss Graef in her pursuit of natural causes.

In spite of her ambition to be a missionary sister, Thérèse Neumann had to start earning her living as a servant in 1914; and, owing to the absence of the men at the war, her work was particularly hard. On the morning of 10 March 1918 a fire broke out in the house where she was employed. For two hours she stood on a chair, handing up buckets of water, then she fell. This, aggravated by a further fall a month later when she was carrying a sack of potatoes, was the beginning of a long period of suffering and illness, during which she lost her sight and became partly paralysed. In 1923 her sight was restored, and in 1925 she was cured of a wound in her foot, of what was alleged to be an organic lesion of the vertebrae, of appendicitis and of pneumonia. Thérèse maintained that she was cured miraculously by St Thérèse after a vision. Dr Madeyski, whom of course Miss Graef follows, holds that these disabilities were due to hysteria initiated by traumatic shock. Let us avoid this much-abused word 'hysteria' and say that these illnesses were psychogenetic, that is, due in some way to the reaction of the mind (not necessarily conscious) on the body. There is much to be said for this contention, for many parallel cases of such symptoms are recorded. Certainly the Medical Bureau at Lourdes would not accept these cures as necessarily miraculous. What follows? Nothing whatever either

Alfred O'Rahilly III: Controversialist

to the disparagement of Thérèse or to the invalidation of her subsequent experiences.

Let us now turn to Thérèse's stigmata, the impression of five wounds recalling those of Christ. The first recorded case is that of St Francis in 1224; since then there have been literally hundreds of instances. Rationalist historians, fearful of admitting a miracle, have been reluctant to admit the genuineness of the phenomenon. Renan suggested that Br Elias manipulated the corpse of St Francis; the Cambridge historian Coulton suggested that the saint used a 'rusty nail'! When the German pathologist in 1874 was told of the case of the Belgian girl Louise Lateau, he declared: 'Wunder oder Betrug – miracle or fraud.' And of course he opted for fraud. Such scepticism is nowadays quite untenable. The stigmata of Thérèse Neumann have been investigated and described by numerous medical men; they have been photographed. Says Fr Siwek, an exigent critic (p. 44): 'I do not believe that the reality of the phenomena of Konnersreuth can be seriously doubted.' Miss Graef, who would be glad to be rid of inconvenient facts, reproduces from Dr Madeyski an account of a certain Dr Martini who, because he did not himself witness the start of the bleeding from the wounds, suggested the possibility of a pious fraud; she even reproduces (p. 64) an insinuation from Waldmann that Thérèse's mother manipulated the bleeding. Such base and unfounded charges are indefensible. There is the moral case against deceit; Thérèse is a daily communicant, neither the Neumann household nor the villagers have derived any profit from the visitors, the parish priest, Fr Naber, is a watchful witness. But above all there have been innumerable competent observers. Says Fr Siwek again (p. 90):

> The spontaneous beginning of the blood-flow has been well observed by a number of doctors, of whom several used a magnifying glass. The quantity of blood is more than could be produced artificially without leaving notable scars ... There is no tendency to the production of pus.

It is unnecessary for me to quote numerous medical men, some of them non-Catholics, who have authenticated Thérèse's stigmata and their periodical bleeding. There can be no question of fraud. But are they a miracle? Or to express it more accur-

Appendix 1

ately: Is it necessary that God should intervene miraculously to produce stigmata? In this matter the Church shows a prudent reserve. Even in the decree approving the heroic virtues of St Gemma Galgani in 1932 it is stated that no decision is given 'concerning the supernatural character of the charismata of the servant of God'. It is true that no authentic case of natural stigmata has yet been adduced. A case described by Dr Lechler is very doubtful; and Miss Graef was ill-advised in adding an appendix on an alleged case reported in German newspapers. Blisters have been produced by hypnotic suggestion, but not bloody wounds and tears. And yet, given the phenomena of psychical research which we must nowadays admit, it would be rash to assert that stigmata must be purely supernatural in origin. If, however, there be a natural cause, we can exclude two extremes. (1) Auto-suggestion in the sense of will or conscious desire. Many stigmatics have been reluctant recipients; and many great devotees of the Passion have lacked stigmata. (2) Any purely physiological cause. For the stigmata are not just wounds, they have a reference to Christ's wounds, they embody an idea, they convey a message. So most Catholic writers today leave it an open question whether God uses some factor in the psychophysical constitution in the production of stigmata.

In this question Miss Graef appears to me to make two mistakes. She assumes (p. 9) that 'a number of cases are explicable by purely natural causes', while others are purely supernatural. But the same phenomenon cannot be explained naturally in one case and miraculously in another. As a result of this false dichotomy, she adopts the possession of conspicuous virtue as the criterion of the supernatural origin of stigmata in any given case. This is bad theology; for whatever be the explanation of stigmata, they are gratuitous favours which do not presuppose high sanctity in the receiver. Thérèse Neumann herself was much more accurate when she said: 'These gifts are not for me, they are for others; I could be damned with them if I did not look to myself' (Teodorowicz, p. 274). Let me cite Fr Siwek once more, as he is a critic whose conclusions largely coincide with those of Miss Graef. Here is how his book ends (p. 168):

> We have laid aside not only the problem of the personal sanctity of Thérèse Neumann but also that of her mystical

Alfred O'Rahilly III: Controversialist

life. Between personal holiness and mystical life on the one hand, and on the other hand the phenomena we have discussed in this book, there exists no necessary or intrinsic relation.

Elsewhere he says (p. 85): 'Personal piety, having no intimate relation with stigmata, cannot serve as a criterion for deciding in any given case whether the stigmata do or do not come from God.' It is a great pity that Miss Graef missed this point. For, having set out to prove that the stigmata and visions of Thérèse Neumann are purely natural phenomena, she finds it necessary to show that Thérèse lacks fundamental virtues and is full of imperfections. This systematic denigration of an inoffensive living person is a grave defect of Miss Graef's book, for it involves a lot of intimate prying, slick insinuations and some really cattish remarks. It is simply absurd for the author to claim that her book is a 'balanced and impartial account', when it is full of irrelevant personal attacks.

Nor do I think that she has dealt fairly with the evidence. For example, she disposes in a few lines (p. 91) of the assertion that Thérèse hears Our Lord speaking Aramaic in her visions of the Passion. She does this by taking one obscure phrase and trying to make out that it is really a corruption of Bavarian dialect. This is not good enough. Why did she not take 'Abbā Shebōk lehōn' – 'Father, forgive them'? Or the unexpected but good Aramaic 'eshe' for 'I thirst' instead of 'sāhēnā'. It is useless to pretend that Fr Wutz, consciously or unconsciously, inspired Thérèse. Fr Robert Leiber, S.J., in a published book, tells us that he became convinced after a long discussion with Wutz. Still more striking is the evidence of the non-Catholic Hans Bauer, professor of Semitic languages in Halle, and of the famous Jewish orientalist, Dr Wessely of Vienna. Both of these were convinced that Thérèse heard Aramaic, the language spoken by Our Lord. Miss Graef's summary dismissal of this extraordinary problem is quite unjustified. Her bias has made her unfair.

I have left myself no time to deal with Thérèse's inedia, that is, her going without solid food since 1922 or without even liquid food since 1926. As in the case of St Catherine of Siena, this is simply due to her inability to eat. Thérèse herself takes a very sensible view. She says: 'I place no value on eating or not eating, because after all what is of importance? Only to come to

Appendix 1

the Lord' (Teodorowicz, p. 20). This alleged abstention from food, especially in the case of a person leading an active life, seems to contradict all we know of the laws of energy; were there not similar recorded instances, we should find it hardly credible. Miss Graef, refusing to attribute conscious fraud, suggests (p. 55) that Thérèse helps herself to food in a state of somnambulism, which could hardly be done without the connivance of her family. Alternatively, she suggests that this abstention from nourishment can occur naturally. Once more I find the discussion quite unsatisfactory.

Miss Graef obviously set out to debunk her fellow-Catholic Thérèse Neumann. She reduces as much as she can to hysteria, she pictures Thérèse as a pigheaded and faulty Bavarian peasant, and she tries to evade facts which are inconvenient. Her book may have a *succes de scandale*. But it is not an objective account of 'the case of Thérèse Neumann'. Nor, even if her theories were true, would it show that God was not using Konnersreuth to revive devotion to the Crucified.

APPENDIX 2

ALFRED O'RAHILLY'S REPLY TO H. G. WELLS IN THE *STANDARD*[1]

I[2]

Introduction

There recently appeared in a weekly English paper what purported to be 'a digest of one of the most important books published in our lifetime'. Ordinarily an Irish Catholic would not pay much attention to this screaming commercial stunt indulged in by an imported paper which also provides illustrated accounts of night clubs[3] and, incongruously and illogically, a life of Our Lord. On this occasion, however, widespread indignation was evoked because the articles, so far from using legitimate arguments, contained offensive guttersnipe references to our religion and to our country. While I agree in general with the editor of the *Picture Post* that a 'reply to Wells's articles under democracy should not be a ban but a reasoned argument', I feel he does not appreciate the difficulty of dealing, not with reasoned arguments on the other side, but with sweeping unproved statements expressed with execrable taste.[4] Speaking of a meeting in Australia, Mr Wells says:

> I had denounced the teaching of the Judaeo-Christian mythology as historical fact, in the most emphatic terms. Not a single Christian teacher appeared to reply to that challenge (*The fate of homo sapiens* (1939) 101).

Now supposing that I myself – in a popular lecture, observe, not in a documented book – had emphatically denounced the teaching of the Darwinian mythology as scientific fact, should I then start proclaiming as a grievance the fact that not a single

1. The articles, constituting the reply, were introduced under the general title 'Mr Wells and ourselves'.
2. *Standard* 12 January 1940.
3. I am not concerned here with this aspect of the *Picture Post*.
4. The three articles referred to are in *Picture Post* (4 Nov. 1939, 46-8), *Picture Post* (11 Nov. 40-2), *Picture Post* (9 Dec. 47-9). The book itself is *The fate of homo sapiens* (1939). Other works of Mr Wells are quoted incidentally to show his background.

Appendix 2

teacher of biology appeared in reply to my challenge? No; I do not think I would take myself quite so seriously, though I believe I know more of biology than Mr Wells does of theology. The last conclusion Mr Wells would come to about himself is that there are a great number of people who refuse to take him seriously. My own reaction to his book was simply this: a bit of vague biology, some journalistic articles on various countries, a lot of secondhand jeering at religion and various 'rude noises' – to use his own expression (*The fate of homo sapiens*, 158) – about us Catholics. Why on earth should any educated person bother to answer this farrago of ill-mannered sciolism? But the editor of the *Picture Post* was anxious for a *casus belli*; so he handed the contents of his wastepaper-basket to Mr Wells and under big headlines published 'H. G. Wells replies to his critics'. And after devouring the authors of these anonymous scraps, Mr Wells starts shouting challenges to Archbishop Richard Downey and Hilaire Belloc. If this kind of thing goes on, it may, in this advertisement-run world, lead many simple people to share Mr Wells's belief in his own importance, omniscience and infallibility. I have therefore thought it worth while to publish a few comments on this unprovoked attack.[5]

The Competence of Mr Wells

When not roaring like a lion, Mr Wells displays the ability to coo like a dove:

> I am no more responsible for the facts in this book than a telegraph-messenger is for the cable he brings; I have been simply gathering up undisputed statements, and they remain intact, however brilliantly I can be discredited personally (*The fate of homo sapiens*, 320).

This is quite an old controversial dodge of Mr Wells.[6] He is the mouthpiece of science, the impartial collector of facts, the unprejudiced purveyor of undisputed statements, the reporter without bias. This smug self-laudation is really a rather obvious

---

5. No reply was received to an offer to publish my criticism in the pages of the *Picture Post*. See pp. 53-4.
6. 'I am a mere reporter of a vast mass of gathered knowledge and lengthened perspectives' (H. G. Wells, *Mr. Belloc objects* (1926) 51).

225

attempt to poison the wells especially against us Catholics. It is his favourite alibi. You are not hitting me, he says in effect (*Picture Post*, 9 Dec., 47), you are attacking Sir James George Frazer – thus neatly daring us to wade through twenty fat volumes. Now unfortunately it is a very difficult – inhuman or almost superhuman – task to catalogue mere facts without personal equation or bias. There is a good deal of truth in George Bernard Shaw's dictum: 'The way to get at the merits of a case is not to listen to the fool who imagines himself impartial, but to get it argued with reckless bias for and against.' However impartial Mr Wells may regard himself in his self-imposed task as 'messenger', he cannot – especially in the case of an author such as Sir J. G. Frazer – disclaim responsibility for the *message* he extracts from huge specialist compilations. Here is the judgment of a competent critic of *The golden bough*:[7]

> It is perhaps this readiness of Frazer to give up his own theories, to swallow like Kronos his own children, that has contributed to the fact that if his works are universally appreciated as most valuable collections of facts his theories have found relatively few adherents. It is a psychological enigma to me why Frazer, so ready to give up so many theories that he might be styled an absolute sceptic, is so enthusiastic in defending absolute truth in one determined direction . . . His picturesque descriptions are often wonderful. It is clear that by such means he exerts on the general reader the same mighty influence which always proceeds from poetical creation. But of course poetical beauties cannot be for ever substitutes for firm and solid truths; and so I fear that many of Frazer's theories will be found to be nothing but spirited fancies (W. Schmidt, S.J., *Anthropos* 4 (1912) 259; A. Muntsch, S.J., *Evolution and culture* (1923) 4).

---

7. Frazer was aware of the tentative nature of many of his theories: 'Hypotheses are necessary but often temporary bridges built to connect isolated facts. If my light bridges should sooner or later break down or be superseded by more solid structures, I hope that my book may still have its utility and its interest as a repertory of facts' (J. G. Frazer, preface to second edition of *The golden bough (the magic art)* i (1913) (3) xix).

Appendix 2

Speaking of Frazer's *Totemism and exogamy* (4 vols., 1910), Fr Schmidt says (*Origin and growth of religion* (1931) 104): 'It will be for all time to come the foundation of all collections of material; the last volume contained also a critical sketch of the various theories of the origin of totemism, among which three hypotheses of Frazer's own appeared – for he had three times changed his opinion on the subject.' Prof. R. H. Lowie in his *Primitive religion* (1924) 147, does not show much respect for Frazer's reasoning: 'Frazer's argument breaks down at every point; and, even if we adopt his definitions, there is no reason to ascribe greater antiquity to magic than religion.' Frazer's views on primitive mentality are severaly criticised in A. A. Goldenweiser's *Early civilisation* (1922) 337-48. So Mr Wells's attempt to shove Frazerism down our throats is preposterous dogmatism. A very pertinent criticism is that uttered by Fr H. Thurston, S.J., in connection with Frazer's theories on 'the feast of the dead':

> When Sir James Frazer is so hopelessly at sea regarding the tone of thought of people who lived nearly four centuries ago, how can we trust his intuitions of the mental processes of prehistoric races about whom nothing but the most meagre fragments and observation are preserved to us (H. Thurston, S.J., *The memory of our dead* (1915) 106).

The same argument will, as we proceed, strike us more forcibly in the case of Mr Wells. When this man so utterly fails to grasp the facts and to understand the spirit of the Catholicism which is all around him, what reliance can anyone place in his imaginative reconstruction of the mind and religion of prehistoric man?

For the following sentence Mr Wells refers us explicitly to Frazer's *The golden bough*:

> The unbiassed reader can realise for himself how the cannibal blood sacrifice has been refined at last into the mystery of the Mass, which will indeed have very little mystery left for him if he faces the facts (*The fate of homo sapiens*, 119).

Observe, whoever agrees with Mr Wells is *ipso facto* 'unbiassed'. And, while dishing up a far-fetched hypothesis popularised by A. F. Loisy and A. Reinach, he soothingly assures his readers – optimistically identified with the readers of Frazer – that he is merely recounting 'facts', whereas obviously he is theorising (at second or third hand) on the hypothetical genetic concatenation of facts. That, as shown by texts and history, the eucharistic rite is the perpetuation of Christ's farewell service instituted in pagan-loathing Jerusalem – that would be too simple and obvious, too favourable to Catholics, to be admitted. So St Paul must nilly-willy be made to sit at the 'table of demons' and a rite which daily lifts up the hearts of millions is forthwith compared to the orgies of cannibals. Mr Wells seems to take a kind of sadistic pleasure in this kind of insulting blasphemy; he fails entirely to shock us. What is really disconcerting is his rather naïve belief that the stuff is new to us:

> These investigations [he continues] into the beginnings of religion have accumulated steadily throughout the past half-century. It is only by great efforts of censorship, by sectarian education of an elaborately protected sort and the like, that ignorance about them is maintained (*The fate of homo sapiens*, 119).

Well, well; what a disappointment it will be to him to learn that we are neither so ignorant nor so gullible as he fancies. I, the product of 'sectarian education', give in a footnote references to Catholic refutations which I have personally read.[8] To these I refer the 'unbiassed reader', who is not inclined to accept the *ipse dixit* of Mr Wells. There is no point in arguing the matter here; for Mr Wells does not argue, he merely pontificates 'neath the shade of the golden bough.

In this Frazer-alibi we have an example illustrating the worthlessness of Mr Wells's boast (*Picture Post*, 9 Dec., 47): 'There is scarcely a statement in my book for which I do not give a sound reference.' Barring the journalistic excursions into foreign affairs – with which we are not concerned – this is certainly

8. E. Jacquier, 'Les mystères païens et S. Paul', *Dict. Apol.* 3 (1916) 1012; Mgr. C. Ruch, 'L'eucharistie et les mystères païens', *Semaine Int. d'Eth. rel.* 4 (1926) 319-25; Père M. J. Lagrange in *Revue Biblique* 16 (1919) 139-217, 419-80; criticism of Loisy in 17 (1920) 420-46; criticism of V. D. Macchioro in 29 (1932) 424-35; and L. de Grandmaison, S.J., 'Gods who died and came to life', *Jesus Christ* 3 (1935) 319-46.

Appendix 2

not true, as we shall presently see. But, even if it were, does he expect every ordinary Catholic to work through Frazer's ponderous tomes for himself and to test the tissue of hypotheses involved? Has Mr Wells done it himself? I am quite certain that he has not; he has neither the training, critical ability nor the time. Apparently he wants to introduce a new form of authoritarianism, to browbeat and ridicule us into accepting uncritically the pronouncements of these agnostic pundits. Believe it or not, Mr Wells, we Catholics are much more sceptical and critical than your modernistic sciolists. We have but one pope whose sphere of infallibility is strictly limted; Mr Wells has dozens of little popes whose theories he accepts as infallible without any independent research of his own. So he does not like 'such a natural born scoffer as Mr Hilaire Belloc' (*The fate of homo sapiens*, 155).[9] And, if I call Frazer 'scrappy and incoherent', Mr Wells replies in a horrified tone: 'This is really not a permissible way of speaking of . . . Sir James George Frazer' (*Picture Post*, 9 Dec., 47). There are physicists who do not mind atheist blasphemy or moral anarchy, but are painfully shocked if you criticise Einstein or talk disrespectfully of the root of minus one. Mr Wells will pat you on the back if, imitating him, you indulge in coarse ribaldry about Christ and his mother. But it really pains him if you venture to speak slightingly of one of the hypotheses not yet abandoned in the latest edition of the works of Sir James George Frazer. Mr Wells's narrow iconoclasm is thus combined with an enormous amount of intolerant credulity.

Have I myself independently investigated all the theories of *The golden bough*? I certainly have not; life is too short for such personal exploration. On one or two points which I examined

---

9. To the Catholic (represented by Mr Belloc) he attributes the tag: *Credo quia absurdum*. This phrase is incorrectly fathered on Tertullian, who, however, uses cognate phrases which merely emphasise that in Christian truths there are superficial paradoxes: 'God's foolishness is wiser than men' (1 *Cor.* 1:25). Cf. M. Grabmann, *Die Geschichte der scholastischen Methode* 1 (1909) 118. 'I have tried to imagine,' says Wells (*The fate of homo sapiens*, 155), what Belloc 'thinks at Mass. But that is just when he suspends all thinking!' Why, Belloc says his prayers, of course. Has not Mr Wells ever seen a missal? But you see, *by definition*, all thinking outside the range of his own narrow little creed is non-existent and inconceivable to Mr Wells. The world of thought consists of Wells and a great void!

Alfred O'Rahilly III: Controversialist

at first hand I have found him entirely unsatisfactory;[10] on matters connected with Catholic faith and practice I have found him grossly inaccurate;[11] and as regards the most important of his claims to have breached the 'venerable walls' of Christianity with his 'battery of the comparative method?', I am satisfied that Frazer has been adequatley refuted.[12] So I have no intention of spending the rest of my life in burrowing amid Frazer's avoirdupois; still less am I inclined with Mr Wells to grovel before this new idol.[13] The up-to-date canon *Credo quia modernum* does not strike me as very reliable.

Without pursuing further Mr Wells's use of expert authorities, I content myself with quoting a non-Catholic scholar's estimate of Mr Wells's performance (as regards Greek and Roman history) in his *The outline of history* (1920):

> The non-expert will always be at sea (although he may not often know it), will not know what expert to follow, nor how far, and may make the most absurd blunders by using the wrong book or misunderstanding the methods of the right one, through ignorance of the sources of opinon . . . However, these defects would be scarcely worth mentioning if the author possessed the other necessary qualifications for work of this kind: namely, perception – that he may see the true line of action and distinguish between the important and the trivial – and the power of expression by means of generalisation and definition . . . None of these qualities, in my judgment, does Mr Wells

---

10. For example, on fire-walking (cf. J. G. Frazer, *Balder the beautiful* 2 (1914) 4). I agree with Fr Thurston: 'The easy confidence with which rationalists like Sir James Frazer dismiss the fire-walking phenomena does not impress me very favourably in regard to their readiness to admit unpalatable evidence or their capacity for weighing it' (*Month* 149 (1932) 203).

11. Cf. H. Thurston, *The memory of our dead* (1915) 231: 'Sir James Frazer's dogmatism'.

12. For instance, Frazer's attempt to connect the crucifixion with the alleged fact that in Western Asia – and even in Jerusalem! – a man was slain yearly in the character of a god. In refutation see: Andrew Lang, 'Mr Frazer's theory of the crucifixion', *Fortnightly Review*, April 1901, 605-62; M. J. Lagrange, *Notes on the Orpheus of M. Salomon Reinach* (1910) 27-36; and K. Kastner, *Jesus vor Pilatus* (1912) 41-51.

13. Similarly it would require a lifetime to follow up Dr G. G. Coulton in his various muck-raking expeditions. But I published a refutation of him concerning the stigmata of St Francis in *Studies* 27 (1938) 177-98.

Appendix 2

possess in sufficient measure (A. W. Gomme (lecturer in Greek in the University of Glasgow), *Mr Wells as historian* (1921) 3).

Mr Gomme's concluding assessment of Mr Wells's qualifications as historian is equally pertinent to his subsequent publications and to his version of the history of Christian theology:

> There is no inquiry in the work, no judgment . . . Starting with a preconceived idea which he is anxious to proclaim, careless of the truth in detail as in general, slovenly in expression, incapable of perceiving the general lines of his story, blind to important things and ready with the irrelevant, indifferent to the qualities that separate race from race and the achievements of one people from another, and possessed with a truly amazing confidence in the ease of the task he has undertaken and his own ability to cope with it, Mr Wells has all the defects of which a historian should be free, particularly one who would write for the general public an outline of the story of mankind (Gomme, 46).

Some of Mr Wells's 'sound references' on topics connected with the Catholic Church are rather peculiar. For example, in *The fate of homo sapiens*, 160, he quotes and analyses W. Teeling's *Crisis for Christianity* (1939). This book is alleged to give us 'the present Catholic outlook', it is 'a fair reflection of the Vatican-centred mentality'. And in conclusion he says (p. 164): 'So much for the Catholic contribution to human adjustment today.' Now this book has no authority whatever, it has been severely criticised in Catholic reviews, and I myself disagree strongly with many things in it. Does Mr Wells seriously hold that because an author happens to be a Catholic – sometimes more or less – the rest of us are bound to agree with his book? Apparently we are all a flock of undifferentiated sheep to him! This kind of thing is really ridiculous. But still more puerile and disingenuous is it to refer us (*The fate of homo sapiens*, 157) to Joseph McCabe's *History of the popes* (1939). 'The Catholic reader,' he says, 'will, I know, feel that my recommendation of that outspoken book is in the worst possible taste.' Not at all, Mr Wells, we do not expect any taste from you; but the *critical* reader will be astonished that you should be so gullible as to

Alfred O'Rahilly III: Controversialist

think Mr McCabe is an authority on Church history.[14] For good measure, you might have included references to G. S. Streatfield, A. S. Rappoport and their ilk.

Mr Wells writes in quite a superior way as if all Catholics were half-educated morons, as if the Church were a house of cards liable to instant destruction by a little puff from every tenth-rate enemy. He does not really think this, he just pretends it to frighten us. When he was a tiny Protestant, he thought God was a 'bogey'.[15] And now he in his turn wishes to play the bogeyman. Hush, hush, here comes Frazer-McCabe-Wells; let us all lie down! But he really does not think we shall be so quickly demolished, that like bewitched rats we shall all so readily and tamely follow the new pied piper:

> For reasons I have made perfectly clear in this book, I do not believe there will be any Roman Catholic Church at all in the fifth millennium A.D. (*The fate of homo sapiens*, 329).

For which millennial relief, many thanks.[16] Mr Wells is rather notorious as a prophet with apocalyptic fervour. Some of us prefer to think that the Gates of Wells shall not prevail against the Rock.

So far we have been discussing Mr Wells's performances based on 'sound references'. But sometimes he prefers to fulminate *ex cathedra* on his own authority, as it were, by lightning-flashes. On Spain, for example:

> Catholicism has waded through blood into its own again (*The fate of homo sapiens*, 319).
> The devout in France or Britain must support the Franco pronunciamento to the infinite injury of their own countries (*The fate of homo sapiens*, 157; *Picture Post*, 9 Dec., 47).

---

15. H. G. Wells, *God the invisible king* (1917) 52; 'Old bogey', *The fate of homo sapiens*, 3.
16. The prophets are becoming cautious. Thirty years ago Mr McCabe said (*The decay of the Church of Rome* (1909) 5): 'Instead of showing signs of increase, the Church of Rome is rapidly decaying; and only a dramatic change of whole character can save it from ruin.' He is not quite so sure now.

Appendix 2

Unfortunately not being one of 'the devout', I do not know on what authority Mr Wells imposes upon them this new article of faith (Francophilism). But, being able to read, I prefer to decide for myself about Spain rather than to accept Mr Wells's oracular pronouncements. Or perhaps he really has the impertinence to expect readers like myself to take his word for it? 'The infinite injury' of England and France is not quite so apparent today; nor would the Finns be ready to accept Mr Wells's appreciation of a Moscow-implanted Red government. But, then, Mr Wells has decided views on everything, views so clear to him that mostly he will not bother even to argue for them. I think it was Lord Melbourne who said: 'I wish to God I were as sure of anything as Tom Macaulay is about everything!' To read Mr Wells is like having a surfeit of predigested pellets; personally I like to do quite a lot of my own digesting.

II[17]

Mr Wells and Catholic priests, explorers, scientists, scholars . . .

Having put Mr Wells's pretentious claims into their proper perspective, we are now in a position to appreciate the impertinent bigotry which he displays in his jibes at Catholic priests.

> [The pope] has the medieval education of a priest, his advisers have worn the mental blinkers of the devout (*The fate of homo sapiens*, 157).
>
> These Catholic prelates . . . are in fact extremely ignorant men . . . They can have read few books, they can have had no opportunities of thinking freely . . . Most of them are trying most earnestly to do right by the dim and dwindling oil-lamps inside their brains . . . [They have] no opportunity of grasping modern ideas without an impossible expenditure of perplexing inquiry (*The fate of homo sapiens*, 165).

And so forth. He does not wish to be too hard on the members of 'the sex-tormented priesthood of the Roman communion',[18]

17. *Standard* 19 January 1940.
18. H. G. Wells, *God the invisible king* (1917) 64.

who not only have no wives but no brains. They just keep mumbling incantations all day, they have no chance of grasping modern ideas. They learn anthropology from the book of *Genesis*, and Belloc teaches them about evolution. Thus, from his superior height, speaks the B.Sc. (hons.) in zoology of London. Why, even as an undergraduate he knew almost everything:

> Now how did we – because I was one of a generation of science students – how did we see the world in '88? Time had opened out for us, and the creation, the fall of man and the flood,[19] those simple fundamentals of the Judaeo-Christian mythology, had vanished. For ever. Instead I saw a limitless universe throughout which the stars and nebulae were scattering like dust, and I saw life ascending, as it seemed, from nothingness towards the stars . . . We knew that our ancestors were apes; and it seemed possible that man would go on to a power and wisdom beyond all precedent (*The fate of homo sapiens*, 11).

Thus in his early twenties, while dissecting frogs, he had exploded the Judaeo-Christian mythology. So after all he need not have quoted Sir J. Frazer at all. Wells, *aetatis* 22, settled all this. *For ever!* It is obvious that we are not really dealing with a mature inquiring reader of *The golden bough* (plus McCabe, etc.), we are up against an excessive prolongation of undergraduate cocksureness. Even then he *knew* he was descended from an ape,[20] but he felt he was ascending 'from nothingness towards the stars'. What a pity that he never suspected he might eventually sink into bathos.

19. Observe the flood as one of our 'fundamentals'!
20. 'The myth of ape-ancestry lingers on the stage, in the movies, in certain anti-naturalistic literature, in caricature of our pedigree, even in certain scientific parlance; but the ape-ancestry hypothesis is entirely out of date, and its place is taken by the recent demonstration that we are descended from "dawn-men", not from "ape-men"' (Prof. H. F. Osborn, *Evolution in religion and education* (1926), cited by W. Schmidt in E. Eyre (ed.), *European civilisation* 1 (1934) 80).

'Huxley was far more subtle a thinker than was Haeckel, and he worked along rather different lines. But, nevertheless, he produced the same popular results – he led people to think that man's origin along the final stages of the scale of life had been scientifically proved to be true' (Prof. F. Wood Jones, *The problem of man's ancestry* (1918) 20f).

Appendix 2

In my Catholic Truth Society pamphlet *Faith and facts* (1917) I adduced several examples of this curious phenomenon that the unbelief of men, like E. Gibbon, J. E. Renan, T. H. Huxley, etc., *preceded* any competent research into the problem; unbelief was not the result but the presupposition of the work which subsequently brought them fame. Loisy is the latest addition to this gallery. We learn from his book *My duel with the Vatican* (1924) that he had lost his faith before he was twenty-one years old, long before he entered upon biblical studies. The cases of Gibbon and Renan are rather relevant to our present dispute, though of course these men should not be compared with a mere populariser like H. G. Wells who is entirely incapable of independent research. The historian Gibbon lost his faith when seventeen and a half years old, owing (he alleges) to his swallowing J. Tillotson's ridiculous argument against transubstantiation. After his lifelong work against Christianity, he began to be appalled by the excesses of the French Revolution. In his *Memoirs* (ed. G. Birkbeck Hill (1900) 237), he says: 'I beg leave to subscribe my assent to Mr Burke's creed on the revolution of France.' A curious alliance! He objects to 'the danger of exposing an old superstition to the contempt of the blind and fanatic multitude' – just what he himself had been doing! Renan – with young P. E. M. Berthelot, the future chemist – abandoned religion at the age of eighteen! He too came to realise that it is easier to destroy than to establish:

> If through the constant labour of the nineteenth century the knowledge of facts has considerably increased, the destiny of mankind has on the other hand become more obscure than ever . . . Candidly speaking, I fail to see how without the ancient dreams the foundations of a happy and noble life are to be relaid (J. E. Renan, *The future of science* (1891) preface, xviii).

In his *Life of Christ* – rehashed by Ludwig in the *Daily Express* – Renan initiated the idea of appealing to the man-in-the street, the policy of issuing popular rationalist editions of alleged research-results for uncritical consumption by the half-educated. Mr Wells has carried on the propaganda on a cosmic scale. He too started as a callow youth by rejecting all religion. On which procedure he has himself written the pithiest

Alfred O'Rahilly III: Controversialist

comment (*The fate of homo sapiens*, 263): 'Few human beings are adult before thirty-five, and most remain puerile to the end.' And he too – as we shall see – has begun to shrink from the nemesis he has created. For years he has been making reiterated and futile efforts to start a new religion – minus God and minus personal immortality. Meanwhile, though ambitioning to be himself our new high priest, he continues to attack Catholic priests – that great organised body of self-dedicated men who stand for those spiritual ideals which are necessary if civilisation is not to crumble. Let us see Mr Wells's intellectual objections to Catholic priests.

To the B.Sc. mind biologist-priests like G. J. Mendel and E. Wasmann must, of course, appear like microbes. But since graduation, Mr Wells has betaken himself not only to fiction but to popularising investigations – other people's of course – into primitive religion. 'It is only by great efforts of censorship, by sectarian education', that Catholics like myself have been kept in ignorance of the subject (*The fate of homo sapiens*, 119). Now, when I read that sentence, I said to myself as piously as Huxley said it about Bishop Wilberforce: 'The Lord has delivered him into my hands.' For if there is one subject in which Catholic priests have been first-hand scientific investigators, it is in the subject of primitive religion. I may refer to Mgr A. Le Roy; and especially to Pater Wilhelm Schmidt, founder of the review *Anthropos*, director of the Missionary-Ethnological Museum of the Lateran, author of many first-class works;[21] and to the splendid book of Père Pinard de la Boullaye, S.J., *L'étude*

---

21. *Die Stellung der Pygmdenvölker in der Entwicklungsgeschichte der Menschen* (Stuttgart 1910); *Der Ursprung der Gottesidee* (Münster, 6 vols., 1926-35); *The origin and growth of religion* (London 1931); *High Gods in North America* (Oxford 1933); *Primitive revelation* (St Louis 1939); 'Primitive man', E. Eyre (ed.), *European civilisation* 1 (1934) 1-82; numerous articles in *Anthropos*.

Fr Schmidt has also written two excellent C.T.S. pamphlets: *The religion of earliest man* and *The religion of later primitive peoples*. He has also edited an Anthropos Library of ethnographic monographs by missionaries; and with Fr G. Hoeltker he has edited fourteen volumes of a linguistic library. A *Festschrift* in honour of Fr Schmidt – to which distinguished ethnologists from all over the world contributed – was published in Vienna in 1928. *Der Mensch aller Zeiten* (4 vols.) has been written by H. Obermaier, F. Birkner, W. Schmidt and W. Koppers. (I have read only vol. III: *Völker und Kulturen* (1924) by Schmidt and Koppers.) I am not sure whether Birkner is a priest or a layman; I have his book *Die Rassen und Völker der Menschheit* (1913). Fr Obermaier's *Fossil man in Spain*

Appendix 2

comparée des religions, I-II (Paris 1922-25). Encouraged and subsidised by the papacy, scientifically trained missionaries have done first-hand pioneer work; for example: Fr Damian Kreichgauer in the solution of Maya inscriptions; Fr P. Schebesta among the pigmies of Malay and Congo; Frs M. Gusinde and W. Koppers among the tribes of Tierra del Fuego. This last investigation is interesting when we remember that Darwin spent a few weeks there and in the neighbourhood in 1832-33. He arrived at the usual hasty generalisations of the tourist – a point which will be duly appreciated by Mr Wells who has the essentially tourist mind.

> Viewing such men, one can hardly make oneself believe that they are fellow-creatures . . . Captain FitzRoy could never ascertain that the Fuegians have any distinct belief in a future life . . . We have no reason to believe that they perform any sort of religious worship (Charles Darwin, *Journal of researches* (1845) 213f).
>
> Their language does not deserve to be called articulate (*Charles Darwin's diary of the voyage of H.M.S. Beagle* (ed. N. Barlow, 1933) 119).

It was left to a Catholic priest to spend several years among this primitive people, to share their material hardships, to learn their languages, to win their confidence – with the unexpected result that he found them possessing 'a well-developed monotheistic belief in God', a high moral code, a régime of private property, and a well-deserved low opinion of their white oppressors.[22]

(1924) has an introduction by Prof. H. F. Osborn. There is a periodical *Primitive man* edited by Rev J. M. Cooper of the Catholic University of Washington. There are English translations of four of Fr P. Schebesta's interesting books: *Among the forest dwarfs of Malaya* (no date); *Among Congo pigmies* (1933); *My pigmy and negro hosts* (1936); *Revisiting my pigmy hosts* (1936) – all published by Hutchinson. An excellent recent book is *Cultural anthropology* (2nd ed., 1936) by Fr A. Muntsch, S.J., on some of the pioneer work of missionaries on Chinese religion, Sanscrit language, etc.; see other references in *Pinard de la Boullaye I* (1922) 181ff. Finally, I may refer to the work on Semitic religions by Père Lagrange, O.P., and to the recent Jesuit Assyriologists J. N. Strassmaier, F. X. Kugler and E. Burrows.

22. Prof. M. Gusinde, S.V.D., 'Zur Ethik der Feuerländer', *Semaine Int. d'Ethnologie religieuse* 4 (1926) 156-71; W. Koppers, S.V.D., *Unter Feuerland-Indianer* (Stuttgart 1924).

Alfred O'Rahilly III: Controversialist

Turn now to the related field of archaeology and anthropology. It will be sufficient to cite a leading anthropologist, Professor H. F. Osborn of Columbia University:

> Among these scholars whose names adorn the honour-roll of anthropology in France, none is more illustrious than the long line of Catholic priests and abbés whose researches and scholarship have notably added to our knowledge of fossil man . . . The Abbé Louis Bourgeois (1819-78) . . . was the first to present and develop the problem of the eoliths in 1863 . . . The Abbé Delaunay collaborated with him in these researches. The Abbé Ducrost, in collaboration with Dr Lartet, published in 1872 . . . the results of the excavations of the station of Solutré . . . It required the co-operation of three enlightened French priests to re-establish and complete our knowledge of the Neanderthal race: namely, the two brothers, the Abbé A. Bouyssonie and the Abbé J. Bouyssonie, and their friend the Abbé Bardon . . . We now reach the names of the two most distinguished men today in the prehistoric archaeology of Europe: the Abbé Henri Breuil . . . and the Abbé Hugo Obermaier . . . Pére Teilhard de Chardin . . . in 1923 discovered at sites in China and Mongolia human industrial remains, together with fossilised bones of animals, many of which are extinct (H. F. Osborn, *Evolution in religion and education* (1926) 198f).

Professor Osborn mentions a journey into the recesses of all the principal prehistoric caverns of France with the Abbé Henri Breuil 'the archaeologist who begins his day in his abbé's dress in religious devotions and then dons his rude miner's costume and lamp for descent into the often perilous recesses of the caverns'. Being a gentleman, a religious-minded man, a man with the tolerance of real scholarship, Professor Osborn did not taunt his colleague with 'suspending all thinking' every morning. Nor did he conceitedly ask the abbé: 'Why do intelligent people accept this strange heap of mental corruption as a religion and a rule of life?' (*The fate of homo sapiens*, 154). No; it was left to a scientific nonentity like H. G. Wells to start thumbnosing his betters. He has succeeded only in making his own swelledheadedness quite ridiculous. This gentleman who is

Appendix 2

never quoted in a single serious work on biology or archaeology, who was never asked – as was Fr Schmidt in 1932 – to give the Upton lectures in religion in Manchester College, Oxford, who prefers the Riviera to Tierra del Fuego, who is more at home in his suburban armchair than in the forests of Malay or the prehistoric caves of France – this gentleman, having solved all the problems of anthropology and religion as an undergraduate, now proceeds to pour abuse on Catholic priests, men of science and trained missionaries, who today stand in the foremost ranks of the world's patient researchers. He is too old to be spanked; he is too noisy to be ignored; he is too cocksure to be argued with; he is too obstinately ignorant to be enlightened. So I just leave him there.

III[23]

Mr Wells and the Catholic Church

For Protestantism Mr Wells has only good-natured contempt:

> Protestantism carried on to its end is a complete acceptance of the limitless impartial and continually more wonderful universe that scientific enquiry is illuminating for us; that is to say, it culminates in atheism without qualification (*The fate of homo sapiens*, 178).

We are not here concerned with this condemnation, which is both summary and unjust; but observe incidentally the cool assumption that science is synonymous with atheism. Catholicism, however, he regards as the 'most highly organised and active expression' of Christianity, as 'certainly the most formidable single antagonist in the way of human readjustment' (*The fate of homo sapiens*, 150, 169). Over a decade ago Hilaire Belloc accused him of being anti-Catholic, an accusation which was vehemently denied:

> He declares that I am violently antagonistic to the Catholic Church, an accusation I deny very earnestly . . . I am conscious of no animus against Catholicism (H. G. Wells, *Mr Belloc objects* (1926) 1).

23. *Standard* 19 January 1940.

Alfred O'Rahilly III: Controversialist

Since then he has owned up to 'anti-Christian bias'.[24] But perhaps he still holds he has no conscious animus against us. I will not argue the point; I merely wonder where the deuce he would find the further vituperative vocabulary if he were *really* prejudiced against us! Anyway, Catholicism is 'intellectually . . . the most extraordinary jumble of absurdities and incompatibilities that has ever exercised and perplexed the human intelligence' (*The fate of homo sapiens*, 151). We have by now learnt that Mr Wells is like King Borria-Bungaloo-Boo, that man-eating African swell: his voice is a hullaballoo, his whisper a horrible yell. So perhaps we may interpret this sentence to be merely the Wellsian scream corresponding to the ordinary opponent's quiet statement that he disagrees with us. Mr Wells has to yell his disagreement at sixteen cat-power. All right, all right, it is on record, Mr Wells; nobody expects *you* to be exercised or perplexed about *anything*.

He does not like the divinity of Our Lord, which *more suo* he refers to as 'the Trinity business' (*The fate of homo sapiens*, 151).

> A hearty laugh at the metaphors of relationships in the triplex composition of the divinity would shatter the whole process. Derision is the deadly enemy of Catholicism (*The fate of homo sapiens*, 154).

That is the trick, Mr Wells; when, owing to the deficiencies of your positivist mind, you cannot argue, just give a guffaw. Once on the continent I met a Jew who spat on the ground, simply to show he did not like me; only you cannot very well do that in a book, Mr Wells, otherwise the gesture would suit you perfectly. The rabbi did not expect me to argue with him; anyway, this salivary kind of disputation does not appeal to my aesthetic or hygienic sense. What do you expect me to do about your Trinitarian difficulties, Mr Wells? You give me nothing to argue about; you just expectorate.[25] In any case, I know from previous publications of yours that you have not even the

---

24. H. G. Wells, *Experiment in autobiography* (1934) ii, 573.
25. 'That stuffed scarecrow of divinity, that incoherent accumulation of antique theological notions, the Nicene deity' (*God the invisible king* (1917) 15); 'A drumming storm of intolerant nonsense' (*The fate of homo sapiens*, 151).

Appendix 2

rudiments of knowledge necessary for adult discussion of the subject;[26] it would be like debating relativity with one of my first-year pass students. So I can only meet you on your own chosen ground; just for a change, I am administering a dose of derision to *you*, Mr Wells; and before I have finished with you I hope to leave you well deflated. Meanwhile might I quote for you some advice from your old master?

> Heterodox ribaldry disgusts me, I confess, rather more than orthodox fanaticism. It is at once so easy, so stupid, such a complete anachronism in England, and so thoroughly calculated to disgust and repel the very thoughtful and serious people whom it ought to be the great aim to attract (L. Huxley (ed.), *Life and letters of Thomas Henry Huxley* II (1900) 322).

So even T. H. Huxley would repudiate his pupil's heterodox ribaldry.

Our author has another ingenious little trick. As he himself admits (*The fate of homo sapiens*, 110f), his 'phraseology no doubt owes much more than he realises to the phrases and assumptions of the liberal protestant progressive world of half a century ago'. He gets rid of the resurrection in a few sentences, with a facility which would have astonished D. F. Strauss and Renan and which must be the envy of Loisy and M. Goguel.[27] Mr Wells never finds any difficulty of disposing of anything that he does not like; just a shake of the pen and the theological gnats fly away from the great man. He has his inhibitions, however; he does not like saying too bluntly that Our Lord was a deceiver and a charlatan. So, according to him, 'the story of the early beginnings of Christianity is the story of the struggle between the real teachings and spirit of Jesus of Nazareth and the limitations, amplifications and misunderstand-

---

26. Take these two statements, for instance: (1) 'The doctrine of the Trinity, as far as the relationship of the Third Person goes, hangs almost entirely upon one ambiguous and disputed utterance in St John's gospel (25:26)' (*God the invisible king* (1917) 11f): (2) 'It was only after three centuries . . . that the cardinal mystery of the Trinity was established as the essential fact of Christianity' (*ibid.*, 3). The Catholic doctrine will be found historically expounded in Père Lebreton's book, of which the first volume has appeared in an English translation: *History of the dogma of the Trinity* (London 1938).

27. H. G. Wells, *Outline of history*, ch. 39, §4-5.

ings of the very inferior men' who were his immediate followers.[28] The misinterpretation, according to Mr Wells, began quite early; it can be seen in the first chapter of the *Acts of the apostles*. Accordingly he is bound to admit that the message which electrified and ultimately transformed the world was not the Sermon on the Mount but the message: 'He is risen from the dead.' The apostles did not preach Jesus as a moralist like Socrates or Epictetus, not even as a humanised Hillel.

But they were wrong, says Mr Wells. These apostles who were deluded enough to work and suffer and die for their faith are just 'inferior men' to Wells in his comfortable armchair. Unequipped in Aramaic or Greek, gifted with a capacious swallow for the latest hypothesis of the latest rationalist, Mr Wells assures newspaper-readers that 'the plain account of Jesus preserved for us in the gospels' is not only inconsistent with the Athanasian creed but clearly with large portions of the gospels themselves. 'No man knows the Father but the Son . . . and him to whom the Son will choose to reveal him' (*Matt.* 11:27). 'He who hears you hears me' (*Luke* 10:6). 'Without me you can do nothing' (*John* 15:5). Mr Wells can no more find room for these amazing claims in his 'plain account' than he can fit in the resurrection. 'Oh Christ, most patient Lord,' writes Tertullian,[29] 'who for so many years has suffered the misinterpretation of the account given of you – that is, until Marcion came to your help!' So Mr Wells is anxious to clear away the accretions and to reveal to us 'the real teachings and spirit of Jesus of Nazareth' as contained in the documentary residue which he decides to accept, quite unhampered of course by any criterion of objective evidence. This is the Jesus of Liberal Protestantism. 'But,' asks Père M. J. Lagrange,[30] 'is this Jesus, this good professor of moral theology, this respected president of a conference of pastors, this useful auxiliary of the State in its endeavour to bring up German children along the path of virtue, the Jesus of the gospel?' This exploded distortion is still the pious ideal of Mr Wells. 'The personal teaching of Jesus' – with the inconvenient bits cut out – 'does seem to mark a new phase in the

---

28. H. G. Wells, *Outline of history*, ch. 39, §5.
29. *Adversus Marcionem* i, 20.
30. M. J. Lagrange, O.P., *The meaning of Christianity according to Luther and his followers in Germany* (1920) 263.

Appendix 2

moral and spiritual life of our race'.[31] But how could this have happened prior to the Strauss-Renan-Wells era, seeing that until then Christianity was built upon a lie?

The early Nazarenes . . . built their faith upon the stories that were told of his resurrection and magical ascension (H. G. Wells, *The outline of history*, ch. 39, §5). St Paul familiarised his disciples that Jesus, like Osiris,[32] was a god who died to rise again and give men immortality (H. G. Wells, *A short history of the world* (1926) 130).

St Paul, writing about A.D. 55, appeals to teaching that he gave the Corinthians some four years earlier, asserting that what he had then taught was what he himself had received from the apostles at his conversion (between A.D. 31 and 36): 'I passed on to you, as of first importance, the account I had received: that Christ died for our sins . . . was raised from the dead' (1 *Cor.* 15:3).[33]

I am not at all clear how Mr Wells gets rid of this testimony, for he scorns to discuss such prosaic details as historical texts. Anyway, in his latest book (*The fate of homo sapiens*, 125), he proceeds – without bothering about such trifles as proofs – to give us 'Paul's reconstruction of the Nazarene cult', namely, that 'his brilliant intelligence seized upon the idea of presenting Jesus as the sacrificial king . . . the lamb by whose blood we were saved'. That is, in plain language and in defiance of the texts, St Paul initiated and *invented* the idea that Christ 'died for our sins'. Now, St Paul pronounced anathema on anyone, even an angel, who would venture to preach another gospel (*Gal.* 1:8). Mr Wells takes the risk, though he is indeed no angel; but he thereby shows himself to be a very inaccurate scholar. That St Paul's soteriology was the faith of the primitive community is

---

31. H. G. Wells, *A short history of the world* (1926) 131.
32. E. Peet, professor of Egyptology in Liverpool University, writes in *The Cambridge Ancient History* 1 (1923) 333: 'The evidence for such a belief [that Osiris was a god of the Nile] is scanty and indecisive, and is outweighed by evidence which suggests that Osiris was either a very ancient king deified or that he was nothing more than a personification of dead kingship. In either case, the essential fact to be grasped is that he is first and foremost a *dead king*.' In Plutarch's version, Set murdered his brother Osiris and afterwards scattered his bones (*ibid.*, 332). But 'Osiris' like 'abracadabra' is good enough for Mr Wells as a rod for believers.

admitted even by liberals like C. von Weiszäcker, P. Sabatier, A. von Harnack and W. Bousset.[34] But up strolls Mr Wells to tell us: 'It is all very plain to anyone who reads these books [of the New Testament] without theological prepossessions' – and, let us add, without any training in scholarship. Curious – is it not? – how 'the unbiassed reader' always agrees with H. G. Wells, while all others – whether anthropologists, biblical scholars, Egyptologists, historians, political thinkers or biologists – are the victims of ignorance and prepossession. There is nothing like having a good conceit of oneself: Wells *Contra mundum*. But I find it rather boring, this prolonged miracle of H. G. Wells being always right without reason assigned.

IV[35]

Mr Wells and the Blessed Virgin

In his *The outline of history* (ch. 30, §9) Mr Wells speaks of 'immaculate conceptions by six-tusked elephants'. He is alluding to the legend that Máyá *dreams* that the future Buddha, of his own accord, enters her side as a six-tusked white elephant. At this stage of his career (1920), he thought that 'immaculate conception' was synonymous with 'incarnation'. After further study he produced this:

> The theologians excogitated a 'sinless' begetting for her. It is difficult to tell these things without a touch of derision. . . . And now all good Catholics must believe in the immaculate conception of the Virgin Mary, though what it is they think they are believing I cannot imagine (*The fate of homo sapiens*, 152f).
>
> I simply cannot understand what is meant by the immaculate conception (*Picture Post*, 9 Dec., 47).

But who on earth asked Mr Wells to imagine or understand this doctrine? Would it not be preferable if he began a bit farther back and examined the proofs for the existence of God? In reality the matter is, from his point of view, quite simple. Mr

---

34. See Mgr P. Batiffol, 'L'idée de rédemption dans le Nouveau Testament', *Semaine Int. d'Eth. rel.* 4 (1926) 305-18.

35. *Standard* 26 January 1940.

Appendix 2

Wells who does not believe in original sin holds that we are *all* immaculately conceived; whereas we hold that this applies only to Our Lady.

Needless to say he does not believe in anything supernatural such as grace. And, of course, what H. G. Wells happens to disbelieve is not arguable; it is unintelligible, unimaginable, worthy only of derision. I am sure he cannot understand the quantum theory of modern physics; yet he takes good care not to boast of this deficiency as a stunning argument. But anything in Catholicism that cannot be pared down to fit into his mental pigeonholes is at once proclaimed to be a monstrous figment. This megalomaniac pose is tremendously convenient. I once had a student who adopted it – but he was plucked.

Now there is considerable astuteness in Mr Wells's tactics; it is an adroit scheme for playing to the gallery. He has always soft-pedalled his atheism; so far from flaunting it, he for many years attempted to mislead the public by writing almost enthusiastically and in biblical language of 'God' – until he was shown up by a more honest fellow-atheist. 'Let there be no mistake about it,' says William Archer (*God and Mr Wells* (1917) 36), 'Mr Wells's ambition is to rank with St Paul and Mahomet as the apostle of a new world-religion.' Driven from this tergiversation, he adopts another method of cozening the ill-educated. He skims lightly over his rejection of Protestantism. He pretends to believe unctuously in a unitarian version of Christ, presumably making this innocuous concession with his tongue in his cheek, careful to avoid alienating possible no-popery recruits. Then, in collaboration with Mr J. A. Kensit, he launches his campaign of invective against us. Next after Catholic priests, the common objective of this brace of ill-assorted bigots is the Mother of Christ. But none of the dirty discredited stories which his predecessor E. H. Haeckel (abetted by his translator McCabe) had disinterred from the late Jewish apocrypha; that did not succeed, it was a bit too foul. So he talks dishonestly of 'the Virgin Mary', deliberately fostering the impression that he is zealously carrying out the reformation-task of freeing unadulerated Christianity from the excrescences of Rome. In this tactical concentration on side-issues, this careful diversion of attention from his materialist creed, he is very dishonest. I would have a great deal more respect for Mr Wells if he were more virile and outspoken about his atheism.

Alfred O'Rahilly III: Controversialist

Mr Wells has a fatal tendency to dabble in Egyptology. He can even smell it! About a visit to Rome he tells us in his *Experiment in autobiography* II (1934) 573: 'In many of the darkened incense saturated churches I felt old Egypt and its mysteries still living and muttering.' He just felt it, he had what Mr Arnold Lunn calls a 'funny inside feeling'. Since then he has read a few books – the data in which he is perfectly incapable of verifying and controlling. After alluding to some later developments of Egyptian religion, he solemnly informs us (*The fate of homo sapiens*, 120) that 'very few Christians know these facts'! He then proceeds to produce a libel which he thinks startlingly new, though it is rather a hoary chestnut:

> The worship of the goddess Isis bearing the infant Horus in her arms anticipated the Catholic adoration of the Virgin Mary down even to minor details (*The fate of homo sapiens*, 120; *Experiment in autobiography* i, 47). With the taking over of Isis and the infant Horus as the Virgin and Child, . . . the Virgin became a divine queen, very beautiful and adorable (*The fate of homo sapiens*, 152).

Let us see the legend. Isis was the sister and wife of Osiris; their son was Horus; so at any rate Isis was not a virgin. Osiris was murdered by his twin-brother Set, and Isis collected the fragments of the body. In one verison Set scattered them again; according to another, Horus embalmed the remains. Afterwards Horus and Set had an undignified fight. Certainly not very promising materials for originating the cult of Our Lady. However, Mr Wells in his *Outline of history* (ch. 29, §5) thinks it was 'a very natural step'. So we have 'the identification of Mary with Isis' and 'the taking over of Isis and Horus as the Virgin and Child'. What on earth is the man talking about? Does he think that Catholics literally *identified* Mary with Isis? Does he maintain that no such people as Mary and her son ever existed, so that the devotion was really to Isis and Horus? Does he really hold that among Catholics today – and back to patristic times – this Egyptian stuff enters as an element into the honour paid to Christ and his mother? Does he think that the only reason why we so act is to be found in this rather sordid bit of mythology? There are limits even to the anti-Catholic obsessions of Mr Wells; so probably he means none of these things. He may be alluding to the appropriation of Egyptian art-forms to Christian worship. I know but little of the

Appendix 2

subject, but I am sure he knows much less. On this interpretation, this whole pother becomes quite innocuous. It is such a commonplace of Church history that pagan festivals and practices were, with practical psychology, 'taken over' and Christianised by the Church, that I should be ashamed to waste space by discussing the subject or giving references. So for all I know some old pagans may have been helped by showing them how superior was Jesus with Mary his mother to these rather disreputable Egyptian myths; and perhaps the Church seized 'the spoils of the Egyptians' and so showed a higher use for these old images. I do not know and Mr Wells does not know; and, if it were true, it would be to our credit and insight.

The more one reads Mr Wells's excursions outside the region of fictional entertainment, the more obvious it becomes that he has not an original idea in his whole composition; he merely collects from other people's dustbins and garbage-heaps. This gibe at Our Lady, for instance, is not very original. Here is a quotation from a book over forty years old:

> The Egyptians were a Horus-worshipping people in Roman times, honouring Isis also as his mother; and the influence this had on the development of Christianity was profound. We may even say that but for the presence of Egypt we should never have seen a madonna. Isis had obtained a great hold on the Romans under the earlier emperors, her worship was fashionable and widespread. And when she found a place in the other great movement, that of the Galileans, when fashion and moral conviction could shake hands, then her triumph was assured; and as the mother goddess she has ruled the devotion of Italy ever since. How much Horus has entered into the popular development of Christianity . . . is seen readily when we note the general popular worship of the child Horus . . . The well-known Christian monogram [the two Greek letters *chi* and *rho*, that is, *Ch* and *r* in Christos] . . . essentially is the sign of Horus and only became Christian by adoption[36] (W. M.

---

36. I find it rather incredible that the combination of the Greek capital or uncial letter X and P came from Egyptian paganism. There are but few pre-Constantine examples, and always as an abbreviation of *Christ* in Greek, usually in conjunction with IH (the first two letters of Jesus in Greek). See C. M. Kaufmann, *Handbuch der altchristlichen epigraphik* (1917) 40f, 163.

Alfred O'Rahilly III: Controversialist

Flinders Petrie, *Religion and conscience in ancient Egypt* (1898) 46).

This quotation is interesting, for it shows us that if we have to 'identify' Our Lady with Isis we must also 'identify' Our Lord with Horus. At this stage it becomes clear that the whole business is a mare's nest, one of those heavy jokes which bookish pedants inflict on long-suffering readers. The matter can be cleared up by referring to some Catholic book on Christian art: say, L. Bréhier, *L'art chrétien* (1928) 49-52; or G. de Jerphanion, S.J., *La voix des monuments* (1930) 37-39. In the first few centuries of the Christian era hellenistic art had become cosmopolitan, stylised, stereotyped. The artist – perhaps originally a pagan – naturally employed the known forms and existing models; realistic art based on nature was almost unknown. Thus the typical orator-form, as exemplified, for example, in a statue of Sophocles, reappears in the first delineations of Christ, as we can see in the second-century cemetery of Praetextatus; curiously enough, the same type was used by other hellenistic artists, working for the king of Jandhara, to represent the founder of Buddhism! The representation of the Good Shepherd is similarly modelled on that of Hermes or of Aristaeus. So, too, what we may call the type of Madonna and Child is based on older art-models which can be seen in Etruscan statuettes, in certain Gallo-Roman effigies, and in a painting in the *Jewish* hypogeum at Palmyra (259 A.D.).

Thus this shallow objection boils down to a commonplace in the early history of Christian art before it acquired its own vigorous expression in Byzantine and medieval times. To say that without Egypt we should never have seen a madonna, is of course childishly ridiculous; it is like saying that without the wall-paintings of Pompeii we should never have had the Fra Angelico or Rembrandt. To say that, because the first steps in Christian art were based on the stylised models of the time, Italian Catholics are 'ever since' devoted to 'the mother goddess', is a lowdown bigoted libel; it is on a level with claiming that when we honour the figure of Christ we are really worshipping Sophocles or Hermes. Is it not really surprising what arrant nonsense even more serious writers than H. G. Wells can utter when influenced by the itch to be smart and a dose of anti-Catholic virus?

Appendix 2

But Mr Wells accuses us of adoring Our Lady.[37] And this professed atheist secures a strange ally in The Protestant Truth Society which assures him that 'she is adored and not merely honoured'. It might be verbally true in an obsolete sense of the word 'adore' – as in the 1582 Rheims version of *Hebrews* 11:22: Jacob 'adored the top of his rod'. Subsequently in the *Picture Post* Mr Wells shifted his vocabulary; we are now told that 'Catholics worship the Virgin Mary' (*Picture Post*, 9 Dec., 47). According to the *New English Dictionary*, to worship means (1) 'to honour or revere as a supernatural being or power or as a holy thing', (2) 'to regard or approach with veneration', (3) 'to adore with appropriate acts, rites or ceremonies'. Mr Wells's last assertion is therefore capable of an accurate interpretation. There is, I believe, a Worshipful Company of Goldsmiths in London; I have myself addressed a justice as 'Your Worship'; and Mr Wells himself speaks of singing the national anthem as an 'act of worship' (*The fate of homo sapiens*, 73).[38]

Leaving aside verbal points, let us inquire if Mr Wells seriously holds that we pay divine honour to Our Lady, that in spite of our subtle doctrine of the Blessed Trinity (which he has been deriding), we are really polytheists and regard the Blessed Virgin as a goddess? His language shows clearly that this is his view. Honestly, I think this is about the last straw in puerile scurrility. I come from Catholic forbears whose consolation amid the persecution of Mr Wells's fellowcountrymen was – after Mass in a bleak field – the recital of the Rosary. I have spent my life as a Catholic amid Catholics, I have travelled in many countries of Europe, I have spent a year in the United States – always closely associated with my co-religionists. I have received a prolonged scientific training, I have studied philosophy and read widely in theology. And I declare solemnly that H. G. Wells's assertion is simply incredible bunkum as well as a foul libel, entirely unworthy or even of an ordinary decent

37. Ducange Anglicus, *Glossarium* (1842), s.v. adorare: 'In Sacred Scripture and in ecclesiastical writers it is often used to mean: to honour and venerate.' *New English Dictionary*, s.v. adore: 'In the usage of the Roman Catholic Church, to reverence with relative or representative honour.'
38. In *God the invisible king* (1917) 6, Mr Wells tells us that his 'new faith . . . worships a finite God'. So after calling on us to *worship* a finite being which is merely a synthetic figment of his imagination, he accuses us of 'worshipping' Our Lady.

Alfred O'Rahilly III: Controversialist

illiterate. But such a protest falls on deaf ears. Mr Wells blandly informs me that Catholics 'do not seem to know their own stuff' (*Picture Post*, 9 Dec., 47). This pooh-bah knows better than ourselves what is in our minds, what we are taught from the cradle. Good heavens, is there any limit to this man's intolerable and intolerant megalomania?

V[39]

Further Libels of Mr Wells

With characteristic oracular brevity Mr Wells utters against us some further libels. He speaks of 'annulments of marriages for the wealthy' (*The fate of homo sapiens*, 160). This accusation comes with very bad grace from a person who declares as follows:

> The family can remain only as a biological fact. Its economic and educational autonomy are inevitably doomed. The modern State is bound to be the ultimate guardian of all children; and it must assist, replace or subordinate the parent as supporter, guardian and educator. It must release all human beings from the obligation of mutual proprietorship, and it must refuse absolutely to recognise or enforce any kind of sexual ownership. It cannot, therefore, remain neutral when such claims come before it; it must disallow them (H. G. Wells, *Experiment in autobiography* (1934) ii, 481).

Though this paragraph is couched in polite terms, its gross implications are obvious, and the State-tyranny advocated is merely a form of Nazism. I am not now engaged in attacking this disgusting doctrine. I am merely pointing out the type of hostile critic that we Catholics have to deal with. If there is any one thing that makes me proud to be a Catholic, it is a lifetime's experience of a long succession of pseudo-science, novels, dramas and movies advocating all that is cheap, easy and nasty. The only organised institution – apart from individuals – that today stands four-square uncompromisingly for all that is loyal, unselfish and noble in family life is the Catholic Church. And

39. *Standard* 2 February 1940.

Appendix 2

this ideal of family life owes much to our celibate priests and religious – to the example of men and women who, inspired by a great ideal, have shown us that passion is not unconquerable and that there are higher things in life than 'biological facts'. Mr Wells with his pawky zoological mind can only sneer at what he nastily fancies are 'sex-tormented' people. For it is plain that his mind is obsessed with biology. 'If then,' he says (H. G. Wells, *Experiment in autobiography* (1934) i, 46), 'we want to know what the future holds for Britain or Germany or Russia we must understand the laws of biology.' How he manages to reconcile this with his 'democracy' is a puzzle; for, as Prof. E. M. MacBride[40] says, 'no zoologist has a right to be a democrat if he bases his political creed on his science'. It is also difficult to reconcile with his newfangled 'religion':

> The survival-value of a religion to a community has lain always in the practical assistance it afforded to the subordination of self and the achievement of co-operative loyalties not otherwise obtainable (H. G. Wells, *The open conspiracy* (1928) 12).

How can self-subordination and co-operative loyalty be built upon the basis of family as 'only a biological fact' which is self-exalting and loyalty-destroying? Presumably Mr Wells solves the contradiction by exalting the State – 'the ultimate guardian of all children', to use his own Nazi expression – into a brutal force-mechanism.

This is merely to illustrate our critic's background so that we may understand *his* philosophy when he stands up to criticise ours. Let us be clear that we are not here concerned with divorce, that is, with the dissolution of a valid marriage, which Catholics do not admit. The question concerns annulments, that is, with the decision that the parties were never married at all.[41] Presumably Mr Wells does not object to the necessary jurisdictional power of nullification; there must somewhere be an authority to decide on validity. Of course he wants this authority lodged in his State-machine, but he admits the

---

40. E. M. MacBride, *Zoology* . . . (1922) 118.

41. It may be necessary to remark that England has a law of nullity quite distinct from its law of divorce. See F. J. Sheed's excellent little book *Nullity of marriage* (London 1931).

Alfred O'Rahilly III: Controversialist

existence of us Catholics until 'the fifth millennium A.D.' His objection is this: our annulments are *for the wealthy*. Once more he gives no reference, no proof, no statistics; he just picks up any stray bit of mud from the gutter-press. Why should I bother to refute this man who obviously holds that the ordinary canons of decency and fair-play can be thrown aside when he is assailing the Catholic Church? I content myself with giving in a footnote indications sufficient for any honest inquirer.[42]

I proceed to consider Mr Wells's second libel:

> Formally other religions are still tolerated, the Roman Catholic for example, but only on condition of ceremonial and practical acquiescence in the main doctrine of the creed: the recognition of the supreme divinity of the Mikado (*The fate of homo sapiens*, 212).
>
> The Japanese Catholic bows in the Shinto temples in acquiescence to the local supremacy of the emperor-divinity over the Vatican (*The fate of homo sapiens*, 330).

And later (*Picture Post*, 9 Dec., 47) he refers to 'Catholicism's new ally Shinto'. The innuendo is craftily worded; he accuses us of acquiescence rather than active participation in idolatry. According to him, we once were Buddhists; then he says we are Egyptians; and now we are Shintoists. The mud of the Ganges and the ooze of the Nile were insufficient; so Mr Wells, knowing the current English antipathy to Japan, then tries to tar us with the brush of Mikado-worship. He is probably also annoyed that, unlike Anglicanism, the Catholic Church is universal and all-embracing, so that a Japanese Catholic can remain a Japanese and – let us add *sotto voce* – an Irish Catholic can continue to be an Irishman. When my parents went to school they were compelled to sing this pharasaical cant:

> I thank the goodness and the grace
> That on my birth have smiled,
> And made me in these Christian days
> A happy *English* child!

42. In addition to Sheed's book, see the synoptical summary of the decisions of the Rota 1922-28 in T. L. Bouscaren, S.J., *Canon law digest* (1937) ii, 291. In 1933 out of a total number of 77 cases decided by the Roman Rota 32 were treated gratuitously.

Appendix 2

And we in this country know the long history of the attempt to give us a denationalising imported religion, down to Gladstone's attempt to work the Vatican against us. Mr Wells, the atheistical descendant of these bible-*cum*-gun bullies, still retains some of the narrower characteristics of his ancestors. Frankly, he does not like the idea of Catholics being really Japanese; and he is probably horrified at the idea of a full-blooded African negro being a Catholic bishop.

Where Mr Wells got this particular libel I do not know; it may be from a book to which he refers and which I have not read. But, having studied his shoddy mind, I am sure this particular piece of bric-a-brac was secured at second or third hand. One need never verify any charge against us Catholics; we are beyond the pale of common decency. Such being his view, it would be futile for me to ask him for any first-hand proof. But for the benefit of fairminded inquirers, I refer to the 'Instruction to the apostolic delegate in Japan on the duties of Catholics to their native land' issued by the Sacred Congregation for the Propagation of the Faith on 26 May 1936.[43] This recounted that the faith is in no wise hostile to national customs provided they are not reprehensible. The particular issue concerned the visiting of the national temples (Jinja). The minister of public instruction assured the archbishop of Tokyo that the cermeony nowadays is purely non-religious, merely patriotic. This was confirmed by an extensive inquiry:

> To the ceremonies usually made in the Jinja (National Temples) administered civilly by the government, the civil authorities – as is shown by repeated and explicit declarations – as well as the common opinion of persons of a certain culture, attribute only a significance of love of country, that is, of filial reverence towards the imperial family and the benefactors of the fatherland.

And so, *pace* H. G. Wells, a Catholic is allowed, and even encouraged, to be a patriotic Japanese. Mr Wells's Mikado-bogey leaves us as unmoved as does his Isis-bogey. Give up this nursery-maid business, Mr Wells; you are not dealing with infants.

43. The Latin text is in *Acta Ap. Sedis* xxviii, 406-9, also in *Irish Eccles. Record*, April 1937, 440-42. There is an English translation in the *Clergy Review* 12 (1936) 247-51, and in Bouscaren, *op. cit.*, ii, 164-6.

Alfred O'Rahilly III: Controversialist

I will here make a brief holocaust of a few more objections which Mr Wells flings at the Church. They are all crammed together on one page (*The fate of homo sapiens*, 157), without reference or argument.

(1) 'The Vatican [is] in entirely unveracious succession to St Peter.' Who would ever think that H. G. Wells had scruples about apostolic succession?, that he was dissatisfied with the firm tradition, confirmed by recent archaeological exploration, of St Peter's residence and martyrdom in Rome? Why should anyone bother with the views of non-Catholic scholars like J. B. Lightfoot and H. Lietzmann now that H. G. Wells has spoken? For obviously what he does not know is not knowledge.

(2) The Vatican is 'sustained by a handsome subsidy from the Fascist government and the less reliable contributions of the faithful at large'. The implication of this appears to be that the central establishment of the Church should live on fresh air. As to the faithful, is Mr Wells advising them to be more 'reliable' or to go on strike? Willing to wound and yet afraid to strike, he emits a nasty innuendo about the bribery of the pope by Fascism. 'Regarding pecuniary indemnities,' says Mgr R. Fontenelle (*His Holiness Pope Pius XI* (1938) 126), speaking of the Lateran Treaty, 'they amounted to the sum of seventeen hundred and fifty million lire, in kindly compensation of the immense damages suffered by the Holy See as a result of the events of 1860-70.' Our new super-Christian critic, so far from applauding the papacy for renouncing temporal dominion, upbraids it for even accepting voluntary compensation for past robbery. In fact, we should take everything lying down: spoliation from Masonic States and calumnies from rationalist busybodies.

As to the cleverly veiled suggestion of subservience to Fascism, did Mr Wells ever hear of the encyclical *Non abbiamo bisogno* of 1931? Let me quote a sentence:

> A conception of the State which makes the rising generations belong to it entirely, without any exception, from the tenderest years up to adult life, cannot be reconciled by a Catholic either with Catholic doctrine or with the natural rights of the family.

This sentence – originally directed against the Fascist government – is equally apposite against the tyrannical socialism

Appendix 2

which Mr Wells has for years been advocating. No wonder he did not refer to the encyclical.

(3) 'In all the democracies the "Catholic vote" obeys the tortuous wisdom of these scheming old anachronisms.' Though this is more forcible than polite, its meaning is quite clear. In *all* the democracies, including our own, the Catholic clergy control the voters. That is, 95% of us take political directions from our priests! Was I not right in retorting on Mr Wells that the only way of dealing with him was to give him a dose of his own derision, to show him up as an unscrupulous and petty bigot who specialises in the discovery of mares' nests? We are reminded of a character which Mr Wells has drawn for us in *The war in the air* (1908):

> Bert Smallways was a vulgar little creature, the sort of pert limited soul that the old civilisation of the twentieth century produced by the million in every country of the world. He had lived all his life . . . in a narrow circle of ideas from which there was no escape. He thought the whole duty of man was to be smarter than his fellows.

These disjointed accusations of Mr Wells are certainly smart and vulgar; they betray the Bert Smallways streak in his mentality. It would be pleasant to take them merely as ebullitions of bad temper; but they seem to be a deliberate exploitation of British no-popery prejudices. They are unworthy of Mr Wells who in reality has a much more fundamental and passionate dislike of Christianity, such as was felt by a Tacitus or a Celsus.

Let us sum up our impressions. The outsider might naturally expect that the difficulties which modern scientific pundits urge against religion would be novel and difficult. Yet when we examine the objections of men, like Bertrand Russell and Sir Arthur Keith, we find them so stale and even childish that at first we are almost tempted to think they are indulging in an elaborate joke. It soon dawns on us that they are in deadly though fatuous earnest, that when these gentlemen get off their specialist beat they display what Mgr Ronald Knox calls 'broadcast minds'. Speaking of psychical research – the remark is capable of wider application – Prof. C. B. Broad[44] says:

[44]. Dr Broad, in this otherwise excellent book, exhibits a few blind spots himself. In one paragraph (p. 484) he dismisses the entire case for Revelation: 'I find nothing to add to Mr Hobbes's statement or to alter in it.' We are asked to

Alfred O'Rahilly III: Controversialist

Whenever we are told that 'science *proves* so-and-so to be impossible' we must remember that this is merely a rhetorical form of 'Professor X and most of his colleagues *assert* so-and-so to be impossible'. Those of us who have the privilege of meeting Professor X and his colleagues daily, and know from experience what kind of assertions they are capable of making when they leave their own subject, will, I am afraid, remain completely unmoved (C. B. Broad, *The mind and its place in nature* (1937) 515).

Now no serious thinker would regard H. G. Wells as expert in scholarship or in science; he is merely a novelist off his beat, an uncritical and gullible follower of agnostic bigwigs. But he, too, displays something of the early pagan's narrow-minded simplicity. There is in him that elemental crassness which would be natural in the first century A.D. All that a rationalist Roman official (Portius Festus) could make of the Christian religion in the year A.D. 60 was this: 'A dispute among Jews concerning a certain deceased Jesus whom Paul affirmed to be alive' (*Acts* 25:19). Which, concisely and without vulgarity, sums up the attitude of Mr Wells. It is not new, and it does not shock us. So also when we are told (*The fate of homo sapiens*, 119) 'how this cannibal blood sacrifice has been refined at last into the Mystery of the Mass', we cannot help thinking of a much older objection (*John* 6:53): 'The Jews debated among themselves: How – they asked – can this man give us his flesh to eat?' And, when today we read the accusation that we are 'extremely ignorant men' who 'have read few books' and are incapable of 'grasping modern ideas', we observe that this is but the echo of the old pagan Celsus[45] who called us 'foolish and low individuals, persons devoid of intelligence, slaves, women and children'. Then there is this seeming-modern cry:

---

believe that one sentence in T. Hobbes's *Leviathan*, published in 1651, has shown Revelation to be impossible. In the next page the metaphysical arguments for immortality – that is, for the substantiality and spirituality of the human soul – are dismissed in two paragraphs; they have been 'refuted by Kant'. In Aldous Huxley's *Ends and means* (1938) – a much more truth-seeking book than that of H. G. Wells and more deserving of a boost in *Picture Post* – 'the stock arguments for theism' are misrepresented and quickly disposed of (p. 277). I have often been tempted to play the *advocatus diaboli* and to show these people some real difficulties against religion!

45. Origen, *Contra Celsum* (A.D. 248) iii, 49.

Appendix 2

The symbol of the crucifixion, the drooping pain-drenched figure of Christ . . . these things jar with our spirit . . . We cannot accept the Christian's crucifix or pray to a pitiful God. We cannot accept the resurrection as though it were an afterthought to a bitterly felt death. Our crucifix – if you must have a crucifix – would show God with a hand or foot already torn away from its nail, and with eyes not downcast but resolute against the sky . . . A Christianity, which shows for its daily symbol a Christ risen and trampling victoriously upon a broken cross, would be far more in the spirit of our worship (H. G. Wells, *God the invisible king* (1917) 121, 123).

But long ago we heard an old pagan (Hierocles) say:

Even if Christ had to suffer . . . yet at least he should have endured his Passion with some boldness and uttered words of force and wisdom to Pilate his judge, instead of being mocked like any guttersnipe (M. Macarius, *Apocriticus* (*circa* A.D. 350) iii, 1).

Why, even on Calvary itself there were those who said (*Matt.* 27:42): 'Let him now come down from the cross – and we will believe in him.' No life or cause ever appeared so hopelessly defeated as that which seemingly ended on Calvary amid dark despair and hostile mockery. Those old gibes still float through the world. But we answer in the words of the convert from Tarsus (1 *Cor.* 15:54, 57): 'Death is swallowed up in victory – thanks be to God who has given us the victory through Our Lord Jesus Christ.' We have the same faith today, the same resilient hope amid decadent pessimism. And Peter's successor re-echoes the words of Simon Peter:

Lord, to whom shall we go? You have the words of eternal life; and we believe – yea, we know – that you are the Holy One of God (*John* 6:69, 70).

Alfred O'Rahilly III: Controversialist

VI[46]

The Catholic Irish

Much as Mr Wells dislikes Catholics in general, he dislikes Irish Catholics even more.[47] So an Irish Catholic when replying to him cannot overlook his special diatribe against us. Let us hear him:

> In Éire (formerly Southern Ireland) and in Spain, the Church rules and we can watch it in operation ... A stringent censorship of books and publications and a fairly complete control of education have produced a first crop of young men as blankly ignorant of the modern world as though they had been born in the thirteenth century, mentally concentrated upon the idea of bringing the Protestant North under Catholic control in the sacred name of national unity ... The Church in Éire may be trusted to see to it that the young men of Ireland learn little and so sustain their tradition that inveterate animosities are dignified and desirable (*The fate of homo sapiens*, 166f).

Upon my word, I rubbed my eyes when I read this. In heaven's name, what started the man rampaging into regions of which he is blandly ignorant? Whence all this senile scurrility? Now I have been engaged in education in this country for over a quarter of a century, I have a position independent of Church and State, I belong to no political party, and I am even notorious for my outspokenness. Furthermore, I do not think it is boastful of me to consider myself at least as well educated as Mr H. G. Wells. In this question at any rate I am, by my extensive and intimate first-hand experience, better equipped than my antagonist. And I declare in good vulgar parlance that Mr Wells is talking through his hat.

First, consider our censorship. Personally, I am not sure that an improved police-law, throwing the personal responsibility on the vendors, would not be better; but let that pass. I examine the list of censored publications: a collection of salacious tripe disguised as fiction plus a few items of the Marie Stopes brand.

46. *Standard* 9 February 1940.
47. This *animus* against Ireland seems to be a badge of the rationalist tribe. See Sir Arthur Keith in *Early man* (1931) 57.

Appendix 2

For all I know, the Censorship Board, being human, may have made a few mistakes – it is only H. G. Wells who never makes any. We have one or two of these censored books in our library; the minister for justice would at once give us a licence for any we want; but we do not wish to clutter our shelves with muck. Shall I send the complete list of censored books to Mr Wells so that he can indicate to me which are the items whose absence is stunting the education of our 'young men'? Or is he merely blathering *in vacuo*?

Mr Wells will be glad to hear that we have not only his own works (non-fiction) in our library, but also those of his predecessors Voltaire, Renan, Haeckel and others.[48]

Does he also want to stuff up our college with pornography? He himself admits (*Picture Post*, 11 Nov., 48) that 'no democratic community could exist without limiting the liberty of the individual'. He agrees with me that the sale of poisons must be controlled and that protection must be given against the adulteration of foodstuffs. But, as far as I can gather, he does not bother whether our minds are poisoned and our morals adultrated by commercialised vice masquerading as liberty. On which point, as he has no coherent philosophy of life, he cannot help being muddle-headed. When 95% of a people agree on certian fundamentals, they are not going to have these flouted for immature minds by people who are mostly ghoulish profiteers. You do the same in England, Mr Wells, you carry out your allegedly moral ideals. You believe in divorce and birth-control – more fools you – and so you spend public money on them; you are even tinkering with the idea of euthanasia. But you are not going to bamboozle us with your 'phrases and assumptions of the liberal protestant progressive world' (*The fate of homo sapiens*, 111). We do not like a lot of your alleged progress; and that is flat. Why, even the *Picture Post* draws the line somewhere: 'Almost the only thing in the nature of a crusade we

---

48. Every single book to which I have referred or which I have quoted in these articles is also to be found in our library. So we have plenty of antidotes to Mr Wells.

I observe that two of Mr Wells's books have been banned. The novel (*The Bulpington of Bulp* (1932)) I have not read. The other (*The work, wealth and happiness of mankind* (1931)) is in our library and I have read it. It is a pretentious bulky compilation without much value. In spite of some coarse pages I personally would not vote for prohibiting it; but perhaps it was banned lest immature students mistake it for a serious work on sociology.

have ever conducted has been our persistent opposition to Nazism.'[49]

That may be all right for an English paper (started by a Hungarian), but it is a rather meagre and negative philosophy. There happen to be some other things which some of us would like to see scheduled for 'persistent opposition'. Why the deuce should Stefan Lorant and H. G. Wells think that they have the sole right to choose what they will persistently oppose, and what they will pander to, not only in England, but in Ireland?

If I wanted to anchor in any century, I would prefer the thirteenth – a confession which will astonish the author of *The outline of history*. At any rate it would be more preferable than to be so frightfully up-to-date as Mr Wells, so much at the mercy of the latest fad or ephemeral stunt. 'Even now Freud is busy, he tells me, in a patient analysis of the legend of Moses' (*The fate of homo sapiens*, 323). You can visualise H. G. Wells gleefully rubbing his hands in anticipation of this cheap sensational – and smutty – book (which has since appeared). Will the man ever mentally grow up? I ask myself. Will he ever develop a critical faculty? Will he ever learn to distinguish solid scholarship from cheap sensationalism? Make no mistake about it, Mr Wells, we respect genuine scholarship and patient industry in our opponents. We have no intention of banning any serious work however much we differ form it, for we learn much in the clash of disputation. But there is a distinction which is almost instinctive in a man who is a gentleman as well as a scholar. As you may not accept it from me, let me give it to you in the words of your old master, Huxley:

> I am ready to go great lengths in defence of freedom of discussion. But I decline to admit that rightful freedom is attacked when a man is prevented from coarsely and brutally assaulting his neighbours' honest belief (L. Huxley, *Life* . . . ii, 407).

Just think over that, Mr Wells, when you plan your next coarse and brutal assault. Huxley *loquitur*.

49. In the publisher's blurb to the Penguin book Lorant's *I was Hitler's prisoner*, we are told that Stefan Lorant 'came to England where he started *Lilliput* and *Picture Post*.' *Lilliput* was banned in Éire last year: the ban has now expired. At present *Picture Post* is banned.

Appendix 2

The distinction is well brought out in a review of Mr Wells's *Ann Veronica* which G. K. Chesterton wrote in the *Daily News* in 1910:

> *Ann Veronica* is not an immoral book in any imaginable sense; but that is not the primary point. The primary point is this, that it is no business of the State or of any coercive power to suppress immoral books. The business of the coercive and collective power is to suppress indecent books; books that violate fixed verbal and physical custom in such a way as to be a public nuisance. We have a right to be guarded against bodily indecency as against bodily attack; but do not let us call in the police to protect our souls; we must protect our souls with the sword of the spirit. If once I am supposed to test books by whether I think them profoundly and poisonously immoral, I could furnish a very long list to the police. I should at once ask the magistrates to forbid the sale of Froude's *History of England*, Burke's *French Revolution*, Hobbes's *Leviathan*, Smiles's *Self help*, Carlyle's *Frederick the Great*; all the works of imperialists, eugenists, theosophists and higher thinkers; and at least half the works of socialists and of jingoes . . . *Ann Veronica* does not urge immorality; it does not urge anything . . . A writer on the *Spectator* – an honest writer, I daresay – wished to suppress *Ann Veronica*. Now *Ann Veronica* is not indecent any more than the *Spectator* is indecent; they both observe civilised traditions of speech; and therefore they should both be allowed to speak . . . But, if once we come to the question of what spreads essential moral error, I should suppress the *Spectator*.

It is quite another question whether since that date Mr Wells has not at times descended to write lubricity and indecency; and it is certainly true that he has ceased to observe civilised traditions of speech. But the question of censorship does not arise in connection with the book I am criticising (*The fate of homo sapiens*); and it arises in connection with *Picture Post* only owing to the accidental fact that excerpts from that book were published in a periodical which *also* – in the view of our Censorship Board and of many other persons in Great Britain and Ireland – indulged in indecency.

Alfred O'Rahilly III: Controversialist

Our censorship is the product of *civil* legislation, for which the Church has no responsibility. There is not a priest or bishop in either house of our legislature; there are several Protestants and at least one Jew. So the attitude of the Church on the question is not relevant. But Mr Wells seems under the delusion that, if the majority of a people are Catholic, 'the Church rules'. General Franco would take that as a good joke. If the majority are Protestant, does *their* Church rule? What, except to muddle readers, is the object of using the word 'church' to denote not the definitely circumscribed authorities of the organisation but to mean laymen and women in their civic capacity, who happen also to belong to a particular Church? Is it to voters like myself or to the members of our legislature that Mr Wells objects? Of is it merely to the additional fact that the majority of us have – in spite of his fellow-countrymen – remained Catholics? Probably the distinction never occurred to him; if it had, it would have quite spoiled his ambiguous rhetoric.

And now, Mr Wells, while you have been vaguely and inaccurately referring to our tiny segregation of a little pornography, are not you forgetting the huge amount of informal but effective censorship that is going on even in peace-time in England? Is it not notorious that British papers are not as free as American? That the royal family, but not Christ our Lord, is fully protected? That English periodicals calmly adopt a generalised Protestant outlook as if it were the only possible philosophy? That even scientific publications are often under the control of a clique? Let me give you two experiences of my own. In October 1920 I published in the *Irish Theological Quarterly* an article entitled 'Some theology about tyranny', wherein Ireland was not so much as mentioned. Whereupon some English journals called in unmistakable terms for my assassination by the Black-and-Tans who were at that moment rescuing us from the thirteenth century – but were unable otherwise to meet the arguments of thirteenth-century thinkers. I was arrested and interned for six months: not a reasoned argument with pens but a ban with bayonets.

In January 1921 there appeared a pamphlet of 68 pages: *Who burnt Cork city? A tale of arson, loot and murder: the evidence of over seventy witnesses.* It was printed by the Caledonian Press, London, and 'published by the Irish Labour Party and Trade Union Congress, Dublin'. What stratagems and adven-

Appendix 2

tures I had to outwit Mr Wells's compatriots. It was I who took the seventy depositions; sometimes I had some of them in my pocket when I narrowly escaped cordons of armed British gangsters who were searching and robbing passers-by. The account was put together at night and in the early morning an Irishwoman took the manuscript – with the map drawn by my friend, A. Farrington, B.E. – to Dublin and thence to England. Eventually it was published in England and circulated even in America. We succeeded in circumventing the British censorship which was combined with robbery and murder. And now Mr Wells soothingly preaches to us about the iniquities of censorship – to us who risked our lives to assert our right to express our views against British tyranny. Somehow it never occurs to him that we are but continuing our assertion of freedom and national individuality when we refuse to allow ourselves and our children to be exploited by British commmercialised vice.

Of late years I have tried to break a lance – metaphorically speaking – with authoritarianism in physics.

And I have discovered that there is a much stricter orthodoxy in science than in theology. It is expected that at least lip-service will be paid to certain tutelary deities; for instance, to J. A. L. Maxwell in electromagnetics; just as a J. C. Lamarckian like Mac-Bride feels bound to refer to C. Darwin's *On the origin of species* . . . (1859) as 'the sacred book of every student of zoology' (*Zoology*. . .85). An amusing instance occurred in connection with Sir Arthur Keith's review of Mr H. Belloc's *A companion to Mr Wells's outline of history* (1927) which review contained a gross historical error concerning the Catholic biologist St George Jackson Mivart. Sir Arthur put his foot in it badly – he had never heard of the important book of L. M. Vialleton, to which Belloc had referred. But Vialetton was only a Catholic and Sir Arthur's face had to be saved. So the editor cut short the discussion with this magisterial declaration: 'As to the particular point under discussion, it has been referred to the leading authority upon the subject, who replies: It is absolutely certain that the birds came from reptiles' (*Nature* 119 (1927) 277). Arguments against Prof. Vialleton? Not at all. The leading British authority is dead certain; enough said! To return to the subject of physics, it has been my experience that at present it is useless to argue against A. Einstein, A. Eddington and J. H. Jeans; one is met not with counter-arguments but with a supercilious smile. Verily, the ways of the scientific heretic are hard.

I envy you, Mr Wells, you are always so wonderfully in the swim; you always manage to be perfectly synchronous with the mind-current of demos.[50] But for heaven's sake, do not be preaching hypocritical claptrap about censorship to people like me.

You do not like our education, Mr Wells, and we do not like yours. I think ours is very defective; but on the whole, as far as my experience goes, I think it is much better than yours. So our young men live in the thirteenth century and are blankly ignorant of the modern world! I wish to heavens they learnt a little about the thirteenth century and were ignorant of a good deal of what is pompously called the modern world. Did you ever study our school programmes? Do you know that we have university institutions? We even read the Penguin books, switch on the radio and go to the pictures – is it not all that frightfully educative and modern? The 'church rules education'. Even lectures on medicine? Even Protestant schools which we protect and subsidise? Do you know, I would not mind if the Church did a bit more ruling in primary and secondary education. For – tell it not in Gath – we are at present being ruled by a bureaucracy which I have never ceased to denounce; and our only refuge against Leviathan is the spiritual liberty championed by the Church. You yourself, Mr Wells, are advocating a new Church-State, which you have pleasantly called 'The open conspiracy'. Your advocacy merely shows that ultimately the only consistent enemy of Nazism is the Catholic Church which fearlessly proclaims that there is something in man beyond the jurisdiction of the praetor's forum. According to you, the entire educational organisation must be recast – by the State, of course, for this the ultimate guardian of all children; the family having – as you delicately put it – been reduced to a crude biological fact, the parents do not count. It is only the Catholic philosophy which makes the family more fundamental than the State and acknowledges parental primacy. Your object

50. 'Nobody who has followed the career of Mr Wells can have failed to notice this representative quality in him; during the war particularly how well he fell in with our fire-eating state of mind in the early stages, with our questioning idealist attitude in the middle of it, with our half-despairing mood at the end of it!' (Mgr R. Knox, *Caliban in Grub Street* (1930) 14).

Appendix 2

presumably is culture, or perhaps I should say *Kultur* with Wells's textbooks substituted for A. Rosenberg's. 'This,' you admit (*The fate of homo sapiens*, 79f), 'may involve, it will almost certainly involve, such a *Kulturkampf* as the world has never seen before.' Dear me, do you propose to outdo Bismarck and Hitler? If I were you, Mr Wells, I should pipe down a bit; you are not made of such stern stuff at all; 'God the invisible king' – whatever that means – never cast you in such a mould. But henceforth do not make me laugh by deploring the lack of liberty and education in my country. We should make a vigorous riposte if you tried any of your Black-and-Tan stuff over here, Mr Wells. You are several centuries too late to emulate Cromwell even in education.

Our author seems to have changed his mind on the so-called Ulster question. In his *The outline of history* (ch. 39, §5), he speaks of 'a Protestant community in necessary permanent conflict with the Catholic remainder of Ireland'. And he calls the Carson-Smith rebellion 'the reactionary effort of a few score thousand people to arrest the world-movement towards democratic law and social justice'. But now he no longer thinks that the running of our own country by ourselves corresponds to the ideal of democratic law and social justice, he regards our unchanged viewpoint as merely a dirty trick for bringing the Protestant North under Catholic control.

He does not dare to suggest that we do not deal generously with Protestants in Éire, he just hints that we *would* be unfair to Northern Protestants. Not a word about the actual – not hypothetical – treatment of Catholics (one-third of the population) by the Northern Protestant ascendancy. Apparently he never heard of the abolition of proportional representation, of the gerrymandering of electoral areas, of Orange bigotry and jobbery. This lover of freedom does not appear to know of the Special Powers Act in force for over seventeen years, nor to have read the report of the British Council for Civil Liberties. Tut, tut, replies Mr Wells, you are only displaying your tradition of inveterate animosity. Which is the Wellsian for: Croppies, lie down.

Let us return to his final point:

> I said the young I.R.A. men confessed and got absolution before they went about their patriotic exploits of killing people in cloakrooms and busy streets . . . They confess

about general sins and say nothing of the thing they have in mind. So, according to their beliefs, they go to this evil business as clean as they can. It is just the mixture of superstition and malignancy in this that makes one realise that Ireland is slipping back into the middle ages (H. G. Wells, *Picture Post*, 9 Dec., 47).

The destruction of the property of others and the endangering of human life are quite indefensible. This is the view of the overwhelming majority of us; these extremists are numerically negligible. To indict a whole nation for their acts is ludicrously unjust and unbalanced. Now, while I concur with Mr Wells in the essential condemnation, I find in him a deplorable smugness and a very onesided bias. The first stone should not be cast by an Englishman, at least not without realising his country's primary responsibility. The idea that these outrages are just the exuberant outcome of superstition and malignancy is simply puerile psychology. It is on a par with his other verdict that Moonlighters – plus Chinese Boxers trying to get rid of their invaders, etc. – are a kind of natural phenomenon which supervenes 'when a country is unable to get rid of its youth by way of war or emigration' (*The fate of homo sapiens*, 42; *Picture Post*, 9 Dec., 47). I wonder if he ever heard of the Irish land war, the attempt to get back the land of which the British invaders had dispossessed us? Mr Wells is ridiculous enough when strutting like Hitler after getting his B.Sc. But he is simply nauseating when he adopts the attitude of Rev Mr Stiggins. He has nothing to say about the murders and tortures perpetrated by the Black-and-Tans and their attempt to burn the city (Cork) in which I am writing these lines; nothing about the Belfast pogroms and the brutal tyranny of the puppet government installed by his fellow-countrymen in the North; and of course nothing about the centuries-long massacres, confiscations and persecutions we have suffered. No; this gentleman, who can write a whole history of the world for the waistcoat pocket and who knows all about the physique and psychology of alleged ape-men, has nothing to account for the desperate actions of a few embittered patriots except to say that they are suffering from a 'mixture of malignancy and superstition'!

Mr Wells, who does not believe in original sin, attributes to us a double dose of it, thereby seeking to divert any rude

Appendix 2

remarks about his countrymen's actual sins. Good gracious, he exclaims with smug suburban respectability, the whole of Ireland is slipping back into the middle ages – which, when translated from Wellsian, means going to hell. For all his atheist rationalism, he has not yet sloughed off the Britisher. To hear him on this subject is like listening to some apoplectic ex-major holding forth in his club: Why, demme, these fellows are quite balmy – what have *we* ever done to them except to try to civilise them?

No, Mr Wells, we are not malignant. We wish the British well – in their own country. But we wish they would get out of ours. If we had sufficient physical force in the morning, we would, I think, clear you out. These men to whom you refer are wrong, however, because such a war can be validated only by the Irish people; they have no right 'to take the law into their own hands'; and of course the murder of innocent civilians is quite indefensible. To call them names while ignoring British guilt is simply a hypocritical attempt to create a moral alibi.

Neither are we superstitious. You would find more shrewd critical acumen in an Irish cabin than in a whole English countryside. We do not believe half the stuff that you swallow and then disgorge, Mr Wells. We do not even take you half as seriously as you take yourself. You may be a tin-god in Brummagem, but you are very small beer in Cork. You see, we know your type of the half-baked encyclopaedist or – to use your own metaphor – the caddis-grub accumulating odds and ends to paste around its tenuous body. We have a philosophy, a body of fundamental doctrine, which keeps us sane, which is in harmony with man and civilisation, which enables what is deep and permanent in us to combine a sense of historical perspective with a sense of humour. It is only when one loses the central core of the faith that one becomes the victim of every ephemeral modern superstition.

Mr Wells appears to know all about the private religious practices of these men. I do not know, and I am not inclined to take his unsubstantiated word for it. But even if it were true, what would follow? It would merely be another instance of men forming a bad conscience for themselves; just as Mr Wells thinks he is doing right in using all means fair and foul to bespatter Catholics, the end justifying the means; or just like a Catholic Black-and-Tan officer I heard about. The misuse of religious

Alfred O'Rahilly III: Controversialist

practices is no more an argument against religion than Haeckel's notorious faking of embryo-illustrations is an argument against biology, no more than Mr Wells's mistakes are arguments against history.[51]

VII[52]

Postscript on *Picture Post*

Since writing last week on 'Mr Wells and the Catholic Irish' I have seen the article: 'We are banned in Éire' which appeared in *Picture Post* for 13 January 1940.

I propose to append a few comments on this piece of consummate bluff. A gentleman called Stefan Lorant – formerly an editor in Munich – started two weeklies: *Lilliput* and *Picture Post*. On grounds of indecency we had first to ban one and then the other. Concerning the prohibition of *Lilliput* (again lifted after three months) there is a significant silence. But the attitude adopted towards our banning of *Picture Post* is rather amusing in its assumption of injured innocence and highbrow idealism, quite reminiscent of the various British proselytising societies founded to uplift benighted Irish papists.

On 16 December 1939 the minister, acting on a report of the Censorship Board of the day before, prohibited the *Picture Post* on the ground that it had been 'indecent'. And this prohibition was published in the *Iris Oifigiúil* for 22 December 1939.

The editor of *Picture Post*, after actually quoting an announcement of the ban from the *Irish News* of 23 December, proceeds to state that 'the decision by the Éire authorities was taken after our issue dated 30 December had been submitted to them'! Next he says he was condemned for the issue of 23 December which 'breathed the spirit of Christmas'. He almost assumes the attitude of a Christian martyr, but he is rather muddled in his chronology.

Now I happen to know that long before this there had been in this country complaints of pornographic tendencies in the *Picture Post*. And the editor himself seems to have forgotten that in the issue of 25 November he published a 'reply to letters

---

51. In *The fate of homo sapiens*, 167, he adds: 'They *take* Mass'!! Did he learn this too?
52. *Standard* 16 February 1940.

Appendix 2

about pictures of the war-time night club', in which he admitted that 'the reason the pictures were objected to was that they were said to have an exciting effect on the young'. In plain words, a vocal section of his British readers considered his illustrations to be indecently suggestive. But he scotches the idea that our Censorship Board might have taken the same view. Not at all, the editor reassures his restive, decent-minded British readers. He informs them that 'the campaign against *Picture Post* was started and carried on for one reason only: 'Because we published, in our digest of his important book *The fate of homo sapiens*, H. G. Wells's criticisms of the Roman Catholic Church of Éire.' But he omits to inform his readers that Wells's book itself has *not* been banned! And, while telling them that an Irish editor refused his offer to reply, he also concealed from them the fact that on 16 December he received a telegraphed offer from me to reply in his paper to Wells. I therefore publicly charge the editor of the *Picture Post* with deliberately trying to deceive his readers in his attempt to escape from the verdict of Irish public opinion that this paper of his, like the other one, has been guilty of pandering to indecency. He hides this nasty rebuke under the shelter of H. G. Wells whom he protected against exposure by me in his columns.

This gentleman takes himself very seriously, even more ponderously than H. G. Wells. He is determined to publish 'vital facts and vital opinions'; he is full of vitality; at one moment he is breathing the spirit of Christmas, the next moment he is inviting us to leer at nude females in a night-club. Large numbers of readers were delighted 'to find that a great national weekly paper realised that the festival of Christmas had something to do with Christ' – apparently one of the 'national' editor's most original discoveries! Other readers were delighted that the paper gave publicity to the atheist H. G. Wells's blasphemies against Christ and his mother. The great thing is to have the paper *vital* and full of stunts – for that will keep up the circulation and make good profits for the gentleman and his associates. To pretend that he is platonically interested in indiscriminate and contradictory *vitality* without a thought of pecuniary gain – that is merely the sickening hypocritical pose of the modern journalist. He must think his British readers are very green and gullible; that kind of humbug would never work in this country, we have not yet become so amenable to mass-suggestion of profiteers disguised as philanthropists. Besides, we decline to put Bethlehem and a brothel on the same level.

Since the *Picture Post* was banned for indecency, it has begun to take an interest in us. In its issue of 20 January it publishes an article 'What is happening in Ireland?' by Edward Hulton. Not bad at all as British pronouncements go, but still marred by puerile shallow psychology and mealy-mouthed hypocrisy about 'the emerald isle':

> There is still a great deal of the Christmas cracker mentality in the Irish . . . The British are the supreme example of orderliness and unity. The Irish never achieved either amongst themselves, and have never gained understanding of the British . . . The inhabitants of the green island are a supreme example of the rebel who will never lie down. Their extreme individualism can be compared to the anarchistic nature of the Spaniards and the Poles . . . Knight errantry still means much to the Irishman . . . In fact it is certain that Ireland will never be 'settled' at all.

And so forth. Like other lesser breeds without the law – such as the Poles – we are a lot of impractical quarrelsome visionaries, who give a lot of trouble to supremely orderly John Bull. Great Britain has never suffered an invasion since it was conquered by the Normans; she has managed to annex a large portion of the world's territory; she has never had a foreign plantation on her soil. Having been hitherto well-off – with iron and coal and foreign tribute – she simply cannot understand the grievances of the have-nots and the difficulties of nations subjected to oppression or partition. Having failed to subdue us with her Black-and-Tans, having partitioned our country, and continuing to subsidise an intolerant clique on portion of our territory, she starts to weep over our perverseness. I weep for you, the Walrus said, I deeply sympathise . . .

And now, having washed his hands like Pilate – that eternal representative of the colonial governor – John Bull begins to bewail our lack of 'culture':

> Under British rule in the eighteenth century, Dublin was the abode of wit and refinement and was the city of Swift,

Appendix 2

Goldsmith and Sheridan. Today it has been compared to the capital of a small Balkan State. Yeats dreamed of an island of poets; but culture will not survive under a censorship.

So wit and refinement went out with the British ascendancy. Poor 'Pat Murphy' failed to appreciate this long-standing British joke. The 'eternal rebel' would not lie down; we will not even apologise for our 'rebellion'. Even if Dean Swifts can no longer flourish here to taunt us, even if modern Goldsmiths have to follow him to London, we intend to guard our religion and our nationality. And if 'culture' is dependent on the importation of British pornography, then we say frankly: 'To hell with your culture!'

VIII[53]

Mr Wells and Man

I have reserved for the end some brief observations on Mr Wells's views on the fundamental problems of man and religion. His treatment is woefully superficial and jejune; his ideas appear to have ossified about the 'nineties in the heyday of Darwinism; he moves within the limits of physical anthropology buttressed with hypothetical genealogical-trees which were once fashionable; of modern ethnological research into primitive peoples and their culture-cycles he seems to be completely ignorant.[54] When we turn from this silly demoded travesty to the work of a man like Fr W. Schmidt – it is like emerging from a stuffy suburban drawingroom into fresh air and sunlight – we begin to surmise that perhaps after all there is something in 'the medieval education of a priest'; it teaches him principles, clear thinking and general culture.

As in the short space of a newspaper article I cannot undertake a detailed investigation, I will merely give a few quotations from Fr Schmidt. I begin with the essential issue of man's soul:

53. *Standard* 23 February 1940.
54. Nevertheless he is quite up-to-date for his popular untrained audience which – in spite of superficial terminology – is always half a century behind the basic trends of science.

That this full development of mind is present even in the very earliest of men, in all its essential features and in a surprising number even of non-essentials, is a fact that modern ethnology and pre-history can demonstrate with scientific certainty. All the earlier attempts to discover within the human race itself 'inferior' transitional types and links with the lower animals may be dismissed as hopeless failures.

At the same time researches into the mental life of the higher animals have been carried out with greater exactitude; and it has been completely and conclusively shown that the chasm which divides them from the primitive man is much wider and deeper than many at an earlier date were inclined to believe (W. Schmidt, in E. Eyre (ed.), *European civilisation* I (1934) 13).

Thus once and for all we may finally abandon any expectation of fresh evolutionary links being established between the spiritual life of man and that of the highest forms of animal life. Even in the earliest representatives of mankind known to us, the soul is so absolutely and completely human that the advance to it from the highest level of the brute creation is more plainly than ever seen to be an impossibility, and any mental development such as evolution requires is utterly excluded (Schmidt, *ibid.*, 76).

And now concerning the much less important issue of the evolution of man's body:

> Everywhere we turn, the 'ape-man' – from whatever point of view we regard him, either as the ancestor or the descendant of the ape – remains a myth, according to the testimony of the most authoritative palaeontologists of the present day . . .
> Our best attitude with regard to the question of the descent of man, so far as his bodily form is concerned, must be a patiently expectant one, with an evenly balanced mind, waiting till further discoveries and researches give us such a decisive result as has already been attained with regard to the question of the descent of the soul of man from some earlier existing forms of life. This latter question has already been settled in the negative with complete certainty (Schmidt, *ibid.*, 81).

Appendix 2

I have thought it better to quote an eminent Catholic ethnologist on these points, lest some unwary reader might be misled by Mr Wells's vehement and dogmatic cocksureness into believing that his popular undocumented books give a fair all-round presentation of modern research, or that Catholics somehow are afraid to face such problems.

As regards man's body, other priest-anthropologists – Bouyssonie, Breuil, Obermaier, Teilhard – go much farther than Fr Schmidt.[55] Let me quote from the work of a Catholic layman, which Prof. M. C. Burkitt has characterised as a 'monumental and remarkable work':[56]

> The conviction of the animal derivation of the human *body* must today be regarded as a commmonplace of research; even orthodox theology is beginning to be friendly to this view. But the matter is otherwise as regards the origin of the human *soul*. In this question dualism and materialism confront each other in a bitter struggle. Monistic materialism views the psychic faculties of man as merely the quite naturally developed qualities of the animal. Dualism is based on the substantiality and essential specificity of the human soul; it regards the sum of its expressions – especially those which world history investigates – as a fully valid proof of the thesis. Since the materialist outlook excludes all belief in revelation while the dualist view is the presupposition for such, there is here a disputed question which moves men as hardly any other does. All theoretical work in science aims at this, all practical outlook on life is dependent on it . . . Anthropology deals with the oldest sources; they are sufficient to make the animal derivation of the human body palaeontologically probable. Concerning the culture and the language of these times, there are beautiful speculations; but it is better to confess that we know nothing about primeval culture and language (Oswald Menghin, *Weltgeschichte der Steinzeit* (1931) 595).

55. See two excellent articles by R. Boigelot, S.J., 'L'origine de l'homme', in *La Cité Chrétienne*, 20 Nov. and 5 Dec. 1938. On the difficulties of transformism, see the section on man's place in nature in L. M. Vialleton, *L'origine des êtres vivants; l'illusion transformiste* (1929) 267-302.
56. *Nature* 127 (1931) 845. In his work *The old stone age* (1933) vii, Burkitt calls it an 'epoch-making book'.

Alfred O'Rahilly III: Controversialist

In the preface to this important work the author says:

> I received from Wilhelm Schmidt the first stimulus to effect the synthesis of archaeological and ethnographic research. Already about 1910 I learnt from one of his lectures about the teaching on culture-areas. But not less than ten years elapsed before I could bring myself to accept the standpoint of Schmidt and [F.] Gräbner.

This brief quotation with the few that follow – no more can be done in a newspaper article – will be sufficient to indicate the modern trend of cultural anthropology which has occurred since Mr Wells formed his convictions and secured his B.Sc. degree. The reaction against the superficial evolutionary schematism has been much more pronounced in America than in Great Britain where a national cult of Darwin has continued to prevail.[57]

> There is scarcely an ethnologist in this country, in France or in Germany, who does not believe the narrow simple method of the classic English evolutionary school to be sterile (A. L. Kroeber, *American anthropologist* 19 (1917) 70).
>
> Most of us have been brought up in the tenets of orthodox ethnology; and this was largely an enthusiastic and quite uncritical attempt to apply the Darwinian theory of evolution to the facts of social experience. Many ethnologists, sociologists and psychologists still persist in this endeavour. No progress will ever be achieved, however, until scholars rid themselves once and for all of the curious notion that everything possesses an evolutionary history; until they realise that certain ideas and certain concepts are as ultimate for man as a social being as physiological reactions are for him as a biologcal entity

---

57. I may mention these non-Catholic American names: F. Boas, A. L. Kroeber, A. A. Goldenweiser, P. Radin, E. Sapir, J. R. Swanton, C. Wissler. Cf. Fr Schmidt's article: 'The abandonment of evolutionism and the adoption of historicism in American ethnology', *Anthropos* 16-17 (1921-22) 487-519. 'Evolutionism . . . was shaken off earlier and more emphatically in America than elsewhere' (W. Schmidt, *Origin and growth of religion* (1931) 197). My reference to British anthropologists does not apply to men like W. H. R. Rivers and B. Malinowski.

Appendix 2

(P. Radin, *Monotheism among primitive peoples* (1924) 66; also in the same author's *Primitive man as philosopher* (1927) 373).

Though similar to the animal in many ways, man differs markedly from even the highest animals, including his closest known relatives the anthropoid apes. Erect gait, shape of the cranium, size of the brain, position of the head, development of the hand; and with these the use of tools, articulate language and the gift of abstract thought – such are some of the traits that set off man as a unique achievement of biological evolution, as a super-animal immeasurably removed from all his precursors . . . Is it not clear then that the races, with their complexes of more or less characteristic traits, cannot be arranged in an ascending series from the animal upward? . . . No proof has been forthcoming of the inferiority of the other racial stocks to the white . . . It is easy to show that the alleged inferiority of early man in the higher mental functions is also based on deficient knowledge and an erroneous point of view . . . The evidence of biology, neurology and psychology fails to supply any data on the basis of which could be inferred either a primitive superiority in sense development or an inferiority of early man in his capacity for abstract thought and in other achievements supposedly peculiar to white man (A. A. Goldenweiser, *Early civilisation* (1922) 3, 6, 9, 12).

Needless to say, I am not now arguing that this anti-evolutionary view of human mentality is correct; such a view is based not only on philosophy and psychology but also on an enormous mass of recently acquired ethnological-cultural data.[58] I am merely pointing out that Mr Wells's contention that in his alleged popularising of science he has been 'simply gathering up undisputed statements' is palpably dishonest. His one-sided dogmatism, his spurious simplification and his blatant ignorance result in a barefaced imposition on the public. The judgment which posterity will pass upon him is that recorded by a distinguished anatomist against E. H. Haeckel:

58. *Cultural anthropology* by A. Muntsch, S.J. (Milwaukee 1936), is an excellent Catholic textbook. A handy smaller book is *Social origins* by Eva J. Ross (London 1936).

Alfred O'Rahilly III: Controversialist

> Upon this subject of the origin of man, the work of Haeckel is perhaps without parallel for its blind dogmatism, its crudity of assertion, and its offensive discourtesy to all opponents (F. Wood Jones, *The problem of man's ancestry* (1918) 19).

And now for a few gems from Mr Wells:

> [Man] belongs to a branch of animal life which millions of years ago chanced [!] to develop that part of the brain situated in front called the cerebral cortex (*Picture Post*, 4 Nov. 1939, 46).
>
> A man is a natural man plus a great cerebral accumulation of directive ideas, prejudices, antagonisms, tolerances and conceptions of what he ought and ought not to do . . . The growth of this mental superstructure upon the primitive ape-man of the later tertiary period can now be traced in its broad lines without very much difficulty (*The fate of homo sapiens*, 36).

No difficulty whatever to Mr Wells; he is quite an adept at this kind of mythological speculation which can be easily performed at one's fireside. The cerebrum became larger and more wrinkled, leading to 'a great *cerebral* accumulation' not of organic *matter*, but of *ideas*; this hypothetical mental growth of the hypothetical ape-man into real man can be traced on paper without very much difficulty.[59] What nice pleasant nature-abhors-a-vacuum kind of stuff; it dispenses with the 'difficulty' of experimental research such as that conducted by Catholic missionaries; the *a priori* is so much easier, you know; you can spin it out of your own head. Elsewhere Mr Wells informs us:

> In civilised man we have (1) an inherited factor, the natural man who is the product of natural selection, the culminating ape . . . and (2) an acquired factor, the artificial

---

59. In *The science of life* (1931) by H. G. Wells, Julian Huxley and G. P. Wells, we find the old theory of hylozoism revived: 'A single universal world-stuff of which – so far as we know – life is the crowning elaboration, and human thought, feeling and willing the highest expression yet attained.' This rather hydraulically expressed theory contains all the difficulties of both pantheism and materialism; there is nothing new in it.

Appendix 2

man . . . In this view, what we call morality becomes the padding of suggested emotional habits necessary to keep the round palaeolithic savage in the square hole of the civilised state. And sin is the conflict of the two factors (H. G. Wells, *Fortnightly review*, October 1896, 594).

On this view – which is completely at variance with the results of ethnological research – the sense of sin has no relation to the deity, it is merely a clash between instincts alleged to be inherited ftom alleged half-human ancestors and those alleged to be acquired and imperfectly transmitted by more recent ancestors; in fact, a battle between two non-existents. But how can this be called Morality (written by Mr Wells with a capital letter)? Whence the sense of right and wrong, duty, obligation, categorical imperative? Not a trace; you cannot get *ought* from what is.[60] This alleged 'conflict' is as non-moral as the action and reaction involved in my gripping my pen. Mr Wells's soothing assurance that our specifically human 'mental structure' just grew – like Topsy – and that *he* can 'trace' the 'growth' 'without very much difficulty' is just so much eyewash to deceive the ill-educated public. Instead of starting from the indubitable qualities and modes of human thought – known in ourselves by observation and now laboriously confirmed by ethnologists – he prefers to explain the actual and known by the hypothetical and unknown; in other words, to substitute *a priori* constructions for scientific research, to bolster up a decadent materialistic theory by *ad hoc* guesses expressed in pseudo-scientific jargon. And after giving 'the biological equivalent of sin' he concludes[61] that 'from the biological point of view we are as individuals a series of involuntary "tries" on the part of an imperfect towards an unknown end'. *Ignotum ad ignotius*, in fact; surely not a very exciting creed. I think Mr Wells's evolutionism is one of nature's worst shoots.

Mr Wells presumably accepts Sir Arthur Keith's 'religion of a Darwinist' as the cult of truth, while, of course, the rest of us

60. Mr Wells professes to think they are synonymous: 'What does moral mean? *Mores* means manners and customs. Morality is the conduct of life. It is what we do with our social lives. It is how we deal with ourselves in relation to our fellow-creatures' (H. G. Wells, *What are we to do with our lives?* (1931) 6). The very title of this book shows that he really does distinguish between what we are to do (that is, ought to do) and what we actually do.

61. H. G. Wells *God the invisible king* (1917) 172.

worship error. But he gives us no account of how he would answer Darwin's difficulty:

> Then arises the doubt: Can the mind of man which has – as I fully believe – been developed from a mind as low as that possessed by the lowest animal, be trusted when it draws such grand conclusions? . . . Would anyone trust in the convictions of a monkey's mind, if there are any convictions in such a mind? (C. Darwin, *Life and letters*, i, 313).

Whence, indeed, our power of forming concepts and our faculty of reasoning? If intellect is merely the culmination of biological processes leading our organisms to respond to stimulus in a way having survival-value, then our judgments are not true or false – or at least did not arise on this score – they are merely advantageous or disadvantageous. And even this is no escape, for Mr Wells holds that this doctrine is true, thereby assigning an absolute value independent of the alleged genetic evolution of his faculty. So the attempt to derive morality and ratiocination from organic processes and blind instincts is a ghastly failure; it ends in a self-contradiction which no amount of scientific phraseology can conceal. Let us conclude with Professor H. E. Osborn:[62]

> The spiritual qualities of man cannot be accounted for by purely evolutionary processes . . . We observe a creative rise of intellectual and spiritual characters of which we have no explanation whatever; and side by side with this we place the creative rise of new anatomical characters which are equally difficult to explain (*Evolution in religion and culture* (1926) 224, 227).

IX[63]

God and Mr Wells

We have seen that, according to Mr Wells, sin is the conflict of two factors within us. One of these he conveniently calls the

---
62. I quote Osborn because he was a pupil of Huxley and because his *Men of the old stone age* (1916) is still regarded as a scientific bible by Wells, McCabe, etc.
63. *Standard* 1 March 1940.

Appendix 2

culminating ape and the other he regards as civilised. But he assigns no reason why we *ought* to allow one to overcome the other. It is all very fine to tell us[64] that 'the survival-value of a religion' lies in its helping 'the subordination of self and the achievement of co-operative loyalties'. But why ought I to subordinate myself? Why should I be loyal to demos? It would almost seem that Saloman Reinach[65] deliberately reversed the Wellsian nomenclature when he defined religion as 'a sum of scruples which impede the free exercise of our faculties'. An inhibition which Mr Wells regards as an emotional habit necessary for civilisation, Reinach regards as a taboo, 'a heritage transmitted to man from the brute'. And Mr Wells too thinks that religion arose from taboos, particularly from 'fear of the old man of the tribe'. 'Out of such ideas and a jumble of kindred ones,' he says,[66] 'grew the first quasi-religious elements in human life.'

As an account of primitive religion, this *a priori* theory – long since discarded by serious thinkers – is ludicrous and inane. But, even if it were true, it would not prove what Mr Wells thinks it proves. The validity of a belief is not vitiated because it had a gradual development. If origin or causation determined validity, our logic would be demolished because we were all once infants and our science would collapse because it probably originated in magic. In reality, the way in which a belief is started or developed is quite irrelevant to the problem of its validity. This applies to knowledge, morality and religion. It is a very simple point, but how many of Mr Wells's ordinary readers will see it? I doubt if Mr Wells himself sees it, for he never bothers to examine the proofs of the existence of God; he thinks it is sufficient to shout evolution.

Moreover, he has been guilty of gross prevarication. In one of his numerous attempts to found a new religion, he wrote *God the invisible king* (1917). Among other astonishing items in this tour-de-force we read on page 66 (in capital letters): GOD IS A PERSON. But in 1928 he tells us:

---

64. H. G. Wells, *The open conspiracy; blueprints for a world revolution* (1928) 12.
65. M. J. Lagrange, *Notes on the Orpheus of M. Salomon Reinach* (1910) 11. He adds: 'Really one would imagine that M. Reinach had done it for a bet!'
66. H. G. Wells, *The outline of history*, ch. 11, §§2, 4.

Alfred O'Rahilly III: Controversialist

Personality is the last vestige of anthropomorphism. The modern urge to a precise veracity is against such concessions to traditional expression (H. G. Wells, *The open conspiracy* (1928) 21).

And in *The fate of homo sapiens* (1939, 177) he declares: 'Even now many atheists prevaricate . . . A God who is not a personality is a contradiction in terms.' Mr Britling having seen through the dodge of adopting a theistic disguise – the rationalist William Archer having published *God and Mr Wells* (1917) – the urge to veracity resumed its sway over the culminating ape. So Mr Wells unobtrusively repaired his 'sin':

> I came to admit that by all preceding definitions of God, this God of Mr Britling was no God at all . . . My phraseology went back unobtrusively to the sturdy atheism of my youthful days . . . In *What are we to do with our lives?* (1932) I made the most explicit renunciation and apology for this phase of terminological disingenuousness (H. G. Wells, *Experiment in autobiography* (1934) ii, 672, 677).

Having abandoned what he euphemistically terms his terminological disingenuousness, he persevered in his efforts to found a new religion; if he could not be the prophet of Allah, he would at least be his own prohpet, he would pontificate *in vacuo*. For 'if there is no sympathetic personal leader outside us, there is in us the attitude towards a sympathetic personal leader'.[67] This is the religion of Attitudinarianism, the creed of the great As-If. There is no God – we have just his word for it – but let us go on behaving as if there were.

> He [H. G. Wells] cannot picture a secular Mass nor congregations singing hymns about the 'Open Conspiracy'. Perhaps the modern soul in trouble will resort to the psycho-analysts instead of the confessional . . . The modern temple in which we shall go to meditate may be a museum; the modern religious house and its religious life may be a research organisation (H. G. Wells, *What are we to do with our lives?* (1931) 100f).

---

67. H. G. Wells, *What are we to do with our lives?* (1931) 30.

Appendix 2

Mr Wells has here considerably lightened my task by becoming his own unconscious caricaturist; I could never have penned so biting a satire. Having robbed thousands among his simple readers of their faith by his pseudo-scientific sciolism, having unleashed powerful passions by his talk of ape-man and his reduction of the family to a biological fact, he starts to repair the damage by founding a new religion of middle-class claptrap. Having ridiculed historical Christianity with coarse buffoonery, he thinks it is the easiest thing in the world to keep the virtues of Christianity without Christ and to retain the attitude towards the non-existent leader after he has blasphemed away his readers' faith in the great leader. Having mocked and jibed at the Catholic Church, he next proceeds to erect a ghostly bloodless caricature of the institution he has defamed: the psycho-analyst is to replace the confessor, museums are to succeed churches, and research organisations are to be the new religious orders.

This jejune and futile scheme is the religion of bathos. It could have been excogitated only by one of those gentlemen of England who live at home at ease, dictating to secretaries and receiving fat royalties. This kind of inanity might have been perpetrated in the heyday of Victorian liberalism, when extended suffrage, universal literacy and free trade were expected to usher in the era of peace and plenty. But apparently this elderly liberal, still basking in the ethics of an after-Christian, does not yet realise the bankruptcy of naturalism. After a generation of godless education, the rationalist democrat is now face to face with the barbarian. To offer this tenuous concoction as the pseudo-intellectual's substitute for Christianity is like fobbing off a tiger with a tomato-sandwich. You are right, Mr Wells; there is no gizz in it; men could not sing hymns about it, nor are they prepared to live and die for museums. The world's drudgery will not be cheerfully performed, men will not check their strong passions, just because they have joined 'The Open Conspiracy' just as they might join a book club. Thousands of men and women have sacrificed all in life to serve Christ's brothers and sisters; they would not do it just because they have read the *Outline of history* or because they want to help a bit of research. When men are weary and heavy-laden they find rest for their souls by turning to Christ; it is mere mockery to refer them to Freud. This new-fangled religion is a paper-scheme; it will not work. Having lived a year in the United States during Prohibition, I can appreciate the negro's verdict on near-beer: 'It looks like be-ah, it smells like be-ah, it tastes like be-ah; but when it gets down inside, it ain't got no authority.' That is what is wrong with the near-religion founded by Mr Wells: it ain't got no authority.

Was there ever such a pitiable confession of defeat, such a clear acknowledgement that he has in the hearts of myriads destroyed something precious and valuable which he is vainly endeavouring to re-establish? 'There is no creed,' he sadly admits (*The fate of homo sapiens*, 291), 'no way of living left in the world at all, that really meets the need of the time.' How myopic he is; he can see nothing in the world beyond the grim area of spiritual devastation caused by a small clique of atheists with their counterfeit science. You have done a lot of damage, Mr Wells, but not at all as much as you think. You might drown a fly by spitting at it; but such tactics are useless against the Rock of Peter. Surely you do not think that 'the need of the time' is to be measured by the narrow gauge of your single-track mind? Is it possible that you imagine you have really demolished our religious orders, our churches, our confessionals?

Please do not delude yourself, do not think you have *this* damage to repair. I assure you the Church is flourishing today and will be still flourishing in the fifth millennium A.D. when you and your pawky ideas have – in J. Tyndall's phrase – melted like streaks of morning cloud into the infinite azure of the past.

And now, Mr Wells, I take leave of you. It was you, not I, who started this controversy. You wantonly insulted Catholics, and in particular, Irish Catholics. And I, an Irish Catholic layman, have accepted your challenge. I would much prefer a serious scholarly discussion; that is, had I found any real scholarship or good manners in you. But you are nothing but a scurrilous large-scale pamphleteer, trotting out other rationalists' hypotheses and discarded scientific junk as the assured conclusions of present-day science. I have no hope of inducing you to reconsider the immature dogmatism which has persisted since your undergraduate days. But by showing you up for what you are – a truculent trumpery sciolist – I hope to put some spunk into those unfortunate non-Catholics whom you have been bamboozling. And I am sure my fellow-Catholics will accept me as

Appendix 2

their mouthpiece on this occasion and will regard these articles as the expression of their just indignation at your clumsy and vulgar blasphemies.

'A little friend of mine,' you tell us, Mr Wells (*The fate of homo sapiens*, 319) 'sent me a card to wish me a Happy Easter.' Your little friend has evidently not yet realised that you claim to have abolished Easter. Now unfortunately I know too much about you to be able to wish you a Happy Christmas, for you fancy you have also abolished Christ-Mass. I think, however, that my day has been well spent in the service of him who was born in Bethlehem as our 'little friend'. And perhaps I have thus done something towards keeping this feast alive in the hearts of my fellows. Once it was Herod who vainly sought the child to destroy him. Now it is H. G. Wells.

Appendix 3

CORK CORPORATION AND THE PROPOSAL FOR A NEW MATERNITY HOSPITAL IN THE CITY

The following quotations (from the only documents accessible) show that the project to replace Erinville hospital by a women's hospital, quite distinct from the proposed regional hospital at Wilton, was unanimously approved by Cork Corporation, was accepted by the government (at least until 1946), and also – with certain modifications subsequently approved by Erinville hospital – advocated by the medical staff of University College, Cork.

The following letter was sent on 15 February 1939 to the Erinville hospital:

> I am directed by the minister for local government and public health to forward for the information of the committee of management of Erinville lying-in hospital the accompanying extract from the minutes of proceedings of the South Cork County Board of Public Assistance at their meeting on Monday, 23rd ultimo, regarding the question of the site of the proposed Cork maternity hospital. In reference thereto, I am to point out that the reasons governing the selection of a site for that hospital on the land formerly used as the terminus of the Cork and Muskerry Light Railway were that:
>
> (a) the location of the institution would be convenient to the homes of the poor people availing themselves of the services of the institution;
>
> (b) the medical staff would be within easy call of confinement cases requiring to be attended in their own homes;
>
> (c) the hospital which is to be an important teaching and training centre would be more easily accessible to the students and teaching staff; and
>
> (d) the site was approved by the committee of management of Erinville lying-in-hospital and by the provisional committee set up to consider the acquisition of a site for the new maternity hospital.
>
> If, however, the committee of management of Erinville lying-in-hospital are of opinion that the question of the site of the new institution should be reconsidered, it would be well for them in the first instance, to discuss the whole

Appendix 3

matter with the medical staff of their hospital and with the Cork University authorities in view of the close connection between the hospital and the medical faculty. The minister will be glad to be furnished with the views of the committee in the matter as soon as possible.

This letter refers to the request made by the lord mayor (Councillor J. Hickey) to the South Cork Board to sell three or four acres of the Wilton site (at the original price of £190 per acre) for the erection of a city maternity hospital, in case the Muskerry site proved unsuitable or too costly. The South Cork Board agreed.

From this document we infer:

(1) In 1939 the South Cork Board of Assistance accepted without demur the establishment of a city maternity hospital, completely distinct from and independent of the proposed regional hospital. Moreover the board was anxious to facilitate the project.

(2) In 1939 the department of local government and public health was decidedly in favour of the Muskerry site.

(3) The department recommended the Erinville hospital to discuss the matter with U.C.C. Unfortunately this was not done.

The following is an extract from a letter sent by the department to Erinville hospital on 11 July 1941 and read at a meeting of Cork Corporation held on 22 July 1941:

I am directed by the minister for local government and public health to state that, as it is contemplated that the new hospital when erected will be administered by a joint board consisting of members of the board of management of Erinville hospital and the corporation of Cork in the agreed proportion, it is desirable that the joint board should be associated with the responsibility for the planning of the hospital. The joint board can only be set up by an establishment order in pursuance of an application made by the board of management of Erinville hospital.

The following are extracts from a letter from the department to the corporation, dated 25 September 1943, in reply to a letter 'enquiring as to the present position with regard to the construction of the Cork regional hospital and of the new Cork maternity hospital:

(1) Cork regional hospital:
Exactly twelve months ago the department conveyed to the South Cork Board of Public Assistance – the body responsible for the planing of the institution – a statement of the views of the department on several aspects of the accommodation to be provided. No representations have since been received in this office in regard to the matter.
(2) The Cork maternity hospital:
As regards the proposed Cork maternity hospital, the conditions governing the architectural competition for the planning of the institution have been settled. But it is considered that the proper body to administer that competition is the joint board composed of representatives of the Cork Corporation and of the present maternity hospital, which is to be constituted for the provision and administration of the new hospital. This was notified to the committee of management of Erinville hospital on 10 October 1940; and they were requested to apply for an establishment order . . . Further action in regard to proceeding with the proposed maternity hospital rests with that committee.

Notice the clear distinction between the Cork regional hospital (pertaining to the South Cork Board) and the Cork maternity hospital (pertaining to Cork Corporation and the Erinville committee).

The above letter was read at a meeting of the corporation on 28 September 1943; and the following resolution was passed:

It was unanimously decided . . . to request the committee of management of Erinville hospital to apply for an establishment order under the Hospitals Act 1939 to enable a joint board for the provision and administration of the new maternity hospital to be constituted.

At the meeting of the corporation held on 11 January 1944 'a letter was read from the secretary, Erinville hospital, stating that the committee of management had applied for an establishment

Appendix 3

order and that the site for the proposed new hospital has been sold to Messrs Dwyer & Co.' The corporation decided to send a copy of the letter to the minister for his observations.[1]

On 16 May 1944 the city manager wrote to the solicitor acting for Erinville hospital. After acknowledging the receipt of the draft application for an establishment order, he says: 'The corporation has agreed in outline to this draft already.' The city manager then made some suggestions for alterations which had been made by the lord mayor after consulting the M.O.H. On 2 June 1944 the solicitor replied that the committee was unable to accept these suggestions.

On 25 March 1945 there appeared in the *Cork Examiner* an official notice that the lady governors of Erinville hospital had applied for an establishment order:

> The application asks for the provision of a new maternity hospital to receive general maternity and gynaecological cases from the Cork County Borough and South Cork County Health District and to act as a regional institution for special maternity and gynaecological cases sent from the remainder of Cork County and from Waterford County and the southern part of Tipperary South Riding and Kerry Counties. It also requests the dissolution of the existing

---

1. At this point in his first draft of this memorandum Alfred included the following: 'It is worth while remarking that, at least five years previously, objections had been made to the Muskerry site on the alleged ground of the cost involved in piling and in building a new bridge. The following is a quotation from the *Cork Co-operator* for April 1939:

> It is understood that the architect has advised the committee of Erinville hospital that proper foundations will cost an extra £5,000 and the erection of a bridge a further £15,000. (A more correct figure would be about £6,000.) The South Cork Board's site at Wilton, less than a mile away, costs £190 per acre. In order to avoid such wasteful expenditure, the lord mayor (Councillor J. Hickey, T.D.) requested the South Cork Board if they would sell about three or four acres of the Wilton site at the price per acre they paid for it, for the erection of the maternity hospital. The South Cork Board agreed. The lady governors and the committee, however, did not approve of the lord mayor's suggestion, as the Muskerry site already fulfilled the department's requirements.

The quotation is interesting as showing how completely it was accepted at that date – not only by the corporation but by the South Cork Board of Assistance – that Cork City was to have a women's hospital completely separate from the regional hospital.'

governing body of the hospital and the transfer of its property, debts, duties and liabilities to a new governing body representative in part of Cork Corporation.

And further take notice that any person who objects to the making of the said establishment order in relation to the said hospital may at any time on or before the 16th day of April 1945 furnish a written statement of his objection to the minister.

On 14 April 1945 the president of U.C.C. wrote to the minister:

After a hurried consultation with some of my medical colleagues, I would like to lodge a provisional objection. The reason I am writing hurriedly is that I understand that the objection must reach you by next Monday. I propose to make the points clearer as soon as I have an opportunity of further consultation with my colleagues. At the moment I happen to be laid up.

The new hospital will be of great importance to us as a medical school and therefore to the future medical graduates who are qualified in Cork. In such a teaching hospital we consider that University College, Cork, should have representation on the board.

On 15 June 1945 the president sent to the minister a long memorandum containing not only objections but constructive counter-proposals. The receipt of this was acknowledged on 22 June by the parliamentary secretary (Dr Ward).

Subsequently this memorandum was shown to the lord mayor and to some of the city T.Ds, who signified their approval.

By way of anticipation it may be observed that this year (1948) the medical staff and the lady governors of Erinville hospital unanimously approved of the principles embodied in the president's memorandum.

The following is an extract from a letter sent by the department to the lord mayor, dated 26 July 1946, in reply to his inquiry 'with regard to the erection of a new maternity hospital in Cork:

The proposals and objections in relation to this project are at present receiving attention. It is expected that the

Appendix 3

minister will be in a position to communicate with the corporation on the matter in the course of a few weeks.

This letter was read at the meeting of the Cork Corporation held on 27 August 1946. Next day the *Cork Examiner*, under the heading 'Cork maternity hospital', quoted the minister's letter and reported as follows:

> Mr J. Horgan remarked that it was nearly time, in view of the fact that this was going on for about eight years.
>
> Mr S. McCarthy, T.D., said that the objections sent to the minister included an important one from U.C.C., where the medical faculty and the president (Dr O'Rahilly) were much concerned about the whole matter.
>
> The lord mayor (Mr M. Sheehan), who presided, said he had discussed the matter with the president of U.C.C., and he could bear out what had been said regarding Dr O'Rahilly's interest being, first and foremost, the welfare of Cork and its citizens.
>
> Mr McCarthy said they were all glad to hear there would be a decision in the near future.

On 28 January 1947 the minister intimated to the lord mayor that the whole matter required further consideration and that 'it has been decided to defer the making of the order pending further review of the general position'. A similar answer was given by the minister (Dr Ryan) in the Dáil on 6 May 1947 in reply to a query from Deputy Anthony. Thus the late government accepted the principle of an establishment order to provide a women's hospital in the city, as requested by the corporation. The matter was deferred owing to the objections and counter-proposals made by U.C.C. These, however, were subsequently accepted by Erinville.

It is fitting to record in conclusion a tribute to the lady governors and the medical staff of Erinville hospital, without whose devoted services during so many years the university medical school could not have continued.

Appendix 4

EDITORIAL DRAFTED BY ALFRED O'RAHILLY IN *STANDARD* 20 APRIL 1951

WANTED – LIGHT, NOT HEAT

So much has been said and written about the government's rejection of the mother-and-child scheme proposed by the late minister for health, Dr Noel Browne, and about the minister's resulting resignation, that there is some danger, if indeed we are not already faced with this result, of a perilous confusion of the public mind on the issues involved. What these issues are will, we think, be clear to anyone who reads the able and comprehensive article in this issue entitled 'The bishops and the people' by the distinguished president of University College, Cork.

It should be clear, first of all, that this is not a question which arose last week, or even last year. Readers of the *Standard* who can cast their minds back six years should have no difficulty in recalling the cogent and clear criticism which we then published of, not one but two, health bills, introduced by the previous administration. The second was passed, let us hope in all good faith, and was about to be challenged as to its constitutionality in the courts by the private action of Mr James Dillon just when the reins of power passed from Mr de Valera's party to the present coalition. Before that point had been reached the bishops drew the attention of the then government to the conflict between the provisions of the bill and Christian moral values. The case made in 1947 was no different if perhaps, in the circumstances, less developed than that made in 1951. In neither case did the bishops make an overt public pronouncement. One frequently hears it said, in relation to grave problems in the social and political field, that 'the Church should do something about it'. The bishops, who are the divinely appointed guardians of the teaching of the Church in Ireland, are naturally reluctant at any time to enter into the arena of public affairs. They will do so only when their clear duty compels them.

It will be obvious to fair-minded observers that, in making a private approach both to this and the previous government, the bishops were discharging that duty in the only way which would at the same time ensure that their intervention and direction could not be taken as 'interfering in politics', or as casting a general aspersion on the personalities or policies of any

Appendix 4

particular party within the State. It is greatly to be regretted that the methods employed by Dr Noel Browne and his adherents and the use made of their disclosure of private documents has provided the enemies of religion, of the nation and of all true concepts of Christian liberty with an opportunity for attack which they have been quick to seize upon.

They have seized upon it, as Dr O'Rahilly points out, in spite of the fact that the principles and the liberties which the Irish bishops are now defending are as valuable to any minority group of Christians or others who believe in God and the dignity and integrity of the human person as they are to the great majority of Irish people who are Catholics.

It would be well for those who from ignorance, from humanitarian sentiment or even from malice, use this opportunity of attacking the Church and its ministers to remember that the Catholic Church fights for the most fundamental human rights on the very outworks of Christian defences. It does not wait until the enemy is within the citadel. There are millions in Europe today who have painful cause to regret that when the Church – the bishops, their priests and the instructed Catholic laity – stepped into the first breaches made in the structure of Western and Christian civilization they were attacked from the rear not alone by the well-trained and thoroughly indoctrinated agents of communist tyranny, but also by so-called 'liberals' whose out-of-date habits of mind had conditioned them to ally themselves to any and every enemy of Catholicism.

The issues which are now in the forefront of the minds of so many people are important. It is vital that they should be clearly understood, that they should not be made the instrument for private vengeance or sectional strategy. We have little doubt, knowing as we do the essential Christian quality of the vast majority of our legislators and popular leaders, of all parties and sections, that the unhappy circumstances of the dismissal of the minister for health will not be allowed to cloud the minds of our people and that the recognition of the supremacy of moral over material values will set a standard in public affairs which will not alone be a guarantee of our future liberties as a Christian people, but also one which other and less fortunate communities may well envy.

To say, for instance, that the bishops' defence of the integrity of the family and the rights of parents should cause any but a manufactured concern to the Protestants of the six counties is to assume a scale of values amongst a large group of God-fearing men and women which insults both their traditions and their intelligence.

APPENDIX 5

'THE DOCTOR, THE STATE AND THE COMMUNITY'

by ALFRED O'RAHILLY[1]

There are three great liberal professions which are directly and intimately concerned with ministering to human beings: those of the clergyman, the teacher, the doctor. Each of these is liable to occupational bias. When Marx called religion the opiate of the people, there was a certain amount of justification in the England of his time. On the plea of being supramundane, religion acquiesced in social injustice; clergymen acted as if men had souls without bodies, as if the supernatural involved the denial of the natural. Teachers – especially in America, under the influence of Dewey – have become infected with the contemporary disbelief in an objective moral order. Hence, many teachers in schools and universities have reduced education to mere instruction and professional equipment; repudiating their own responsibility they have placed an intolerable burden on immature youth.

Medical men have also largely become the victims of the contemporary naturalism of biologists and sociologists. Even when slowly and reluctantly they diluted their materialism by admitting psychosomatic causation, many of them succumbed to Freud's fragmentation and depersonalisation, which was the continuation of Darwin's dehumanisation. In other words, the doctor, playing the double role of scientist and of human helper, tends to become assimilated to the engineer who deals with inanimate matter and to the biologist who is concerned with animals. Lacking a humanist philosophy in his education, and influenced by the Zeitgeist of naturalism, the medical man is tempted to extricate himself from the moral order and even sometimes godlike to decide on life and death.

In addition to being liable to this internal one-sidedness, each of these great professions is nowadays subject to increasing efforts at subjugation by the centralised power of the modern State. We can see this pressure operating in an extreme form in totalitarian countries. Communism aims to destroy the

1. This is the text of an address given by Alfred on 8 July 1952 during an international conference of members of the Guild of SS. Luke, Cosmas and Damian at Newman House, Dublin. The address was later published as part of a supplement in the *Standard* in November 1953.

autonomous and international character of the Church, to nationalise it in order to domesticate its ministers and to make them the tools of the government. The teachers become civil servants, mouthpieces of the political party in power. Like the pope, the parents are to be superseded. As to the doctors, we can learn from Buchenwald and Auschwitz to what depths of degradation men of great scientific attainments can sink under a false philosophy of the State.

In democratic countries the results are not so drastic. Nevertheless the danger is real, if more subtle and gradual. Governments resent moral criticisms of their measures; they object to any criterion except the arithmetical verdict of the electorate. Religion is a private affair; the priest must stay in the sacristy. In education the parents are not altogether ignored; but those who do not accept agnostic secularism, or at the best an amalgam called an agreed syllabus, are financially penalised if they wish to have a real say in the education of their children. In other words, most contemporary democracies openly or implicitly adopt the unitary concept of the State. Man's social nature is adequately expressed in the political community, which is the final depositary of authority and from which alone all other aggregations – churches, families, professions – derive any right to exist and to function.

In this striving of the modern democratic State to dominate or to absorb all other natural groups, the medical profession is in the front line of battle. Apart from the occasional grumblings of an out-of-date Voltairianism, the Churches have not been impeded. There still exists – though with increasing financial burdens – a large body of independent teachers, clerical and lay. The most active drive today is to rope in the doctors, to make them agents of the public authority, to use them to penetrate the family and to condition the workers, in some countries even to regulate parenthood and to sterilise undesirables.

We see then how great is the responsibility of medical practitioners and how important it is that they should be trained in sound philosophy and in social principles. For the doctor of today is subjected to a double tension: that between the human and the scientific aspects of his profession, and that between personal and collective responsibility. These dilemmas cannot be solved by accepting either extreme alternative. He must

Appendix 5

gradually find a position of equilibrium which does justice to the varied and often conflicting loyalties involved in his work.

Let us examine the first of these internal tensions between science and humanity in medical practice. Undoubtedly, a doctor must be a man of science in his training and in his methods. The scientific renaissance culminated during the nineteenth century in its application to human beings as subject to scientific laws and procedures. Hence, arises the problem of our time: How far can humans, endowed not only with individuality, but with personality, be the object of scientific experiment and control? Is the sick person merely a case, a number in a hospital bed, the subject of standard treatment, material for research?

When a patient asks help, he appeals to the doctor primarily as a man of science acquainted with such bodily infirmities. Now science is concerned with the general, not with the particular. If the patient wishes to be cured, he must submit to being regarded, not solely as a free person worthy of love and service, but also as an object or a nature, a body governed by physical laws. He must, therefore, acknowledge the legitimacy of this science, and, consequently, of the experimentation required for establishing a body of verified hypotheses. Naturally the first step should be trial in the laboratory and on animals. Human beings should not be regarded as guinea-pigs; nor should hazardous procedures be tried out on the defenceless and on the poor. But when we come to human patients in the concrete, there must always be an element of risk difficult to estimate. Each individual case must be decided by the conscience of the doctor who is given a large measure of legal immunity.

This limited legitimacy of experimentation – which was denied by some of the older moral theologians who wrote before scientific method was understood – places a heavy onus of moral responsibility upon the doctor, who must accordingly have a serious training in medical ethics.

We see in the case of Nazi Germany how far false ideological postulates can gradually corrupt a great professional body. Brutal experiments – on refrigeration, altitude, phosgene, phenol poisons, burns, typhus, paludism – were performed on prisoners regarded as sub-human and involved enormous suffering and mortality. Such an example of degenerescence ought to lead to an examination of conscience. An American doctor writes:

Alfred O'Rahilly III: Controversialist

My experience at the Nürnberg medical trials emphasised the great practical and humanitarian importance of medical ethics. It caused me to realise that my medical education in that regard had been deficient and that medical education today is negligent in teaching the relation of the ethics of medicine to the economics of medicine . . . More instruction regarding the meaning of medical ethics should be given to the medical student and the layman (A. C. Ivy, M.D., 'Nazi war crimes of a medical nature', *Journal of the American Medical Association* 139 (1949)).

But, while duly expressing horror, we should not use this Nazi performance as by contrast providing a complete exoneration of medical practice in other countries. The writer of the above quotation, when himself interrogated at the Nürnberg trials, made a very poor defence of American milder experiments on conscientious objectors and prisoners. It is even more pertinent to point out that the Jewish doctor, Alfons Fischer, by his propaganda for eugenics and for the elimination of hereditary taints, by his approval of the 1933 law, and his attacks on the stand made by Catholic doctors, paved the way for the medical horrors of the concentration camps which he escaped by death, but in which several of his relatives perished.

The lesson to learn is to make sure that the medical practitioners of democratic countries are not themselves indoctrinated with the false philosophy of which these horrors are merely the full logical development. We must learn to abhor the wrong principle involved and not merely the accidental concomitant of large-scale cruelty. For otherwise we are merely making a sentimental protest.

This is especially true of those scientific and medical men who deny the specifically human. If man is merely an animal, there can be no rational objection to selecting batches of patients as guinea-pigs. The only sensible procedure would be to kill off the feeble-minded and the unfit, or to prevent them from being born. Sterilisation, or in hopeless cases the lethal chamber, is the efficient economic and scientific method of solving the social problem. Inhuman? Nonsense. We slaughter cattle; we must stamp out foot-and-mouth disease. Why not similarly liquidate the unfit and the recalcitrant? Or, at least, why not enslave them as the Russians do? Many a modern

Appendix 5

philosopher or doctor would be hard pressed to give any answer except a confession of squeamishness. Mr C. E. M. Joad, for example, in *The Book of Joad* (1942), writes: 'Whether I have a conscience or not, I do not know. But elsewhere he tells us:

> I would affirm that the individual is an end in himself. Souls are souls even if their life here is transitory; and though they may not be immortal, it is none the less the business of the government to treat them as if they were (*For civilization* (1940) 20).

This piece of make-believe he affirms to be 'the great gift of Christianity to the world.' Joad does not know whether or not he has a spiritual soul and a conscience; but he declares that it is the duty of the government to treat him as if he had. The government, which is not composed of academic as if's, may well ask why. If men repudiate their unique status as amenable to the moral order as well as living in the physical and biological world, then they should be sufficiently honest to accept the practical consequences of this repudiation. Unless man has natural rights, rights due to his nature and beyond the jurisdiction of the collectivity, he is not a person in an objective moral order, he is just one of a herd. As General Eisenhower said in his parting message to Holland:

> Free government without spiritual values and religion is impossible. Do not be afraid to say men have souls; for if they have not, then what we are fighting for is silly.

This 'doctrine of the bestiality of man' – to use Mivart's description of Darwinism – has had disastrous consequences, not only on medical practice, but on personal conduct. Charles Darwin wrote his *The descent of man* (1871) 'to show that there is no fundamental difference between man and the higher mammals in their mental faculties' and moral outlook. This was immediately popularised by the elder Huxley in lectures to working-men. 'By next Friday evening,' he wrote, 'they will all be convinced that they are monkeys.' The Catholic Mivart denounced this school which logically denies all absolute individual rights, asserting that man is essentially no better than the brutes, and may, like brutes, be treated in any way useful for material ends without regard to any divine law' (*Quarterly Review* (1874) 20). Darwin, Huxley and Hooker boycotted Mivart for daring to assert that their dehumanising doctrine would lead to totalitarianism, or even to any disturbance of the domestic fidelity exemplified in the good Queen Victoria. But Mivart was prophetically right. The most brutal and forthright enunciation of the consequences can nowadays be found in the writings of scientific and medical men. Here are two quotations from a book by two Yale professors, published last year in England by *The Practitioner*:

> Perversion: A term without scientific meaning. It refers to any form of sexual activity which a given social group regards as unnatural and abnormal. Activities that are classified as perversions by one society may be considered normal in another.
> In view of the extremely widespread occurrence of autogenital stimulation throughout the class mammalia, it seems illogical to classify human masturbation as abnormal or perverted (C. S. Ford and F. A. Beach, *Patterns of sexual behaviour* (1952) 163, 283).

Here we have the crude assumptions that objective moral principles do not exist, that ethical judgements merely reflect existing social taboos, that what is humanly normal or morally perverse is to be gathered from a factual survey of primitive societies and from a study of monkeys.

What strikes one most about this, and similar pronouncements, is the entire unconsciousness and bland insouciance with which so many medical men go beyond their beat, as if technical skill in biology or therapeutics *ipso facto* conferred on them competence to decide questions of value or fundamental moral issues. Thus, we find medical associations making pronouncements on the institution of marriage and the World Health Organisation deterred only by Italy and Ireland from establishing a committee on birth control as if it were only a question of 'health'.

Until we lay the axe to this pestiferous doctrine of bestiality, it is useless to discuss the relation of the doctor to his patient, or to the community, or indeed to raise any issues of medical

Appendix 5

ethics except certain trade-union amenities and existing legal restrictions.

Against this degradation of a great profession, we maintain that medical practice, as in the case of all technics, must observe absolute respect for the human personality in ourselves and in others. The patient is never an anonymous entity, never merely an organism in disequilibrium, never just a means. Nothing – not medical research, not even the propagation of the faith – justifies the least violation of his fundamental rights. Even as regards scientific progress it is this view which has led to the greatest advances. The excuses for therapeutic abortion have been ousted by new methods of treatment; the so-called incurable diseases paraded by advocates of euthanasia have been steadily lessened by new discoveries. But, even if this were not so, the doctor should be so trained as to be immunised against scientism – the current fallacy that a study of what is settles what ought to be, and that applied science is exempt from moral criteria.

It is when we come to consider the status of the physician *vis-à-vis* the community that the need for a proper philosophy becomes most evident. The doctor-patient society is – like husband-wife, priest-penitent, teacher-pupil – one of the oldest and primary of human relationships. Though it has subsisted through all the changes of social structures, its integrity is now gravely menaced. In the so-called Hippocratic oath, dating from about 480 BC, the doctor swears 'by Apollo Physician, by Asclepius, by Health, by Panacea and by all the gods and goddesses' to carry out his ministrations faithfully, never to administer a poisonous drug, never to abuse bodies, and to observe professional secrecy.

The pagan deities were dethroned by Christ: Great Pan is dead! The modern post-Christian doctor has left himself no power to swear by, except Caesar, and so he is defenceless against the encroachment of the State against which he has no court of appeal. Illogically he strives to evade the ineluctable consequence of his herd-philosophy, namely, that all his professional privileges are concessions from the State and may be revoked by it.

Against this doctrine of social permission, we maintain that medical secrecy is primarily personal and not just a working arrangement exacted and limited by public order. It is based on the fundamental right of the human person to confide, integrally and with impunity, in another who can supply moral or material aid. A person thus entering into intimate contact with another is subject to a duty which results not from a special contract or from public order, but from the confidential nature of the relationship. *A fortiori* this is true of the doctor-patient association, which, being a traditional and quasi-natural institution, possesses objective natural rights independent of the political community.

But, since this association is not a complete society, its independence is not unlimited. This is more obvious to us than it was to Hippocrates who lived before the emergence of the State as we know it and when the idea of contagion – for example, syphilis, epidemics – did not exist. So the medical practitioner of today feels the tension between his personal and his social obligations. Hence, many acute conflicts arise, and these are not easy of solution. This is not the occasion for discussing such cases of conscience. But it is important to make, again, the general assertion that medical secrecy, though loaded with certain obligations to society, is based primarily and intrinsically upon the doctor-patient relationship independently of the general community. Here, as in the case of the family, it is necessary to consolidate our defence of institutional autonomy against increasing political invasion, for the intervention of public law cannot go on indefinitely.

In medicine, responsibility must be indivisible and exclusive. The excuse made by many of the participants in Nazi medical experimentation was that they were not only doctors, but army officers. A similar, though lesser, dilution of medical autonomy is taking place in our own society, where the same individual so often combines the position of medical adviser and of health policeman. Already in the case of a doctor to a group (for example, a factory), the treatment is not of individuals as such, but of members. The State, however, is going much further and is not content to authorise the doctor to use the permission of disclosure usefully and voluntarily given by the patient, so far as the rights of a third party are not violated. It has imposed upon the doctor a legal obligation not applied to other citizens with similar knowledge. It is understandable that the victim of certain diseases, or anyone else with a knowledge of his state, should be bound to notify the public authorities for the pro-

Appendix 5

tection of the community. But what we have all too readily acquiesced in is the exclusive saddling of the medical attendant with this general obligation. Using a tacit threat of professional disbarring, the State selects as its agent, the doctor who, in virtue of his relationship to the patient, is under the least obligation to violate confidence.

The general good will ultimately suffer, not only because the individuals whose confidence is no longer protected will hesitate to consult or confide fully in their medical adviser, but also because the State will be encouraged more and more to ride roughshod over all other human associations.

For, ultimately, there is a fundamental social principle of which the doctors should be the leading defenders. This is the principle of institutional plurality, described as follows by Pius XI in *Quadragesimo Anno* (1931):

> It is an injustice, a grave evil and a disturbance of right order for a larger and higher association to arrogate to itself functions which can be performed efficiently by smaller and lower societies. This is a fundamental principle of social philosophy, unshaken and unchangeable.

This is directly opposed to the conception of the unitary State now so generally accepted even in democracies. This idea may be said to have started with Rousseau's false view of the human will as determining itself without any prior assignment or end. That is the assertion of the supremacy of will in the individual and in the group without any consideration of an objective moral order existing independently of man's volition. The anarchic free will of men in the state of nature led in Rousseau's mind to the authoritative will of the government in the state of society. Hence, the theory of State monopoly started its modern career at the French Revolution, when (in 1791) all lesser associations were dissolved, and it was sought to pulverise society into atomic individuals face to face with the sovereign State. Subsequently, indeed, combinations and trade unions came to be recognised, but only as legal creations of the State. And in our day, with the technological accumulation of power, the State has once more begun to monopolise all social relationships under its domination and control. To use the papal language, the larger and higher association called the State is more and more arrogating to itself functions which can be performed more efficiently and humanly by the smaller societies, such as the family, the professions and private enterprise. The individual is losing his institutional liberties and becoming a cog in a vast impersonal machine.

How does all this concern the doctor? In the first place, his professional autonomy is being filched from him when he is saddled with incompatible duties as health-policeman and the State obtrudes itself into his relations with his patients. In the second place, he is being used as a tool by the State for usurping the natural rights of the family. The latter perversion is, unfortunately, facilitated by the false philosophy with which so many doctors are imbued. Their attitude to marriage and sex is inspired by the same erroneous voluntarism which lies at the root of modern totalitarianism. To quote Pius XI again, God has given to private individuals 'no other power over the members of their bodies than that which pertains to their natural ends'. In other words, there is a natural order which is morally obligatory on the human will. Thus the reproductive function as such is not directly subordinated to the good of the individual, as is the appendix or the gall-bladder or the foot; nor is the life of the child subordinated to the life and well-being of the mother. Relationship to another is essentially involved. Yet, ignoring this social reference, how many surgeons without scruple engage in procedures which directly and intentionally result in sterility or abortion. They regard sexual functions and maternity as completely subject to human decisions, without taking the smallest notice of that natural teleology which indicates God's purpose.

By so acting, these medical practitioners have sold the pass; they have betrayed their own professional autonomy as well as the natural rights of the family, for a valid defence of either cannot be made without assuming an objective moral order to which the human will must conform.

How can these doctors, who arbitrarily play fast and loose with human life and life-giving functions, make a stand against the State when it prescribes or practises sterilisation on sections of the population, or allows euthanasia?

Moreover, these medical men, who thus repudiate the inviolability of the natural order of the family and regard marital relations as subject to arbitrary interference, are really claiming

Appendix 5

for themselves powers which they would inconsistently deny to the State. Hence they have deprived themselves of the strongest argument against their being turned into State employees commissioned to direct and to inspect mother and child. The only solid defence of the family is to uphold the pluralistic view of social life, to deny that the political community is all-inclusive, to maintain that other associations – in particular the family – have independent natural rights and duties, internal and external. In his encyclical *Divini Illius Magistri* of 1929, Pius XI declared:

> God directly communicates to the family, in the natural order, fecundity (which is the principle of life) and hence, also, the principle of education to life together with authority (the principle of order) . . . The family, therefore, holds directly from the creator the mission, and hence, the right to educate the offspring; a right inalienable because inseparably joined to the strict obligation, a right anterior to any right whatever of civil society and of the State, and, therefore, inviolable on the part of any power on earth.

A further quotation will show us that this strong declaration affects not only the status of the children's teacher, but also that of the family doctor:

> As this duty on the part of the parents continues up to the time when the child is in a position to provide for itself, the same inviolable parental right of education also endures . . . The obligation of the family to bring up children includes, not only religious and moral education, but physical and civic education as well, principally in so far as it touches upon religion and morality.

From this it follows that, like the teacher, the doctor is *in loco parentis*, he is helping the parents to fulfil their natural right and duty in 'physical education', that is, in safeguarding the health of the children – a function which can never be completely dissociated from principles of religion and morality.

In conclusion, I wish to excuse myself for my daring in addressing a medical audience. I have no qualifications except my having been lecturer in sociology and my being head of a medical school. I have avoided dealing with specifically medical problems beyond my competence. The wonderful advances made by medical science are especially clear to one who is old enough to remember the first news of Roentgen's discovery and J. J. Thompson's first exploration of beta-particles, who had teeth extracted without an anaesthetic, and who recalls when appendicitis was unrecognised and irremediable. But, unfortunately, instead of progress there has actually been regression in other, even more important, aspects of medical practice.

The idea has become widespread that moral assessment of human actions is inapplicable to the operating theatre, that a medical man can behave much as a veterinary surgeon (for example, as regards artificial insemination). We discuss the grave issues raised by the atomic bomb; but an equally serious problem has arisen regarding the use of medical discoveries for dehumanising personal and social action. The influence of medical materialism has become a major factor in modern life.

It is, therefore, vital that medical ethics should be an integral part of the education of a doctor. I do not mean a few jejune remarks such as are contained in existing codes, do not advertise or poach, do not be grossly negligent or drunk. I mean a systematic course of social and medical ethics. There is, however, little prospect of its introduction into the so-called liberal medical schools, where there is no agreement on the fundamentals of ethics. All the more important, then, is the task which is incumbent on Catholic doctors and on their organisations.

I suggest that the Guild of SS. Luke, Cosmas and Damian could fruitfully extend its work by admitting and catering more for medical students, and by arranging systematic courses in medical ethics in connection with British universities. There is a project which I am going to propose to the Irish guild: the establishment of small lending libraries in the various branches. For this purpose, I hope to have a suitable list of books printed shortly. Even in this country, it is important that Catholic doctors should be well grounded in social principles and should be able to explain these to the public in defence of their stand. For there is widespread ignorance and the general public are inclined to attribute motives of self-interest to any concerted action of medical men.

APPENDIX 6

PSYCHOLOGICAL PROFILE OF ALFRED O'RAHILLY

The difficulties and nervous tension which forced Alfred to leave the Society of Jesus in May 1914 began towards the end of 1912. Three weeks before Christmas he shared his anxieties with Fr Michael Maher, S.J., rector of St Mary's Hall, Stonyhurst, for whom he had a high regard. Maher (1860-1918) arranged for Alfred to spend his Christmas vacation at Stonyhurst. This and a meeting in London with some of his former Stonyhurst colleagues helped him to regain his equilibrium.

On his return to St Ignatius' House of Studies, Leeson Street, Dublin, Alfred wrote to Maher and gave him permission to discuss the difficulties he was experiencing with Fr Thomas V. Nolan, S.J., the Irish provincial. Maher lectured in psychology, was the author of *Psychology: empirical and rational* (London, 6th ed., 1908) and had considerable experience as a confessor and counsellor. He advised Nolan that Alfred would require 'delicate handling' and described his condition as follows:

> The immediate assault is the resultant of a combination of forces which, as far as I feel myself free to speak, are mainly these: an old-standing continuous temptation from a persuasion that he is 'unlike other Jesuits, cannot get on with people, is solitary, not understandable by superiors', etc., and so probably not really designed for life in the Society. This apparently became unusually vivid last term. Again there has been a growing anxiety about possible intellectual difficulties in the future. Not so much, I think, present doubtings about matters of faith, as doubts whether his leaning towards broad interpretations may not bring him into conflict with the somewhat strict attitude of the Society later on; and whether this disposition again is not a symptom that he is not made for the Society. These things do not look much on paper and, of course, I dealt with them in detail in our talks, but they undoubtedly had gained considerable hold. But they had been enormously intensified by another recent trouble of an extremely acute kind [see J. A. Gaughan, *Alfred O'Rahilly I: Academic*, 53-4].

Maher told Nolan that Alfred had been impressed by the kind and sympathetic manner in which he had been received by the provincial and continued:

Alfred O'Rabilly III: Controversialist

> He is very singularly constituted. And though, recognising his potentialities for work of rare value, I had observed and cultivated him pretty closely for the three years here, it was only at the end and from his correspondence afterwards that I came to get a real understanding of him.
>
> He is, as everybody knows, a man of extraordinary intellectual ability; but very few realise that the feeling or emotional faculty in him is not less powerful or intense. His manner, a little shy, and sometimes brusque, occasional sarcasm, with outbreaks of the dogmatism of youth and his consciousness of clearer knowledge, and a certain abrupt undiplomatic directness in conversation tend to prejudice people a little against him, at least in the beginning. And I was not altogether at ease myself with him during the first couple of years, in spite of my best efforts. He finds great difficulty in opening out, and has been wont to settle most difficulties for himself.
>
> All this has made him solitary and led many to look on him as a dry intellectual book-worm. And yet the very contrary is the case. There is a curiously intense craving for friendship in his nature, and he is liable to feel his loneliness at times most acutely. The intensity of this side of his character became known to me especially after he left from his correspondence with two or three friends here to whom he became in a way spiritual adviser.

Maher concluded this part of his assessment by adding that Alfred was 'in fact extremely Celtic in natural temperament'.

On Alfred's suitability to be a member of the Society, Maher stated:

> I am glad to be able to say that the three years experience of him convinced me that he was solidly good. He is thoroughly straight. One can fully rely on his promise. His judgement too is sound; and he is constantly on the right side when any question rises in the community, though he will speak with considerable frankness to superiors himself. Further, one can rely on his strict obedience. But here I learned earlier that we have to be cautious. If he gets an order in hard matter, after he has indicated his difficulty, he will set his teeth tight and do his level best to carry it out

Appendix 6

faithfully, but the vividness of his imagination and the strength of the impulsive elements underneath can set up a very severe struggle when the work is very much against the grain, so that on such occasions one has to be very carefuly as to the strain put on.

Further, he is faithful to prayer. It is the good proportion of this religious element in him which has given me most confidence in regard to the possible intellectual difficulties which a man of his mental constitution is likely to experience.

It seems to me, therefore, quite clear that, in spite of present difficulties or temptations, he has the essential qualities and his whole history points to a career of work of a high order in the religious life.

Maher's observations, particularly with regard to the strong emotional side to Alfred's character, are borne out by entries in Alfred's extant diaries.

In March 1925 Alfred applied for the chair of ethics and politics in U.C.D. His submission included testimonials from Frs William Delany, S.J., and Michael Maher, S.J. Apart from drawing attention to Alfred's brilliant mind, Delany referred to his 'solidly religious and moral character which entitled him to the esteem of all who knew him' and Maher recalled his 'kind and unselfish disposition and high rectitude'. They did not refer to two qualities which became more obvious as Alfred grew older, his single-minded ambition and an extraordinary child-like vanity. Alfred's attempts to deal with the latter caused considerable merriment to his friends, as they gave rise to situations wherein, as Con Murphy recalled: 'Alfred would be seen to be taking pride in his humility!' With regard to these two traits, Alfred's diaries indicate that he had a remarkable capacity for posturing and self-delusion. In addition, the diaries provide evidence that his married life and family life involved more than the usual measure of disappointment and pain.

A number of other qualities also became more pronounced as he grew older. His tendency to be combative is most remembered by contemporaries, as well as his seemingly boundless energy and enthusiasm. Patriotism, manifested by a strong commitment to Irish independence, inspired many of his

Alfred O'Rahilly III: Controversialist

contributions to public life.[1] There was the urge to champion the underprivileged and the deprived, his inability to be a team-man, his impatience and his self-righteousness.[2] Finally, for Alfred the spiritual dimension was all-important. He wrote in his diary on 13 September 1954: 'Lately, after a friend (Kathleen O'Flaherty) had impressed on me that someone was sure to write about me – perhaps a whole volume – after I am dead, I have become more chary of destroying intimate documents. I honestly do not think I am worth writing about; but I have no means of stopping prurient curiosity and the present-day *cacoethes scribendi* [incurable itch to write]. So I want to leave some materials for reconstructing the otherwise unrecorded thoughts and aspirations which have meant so much more to me than my external activities. This is not an attempt to gloss over my faults or to excuse my uncharitabaleness. On the contrary, my weakness and mediocrity will be much more apparent. But it may help others to know that, like them, I too have had to struggle with darkness and difficulties.'[3]

---

1. During an exchange with U.C.C. students, members of a 'Republican Club', who had defaced the entrance to the college, Alfred wrote in the *Cork Evening Echo* of 3 February 1939: 'If people want to efface British influence here, let them back people like me who strongly advocate financial independence, development of our resources, social betterment and neutrality in England's wars. Insistence on breaking the link with sterling would be more effective patriotism than chipping dead unicorns, growing trees would be better for the country than hacking the face of a stone lion . . .'
2. Those who crossed swords with Alfred at U.C.C. would have been amused or infuriated to read the entry in his diary for 3 May 1954. In a reference to his clash with Fr James O'Brien, the dean of residence (see J. A. Gaughan, *Alfred O'Rahilly I: Academic*, 102-3), he wrote: 'The longer I live the more astonished I am at the facility with which holy people can subjectively justify what is objectively wrong.'
3. J. A. Gaughan, *Alfred O'Rahilly I: Academic*, 170-1; diaries of Alfred O'Rahilly, 15 July-25 December 1928, 26 January 1929-19 January 1930; 23 December 1953-19 January 1954, 8 April-1 May 1954, 2 May-23 May 1954, 24 May-7 July 1954, 11 July-12 September 1954, 13 September-26 October 1954, 27 December 1954-28 February 1955, 1 March-9 November 1955, 13 November-25 December 1956; Irish Jesuit Archives, correspondence from English Province, 1906-1920, letter, dated 24 January 1913, from Fr Michael Maher, S.J., to Fr Thomas V. Nolan, S.J., and interview with Con Murphy.

ADDENDUM TO WRITINGS OF ALFRED O'RAHILLY[1]

A

BOOKS AND PAMPHLETS

The constitutional position of education in the Republic of Ireland (pamphlet, Cork 1952).

Foreword in P. Power's *The place-names of Decies* (pamphlet, Cork 1952).

B

ARTICLES AND BOOK REVIEWS IN COLLECTIONS AND PERIODICALS

'Socialism and co-operation', *Irish Commonwealth*, March 1919.

Review of Jan Herben's *John Huss and his followers*, *The Irish Tribune, a weekly review of affairs* 19 March 1926.

'Senator Yeats as theologian', *The Irish Tribune, a weekly review of affairs* 23 April 1926.

'Some thoughts on "St Joan"', *The Irish Tribune, a weekly review of affairs* 14 May 1926.

Review of R. H. Murray's *The political consequences of the Reformation*, *The Irish Tribune, a weekly review of affairs* 21 May 1926.

Letter 'The cherry tree carol', *The Irish Tribune, a weekly review of affairs* 4 June 1926.

Review of F. M. Laird's *Personal experiences of the great war*, *The Irish Tribune, a weekly review of affairs* 25 June 1926.

Letter 'Mr T. P. Gill', *The Irish Tribune, a weekly review of affairs* 9 July 1926.

Review of Bede Jarrett's *Social theories of the middle ages*, *The Irish Tribune, a weekly review of affairs* 23 July 1926.

'The university and the people' (an unsigned editorial), *The Irish Tribune, a weekly review of affairs* 22 October 1926.

Letter 'The Gaol', *The Irish Tribune, a weekly review of affairs* 17 December 1926.

'Religion and the university', *Catholic Mind*, February 1930.

1. See J. A. Gaughan, *Alfred O'Rahilly I: Academic*, 204-40.

Alfred O'Rahilly III: Controversialist

'A layman's thoughts – No 1. Want of principle', *Catholic Mind*, October 1931.
'A layman's thoughts – No 2. Bedrock', *Catholic Mind*, November 1931.
'A layman's thoughts – No 3. The average person', *Catholic Mind*, December 1931.
'Sinn Féin and Bedrock', *Catholic Mind*, December 1931.
'A layman's thoughts – No 4. Fianna Fáil and the treaty', *Catholic Mind*, January 1932.
'A layman's thoughts – No 5. Any chance of a policy', *Catholic Mind*, February 1932.
'A layman's thoughts – No 6. On what did we vote?', *Catholic Mind*, March 1932.
'A layman's thoughts – No 7. A reply to Mr Churchill', *Catholic Mind*, April 1932.
'A layman's thoughts – No 8. Bread-rock', *Catholic Mind*, June 1932.
'A layman's thoughts – No 9. After the Congress', *Catholic Mind*, July 1932.
'A layman's thoughts – No 10. Wake up on the back benches', *Catholic Mind*, October 1932.
'A layman's thoughts – No 11. An American theologian on the war-path', *Catholic Mind*, November 1932.
'Address at conferring of diplomas on twenty-four workers', *Cork University Record*, Christmas 1948.
'The adult education movement', *Blackfriars*, February 1951.
'Education and the Constitution', *Educational Year Book 1951*.
'Address on conferring day 1952', *Cork University Record*, Christmas 1952.
'Catholics and socialism', *Hibernia*, December 1956.
'The problem of North and South', *Hibernia*, January 1957.
'What is the proper attitude to the problem of partition: past history, present reality and future policy', *Hibernia*, Feb. 1957.
'Partition and force: the ethics of revolt' (A reply to Ciarán Mac an Fhailí), *Hibernia*, March 1957.
'Little Christmas', *Hibernia*, December 1958.
'Need for clarification and more information: University College, Limerick – The problems', *Hibernia* 29 January 1960.
'Students do not go to nearest college: Limerick's demand for a university, a reply to Mr P. M. McCarthy', *Hibernia* 19 February 1960.

Addendum to Writings of Alfred O'Rahilly

'What does Limerick want?', *Hibernia* 11 March 1960.
'U.C.D., Trinity and Limerick', *Hibernia* 15 April 1960.
'The U.C.D. fracas', *Hibernia*, 6 May 1960.
'The U.C.D. bill', *Hibernia*, 10 June 1960.
'The Irish university question', *Studies*,[2] Autumn 1961.

C

CONTRIBUTIONS TO NEWSPAPERS

'Cork notes', *New Ireland* 26 August 1916.[3]
'Cork notes', *New Ireland* 2 September 1916.
'Gleanings', *New Ireland* 6 January 1917.
Review of M. Quinn's, *The problem of human peace: studied from the standpoint of a scientific Catholicism*, *New Ireland* 20 January 1917.[4]
'An Irish mission to Russia', *New Ireland* 9 June 1917.
'The old Party and the new', *New Ireland* 28 July 1917.
'Who said Parnell!', *New Ireland* 11 August 1917.
'Mgr Battifol and Sinn Féin', *New Ireland* 5 January 1918.[5]
'The law and the land', *New Ireland* 16 March 1918.[6]
Review of Labhrás Mac Fhionnghail's *D.O.R.A. at Westminster*, *New Ireland* 27 April 1918.[7]
'Women's day and St Columcille', *New Ireland* 8 June 1918.[8]
'The issue', *New Ireland* 24 June 1918.
'Cork notes', *New Ireland* 24 June 1918.
'Cork notes', *New Ireland* 8 July 1918.
'Chaos in Cork', *New Ireland* 22 July 1918.
'Ginnell in Cork', *New Ireland* 29 July 1918.

---

2. At Alfred's prompting his brother, Michael Anthony, Fr Aloysius of the Cistercian community of Mount St Joseph, Roscrea, County Tipperary, compiled an index to *Studies* (see *Standard* 28 May 1943).
3. Alfred published these and subsequent 'Cork notes', as well as 'Chaos in Cork' and 'Ginnell in Cork', over the pseudonym Corcaig. The rest of the contributions by Alfred to *New Ireland* listed here, apart from those referred to in footnotes, were over the pseudonym 'Lector'. By the end of 1916 *New Ireland* had an impressive list of subscribers, including Hilaire Belloc.
4. Over Alfred Rahilly.
5. Over M.A.
6. Over M.A.
7. Over A.M.
8. Over A.M.

Alfred O'Rahilly III: Controversialist

'Can the leopard change his spots?', *New Ireland* 5 Aug. 1918.[9]
'Cork notes', *New Ireland* 19 August 1918.
'Cork notes', *New Ireland* 26 August 1918.
'Elsewhere, of course', *New Ireland* 1 March 1919.[10]
Letter 'The university plot', *New Ireland* 19 April 1919.[11]
Letter 'The Cork presidency', *Irish Independent* 4 Dec. 1919.[12]
Letter 'The Cork presidency', *Irish Independent* 5 Dec. 1919.[13]
Letter 'Sinn Féin and the Law', *Cork Examiner* 29 January 1920.
Letter 'Irish government. An appeal to principle', *Irish Independent* 16 August 1920.[14]
Letter 'Confederation of Ireland. The only solution of the "Ulster" question', *Irish Independent* 8 January 1921.[15]
Letter *Cork Examiner* 19 October 1923.
Letter 'The National University Contest', *Irish Independent* 25 Oct. 1923.[16]
Letter 'Ford factory in Cork', *Cork Examiner* 29 April 1924.
Letter 'Ford's and the budget', *Cork Examiner* 30 April 1924.
Letter 'What next?', *Irish Independent* 20 September 1927.[17]
'A reply to Mr Gorey', *The Leader* 17 May 1930.
'Milling and myself', *The Leader* 14 June 1930.
Letter 'Mr Cosgrave's recent speech', *Irish Press* 1 Feb. 1932.
Letter 'The general election', *Cork Examiner* and *Irish Press* 4 February 1932.
'The end of a neutral', *Irish Press* 15 February 1932.
'The new Cromwell', *Irish Press* 27 February 1932.
'The conversion of Mr Rank', *The Leader* 24 May 1932.
'Do not play England's game', *Irish Press* 25 July 1932.
'We can win', *Irish Press* 29 July 1932.
'Murphy versus Bull', *Irish Press* 10 January 1933.
'People stand for your rights', *Irish Press* 14 January 1933.
Letter 'University vote', *Irish Press* 16 January 1933.
'Now Pat Murphy get on your feet', *Irish Press* 21 January 1933.
'Voters, do your duty', *Irish Press* 28 January 1933.

   9. Over The Free Lance.
  10. Over M.A.
  11. Over Cork student.
  12. Over A voter.
  13. Over An old graduate.
  14. Over A. O'Rahilly.
  15. Over Alfred O'Rahilly.
  16. Over A university voter.
  17. Over Civis.

Addendum to Writings of Alfred O'Rahilly

Letter, 'The Corporate State', *Cork Examiner* 5 May 1934.
Letter 'The U.C.C. raid', *Cork Evening Echo* 3 February 1939.
Letter 'The U.C.C. raid', *Cork Evening Echo* 6 February 1939.
Letter 'The U.C.C. raid', *Cork Evening Echo* 9 February 1939.
Letter 'O'Rahilly replies', *Standard* 23 February 1940.
'Hear the chairman', *Standard* 15 January 1943.
'What do bankers do?', *Standard* 22 January 1943.
'Against the growing power of the State the Church is your protector', *Standard* 19 February 1943.
'Further reply to Professor W. B. Standford', *Standard* 26 May 1944.
Review of Peter McKevitt's *The plan of society*, *Standard* 15 December 1944.
Review of Erwin Schrödinger's *What is life? The physical aspects of the living cell*, *Standard* 23 February 1945.
'National schools and the State', *Standard* 25 October 1946.
'At it again!: Picture Post piffle I', *Standard* 27 June 1947.
'*Picture Post* piffle II: a modern priest in mufti', *Standard* 4 July 1947.
'Everyone is infallible except the pope', *Standard* 1 Aug. 1947.
'*John O'London's Weekly*', *Standard* 1 August 1947.
Letter 'The censorship', *Standard* 15 August 1947.
'Fred and Mollie – a study in prejudices', *Standard* 29 August 1947.
Review of M. P. Linehan's *Canon Sheehan of Doneraile*, *Standard* 11 July 1952.[18]
Review of J. Crehan's *Father Thurston, a memoir with a bibliography of his writings* and of H. Thurston's, S.J., *The physical phenomena of mysticism*, *Standard* 31 Oct. 1952.
Review of J. Fennelly's *A children's Mass book*, *Standard* 31 October 1952.
Letter 'Cork County Council and University College, Cork', *Cork Examiner* 17 December 1952.
Editorial 'Freedom and the health bill', *Standard* 6 March 1953.
Review of E. F. Barrett's (ed.), *University of Notre Dame Law Institute Proceedings* V, *Standard* 30 October 1953.[19]
'Debate in U.C.D., statement by Rev. Dr Alfred O'Rahilly', *Irish Independent* 10 May 1960.

18. This and the articles in the *Standard* of 1 and 29 August 1947 were over the pseudonym Ollamh.
19. Over Lector.

CORRECTIONS TO VOLUMES I, II and III (1)

VOLUME I

page 21, line 40 **read** 1881 **for** 1880
p. 52 ls. 13-15 **read** In 1955 and in 1958 **for** In 1955 **read** in replies **for** in a gracious reply
p. 61 l. 14 **read** honeymoon – four days – **for** honeymoon
p. 61 l. 15 **read** Villas, Victoria Road, **for** Villas,
p. 79 l. 5 (of caption) **read** Mrs Earnán de Blaghd (*nèe* Annie McHugh); **for** unidentified lady;
p. 83 ls. 1-2 (of caption) **read** An tOllamh Tadhg Ó Donnchadha (Tórna), Dr Eibhlín Ní Dhonnchadha (later Mrs Labhrás Ó Dúill) **for** unidentified, unidentified
p. 91 l. 3 **read** Alfred **for** Aflred
p. 140 l. 14 **read** mid-March **for** mid-march
p. 145 l. 33 **read** 1955 **for** 1954
p. 175 caption **add** In the background is Isaac Swain, professor of geography and geology and supervisor of examinations
p. 204-40 Index references to these pages are listed one page ahead of their pagination
p. 215 l. 24 **read** Our **for** One
p. 218 l. 8 **read** 'Black is White' **for** 'Black and White'
ls. 20-3 **transpose** Review of R. H. Benson's . . . and Review of E. D. Morel's . . .
p. 219 l. 3 **read** 2 March 1918[79] **for** 16 February 1918[79]
p. 221 l. 7 **exclude** 'As others see us', *New Ireland* 30 August 1919
p. 222 l. 25 **read** Letter, *The Tablet* **for** *The Tablet*
p. 225 l. 24 **read** 13 **for** 12
p. 340 l. 18b **read** Dowdall, Senator James Charles **for** Dowdall, Senator T. P.
p. 352 l. 34b **read** -1744, 84 **for** -174484

VOLUME II

p. 74 l. 21 **add** (In Jan. 1921, 500 offprints of it were distributed by Sinn Féin.)
p. 89 l. 14 **read** acting **for** the

314

Corrections

p. 106 l. 23 **add** (The extent of Alfred's service to the Sinn Féin movement could scarcely be exaggerated. Apart from the activities already referred to, at the end of 1919 he helped Robert Barton to draft 'the Land and Bank Proposals' which were presented to Dáil Éireann. He was director of education in the Cork City Sinn Féin executive, a member of the Cork City Arbitration Court, a member of the organisation's Commission of Inquiry into the Resources and Industries of Ireland and Sinn Féin's representative on a Council of Agriculture, set up by the department of agriculture and technical instruction. In addition, he contributed generously to Sinn Féin's Irish Republican Prisoners Dependents Fund, its 'Munition Crisis National Fund', and was a member of the Cork Relief Committee and the executive committee of the Irish White Cross. Besides being close to Tomás MacCurtain, he was a friend of George Clancy, Sinn Féin mayor of Limerick, who, like MacCurtain, was assassinated by the British forces and whose funeral he attended on 10 March 1921. Alfred's standing in Sinn Féin was generally recognised. When the movement was asked to send some prominent Irish Catholic laymen to attend the beatification of Oliver Plunkett on 23 May 1920, he was unsuccessfully importuned by Arthur Griffith and George N. Count Plunkett to represent the organisation at the ceremonies and festivities in Rome.)

p. 182 l. 2 (of footnote) **read** Micheál Ó Cuill **for** a colleague

p. 361 l. 14 (of footnote) **read** 29 January **for** 24 January

p. 377 l. 2 (of caption) **read** *Left to right:* Jack Horgan, Professor John Busteed, 'Busty' O'Donoghue (auditor), Alfred, Seán MacBride (minister for external affairs), Derry Cantillon, Frank McElligott, Professor M. A. Mac Connaill, Bob Stanton **for** Alfred is in the centre of the group with MacBride on his left

Alfred O'Rahilly III: Controversialist

p. 380 l. 18 **add** (This was on 9 Nov. 1919 at a function in Cork City Hall, sponsored by 'Cummanacht na hÉireann', to mark the 2nd anniversary of the '1st Russian Workers' Republic'.)
p. 384 l. 1 (of footnote 24) **read** Seventeen **for** Twenty
p. 404 l. 6 **read** election **for** eleciton
p. 408 l. 3 **read** Notwithstanding **for** Notwithtanding
p. 511 l. 45 (of first column) **read** 369 **for** 368

VOLUME III (1)

p. 45 l. 1 (of caption) **read** on 23 June 1948. **for** in summer of 1952.
read James Hickey (later T.D.), **for** James Hickey, T.D.,
p. 52 l. 6 (of footnote 2) **read** as **for** was
p. 54 **add** (to footnote 21) Another explanation for the title invariably given to Eoin O'Mahony survives. It seems that during his time at Clongowes Wood College he was compulsorily involved in a game of rugby. He was in the front row of the scrum and still standing when the two scrums attempted to interlock. The languid Jesuit scholastic in charge of proceedings said: 'Would the "visible head" please get down?' The tag stuck to Eoin with the 'visible head' becoming 'the pope'.
p. 106 l. 30 **read** Most of the **for** That
p. 119 l. 26 **read** 19 **for** 17
p. 146 l. 2 (of footnote 28) **read** election **for** eleciton
p. 159 l. 1 (of caption) **read** Unidentified, Pádraig Ó Caoimh (secretary, G.A.A.), **for** Unidentified, unidentified,
p. 281 l. 31 **read** Copy **for** Cope
p. 292 l. 8 (of second column) **read** 44, **for** 44-5

SOURCES

1. SOURCES IN GENERAL

Writings of Alfred O'Rahilly and sources as listed in J. A. Gaughan, *Alfred O'Rahilly I: Academic* (Dublin 1986), *Alfred O'Rahilly II: Public figure* (Dublin 1989) and *Alfred O'Rahilly III: Controversialist, Part 1: Social Reformer.*

2. PRIMARY SOURCES CITED

(a) Manuscripts

Cork, Archives Institute
   Papers of Liam de Róiste.
Cork, University College
   Papers of William O'Brien, M.P.
Dublin, Archdiocesan Archives
   Alfred O'Rahilly file.
Dublin, Holy Ghost Fathers' Provincialate, Temple Park, Archives
   Papers of Fr Denis Fahey, C.S.Sp.
Dublin, Irish Jesuit Archives, 35-36 Lower Leeson Street
   Papers of provincials.
Dublin, University College, Archives Department
   Papers of W. P. Ryan.
Dublin, County, Fr Michael F. McCarthy, C.S.Sp., Blackrock College
   Papers of Alfred O'Rahilly, including diaries of Alfred O'Rahilly.
Dublin, County, Cornelius Murphy, 8 Sycamore Crescent, Mount Merrion, Blackrock
   Alfred O'Rahilly file.
Dublin, County, Mrs Melissa Webb, 2 Mount Salus, Knocknacree Road, Dalkey
   Typescript containing 'Memoirs of Professor W. B. Stanford (1910-84)'.

(b) Newspapers

Bulletin of the Catholic Societies Vocational Organisation Conference, October 1954.

Alfred O'Rahilly III: Controversialist

Catholic Herald 26 November 1921; 7 June 1929; 27 May 1938; 10 February, 29 December 1939; 2 January 1940; January 1941; 26 November 1943; 21 January 1944; 12 March, 21 September 1945; 18 January 1946; 6 August 1948.
Catholic Mind, July 1932; April 1937.
Catholic Review (New York), August 1914.
Catholic Times (Capetown), 19 January 1940; January (vol. XV, no. 1) 1949.
Church of Ireland Gazette and Family Newspaper 15 December 1950; 20 April 1951.
Comhar, Bealtaine, Meitheamh, Iúl 1951.
Cork Evening Echo 13 September 1926.
Cork Holly Bough, Christmas 1932.
Cork Examiner 19 November 1925; 15 October 1930; March 1931; 8 January, 9 March, 20 June 1932; 13, 21 May 1933; 13 April 1934; 6 March, 30 November 1936; 25 January, 1, 4, March 1937; 15 March, 10 October, 28 November 1938; 27 March, 5 June 1939; 15 January, 4 May 1940; 6 March, 9 November 1942; 24, 31 January, 7, 14, 21, 28 February, 6, 15, 21 March 1944; 26 February, 5, 12, 19, 26 March, 1, 8, 15, 21 May 1945; 7, 14, 21, 28 January, 4, 11, 18, 26 February, 8 March, 15 April, 14 October, 11 November, 2, 16 December 1946; 8 March, 31 October 1947; 14 January, 22 March, 14 July, 27 October 1948; 11, 19 January, 13 July 1949; 7 April, 19 July, 25 September, 23 November 1950; 17 January, 25 February, 5 March, 23 April 1951; 19 January, 12 June, 9 July 1952; 17 June, 15, 16, 17, 18 September 1953; 14, 15 July, 21 September 1954; 4, 6, August 1969.
Freeman's Journal 5 August 1921.
Hibernia, February 1937; January, February, March 1957; March 1958; 29 January, 12, 19 February, 4, 11 March, 15 April, 6 May, 10 June 1960.
Irish Catholic 1 December 1938; 9, 16 November 1939.
Irish Independent 15 October 1930; 30 November 1936; 23 November 1937; 14 April, 30 May, 10 October, 28 November 1938; 5 June, 8 August 1939; 6, 7 May 1940; 9 November 1942; 8, 17 April 1951; 9 July 1952; 22, 25 January 1954; 6, 11 August, 7 September, 13 December 1955; 4, 9, 10, 12, 19, 25 May 1960; 4, 6 August 1969.
Irish News and Belfast Morning News 22 January 1949.

Sources

Irish Press 15 September 1931; 24 May 1935; 7, 9 March, 30 November 1936; 10 October 1938; 19, 20, 21 March 1940; 19, 20 February 1946; 11, 12, 13, 14 April 1949; 15 April 1954; 26 July 1955; February-April 1956; March-April 1957.
Irish Times 3 August 1931; 4, 23 February, 16 April 1943; 29 September 1945; 28 February 1946; 24 November, 15 December 1950; 2, 12, 16, 19, 24, 25, 28 April, 2, 8, 11, 12, 16, 17, 18, 19, 21, 25 May, 27 July 1951; 9 July 1952; 15 February 1958; 31 March, 2 May 1960; 4 August 1969.
Irish Tribune, a weekly review of affairs 19 March, 23 April, 14, 21, 28 May 1926.
Kerryman 12 February 1938; 1 March 1947; 12 January 1957; 9 August 1969.
Leader, The 31 October, 7, 14 November, 5 December 1925; 28 February, 28 March 1953.
Limerick Leader 23 May 1945; 29 June, 16 October, 14 December 1946; 31 March 1947; 1, 8 August, 26 September, 10 October, 2, 9, 23, 28, 30 November, 2, 9 December 1959; January-March 1960.
Listener, The 11 September 1947.
Manchester Guardian 5 August 1950; 24 February 1958.
Observer 1 January 1967.
Picture Post 4, 11 November, 9, 16, 30 December 1939; 13 January 1940; 7 June 1947.
Southern Cross (Capetown) 20 October 1954.
Standard 5, 12, 19, 26 January, 2, 9, 16, 23 February, 1, 8 March 1940; 25 July, 22 August 1941; 30 January, 6, 13 March, 3, 10 April, 11, 18 December 1942; 9, 16, 23, 30 April, 7 May, 25 June 1943; 21, 28 April, 5, 19, 26 May, 16 June, 1 December 1944; 9, 16, 23 February, 2, 9, 16, 23 March, 13 April 1945; 1, 15 March, 14 June, 29 November, 13, 20 December 1946; 14 March, 27 June, 4 July, 1, 15, 22, 29 August, 24 October 1947; Easter Number, 24 September 1948; 11, 18, 25 March, 1, 8, 15, 29 April, 9 December 1949; 24 February, 3, 10, 17, 24, 31 March, 1, 8, 15, 22, 29 September, 1, 8, 15, 22, 29 December 1950; 5, 12, 19, 26 January, 2, 9, 16, 23 February, 9, 16, 23, 30 March, 27 April, 4, 11, 18, 25 May, 22 June, 27 July, 3, 10, 17, 24, 31 August, 14 September 1951; 11 April, 31 October 1952; 6 March, November (supplement) 1953; 24 September 1954; 23 December 1955; 4 May, 22 June 1956; 6, 13 December 1957; 28 February,

Alfred O'Rahilly III: Controversialist

14 March 1958; 9 May 1958 – 28 August 1959; 12, 26 April 1963.
Sunday Chronicle 16 October 1955.
Sunday Dispatch 19 September 1954.
Sunday Express 11 July, 19 September 1954.
Sunday Independent 19 September 1954.
Sunday Press 24 November 1957 – 1 June 1958.
Times, The (London) 5 January 1968.
Universe 17 October 1930; 24 September 1954.
Waterford Star 1 October 1954.

(c) Official Publications

Catholic Church: *Rerum Novarum* (London 1891).
—— *Quadragesimo Anno* (London 1931).
Church of England: *Doctrine in the Church of England* (Canterbury 1938).
Dáil Éireann: *Díospóireachta parlaiminte, tuairisc oifigiúil: Parliamentary debates, official report*, vols 180, 8 March – 7 April 1960; 181, 26 April – 19 May 1960; 182, 24 May – 16 June 1960; *passim*.
Department of Health: *Proposals for improved and extended health services*, July 1952.
Readers' Union: *Readers' News*, spring 1943.
Seanad Éireann: *Díospóireachta parlaiminte, tuairisc oifigiúil: Parliamentary debates, official report*, vol. 52, 20 January – 21 July 1960, *passim*.
University College, Cork, Students' Union: *Quarryman*, March 1937; 1953.

(d) Persons

Bastible, Canon James P., St Patrick's presbytery, Cork.
Caomhánach, An tOllamh Séamus, Irish department, University College, Cork.
Dixon, Mrs Clare, The Point, Crosshaven, County Cork.
Evans, Dr John, 59 Waltham Terrace, Blackrock, County Dublin.
Feehan, Captain Seán, Mercier Press Ltd., 4 Bridge Street, Cork.
Fehily, Mgr G. Thomas, 4 Eblana Avenue, Dún Laoghaire, County Dublin.

Sources

Good, Fr James, St Augustine's Seminary, PO Box 150, Bungoma, Kenya.
Hogan, Peter, Associate professor of mathematical physics, University College, Dublin.
Hughes, S.J., Fr Seán, 135 North Circular Road, Dublin 7.
Humphreys (*née* Flanagan), Mrs Deirdre, 34 Sycamore Road, Mount Merrion, County Dublin.
Jordana, O.P., Mother M., Domincan Convent, Cabra, Dublin 7.
Kinlen, S.C., Dermot P., 69 Merrion Road, Dublin 4.
Lyons, Dr J. B., 'Claydon', Coliemore Road, Dalkey, County Dublin.
Lysaght, D. R. O'C., c/o National Library of Ireland, Kildare Street, Dublin 2.
McCarthy, C.S.Sp., Fr Michael F., Blackrock College, Blackrock, County Dublin.
McConnell, Mgr James, Dublin Institute for Advanced Studies, Burlington Road, Dublin 4.
McDonagh, Bernard, Truskmore, Strandhill, Sligo.
McMahon, Mrs Margaret, Apartment 14, 'Belville', Donnybrook, Dublin 4.
McRedmond, Louis, 11 Westerton Rise, Dublin 16.
Maume, Patrick, 58 Marlborough Road, Dublin 4.
Mercier (*née* Dillon), Mrs Eilís, 7 Templemore Avenue, Dublin 6.
Murphy, Cornelius, 8 Sycamore Crescent, Mount Merrion, County Dublin.
Murray, Fr Patrick, 64 Newtownpark Avenue, Blackrock, County Dublin.
O'Carroll, C.S.Sp., Rev. Dr Michael, Blackrock College, Blackrock, County Dublin.
Ó Ceallaigh, Professor Cormac, 46 Killiney Road, County Dublin.
Ó Cearbhaill, Tadhg, 'Tinode', Roebuck Road, Dublin 14.
O'Connell, William Declan, Kilmurray, Uamvar Estate, Bishopstown, Cork.
Ó Faoláin, Seán, 17 Rosmeen Park, Dún Laoghaire, County Dublin.
O'Flaherty, Professor Kathleen, 'Ard na Gréine', Coolgarten Park, Cork.
O'Flaherty, N.T., Richard, 2 Church Street, Listowel, County Kerry.
O'Meara, Professor John J., 15 Maple Road, Dublin 14.

Alfred O'Rahilly III: Controversialist

O'Rahilly, Professor Ronan, Rue du Coteau 57, Villars sur Glâne, CH – 1752, Switzerland.
Ó Snodaigh, Pádraigh, 127 Bóthar Trágha, Átha Cliath 4.
Quinn, Professor Patrick Joseph, 21 Avondale Lawn Extension, Blackrock, County Dublin.
Sheehan, M.S.C., Fr Patrick, 'San Antone', Newtownpark Avenue, Blackrock, County Dublin.
Sheehy, Mgr Gerard, Archbishop's House, Dublin 9.
Tierney, Dr Niall, 33 Morehampton Terrace, Dublin 4.
Tuohy, Fr Patrick, St Mary's, Rathfarnham, Dublin 14.

(e) Radio Telefís Éireann

Sound Archive

'Marian Finucane Show', interview with Gerald Y. Goldberg, 27 July 1983.

Television Archive

'Gerald Y. Goldberg: a Jew, a Corkman and an Irishman', November 1983.

Written Archive

Alfred O'Rahilly file.

(f) University of Limerick

Archives Department

Video recording 'A university for Limerick'.

3. SECONDARY SOURCES CITED

Books, collections, pamphlets and articles

Acts of the Apostles (New York 1938).
Bancroft, George, *The conquest of disease: the story of penicillin* (London 1946).
Barrington, Ruth, *Health, medicine and politics in Ireland 1910-1970* (Dublin 1987).

Sources

Bell, J. B., *The secret army* (London 1970).
Bennett, Victor, 'The assumption of the virgin and papal infallibility', *Theology*, September 1948.
Blackrock College Annual 1957.
Blanton, M. G., *Bernadette of Lourdes* (London 1939).
Browne, Noel, *Against the tide* (Dublin 1986).
Cahill, S.J., Edward, *Freemasonry and the anti-Christian movement* (Dublin 1924).
—— *The framework of a Christian state* (Dublin 1932).
Coren, Michael, *The invisible man: the life and liberties of H. G. Wells* (London 1993).
Costello, Peter, and van de Kamp, Peter, *Flann O'Brien: an illustrated biography* (London 1987).
Coyne, S.J., Edward, 'Mother and child service', *Studies*, summer 1951.
Crane, S.J., Paul, 'Who pays for the Welfare State in England', *Christus Rex*, October 1951.
Cronin, Anthony, *No laughing matter* (Dublin 1989).
Cros, S.J., L. J. M., *Histoire de Notre Dame de Lourdes* I-III (Paris 1926-7).
Curie, Eve, *Madame Curie* (London 1942).
Davis, Charles, *A question of conscience* (London 1967).
Deeny, James, *To cure and to care: memoirs of a chief medical officer* (Dublin 1989).
Derrick, Paul, *Lost property: proposals for the distribution of property in an industrial age* (London 1947).
Dignan, John, *Catholics and Trinity College* (Dublin 1933).
Ernst, O.P., Cornelius, *Charles Davis and his book* (London 1967).
Fahey, C.S.Sp., Denis, *The kingship of Christ according to the principles of St Thomas Aquinas* (Dublin 1931).
—— *The mystical body of Christ in the modern world* (Dublin 1935).
—— *The rulers of Russia* (Dublin 1939).
—— *The kingship of Christ and organised naturalism* (Dublin 1943).
—— *Money, manipulation and social order* (Cork 1944).
—— *The mystical body of Christ and the re-organisation of society* (Cork 1945).
—— *The kingship of Christ and the conversion of the Jewish nation* (Dublin 1953).

Alfred O'Rahilly III: Controversialist

—— *The Church and farming* (Cork 1953).
Fennelly, John, *A children's Mass book* (Dublin 1952).
Gaughan, J. A. (ed.), *The Crucified* (Dublin 1985).
—— *Alfred O'Rahilly I: Academic* (Dublin 1986).
—— *Alfred O'Rahilly II: Public figure* (Dublin 1989).
—— *Alfred O'Rahilly III: Controversialist, Part 1: Social Reformer* (Dublin 1992).
Golden Hour, November-December 1929.
Gordon David, 'The twilight of the Celtic twilight', *America* 24 July 1937.
Gräf, H. C., *The case of Thérèse Neumann* (Cork 1950).
Gray, Tony, *Mr Smyllie, Sir* (Dublin 1991).
Gwynn, Denis, 'Monsignor Alfred O'Rahilly (1884-1969)', *Studies*, winter 1969.
Herben, Jan, *John Huss and his followers* (London 1926).
Higgins, F. R., *The gap of brightness: lyrical poems* (London 1940).
Hirsch, E. A., 'Veterinary education in Ireland: a historical review', *Irish Veterinary Journal* 23 (1969).
Howell, S.J., Clifford, *The work of our redemption* (Oxford 1953).
Jones, H. A., *My dear Wells. A manual for the haters of England, being a series of letters on Bolshevism, collectivism, internationalism and the distribution of wealth addressed to Mr H. G. Wells, by Henry Arthur Jones* (New York 1921).
Kearney, Pat, 'Limerick's campaign for a university: 1838-1845', *Old Limerick Journal*, No. 26, winter 1989.
Knox, Ronald, *The belief of Catholics* (London 1937).
Letters and notices (published by the English province of the Society of Jesus), Easter 1981.
Lyons, Eugene, *Assignment in Utopia* (New York 1937).
Mac an Fhailí, Ciarán, 'From arrows to atoms: a Catholic voice on the morality of war', *Doctrine and Life*, June 1959.
McCormick, W. J. (ed.), *Memoirs of a wild goose* (Dublin 1990).
McDougall, William, *Modern materialism* (London 1929).
McDowell, R. B., and Webb, D. A., *Trinity College, Dublin, 1592-1952: an academic history* (Cambridge 1982).
McKee, Eamon, 'Church-State relations and the development of health policy: the mother-and-child scheme 1944-1953', *Irish Historical Studies*, XXV (1986-7).
McQuaid, J. C., *Wellsprings of the faith* (Dublin 1956).

Sources

Manly, D. H., 'The Fahey theory', 'Sound history?', 'Fr Fahey and Irish Catholicism', *Ballintrillick Review*, No. 28 (1990).
Miller, René Fülöp, *The power and the secret of the papacy* (London 1937).
Moran, P. F. (ed.), *The pastoral letters and other writings of Cardinal Cullen, archbishop of Dublin, etc.* II (Dublin 1882).
Morrissey, S.J., T. J., *A man called Hughes* (Dublin 1991).
Murray, R. H., *The political consequences of the Reformation; studies in sixteenth-century political thought* (London 1926).
Nolan, J. M., 'The unfortunate affair at Macon', *Intercom*, December 1990.
Noyes, Alfred, *Voltaire* (London 1938).
O'Brien, C. C., 'The Fourth Estate – 5: The Catholic Press', *The Bell*, April 1945.
Ó Faoláin, Seán, 'First Confession', *The Bell*, February 1946.
—— 'The Dáil and the bishops', *The Bell*, June 1951.
—— 'The bishop of Galway and *The Bell*', *The Bell*, September 1951.
O'Flaherty, Kathleen, *Voltaire, myth and reality* (Cork and Oxford 1945).
—— 'Dr O'Rahilly and U.C.C. An appreciation', *Cork University Record*, summer 1955.
—— 'Professor Alfred O'Rahilly, An appreciation', *University Review*, spring 1955.
—— 'Obituary: Right Reverend Dr Alfred O'Rahilly', *Cork University Record*, 1970.
O'Rahilly, Alfred, *Faith and facts* (London 1917).
—— *The mission of the university man* (Cork 1919).
—— *Father William Doyle, S.J. A spiritual study* (London 1920).
—— 'The Syllabus', *Irish Ecclesiastical Record*, January 1933.
—— *Electro-magnetics. A discussion of fundamentals* (London 1938; 2nd ed., New York, 1965).
—— 'The stigmata of St Francis', *Studies*, June 1938.
—— *Money* (Cork 1941).
—— *Religion and science* (Cork 1948).
—— *Social principles* (Cork 1948).
—— *Moral principles* (Cork 1948).
—— *The family at Bethany* (Cork 1949).
—— *Gospel meditations* (Dublin 1958).
—— 'The Irish university question', *Studies*, autumn 1961.

Alfred O'Rahilly III: Controversialist

—— 'The Irish university question', *Studies*, winter 1961.
—— 'The Irish university question', *Studies*, spring 1962.
—— 'The Irish university question', *Studies*, summer 1962.
O'Rahilly, Ronan, *Benjamin Alcock, the first professor of anatomy and physiology in Queen's College, Cork* (Cork 1948).
—— *A history of Cork Medical School 1849-1949* (Cork 1949).
Randles, I.B.V.M., Eileen, *Post-primary education in Ireland 1957-1970* (Dublin 1975).
Ricciotti, Giuseppe, *The life of Christ* (Milwaukee 1952).
Ryan, Mary, *Alfred Noyes on Voltaire* (Dublin 1938).
Saunders, Edith, *Lourdes* (London 1940).
Schrödinger, Erwin, *What is life? The physical aspect of the living cell* (Cambridge 1944).
Sertillanges, O.P., A. D., *The intellectual life: its spirit, conditions, methods* (Cork 1947).
Sheehy-Skeffington, Andrée, *Skeff* (Dublin 1991).
Sherry, Richard, *Holy Cross College, Clonliffe, 1859-1959* (Dublin 1962).
Siwek, S.J., Paul, *The riddle of Konnersreuth, a psychological and religious study (Dublin 1954).*
Stanford, W. B., *A recognised Church: the Church of Ireland in Éire* (Dublin 1944).
Strachey, John, *A faith to fight for* (London 1941).
Syllabus or collection of modern errors (Rome 1864).
T.C.D.: a college miscellany 26 February 1942.
Thurston, S.J., Herbert, 'The history of the name "Roman Catholic"', *Month*, September 1911.
University of Limerick, degree programmes 1992-1994 (Limerick 1991).
von Pastor, Ludwig, *The history of the popes, from the close of the middle ages. Drawn from the secret archives of the Vatican and other original sources* I-XXXIV (English trans., London, 1938-   ).
Walsh, J. J., *The thirteenth, greatest of centuries* (New York 1913).
Walsh, T. J., *Nano Nagle and the Presentation sisters* (Dublin 1959).
Waugh, Evelyn, 'The American epoch in the Catholic Church', *Month*, November 1949.

Sources

Webb, Sidney and Beatrice, *Soviet communism: dictatorship or democracy?* (London 1936).
Wells, H. G., *The fate of homo sapiens* (London 1939).
—— *The rights of man* (London 1940).
—— *The outlook for homo sapiens* (London 1942).
Werfel, Franz V., *The song of Bernadette* (New York 1942).
Whyte, J. H., *Church and State in modern Ireland 1923-1979* (2nd ed., Dublin, 1980).
Woods, Thomas [Thomas Hogan], 'Voltairiana', *The Bell*, November 1945.

INDEX

A children's Mass book 52
A colour atlas of human embryology 91
A companion to Mr Well's outline of history (book) 263
A faith to fight for (book) 55, 57
A history of the Cork Medical School 1849-1949 (book) 91
A man called Hughes (book) 202
A question of conscience (book) 206
A recognised Church: the Church of Ireland in Éire (pamphlet) 26
A short history of the world (book) 243
Abbey Theatre (Dublin) 69, 72, 146
Aberdeen Hall (Gresham Hotel), 16, 36
Academy of St Thomas (U.C.C.) 36, 48-9, 81
Acta anatomica (periodical) 91
Acta Apostolicae Sedis (book) 253
Acton, Lord J.E.E.D. (historian) 105
Acts of the Apostles (*New Testament*) 14, 242, 256
Adeste fidelis (hymn) 74
Adult Education Movement (U.C.C.) 130
Adversus Marcionem (book) 242
Against the tide (book) 91, 127
Agricultural Institute (Dublin) 186
Albert the Great (theologian) 48
Alfred Noyes on Voltaire (book) 66
Allgood, Sara (actress) 72
America, see United States of America
America (weekly) 82
American anthropologist (periodical) 274
  Medical Association 90, 177
Among Congo pigmies (book) 237
Among the forest dwarfs of Malaya (book) 237
An atlas of the anatomy of the ear 91
An Cumann Aontacht (1925) 68
An Ríoghacht (the League of the Kingship of Christ – a Catholic organisation) 45
Anatomy. A regional study of human structure (book) 91
Anglican archbishops of Canterbury and York 20, 22, 104

Church 204, 252; see also Church of England
Anglicans 21, 23, 104
Anglo-Irish songs 41
Animal Farm (book) 61
Ann Veronica (book) 261
Annual Catholic Social Congress (France) 122
Anti-Partition of Ireland League (1951) 120
Anthony, T.D., Richard 289
Anthropos (review) 226, 236, 274
Antonia, Sister M. (sister of Alfred) 34, 129, 131; see ill. 2
Antrim (county) 142
Apocriticus (book) 257
Apocrypha (*Old Testament*) 107, 245
Apollo (mythological figure) 299
Aquinas, Thomas, see St Thomas Aquinas
Aramaic (language) 130, 222, 242
Arcadia Theatre (Cork) 37
Archer, William (writer) 245, 280
Argentina (country) 124
Aristaeus (mythological figure) 248
Aristotle (philosopher) 47, 49, 77, 130
Arklow (Wicklow) 170
Armagh (archdiocese) 175
  (county) 142
  South 142
Asclepius (mythological figure) 299
Asia (continent) 60, 230
Assignment in Utopia (book) 59
Assisi (Italy) 35
Assumption of Mary (dogma) 20-3, 25-6
Atkins, Professor Henry St J. 162, 166, 172, 208
Auschwitz (concentration camp) 294
Australia (country) 224
Averroes (philosopher) 78

Bacon, Roger (scientist) 48
Balder the beautiful (book) 230
Baldwin, Monica (writer) 206
Ballsbridge (Dublin) 181
Ballymun (Dublin) 193
Baltimore (Maryland) 91
Bancroft, Dr George (writer) 34
Bantracht na Tuatha (I.C.A.) 85

328

Index

Baptists 116
Barbadoes (country) 32
Bardon, Abbé (anthropologist) 238
Barrington, Ruth (writer) 91-2
Bastible, Canon, Fr James P. 17, 128; see ill. 12
Batiffol, Mgr P. (writer) 244
Bauer, Professor Hans 222
Bavaria (Germany) 217-18, 222-3
B.B.C., see British Broadcasting Corporation
Beach, F. A. (writer) 298
Becquerel, Henry (scientist) 76
Beirt Fhear (J. J. Doyle) (writer) 70
Belfast (city) 36, 69, 95, 100, 119, 142, 145, 147-8, 162, 166, 170, 187, 200, 266
Belfield (Dublin) 152, 158, 160, 171, 194, 197
Belgium (country) 21, 31
Belloc, Hilaire (historian) 80, 82, 225, 229, 234, 239, 263
Benedict XIV (pope) 26
Benediction (Catholic devotion) 14
Benjamin Alcock, the first professor of anatomy and physiology in Queen's College, Cork (book) 90-1
Bennett, Victor (theologian) 20
Beran, Archbishop Josef 102
Berehaven (Cork) 79
Berkeley, Bishop George (philosopher) 73
Berlin (Germany) 35, 41, 85 (diocese) 94
Bernadette of Lourdes (book) 34
Berthelot, P.E.M. (chemist) 235
Bethany (Holy Land) 136, 174
Bethlehem (Palestine) 270, 283
Bevan, M.P., Aneurin (Brit. min. for health) 92
Bewley, K.C., Charles (diplomat) 80
Binchy, Judge Michael 161
Birbeck Hill, G. (editor) 235
Birkner, F. (anthropologist) 236
Birmingham (archdiocese) 217 (city) 267
Bismarck, Prince Otto von 265
Black and Tans (Brit. forces) 64, 73, 75, 262, 265-7, 270

Blackrock (Dublin) 38, 170, 173-4, 179, 190, 198, 200, 208-11, 213
College (Dublin) 36, 38, 111, 128-9, 131-3, 170, 173-4, 179, 190, 198, 200-1, 208-11, 213
Annual 171
Blackwells (Oxford publisher and bookseller) 66
Blanton, Margaret Gray (writer) 34
Blarney (Cork) 74
Blessed Sacrament (a Catholic devotion) 22
Bloomsday (a Joyce adaptation) 146
Blossoms in the dust (film) 74
Blueshirts 110
Boas, F. (anthropologist) 274
Bohemia (country) 72
Boigelot, S.J., R. 273
Bolton Street (Dublin) 157
Bon Secours Home (Cork) 128
Boston (Massachussetts) 62, 136
Boundary Commission (1924-5) 68
Bourgeois, Abbé Louis (anthropologist) 238
Bouscaren, S.J., T. J. (canon lawyer) 252-3
Bousset, W. (writer) 244
Bouyssonie, Abbé A. (anthropologist), 238
Bouyssonie, Abbé J. (anthropologist) 238, 273
Braybrooke, Neville (writer) 206
Bréhier, L. (writer) 248
Breuil, Abbé Henri (archaeologist) 238, 273
Britain, see Great Britain
British Biological Institute 183
Broadcasting Corporation (B.B.C.) 74, 83
Commonwealth 64, 139
Council for Civil Liberties 265
government 28
Broad, Professor C. B. 255-6
Brookeborough (Fermanagh) 137
Browne, Bishop Michael 36, 110, 117, 195-6; see ill. 15
Browne, T.D., Dr Noel C. (min. of health) 87, 89, 91-4, 97, 104-5, 109, 112, 118-19, 126-7, 159, 161, 290-1

329

Buchenwald (concentration camp) 294
Budapest (Hungary) 14
Buddha 244
Buddhism 248, 252
Bull, John 270
Bulla Cruciatae 33
Bureaucracy 122, 125, 155, 207-8
Burghley, Lord William Cecil 75
Burke, Edmund (statesman) 235, 261
Burkitt, Professor M. C. (anthropologist) 273
Burrows, S.J., Fr E. (Assyriologist) 237
Busteed, Professor John 23, 70
Byrne, C.S.Sp., Bishop Joseph 131
Miss Julia (nurse) 211
Laurence P. (journalist) 68-9, 71
T.D., Patrick 158

Caesar (supreme secular authority) 42, 57-8, 107, 117, 299
Cahill, S.J., Fr Edward (writer) 45-6, 202
Calder, Ritchie (journalist) 104
Caledonian Press (London) 262
Caliban in Grub Street (book) 264
California (U.S.A.) 91
Callistus III (pope) 33, 72
Calvary (Jerusalem) 257
Calvin, John (Reformer) 73
Cambridge (England) 35, 76, 220
University 35, 76, 220
Press 76
Canon law digest (book) 252
Canterbury (England) 20, 22, 61, 104
Capitol Cinema (Cork) 32
Cardiff (archdiocese) 132
Carlyle, Thomas (historian) 261
Carmelite Monastery (Blackrock) 209
Carnegie Embryological Collection (Washington) 91
Institution of Washington (Baltimore) 91
Carraroe (Galway) 193
Carson, Edward Henry (politician) 265
Carty, James (writer) 70
Cashel (archdiocese) 132
Castle (Blackrock College) 129, 132
Catholic Action 42, 45-6, 80

apologetics 17, 130, 173, 213
bishops 21, 91-6, 98-105, 109-10, 115, 118-21, 123, 126-7, 131, 140-1, 153, 155-6, 158, 167, 174-6, 178, 180, 185, 192-6, 198, 253, 290-1
Church 15-18, 20-6, 28-9, 32, 38, 42-3, 53, 55, 62, 65, 68, 72-4, 81, 93-4, 96-7, 99-102, 107, 112-19, 122, 127, 189, 203-7, 211, 214-15, 221, 231-2, 239, 245, 247, 249-50, 252, 254, 258, 262, 267, 269, 281-2, 290-1, 294
culture 14
doctrine 13, 103
priests 18, 73, 238
scholars 20, 238
theologians 21
Digest (periodical) 62
Evidence Guild (London) 13
Headmasters' Association 196
Herald (newspaper) 29, 32, 52, 54, 79-80, 133, 214
Library Institute (Limerick) 36
Literature Guild (St Angela's College) 36
Mind (periodical) 13, 27
Review (New York) 51
School Managers' Association 195
Times (South Africa) 50, 81
Truth Society of Ireland (C.T.S.I.) 14, 41, 53, 235-6
University (Ireland) 64
University of the Sacred Heart (Milan) 103
University of Washington 237
Women's Federation of Secondary School Unions 45
Workers' College (Dublin) 188
Young Men's Society (Cork) 31, 36
Catholicism 13, 27, 29, 35, 62, 65, 68, 70, 72, 76, 79, 82, 84, 172-3, 199, 202, 214, 227, 232, 239-40, 245, 252, 291
Catholics 19, 22-5, 27-8, 45, 58, 63-4, 73, 75, 89, 94-9, 101-3, 111-16, 118, 122, 126, 136, 139, 141, 159-60, 167, 172, 174-6, 178-9, 184, 186, 190-2, 194, 197-8, 203-4, 218, 220, 225-6, 228-9, 231-2, 236,

Index

244, 246, 248-9, 250-3, 258, 262, 265, 267, 282, 291, 296, 304
and *Trinity College* (pamphlet) 179
Celsus (Latin author) 22, 255-6
Celtic Studies 69, 79
  Studies department (U.C.C.) 69
Censorship Board (Éire) 54, 259, 261, 268-9
Chalcedon, Council of (451) 130
Charles Darwin's diary of the voyage of H.M.S. Beagle (book) 237
Davis and his book (pamphlet) 206
Charter Schools (Ireland) 32
Chesterton, G. K. (writer) 40, 80, 261
China (country) 238
Chinese Boxers (revolutionaries) 266
Christ 14-15, 19, 21, 25, 30, 35-7, 42, 45-6, 50-1, 58, 136, 170, 174, 205, 207, 214, 217, 219-21, 228-9, 242-3, 245-8, 256-7, 262, 269, 281, 283, 299
Christian Brothers School (Sexton Street), 152
  Union (Protestant) 172
Christianity 16-19, 38, 42, 45, 49-50, 52-3, 56, 58-9, 65, 82, 84, 93, 100-1, 230-1, 235, 239, 241-3, 245, 247, 255, 257, 281, 297
Christians 21-4, 26, 42, 45-7, 57, 114, 203-6, 215, 224, 246, 291
Christus Rex (a Catholic Society) 171
Rex (periodical) 103
Church and State in modern Ireland 1923-1979 (book) 91
  of England 20-2, 28, 104; see also Anglican Church and Anglicans
  of Ireland 23-4, 26-8, 100
  of Ireland Gazette and Family Newspaper 25, 101, 120
  Times (newspaper) 23
  of the Sacred Heart (Donnybrook) 31
Citizen Kane (film) 74-5
City Hall (Cork) 36
Clann na Poblachta (party) 92
Clare (county) 38, 154-5
Clergy Review (periodical) 203, 253
Clermont convent (Rathnew) 172
Clonfert (diocese) 179
Clonliffe (Dublin) 190, 209
  College, see Holy Cross College, Clonliffe
Codicote (Hertfordshire) 60
Cohalan, Bishop Daniel 81
Colleges Act, Bill (1845) 147-8
Colley, T.D., George (min. for ed.) 195-6, 198
Collins, Michael (Irish leader) 172
Columbia University (New York) 238
Comhar (periodical) 117-19
Commission on Higher Education (1960-67) 157, 184-5, 197-8
  on Vocational Organisation (1939-43) 85
Communism 13, 43-4, 55, 59, 61, 83, 85, 95, 97, 102, 141, 199, 291, 293
Communist Party of Ireland 62
  of Russia 202
Conference of Convent Secondary Schools 195
Congo (region) 237
Conimbricenses (theologians) 130
Connacht (province) 63
Constantinople (Turkey) 33
Constitution (1937) 144, 159
Contra Celsum (book) 256
Convent of St Mary of the Isle (Cork) 51
Convocation (N.U.I.) 162
Cooper, Rev. J. M. (editor) 237
Cootehill (Cavan) 193
Corinth (Greece) 38, 243
Corinthians, Letter to the (New Testament) 229, 243, 257
Cork and Muskerry Light Railway 284
  (city) 17, 27-9, 31-2, 36-8, 41, 46-7, 51, 53, 65-72, 74, 79-81, 83-91, 93, 99, 106-8, 110-111, 121, 123, 128-30, 132-4, 147-51, 153, 156-7, 162-5, 167-8, 170-3, 176-80, 184, 187, 193, 198, 200, 202, 208, 210, 212-14, 216-17, 266-7, 284-90, 308
  (county) 74, 86, 154-5, 287
  North 155
  South 155
  (diocese) 27, 175
Co-operator (newspaper) 287
Corporation 88, 284-9
District Hospital 89
Evening Echo (newspaper) 80, 308
Examiner (newspaper) 27, 31, 36, 72, 81, 84, 128, 151, 171, 287, 289

331

Alfred O'Rahilly III: Controversialist

Free Press (newspaper) 70
Holly Bough (annual) 81
Savings Bank 27
University Graduates' Club 36
University Press 46, 66, 128, 130
University Record 216
Corkery, Professor Daniel (writer) 70
Corry, T.D., Martin J. 90
Cosgrave, William T. (former head of govt.) 172
Costello, T.D., John A. (Taoiseach) 92, 95, 102, 113, 117
  General Michael J. 172, 189
  Peter (writer) 111
Coulton, George G. (historian) 32, 220, 230
Council of Administration for Primary Schools (archdiocese of Dublin) 186
  of the Royal College of Veterinary Surgeons (London) 181
Cowan, T.D., Captain Peadar 102-4, 118-19, 183
Cox, Dr Michael (St Vincent's hospital) 210
Coyne, S.J., Fr Edward 107, 122
Crane, S.J., Fr Paul (writer) 103
Crisis for Christianity (book) 231
Cromwell, Oliver (dictator) 265
Cronin, Anthony (writer) 110
Cros, S.J., Fr L. J. M. (writer) 34
Cultural anthropology (book) 237, 275
  Commission (Dublin Corporation) 183
Cumann na nGaedheal (party) 160
Curie, Eve (writer) 76
  Marie (scientist) 76
Cushing, Cardinal Richard 133, 136
Czechoslovakia (country) 217

Dáil Éireann 44, 87, 95, 102-3, 112, 116, 119-20, 127, 138, 158, 161-3, 166-8, 180, 188, 289
Daily Express (newspaper) 235
  News (newspaper) 261
  Worker (newspaper) 22
Dalkey (Dublin) 59
D'Alton, Cardinal John 81; see ill. 15
Dante Alighieri (poet) 114

Darwin, Charles (scientist) 18, 40, 133-4, 224, 237, 263, 271, 274, 277-8, 293, 297-8
Davis (California) 91
  Fr Charles (theologian) 203-7
de Blacam, Aodh (writer) 70
De Brosses, President Charles 67
de Brún, Mgr Pádraig (polymath) 131, 174-7
de Chardin, Père Teilhard (anthropologist) 207, 238, 273
de Grandmaison, S.J., L. (writer) 228
de Jerphanion, S.J., G. (writer) 248
de la Boullaye, S.J., Père Pinard (anthropologist) 236-7
de Valera, T.D., Eamon (Taoiseach) 92, 123, 126, 128, 135, 148-9, 208, 211-2, 290; see ill. 15
Deeny, Dr James (writer) 91
Delany, S.J., Fr William 307
Delaunay, Abbé (anthropologist) 238
Dengel, Dr Anna (founder of a religious institute) 38
Dental Hospital (Dublin) 182
Der Mensch aller Zeiten (book) 236
  Ursprung der Gottesidee (book) 236
Derrick, Paul (writer) 41
Derry (city) 142
  (county) 142
  Journal (newspaper) 23
Developmental stages in human embryos (book) 91
Devon (England) 35, 129
Dewey, John (educationalist) 293
Die Geschichte der scholastichen Methode (book) 229
  Rassen und Völker der Menscheit (book) 236
  Stellung der Pygmdenvölker... (book) 236
Dignan, Bishop John 179
Dillon, T.D., James 161, 167, 180, 290
Dinan, C.S.Sp., Fr Vincent J. 129-30, 132, 136; see ills. 13 and 14
Divine Office 209
Divini Illius Magistri (papal encyclical) 303
Dixon, Mrs Clare (nurse) 211
'Dr Kildare' films 75

332

Index

Doctrine and Life (periodical) 143 in the Church of England (pamphlet) 21
Dominican Convent (Galway) 36 Order 48, 51, 75
Donegal (county) 142
Donnybrook (Dublin) 31, 51
Donovan, Thomas D. (writer) 70
Douglas, Major C. H. (economist) 201
Douglasism (a theory of money popularised by Major C. H. Douglas) 201
Dover Publications (New York) 174
Down (county), 142 South 142
Downey, Archbishop Richard 225
Doyle, Jack (boxer) 84
S.J., Fr William 31, 49, 174
Drake, Francis (pirate) 75
Dublin (archdiocese) 94, 96, 129-30, 136, 146, 175, 182-3, 186
(city) 13-16, 26-8, 31, 36, 43-4, 50, 54, 58-9, 61, 64-5, 69, 76-7, 79-80, 85, 91, 100, 107, 110-111, 116, 121, 124, 128, 130, 135, 142-4, 147, 150-2, 154, 156-68, 170-2, 174-80, 182-91, 193-4, 197-200, 208, 212, 262-3, 270, 293, 305, 307
(county) South 171
Adult Education Committee 188
City University 158
Corporation 183
Institute for Advanced Studies 76-7, 79, 111
Institute of Catholic Sociology 171, 188, 200
Ducange Anglicus (writer) 249
Ducrost, Abbé (anthropologist) 238
Duff, Frank (co-founder of Legion of Mary) 172, 199; see ill. 16
Dugmore, C. W. (lecturer, University of Manchester) 21
Duignan, Professor Michael 162
Dún Laoghaire (Dublin) 210
Dundalk (Louth) 171
Durham (England) 90
Dwyer & Co., Messrs (Cork) 287

Earlsfort Terrace (Dublin) 152, 158, 197

Early Civilisation (book) 227, 275 man (book) 258
Easter Rising (1916) 209
Eddington, A. (scientist) 263
Egypt (country) 246-8
Egyptology (chair) 243-4, 246
Einstein, Albert (scientist) 79, 100, 263
Éire 54, 100, 119, 258, 265, 268-9
Eisenhower, General Dwight 297
Electricity Supply Board (E.S.B.) 208
Electro-magnetics. A discussion of fundamentals (book) 174
Elias, O.F.M., Br (companion of St Francis) 220
Elizabeth I (queen) 75
Elphin (diocese) 193
Ely Place (Dublin) 171
Ends and means (book) 256
England (country) 21-2, 35, 62, 64-5, 72, 75, 115, 193, 206, 233, 241, 251, 259-60, 262-3, 281, 293, 298, 308
English (language) 119, 217
Epictetus (philosopher) 242
Erinville Hospital (Cork) 86, 88, 90, 284-9
Erne (lake) 145
Ernst, O.P., Fr Cornelius (writer) 206
Established Church (U.K.) 28; see also Church of England
Etudes Carmélitaines (periodical) 217
Eucharist, The 13-14
Eucharistic Congress (Budapest) 14
Eucharistic Congress (Dublin) 13
Europe (continent) 33, 47, 65, 114, 238, 249, 291
European civilisation (book) 234, 236, 272
Evans, Harvey (T.C.D.) 26
Professor John (U.C.D.) 172
Evolution and culture (book) 226 in religion and culture (book) 278 in religion and education (book) 234, 238
Experiment in autobiography (book) 240, 246, 250-1, 280
Eyre, E. (writer) 234, 272

Fabian Society 60
Fahey, C.S.Sp., Fr Denis (writer) 198-202

Alfred O'Rahilly III: Controversialist

Faith and facts (pamphlet) 13, 235
Fallon, Gabriel (writer) 146
Farren, Robert (poet) 83
Farrington, B.E., A. 263
Fascism 254
Fr O'Leary Total Abstinence Hall (Cork) 36
Father William Doyle, S.J., A spiritual study (book) 31, 174
Faulhaber, Cardinal Michael von 217
Fawsitt, J. L. (writer) 70
Feehan, Matthew (ed., *Sunday Press*) 35
Feehan, Seán (writer and publisher) 46
Feeney, S.J., Fr Leonard 62
Fehily, Fr G. Thomas 200
Felici, Most Rev Ettore (apostolic nuncio) 38
Fennelly, Fr John (writer) 52
Fermanagh (county) 137, 142
Ferns (diocese) 199-200
Fianna Fáil (government) 92, 123, 126-7, 161
(party) 89, 126, 161
Fine Gael (party) 160-1
Fire over England (film) 75
Fírinne (Irish-speaking subsidiary of Maria Duce) 200
Firmin Didot (edition of works of Voltaire) 67
Fischer, Alfons (eugenicist) 294
Fitzgerald, Barry (actor) 72
FitzRoy, Captain (colleague of Charles Darwin) 237
Flanagan, Deirdre (daughter of Frank) 209
Frank (brother-in-law of William T. Cosgrave) 172, 209
Flann O'Brien: an illustrated biography (book) 111
Fleet Street (London) 214
Flinders Petrie, W. M. (writer) 247-8
Flinn, Hugo V. (writer) 70
Fontenelle, Mgr R. (biographer) 254
For civilisation (book) 297
Ford, C. S. (writer) 298
Fordham University (New York) 218
Fort Worth (Texas) 74
Fortnightly Review 230, 277
Fossil man in Spain (book) 236

Fra Angelico (painter) 248
France (country) 68, 122, 128, 202, 232-3, 235, 238-9, 274
Franciscan Tertiaries 44
Franco Bahamonde, Generalissimo Francisco (dictator) 232-3, 262
Frazer, Sir James George (anthropologist), 226-9, 230, 232, 234
Frederick the Great (book) 261
Freeman's Journal (newspaper) 53
Freemasonry 199, 201-2, 254
and the anti-Christian movement (book) 202
French (language) 46-7, 136, 199, 218
Revolution 46, 235, 301
Revolution (book) 261
Seán (lord mayor of Cork) 80
Freud, Sigmund (founder of psychoanalysis) 260, 281, 293
Frezenberg (Belgium) 31
Fribourg (Switzerland) 38
University 38
Friends of Soviet Russia 62
Froude, James Anthony (historian) 261

Gaiety Theatre (Dublin) 31, 43
Gaitskell, M.P., Hugh (Brit. chancellor) 92
Galatians, Letter to the (*New Testament*) 243
Galileo Galilei (astronomer) 18
Gallagher, Frank (writer) 70
Galway (city) 36, 50, 87-8, 117, 147-8, 151, 155, 157, 162, 175-7, 184, 195, 198
(diocese) 110, 175
Ganges (river) 252
Garde, O.P., Fr Thomas 51
Gemelli, O.F.M., Fr Agostino (psychologist) 103-4
General Council of County Councils 180
Genesis (*Old Testament*), 24, 234
Geneva (Switzerland) 13
George's Hill (Dublin) 170
Germany (country), 35, 81, 218, 242, 251, 274, 295; see also Third Reich
Gibbon, Edward (historian) 235
Monk (writer) 39, 70

334

Index

Gladstone, William (Brit. prime minister) 253
Glasgow (Scotland) 231
Glenade (Mt Merrion Avenue) 172
Glenties (Donegal) 193
Glossarium (book) 249
God and Mr Wells (book) 245, 280
God the invisible king (book) 232-3, 240-1, 249, 257, 265, 277, 279
Goguel, M. (writer) 241
Gold Standard, The 201
Goldberg, Gerald Y. (solicitor) 202
Golden Hour (periodical) 51
Goldenweiser, A. A. (anthropologist) 227, 274-5
Goldsmith, Oliver (poet) 271
Goldstein, David (writer) 199
Gomme, A. W. (writer) 231
Good, Rev Professor James 171
Good Shepherd Convent (Belfast) 171
Shepherd Sisters 208
Gordon, David (writer) 82
Gospel meditations (book) 173
Grabmann, Martin (theologian) 229
Gräbner, F. (anthropologist) 274
Gräf, Dr Hilda C. (writer) 35, 41, 171, 217-23
Grand Central Cinema (Limerick) 36
Lodge (of freemasons of France) 202
Orient (freemasonry) 202
Grant, Bishop 64
Gray, Tony (writer) 108
Great Britain 22, 66, 103, 123-4, 139-40, 142, 144, 232, 251, 261, 270, 274; see also United Kingdom and Bull, John
Northern Railway 145
Greek (language) 26, 130, 231, 242, 247
Greek metaphysics 205
Gresham Hotel (Dublin) 15-16, 36, 170
Griffin, C.S.Sp., Fr Francis (father general) 38
Guild of SS Luke, Cosmas and Damian (Catholic organisation) 37, 123-5, 293, 304
Gusinde, Fr M. (writer) 237
Gwynn, Professor Denis 128, 211, 216; see ill. 10

Haeckel, E. H. (writer), 234, 245, 259, 268, 275-6
Halle (university, Germany) 222
Handbuch der altchristlichen epigraphik (book) 247
Hanly, Bishop Vincent 193
Harrington, T. R. (ed., *Irish Independent*) 44
Harvard (university, Boston) 68, 70, 80, 85, 133
Hayes, Senator Michael 168
Health Act (1947), 97, 120 (1953) 126-7, 177
medicine and politics in Ireland 1900-1970 (book) 91
Service (Brit.) 92
Healy, M.P., Timothy 70
Hearne, John (dept. of ext. affairs) 172
Hebrew (language) 130
Hebrews, Letter to (*New Testament*) 249
Heidelberg (Germany) 100
(university) 100
Henry VIII (king) 16, 62
Herben, Jan (writer) 72
Herder (publisher) 217
Hermes (mythological figure) 248
Herod Antipas (Palestine) 283
Hertfordshire (England) 60
Hesiod (Greek poet) 216
Hibernia (newspaper) 45, 126, 137, 139, 142, 144, 146, 152-6, 158, 162-3, 167
Hickey, Councillor J. (Cork Corporation, lord mayor) 287-8
Councillor J. C. (mayor of Limerick) 149-50
Hierocles of Alexandria (Greek writer) 257
Higgins, F. R. (poet) 29, 70
High Gods in North America (book) 236
Hillel (Jewish rabbi, writer) 242
Hillery, T.D., Dr Patrick (min. for ed.) 159-60, 188, 194-5
Hippocrates (mythological figure) 299-300
Hirsch, E. A. (writer) 182
His Holiness Pope Pius XI (book) 254

335

Alfred O'Rahilly III: Controversialist

Histoire de Notre Dame de Lourdes (book) 34
History of England (book) 261
 of the dogma of the Trinity (book) 241
 of the popes (book) 29, 231
Hitler, Adolf (dictator) 37, 265-6
Hobbes, Thomas (philosopher) 255-6, 261
Hoeltker, Fr G. (editor) 236
Hogan, Professor J.J. 162
 Professor James 70
 Thomas, see Woods, Thomas
Holland (country) 192-3, 297
Holles Street hospital (Dublin) 155
Hollywood (California) 49, 74
Holy Cross College (Clonliffe) 190, 209
 Ghost Fathers 37-8, 210, 212
 Ghost Missionary College (Kimmage) 199
 Ghost Order 129, 132, 170, 190, 200
 Land 132, 170-1, 208
 See (Rome) 21, 80, 254
 week liturgy 213
Hooker, Sir J. D. (botanist) 298
Honan chapel (U.C.C.) 128
Horgan, John (Cork Corporation) 289
Horus (mythological figure) 246-8
Hospitals Act (1939) 286
House of Commons (Brit.) 92, 147
 of Lords (Brit.) 105
Howell, S.J., Fr Clifford (liturgist) 52
Hughes, S.J., Fr Seán (educationalist) 196-7
Hulton, Edward (prop., *Picture Post*) 54-5, 270
Human embryology and teratology (book) 91
Hungary (country) 145
Hutchinson (publisher) 237
Huxley, Aldous (writer) 256
 Julian (writer) 276
 Leonard (writer and broadcaster) 40, 240, 260
 Thomas Henry (scientist) 18, 40, 134, 234-6, 241, 278, 297-8
Hyde, Douglas (journalist) 214

I leap over the wall (book) 206
I was Hitler's prisoner (book) 260

Imperial Deputy Grand Chaplain (Orange Order) 95
Incarnation (doctrine) 73
India (country) 139
Indians (U.S.A.) 75
Indulgences (a Catholic devotion) 32-3
Inquisition, see Spanish Inquisition
Institute of Catholic Education (archdiocese of Dublin) 182
 of Electrical Engineers 157
 of Mechanical Engineers 157
Intercom (periodical) 78
International Catholic Girls Protection Society 41
 Labour Organisation (I.L.O.) 13
I.R.A., see Irish Republican Army
Ireland (country) 14, 21, 23-4, 26-8, 37, 41, 48, 50, 53-5, 62, 64-5, 69, 72-3, 80, 82-3, 90-3, 95, 98-101, 105, 114-16, 119-21, 123, 128, 131-2, 136-45, 147-64, 166-8, 174-85, 187, 190, 192, 194, 197-8, 202, 211, 213, 258, 260-2, 265-7, 270, 290, 298; see also Éire and Irish Free State
 Act (1949) 144
Iris Oifigiúil 268
Irish (language) 55, 118, 121
 Academy of Letters 112
 -Americans 62-4
 Association of Catholic University Students 171
 Catholic (newspaper) 53, 83
 Christian Brothers 73
 Ecclesiastical Record (periodical) 15, 200, 253
 Free State 13, 144, 202
 Historical Studies (periodical) 91
 Hospitals' Sweep Fund 138
 Independent (newspaper) 15, 29-30, 44, 65, 166-8, 175-6, 199
 Labour Party 69
 Labour Party and Trade Union Congress 262
 Medical Association 100, 123, 126-7
 News (newspaper) 268
 Nurses Organisation (I.N.O.) 123
 Opinion: a weekly journal of industrial and political democracy (newspaper) 69

336

Index

Press (newspaper) 30, 43, 173-4
Republican Army (I.R.A.) 137-8, 140-6, 265
-Soviet Friendship Society 61-2
Statesman (periodical) 69-70
Theological Quarterly (periodical) 262
Times (newspaper) 23, 26, 39, 60, 66, 92-6, 99-101, 104-11, 115, 117-23, 141, 146-7, 151, 158, 189-90
Times Ltd 109
Trade Union Congress 112
Tribune, a weekly review of affairs (periodical) 68-72
Universities Act (1908) 153
Veterinary Journal 182
Isis (mythological figure) 246-8, 253
Italy (country) 103, 247, 298
Ivy, A. C. (writer) 296

Jackson, T. A. (militant atheist) 22
Jacob (*Hebrews*) 249
Jacquier, E. (theologian) 228
Jandhara (India) 248
Jansenism 65
Japan (country) 252-3
Jeans, J. H. (scientist) 263
Jerusalem (Palestine) 228, 230
Jesuits, see Society of Jesus
Jesus Christ (periodical) 228
vor Pilatus (book) 230
Jews 95, 97, 101, 126, 194, 199, 202, 240, 256, 262, 296
Jinja (Japanese national temples) 253
Joad, Professor Cyril Edwin Mitchenson 17, 296
John Huss and his followers (book) 72
O'London's Weekly (periodical) 29
Scotus Eriugena (philosopher) 27, 73
Jones, Henry Arthur (playwright) 53
Jordana, O.P., Mother M. (educationalist) 196-7
Journal of researches (book) 237
Journal of the American Medical Association (periodical) 296
Joyce, James (writer) 82, 146
Juno and the paycock (play) 72

Kant, Emmanuel (philosopher) 50, 256
Kanturk (Cork) 37

Kastner, K. (writer) 230
Kaufmann, C. M. (writer) 247
Kavanagh, Fr James (sociologist) 99
Kearney, Pat (writer) 148
Keith, Sir Arthur (writer) 255, 258, 263, 277
Kenny, John (assist. lecturer, U.C.D.) 161
Kensit, J. A. (anti-Catholic bigot) 245
Kerry (county) 69, 151, 154, 287
North 155
(diocese) 81
Kerryman (newspaper), 41, 139
Kevin Street (Dublin) 157
Kharkov (Soviet Union) 61
Kiernan, Dr Thomas J. (dir., Radio Éireann) 40-1
Killanin, Lord (writer) 104
Killarney (Kerry) 36-7, 43, 81
(parish) 81
Killeshandra (Cavan) 171
Killiney (Dublin) 184
Kilroy, P. J. (Anti-Partition of Ireland League) 120
Kimmage Manor (Dublin) 170, 199, 212
Kinane, Archbishop Jeremiah 132
Kinlen, S.C., Dermot P. 157
Kirov (Soviet leader) 60, 76
Kitty Foyle (film) 74
Knighthood of St Gregory the Great 132
Knights of St Columbanus 171
Knox, John (Reformer) 73
Mgr Ronald (writer) 24, 255, 264
Konnersreuth (Germany) 35, 129, 217-20, 223
Koppers, Fr W. (anthropologist) 236-7
Korea (country) 92
Kreichgauer, Fr Damian (anthropologist) 237
Kremlin (Moscow) 59
Kroeber, A. L. (anthropologist) 274
Kronos (mythological figure) 226
Kugler, S.J., Fr F. X. (Assyriologist) 237
Kulturkampf 265

La Cité Chrétienne (periodical) 273
La Prensa (newspaper) 109

337

La voix des monuments (book) 248
Labour Party 202
Lagrange, O.P., M. J. (writer) 228, 230, 237, 242, 279
Lamarck, J. B. (naturalist) 263
Lang, Andrew (writer) 230
Larkin, James (Labour leader) 58
L'art chrétien (book) 248
Lartet, Dr Edward (archaeologist) 238
Lateau, Louise (stigmatist) 220
Lateran (palace) 236
Lateran treaty (1929) 254
Latin (language) 47, 130, 253
Latin America 21
Laughing Irish Eyes (film) 74
Laurentian Society (T.C.D.) 172-3
Le cas de la visionnaire stigmatisée Thérèse Neumann de Konnersreuth (book) 218
Le Roy, Mgr A. (anthropologist) 236
Leader (newspaper) 68, 80
League of Militant Atheists (Great Britain) 22
Lebreton, Père (theologian) 241
Lechler, Dr (writer) 221
Lecky, W. E. (historian) 27
Leeson Street (Dublin) 305
Legion of Mary (a Catholic organisation) 15-16, 36-7, 43, 130, 171-2, 187-8, 199-200
Leiber, S.J., Fr Robert (writer) 222
Leinster House (Dublin), 117, 119, 140-1, 143
Lemberg (archdiocese) 217
Lenihan, T.D., Brian (min. for ed.) 198
D. M. (writer) 70
Leo XIII (pope) 15
Letters and notices (book on Society of Jesus) 52
L'étude comparée des religions (book) 236-7
Leviathan (book) 256, 261, 264
Liddy, Mrs Margaret (sec., Limerick University Project) 152
Lietzmann, H. (scholar) 254
Life and letters (book) 278
Life and letters of Thomas Henry Huxley (book) 241, 260
Life of Christ (book) 235
Liffey (river) 69
Lightfoot, J. B. (scholar) 254
Lilliput (newspaper) 260, 268
Limerick (city) 36, 55, 87, 137, 147-54, 156-8, 160, 200
(county) 151, 154-5
(diocese) 163
Chamber of Commerce 148-9
Teachers' Training College 153
Technical Institute 151, 157
University Project 147-53, 156-7, 160
Leader (newspaper) 152
Lisieux (France) 131
Listener (periodical) 83
Listowel (Kerry) 131, 151
Urban District Council 151
Literary and Philosophical Society (U.C.C.) 41, 202
Little, T.D., Patrick J. (min. for posts and telegraphs) 41, 70, 172
Liverpool (England) 33-4, 243
Cathedral 33
University 243
Living anatomy (book) 91
Llorente (historian) 76
Local Appointments Commission 87-8
Loisy, A. F. (writer) 228, 235, 241
London (England) 13, 53-4, 59, 73, 79-80, 84, 104, 128, 153, 181, 214, 217, 234, 249, 262, 305
University 153, 234, 271
Lorant, Stefan (publisher) 260, 268
Loreto Convent (George's Hill) 170
L'origine des êtres vivants; l'illusion transformiste (book) 273
Lost property: proposals for the distribution of property in an industrial age (book) 41
Lourdes (France) 19, 29, 34, 219
Lourdes (book) 34
Louvain (Belgium) 136
University 136
Lowie, Professor R. H. (anthroplogist) 227
Lucey, Bishop Cornelius 81, 128, 132, 134, 175-6, 179; see ill. 12
Lunn, Arnold (writer) 32, 246
Luther, Martin (Reformer) 15-16, 50, 242
Lynch, T.D., Jack 161, 212

Index

Lyons, Eugene (writer) 59
Dr J. B. (physician) 211
Mac an Fhailí, Ciarán (solicitor) 142-6
Mac Aonghusa, Críostóir (writer) 70
Macarius, M. (writer) 257
MacArthur, General Douglas 92
Macaulay, Lord Thomas (writer) 25, 233
MacBride, Professor E. M. (zoologist) 251, 263
MacBride, T.D., Seán (min. for ext. affairs) 92, 95, 127
McCabe, Joseph (writer) 231-2, 234, 245, 278
McCarron, E. P. (sec., dept. of loc. govt.) 172
McCarthy, C.S.Sp., Archbishop John J. 133; see ill. 14
C.S.Sp., Fr Michael 198, 203, 210-12, 216
Professor Michael D. 154; see ill. 9
P. M. (Limerick University Project Ctee) 153-6
T.D., Seán 289
Macchioro, V. D. (writer) 228
McConnell, Provost Albert J. 197-8, 212
McCormick, W. J. (biographer) 80
Mac Curtain, Tomás (Republican) 202
McDonogh, Bernard (painter) 137
McDowell, R. B. (historian) 29
McDougall, William (writer) 78
McElligott, James (sec., dept. of fin.) 172
Mac Eoin, General Seán 172; see ill. 16
McGilligan, T.D., Patrick 167, 182, 196
McGrath, Archbishop Michael 132
McGreevy, Thomas (poet) 83
Machiavelli, Nichola (writer) 73
McLaughlin, Dr Thomas A. (architect of E.S.B.'s Shannon scheme) 208
McMahon, S.J., Fr John (provincial) 213
McManus, Francis (writer) 171
MacEntee, T.D., Seán 70
McNamara, Brinsley (writer) 39
Mâcon, Council of (585) 78
McQuaid, Archbishop John C. 96, 124, 126-7, 129-34, 136, 146-7, 170-2, 174-91, 193-8, 200, 209, 211-12; see ills 13 and 15
McQuillan, T.D., Jack 159, 161-2, 167
Macra na Feirme 85
McRedmond, Louis (writer) 82
Madame Curie (book) 76
(film) 76
Madeyski, Dr Boleslas de Poray (physician) 218-20
Mafia (Sicilian) 141
Magnificat Society (U.C.D.) 150
Maguire, B. Waldo (T.C.D.) 28-9
Maher, S.J., Fr Michael (psychologist) 305-7
Mahomet (prophet) 245, 280
Malay (region) 237, 239
Malin Head (Donegal) 119
Malinowski, B. (anthropologist) 274
Mallow (Cork) 37, 69
Malone, Andrew E. (*nom-de-plume*) 68, see also Byrne, Laurence P.
Manchester (England) 21, 85, 239
College (Oxford) 239
Guardian (newspaper) 147
Manning, Cardinal Edward 105
Mansion House (Dublin) 61, 130, 170
Marcion (heresiarch) 242
Marian Hall (Milltown) 170
Shrine (Lourdes) 34
Year (1954) 129
Maria Duce (a Catholic organisation) 200
Mariana (theologian) 73
Maritain, Jacques (philosopher) 105
Martha (sister of Lazarus, *New Testament*) 135
Martin, Rev Professor Conor 124, 187
Kingsley (ed., *New Statesman*) 22
Fr Liam (sec., A.B. McQuaid) 182-3, 186, 188-9, 190-1, 195
Mother Mary (foundress of Medical Missionaries of Mary) 38
Martini, Dr (physician and visitor to Konnersreuth) 220
Marx, Karl (philosopher) 40, 49, 293
Marxism 57, 83, 102
Mary (Mother of Christ) 15-16, 20-1, 25, 34, 36, 43, 135, 171-3, 187-8, 199-200, 209, 244-9, 269, 305
(sister of Martha, *New Testament*) 135

339

Alfred O'Rahilly III: Controversialist

Mass 13-14, 29, 32-3, 52, 81, 132, 134, 136, 146-7, 171, 208-9, 212, 214, 227, 229, 249, 256, 268, 280, 283
stipends 32
Mater Hospital (Belfast) 138
(Dublin) 182
Matrimonial Causes Bill (Brit. 1951) 104
Maxwell, J. A. L. (scientist) 263
Maya (civilisation) 237
(mythological figure) 244
Maynooth (Kildare) 81, 100, 112, 116-17, 141, 152
Mayo (county) 154
Medical Bureau (Lourdes) 219
Missionaries of Mary 38
Missionary Society (U.C.C.) 130
Melanchton, Philipp (Reformer) 73
Melbourne, Lord W. L. 233
Memoirs (book, Gibbon's) 235
Memoirs of a wild goose (book, C. Bewley's) 80
Men of the old stone age (book) 278
Menchen, H. L. (writer) 75
Mendel, G. J. (biologist) 236
Menghin, Oswald (anthropologist) 273
Merchants Quay (Dublin) 171
Mercier, Vivian (writer) 66
Press (Cork) 46, 217
Merrion Square (Dublin) 172
Mexico (country) 15
Middleton, Mr (English broadcaster) 39
Mikado (Shintoism) 252-3
Milan (Italy) 103
Miller, René Fülöp (writer) 15
Milltown (Dublin) 170
Park (Dublin) 170, 210
Milroy, T.D., Seán 70
Mindszenty, Archbishop Joseph 102
Missionaries of the Sacred Heart (Cork) 37
Missionary – Ethnological Museum (Lateran) 236
Mitchell, Rev. Frederick R. (Monasterevan) 101
Mivart, St George Jackson (biologist) 133-4, 263, 297-8
Modern materialism (book) 78
Monasterevan (Kildare) 101

Money (book) 82-3, 201
manipulation and the social order (book) 199, 201
Mongolia (country) 238
Monotheism among primitive peoples (book) 275
Montalembert, Charles Forbes R. de (historian) 25
Monte Cassino (monastery, Italy) 19
Month (periodical) 28, 62, 230
Montini, Mgr Giovanni Battista 122
Moonlighters (agents of agrarian unrest) 266
Montpellier (France) 91
Moral principles (pamphlet) 38
Moran, P. F. (writer) 193
More-O'Farrell, Edward (member of a Patrician Conference) 172
Morning Star Hostel (North Brunswick Street) 43
Morrissey, S. J., Fr T. J. (writer) 202
Mortished, R. J. P. (writer) 70
Moscow (Russia) 23, 41, 61, 85, 233
Moses (*Old Testament*) 260
Moshi (diocese in Tanzania) 131
Most, Johann (writer) 83
Mother-and-child scheme, service 85, 89, 91-2, 96-7, 107, 111, 117, 119, 121, 123, 126-7, 141, 177, 290
Mount Kilimanjaro (Kenya) 38
Merrion Avenue (Dublin) 172
St Joseph's Abbey (Roscrea) 134
Moynihan, Fr Denis (adm., Killarney) 81
Maurice (sec., cabinet) 172
Mr & Mrs Smith (film) 74
Mr Belloc objects (book) 225, 239
Mr Smyllie, Sir (book) 108
Mr Wells as historian (book) 231
Muckross Park Convent (Donnybrook) 51
Muintir na Tíre 85
Mulcahy, T.D., Richard 167
Munich (Germany) 268
Munster (province) 70, 147, 156
Muntsch, S.J., Fr A. (anthropologist) 226, 237, 275
Murnaghan, Mr Justice George 161
Murphy, Con (organiser of ad. ed.) 128, 172, 210, 307

Index

Fr John J. (Bob) (adm., Killarney) 37
Murray, C.S.C., Fr Edward (Notre Dame) 128
S.J., Fr John Courtney (theologian) 207
R. H. (writer) 73
Muskerry (Cork) 284-5, 287
Muslims 44
My dear Wells (book) 53
My duel with the Vatican (book) 235
My pigmy and negro hosts (book) 237
Myles na gCopaleen (writer) 108-11
Mystical phenomena in the life of Thérèse Neumann (book) 217

Naber, P.P., Fr (Konnersreuth) 35, 129, 220
Nagle, Nano (foundress of Presentation Sisters) 31-2
Nairobi (archdiocese in Kenya) 133
Naples (Italy) 48
Napoleon (dictator) 59
Nash, S.J., Fr Robert (writer) 171
National Institute of Higher Education (Limerick) 157
Socialist Party (Nazi Party) 94, 100, 141; see also Nazism
University of Ireland (N.U.I.) 38, 48, 50, 89-91, 128, 131, 148-64, 166-8, 174-85, 187, 190, 197-8
Club 128
Nature (periodical) 263, 273
Nazareth (Palestine) 241-2
Nazism 250-1, 260, 264, 295-6, 300; see also National Socialist Party
Nether Edge Hospital (Sheffield) 90
Neumann, Thérèse (stigmatist) 34-5, 41, 129, 173, 217-23
Nevin, Professor T. E. 162
New English Dictionary 249
Ireland (newspaper) 69
Orleans (Louisiana) 64
Statesman (periodical) 22, 104
Testament (Bible) 15, 66, 130-1, 174, 244
York (U.S.A.) 62, 174
Zealand (country) 201
Newman, Cardinal John Henry (writer) 64, 155, 204, 207
House (Dublin) 124, 293

Society (Belfast) 36-7
'Nichevo' (*nom-de-plume*) 106-7
Nicholson, Professor J. A. 182
Nigeria (country) 38
Nile (river) 243, 252
No laughing matter (book) 110
Nobel Prize 76
Nolan, Mgr J. M. (psychologist) 78
S.J., Thomas V. (provincial) 305
Non abbiamo bisogno (encyclical) 254
North Brunswick Street (Dublin) 43
Infirmary (Cork) 86
of Ireland 69, 116, 120, 145
Northampton (diocese) 136
Northern Ireland 95, 98, 100, 137-44, 258, 266, 292; see also North of Ireland
Notes on the Orpheus of M. Salomon Reinach (book) 230, 279
Notre Dame (university, Indiana) 64, 128
Noyes, Alfred (writer) 65-7
N.U.I., see National University of Ireland
Nullity of marriage (book) 251
Nürenberg (Germany) 296
Nys, M. (philosopher) 136

Obermaier, Abbé Hugo (anthropologist) 236, 273
O'Brien, Conor Cruise (writer) 83-4
Professor George (economist) 82, 172
Fr James (dean of residence, U.C.C.) 308
Mrs Sophie (wife of William) 70, 80
M.P., William 69-70, 80
Judge William 210
Ó Broin, León (writer) 172
Observer (newspaper) 204, 206
Ó Cadhlaigh, Cormac (writer) 70
O'Carroll, C.S.Sp., Rev. Dr Michael (writer) 129, 131, 171, 198-200, 203, 207
O'Casey, Seán (playwright) 69, 72, 146
O'Connell, William Declan (journalist) 171-2
O'Connor, Frank (writer) 70
Ó Cuív, Shán (writer) 70

341

Alfred O'Rahilly III: Controversialist

O'Curry, Peadar (ed., *Standard*) 55, 83-4
O'Doherty, Rev. Professor E. F. (psychologist) 187
O'Donnell, Donat 83; see also O'Brien, Conor Cruise
O'Donnell, Peadar (writer) 61-2, 117
O'Donoghue, Eamon (lecturer, U.C.C.) 69-70
O'Donovan, Professor James M. 86
O'Driscoll, C.S.Sp., Fr Timothy 211-12
Ó Faoláin, Seán (writer) 70-1, 84, 112-17
O'Flaherty, Dr Kathleen (writer) 66-8, 83, 215-16, 308
O'Grady, S.J., Fr Michael (provincial) 132-4, 215
O'Hanlon, Fergal (I.R.A. activist) 137
O'Hara, Archbishop Gerald P. 130; see ill. 12
O'Kelly, Count Gerald 80
Ó Laoghaire, An tAthair Peadar (writer) 119
Old Limerick Journal 148
O'Mahony, Mrs Anna (friend of Alfred) 208
  Eoin (writer) 70, 172
  Frank (book-seller, Limerick) 55
  Timothy (friend of Alfred) 208, 210; see ill. 6
O'Malley, T.D., Donogh 158, 198
O'Meara, Professor John J. (writer) 189
O'Neill, Manus 84; see also O'Curry, Peadar
O'Neill, Bishop Patrick 183
O'Nolan, Brian (writer) 108; see also Myles na gCopaleen
O'Rahilly, Agnes (wife of Alfred) 128-9
  Professor Cecil (sister of Alfred) 128, 208, 210-11; see ill. 13
  Ena (sister of Alfred) 208
  O.C.S.O., Fr Michael Anthony (brother of Alfred) 134; see ill. 13
  Professor Ronan (son of Alfred) 90, 128, 210
  Professor T. F. (brother of Alfred) 70; see ill. 2

Orange Order 95, 116-17, 265
O'Reilly, Francis (sec., C.T.S.I.) 14, 41, 53-4
Origen (Latin Church Father) 256
Origin and growth of religion (book) 227, 274
O'Rourke, Dr P. D. (physician) 211
Orthodox Church 204
Orwell, George (writer) 61
Osborn, Professor H. F. (anthropologist) 234, 237-8, 278
O'Shiel, Mrs Cecil (friend of Alfred), 129
Osiris (mythological figure) 243, 246
O'Sullivan, S.J., Fr Donal 213
O.C.S.O., Fr Hilary (Mt St Joseph's, Roscrea) 134
Our Boys (comic) 73
Oxford (university, England) 62-4, 66, 106, 217, 239

Palace Theatre (Cork) 72
Palmyra (Palestine) 248
Pan (mythological figure) 299
Panacea (mythological figure) 299
Papal infallibility 15
Paris (France) 46-7, 76
Parker, Fr Anselm (writer) 136
  Bishop Leo 136
Parnell, M.P., Charles Stewart 127
Pasteur, Louis (scientist) 214
'Pat Murphy' column (*Standard*) 28, 61, 74, 82, 135, 202, 271
Patterns of sexual behaviour (book) 298
Pax Christi (a Christian organisation) 142-3
Pax Romana (U.C.D.) 189-90
Peet, Professor E. (Egyptologist) 243
Penguin (publisher) 260, 264
Pesch, S.J., Fr Christian (theologian) 130
Peter II (New Testament) 24
Petrus de Hibernia, O.P. (Peter from Ireland) 48
Philbin, Rev. Professor William J. (Maynooth) 81
Phillips, William (leader of Catholic Action) 172
Phoenix Park (Dublin) 13-14

Index

Pia, Secondo (photographer) 36
Picture Post (newspaper) 53-5, 224-6, 228-9, 232, 244, 249-50, 252, 256, 259-61, 266, 268-70, 276
Pilate, Pontius (Roman gov.) 137, 257, 270
Pioneer Total Abstinence Association 31, 36
Pius IX (pope) 15
  XI (pope) 301-3
  XII (pope) 20
Pliny (historian) 117
Plutarch (poet) 243
Pohle, J. and Preuss, A. (Pohle-Preuss) (theologians) 130
Poland (country) 21, 59
Pompeii (Italy) 248
Pontifical Academy of Sciences (Rome) 103
Portius Festus (Roman official) 256
Portland Row (Dublin) 171
Portugal (country) 201
Post-primary education in Ireland 1957-1970 (book) 197
Praetextatus (cemetry) 248
Presentation Sisters 31
Priestley, J. B. (writer) 39
Primitive man (periodical) 237
  man as philosopher (book) 275
  religion (book) 227
  revelation (book) 236
Principle of Subsidiarity (*Quadragesimo Anno*) 105
Prohibition (U.S.A.) 282
Proposals for improved and extended health services (pamphlet) 124
Protestant Truth Society 249
Protestants 21-5, 95, 97, 100-2, 107, 109, 114-16, 119, 126, 138, 140, 158, 160, 180, 183, 190, 193-4, 232, 239, 245, 258, 262, 264-5, 292
Proust, Marcel (writer) 111
Proverbs (*Old Testament*) 106-7
Psychology: empirical and rational (book) 305
Puritanism 64

Quadragesimo Anno (papal encyclical) 105, 124, 301

Quarryman (U.C.C. students' magazine) 84
Quarterly Review 297
Quebec province (Canada) 193
Queen's Colleges 89
  University of Belfast 162, 166, 187
Quinlan, Senator, Professor Patrick M. 168, 180; see ill. 9

Radbruch, Professor (Heidelberg) 100
Radin, P. (anthropologist) 274-5
Radio Éireann 13, 17, 34-5, 41, 49, 135, 171, 202, 216-17
Telefís Éireann 217
Rafroidi, Mrs Connie (sister of Alfred) 208
Randles, Sister Eileen (writer) 197
Raphoe (Donegal) 193
Rappoport, A. S. (writer) 232
Rathfarnham (Dublin) 132, 170
  Castle (Jesuit community) 132, 176
Rathnew (Wicklow) 172
Rawalpindi (Indian province) 38
Readers' News (organ of Readers' Union) 55
Readers' Union (U.K.) 55
Reformation, The 17, 24, 73, 205, 215
Reidy, T.D., Alderman James M. 148
Reinach, A. (writer) 228
Reinach, Salomon (writer) 279
Religion and conscience in ancient Egypt (book) 248
  and science (pamphlet) 19
Rembrandt (painter) 248
Renan, J. E. (writer) 220, 235, 241, 243, 259
Renouf, Professor Louis P. 133-4
Republic of Ireland 95, 116, 137, 139, 143, 145, 158
Republican Club (U.C.C.) 308
Rerum Novarum (papal encyclical) 85
Revisiting my pigmy hosts (book) 237
Revue Biblique 228
Rheims (France) 249
Ricciotti, Giuseppe (writer) 30
Rivers, W. H. R. (anthropologist) 274
Riviera (France) 239
Roche, Barney (businessman) 172
Rockwell College (Cashel) 28, 45
Roentgen, W. C. (scientist) 76, 304

Roman Rota (court) 252
Rome (Italy) 23, 25, 58, 131, 193, 195, 232, 245-6, 254
Rosary 13, 209, 214, 249
Roscrea (Tipperary) 134
Rose Tattoo (play) 146
Rosenberg, A. (writer) 265
Ross (diocese) 81
Eva J. (writer) 275
Rostov (Soviet Union) 61
Rousseau, J. J. (writer) 50, 301
Royal College of Science (Dublin) 156
College of Surgeons (Dublin) 188
Hospital (Sheffield) 90
Ulster Constabulary (R.U.C.) 137
University of Ireland 153, 155
Ruch, Mgr C. (theologian) 228
Russell, Bertrand (philosopher) 17, 40, 255
George (A.E., writer) 70, 82
Russia (country) 15, 59-62, 79, 202, 251; see also Soviet Union
Ryan, Mgr A. H. (writer) 39
Desmond (writer) 69-70
Dr James (min. for loc. govt. and pub. health) 87, 89-90, 124, 177, 289
Professor Mary 46, 66-7
S.C., Michael Joseph 176
W. P. (writer) 69-71
Rynne, Stephen (writer) 80

Sabatier, P. (writer) 244
Sacred Congregation for the Propagation of the Faith (Rome) 253
Congregation of Rites (Rome) 218
St Angela's College (Cork) 36
Athanasius 93
Augustine 82, 215
Bartholomew 66, 73
Bernadette Soubirous 34
Catherine of Siena 222
Catherine's Domestic Science College (Sion Hill) 170
Cosmas 37, 123, 125, 293, 304
Damian 37, 123, 125, 293, 304
Dominic 51
Francis of Assisi 35, 44, 220, 230
Francis Xavier 31, 171
Francis Xavier hall (Upper Sherrard Street) 31, 171

Gemma Galgani 221
Gregory the Great 132
Ignatius Loyola 305
Ignatius' House of Studies (Leeson Street) 305
Joan of Arc 66, 71-2
John's gospel (*New Testament*) 241-2, 256-7
John's Theatre (Tralee) 36
Joseph the Worker (feast-day) 171
Joseph's Home for the Aged (Portland Row) 171
Joseph's Young Priests' Society 172
Louis (Missouri) 91
Louis University 91
Luke 37, 123, 125, 242, 293, 304
Luke's gospel (*New Testament*) 242
Mary's College (Stonyhurst) 85
Mary's Dominican Convent (Belfast) 170
Mary's Hall (Belfast) 36
Mary's Hall (Stonyhurst) 305
Matthew's gospel (*New Testament*) 242, 257
Michael's Hospital (Dún Laoghaire) 210
Patrick 14, 27, 62, 81, 135
Patrick's Cathedral (Dublin) 27
Patrick's College (Maynooth) 81, 152
Paul 82, 228, 243, 245, 256
Peter 16, 254, 257, 282
Scholastica's Abbey (Teignmouth) 35, 129
Thérèse of Lisieux 131, 219
Thomas Aquinas 40, 47-51, 77-8, 81-2, 130
Vincent de Paul 36, 43, 130, 171
Vincent's Hospital (Dublin) 182
Sandy Row (Belfast) 117
Orange Hall 100
Sanscrit (language) 237
Sapir, E. (anthropologist) 274
Saunders, Edith (writer) 34
Savoy Cinema (Cork) 36-7
Schebesta, Fr P. (anthropologist) 237
Schmidt, S.J., Wilhelm (anthropologist) 226-7, 234, 236, 239, 271-4
School Attendance Bill (1943) 120-1
Schrödinger, Professor Erwin 76-9

Index

Scoileanna Réalta na Maidne (Listowel) 131
Seanad Éireann 167-8
Self help (book) 261
Sertillanges, O.P., Père A.D. (writer) 46
Set (mythological figure) 243, 246
Sexton Street (Limerick) 152
Shanahan, C.S.Sp., Bishop Joseph 133
Shannon (Clare) 193
 (river) scheme 208
Shaw, G. Bernard (writer) 58-61, 71-2, 226
Sheed, F. J. (writer) 251-2
Sheehan, Michael (lord mayor, Cork) 289
Sheehy, N.T., Frank (Listowel) 131
Sheehy Skeffington, Andrèe (writer) 91
Sheffield (England) 90
Shelbourne Hotel (Dublin) 171, 178
Sheridan, John D. (writer) 199
Sheridan, R. B. (playwright) 271
Shintoism 252
Shroud of Turin 36, 130, 170-1
Siena (Italy) 222
Simms, Archbishop George Otto 208
Sinn Féin 68-9, 73
Sion Hill Convent (Blackrock) 170
Siwek, S.J., Fr Paul (writer) 35, 218, 220
Skeff (book) 91
Sligo (town) 137
Smallways, Bert (*The war in the air*) 255
Smiles, Samuel (writer) 261
Smith, Sir F. E. 265
Smyllie, R. M. (ed., *Irish Times*) 92, 99-100, 105-6, 108, 119-21, 123; see also 'Nichevo'
Social origins (book) 275
 principles (pamphlet) 38
 Welfare Act (1952) 126, 177
Socialism 56, 254
Society of Catholic Medical Missionaries 38
 of Jesus 52, 73, 130, 133, 136, 190, 210, 213-15, 305-6
 of St Vincent de Paul 36, 43, 130
Solutré (excavation at) 238
Sophocles (playwright) 248
Socrates (philosopher) 242
Sorbonne (university, Paris) 63, 76; see also University of Paris
South, Seán (I.R.A. activist) 137
South Africa (country) 50, 81
South Cork Board of Public Assistance 87-90, 284-7
Southern Ireland – Church or State? (pamphlet) 119
Soviet communism: dictatorship or democracy? (book) 60
Soviet Union (country) 59, 61-2, 143, 145; see also Russia
Spain (country) 15, 21, 33, 75, 232-3, 258
Spanish civil war 76
 Inquisition 75-6
Special Powers Act (Northern Ireland) 265
Spectator (periodical) 22, 261
Spinoza (philosopher) 78
Stalin, Joseph (dictator) 60, 62, 102, 117, 119
Standard (newspaper) 13, 20-30, 34, 52, 54-5, 58, 61-2, 74-6, 83-5, 92, 99, 104-12, 117-19, 122-3, 126, 135, 146-7, 173, 201-2, 208, 224, 233, 239, 244, 250, 258, 268, 271, 278, 290, 293
Stanford, Professor W. B. 26-8
Staunton, Bishop James 199-200
Stepinac, Archbishop Aloysius 102
Stiggins, Rev Mr (attitude of) 266
Stockley, Professor W. F. P. 70, 81
Stonyhurst (near Blackburn) 85, 305
Stopes, Marie (writer on birth-control) 258
Strachey, John (writer) 55-8
Strassmaier, S.J., Fr J. N. (Assyriologist) 237
Strauss, D. F. (writer) 241, 243
Streatfield, G. S. (writer) 232
Student Christian Movement 172
Studies (periodical) 34, 107, 188, 190-1, 230
Suarez, S.J., Franciso (theologian) 73, 130
Summa Theologica (book) 48
Sunday Press (newspaper) 35, 124, 173

Sunday Times (newspaper) 66
Swanton, J. R. (anthropologist) 274
Swift, Jonathan (writer) 270-1
Switzerland (country) 91, 111
Syllabus or collection of modern errors (book) 15
Syriac (language) 130

Tacitus (Latin writer) 22, 117, 255
Taft, W. H. (U.S. ambassador) 128
Tanzania (country) 131
Tarsus (Asia Minor) 257
T.C.D.: a college miscellany (periodical) 28
Teeling, W. (writer) 231
Teevan, Mr Justice Thomas 161
Teignmouth (Devon) 35
Teodorowicz, Archbishop Josef 217, 221, 223
Teresa, O.S.B., Mother (St Scholastica's Abbey) 35, 129
Tertullian (Latin Father) 229, 242
Texas (U.S.A.) 74
The belief of Catholics (book) 24
The Bell (periodical) 67, 71, 83-4, 112-13, 117-18
The Bible 18, 24, 106-7
The Book of Joad (book) 296
The Bulpington of Bulp (book) 259
The Cambridge Ancient History (book) 243
The case of Thérèse Neumann (book) 35, 217
The Catholic Church against the twentieth century (book) 29
The Church and farming (book) 199
The conquest of disease: the story of penicillin (book) 34
The Crucified (book) 36, 174
The decay of the Church of Rome (book) 232
The descent of man (book) 297
The drums of Father Ned (play) 146
The embryonic human brain: an atlas of developmental stages (book) 91
The family at Bethany (book) 174
The fate of homo sapiens (book) 53, 55, 224-5, 227-9, 231-4, 236, 238-41, 243-4, 246, 249-50, 252, 254, 256, 258-61, 265-6, 268-9, 276, 280, 282-3
The future of science (book) 235
The framework of a Christian State (book) 202
The gap of brightness: lyrical poems (book) 29
The golden bough (book) 226-9, 234
The intellectual life: its spirit, conditions, methods (book) 46
The invisible man: the life and liberties of H. G. Wells (book) 53
The kingship of Christ according to the principles of St Thomas Aquinas (book) 199
The kingship of Christ and organised naturalism (book) 199
The kingship of Christ and the conversion of the Jewish nation (book) 199-200
The life of Christ (book) 30
The meaning of Christianity according to Luther and his followers in Germany (book) 242
The memory of our dead (book) 227, 230
The mind and its place in nature (book) 256
The mission of the university man (pamphlet) 46
The mystical body of Christ and the re-organisation of society (book) 199
The mystical body of Christ in the modern world (book) 199
The old stone age (book) 273
The open conspiracy (book) 251, 264, 279-81
The O'Rahilly (1916 leader) 209
The origin and growth of religion (book) 236
The origin of the species (book) 263
The outline of history (book) 230, 241-4, 246, 260, 265, 279, 281
The outlook for homo sapiens (book) 55
The pastoral letters and other writings of Cardinal Cullen . . . II (book) 193
The plough and the stars (play) 69

Index

The power and secret of the papacy (book) 15
The Practitioner (periodical) 298
The problem of man's ancestry (book) 234, 276
The Proclamation of 1916, 209
The religion of earliest man (pamphlet) 236
The religion of later primitive peoples (pamphlet) 236
The riddle of Konnersreuth, a psychological and religious study (book) 35
The rights of man (book) 54
The rulers of Russia (book) 199
The science of life (book) 276
The song of Bernadette (book) 34
The thirteenth, greatest of centuries (book) 81
The war in the air (book) 255
The work, wealth and happiness of mankind (book) 259
Theatre Royal (Dublin) 44
Theology (periodical) 20
Third Reich (Germany) 56
Thirty-Nine Articles (of Church of England) 21
Thomism (philosophical system) 83
Thompson, J. J. (scientist) 304
Thrift, T.D., William E. 44
Thurston, S.J., Fr Herbert 28, 227, 230
Tierney, Professor Michael 160-3, 174-82, 185-6, 197-8, 216; see ill. 15
Dr Niall (physician) 216
Tierra del Fuego (Argentina) 237, 239
Tillotson, J. (writer) 235
Times, The (newspaper) 206
Tipperary (county) 154-5, 287
North 155
South 287
To cure and to care: memoirs of a chief medical officer (book) 91
Tokyo (archdiocese) 253
Torca Hill (Dalkey) 59
'Tórna' (An tOllamh Tadhg Ó Donnchadha) 70
Tóstal, An (annual festival) 146-7
Totemism and exogamy (book) 227

Town Hall (Killarney) 36-7
Tralee (Kerry) 36
Trent, Council of (1545-63) 21
Trinity College, Dublin 26-7, 29, 50, 77, 104, 135, 159-60, 167, 172, 174, 178-86, 188-91, 194, 197-8, 212; see also University of Dublin
Trinity College, Dublin, 1592-1952: an academic history (book) 29, 158, 166
Truman, President Harry 202
Tullabeg (Offaly) 170, 213
Tuohy, Fr Patrick (dean of residence, U.C.D.) 186-7
Turin (Italy) 36, 130, 170
Turks 33
Tyndall, J. (writer) 282
Tyrol (Austria) 38
Tyrone (county) 142

Ulster (prov.) 119-20, 140, 142, 144-5, 265
Ulster Unionist Council 119-20
Ulysses (book) 146
Une stigmatisée de nos jours (book) 218
United Kingdom (U.K.) 64, 182; see also Great Britain
Nations (U.N.) 92, 139
States of America (U.S.A.) 21, 38, 62-3, 74, 82, 116, 122, 124, 128, 139, 143, 249, 263, 274, 282, 293
Universe (newspaper) 80
Université de Montpellier 91
University College, Cork (U.C.C.) 17, 29, 36-8, 41, 46-7, 53, 66, 69-70, 79, 81, 83-91, 93, 99, 106, 110-11, 123, 128-30, 132-4, 149-51, 153, 155-7, 162-5, 167-8, 170-1, 173, 176-80, 184, 187, 198, 202, 208, 210, 212-14, 216, 284-5, 288-90, 308
Medical School 86, 88-91, 165, 177
University College, Dublin 124, 150-2, 154, 156, 158, 160-7, 174-9, 181-91, 194, 197-8, 212, 307
Bill (1960) 161, 167-8
University College, Galway 50, 88, 151, 155, 162, 175-7, 184, 198
University College, Limerick 153

347

Alfred O'Rahilly III: Controversialist

University Education (Agriculture and Science) Act 1926, 156
University of California, Davis 91
of Dublin 160, 183, 197-8; see also Trinity College, Dublin
of Durham 90
of Fribourg (Switzerland) 91
of Glasgow 231
of Manchester 21
of Limerick Act (1989) 157
of Paris 76; see also Sorbonne
of Sheffield 90
Review 216
Unter Feuerland – Indianer (book) 237
Upper Sherrard Street (Dublin) 31
Upton lectures (Manchester College) 239
Ussher, Arland (writer) 83

van de Kamp, Peter (writer) 111
Vatican (Rome) 104, 122, 193, 195, 197, 205, 207, 215, 231, 235, 252-4
Council (I) 15, 231
(II) 193, 195, 197, 205, 207, 215
Veterinary College (Ballsbridge) 181-2
Veuillot, Louis (writer) 25
Vialleton, L. M. (anthropologist) 263, 273
Victoria, Queen (Brit.) 298
Vienna (Austria) 236
(university, Austria) 222
Völker und Kulturen (book) 236
Voltaire (literateure) 23, 54, 65-8, 83, 259, 294
Voltaire (book) 65-6
myth and reality (book) 66-7
von Harnack, A. (writer) 244
von Pastor, Ludwig (historian) 29
von Weisl, Dr Wolfgang (Jewish physician) 218
von Weiszäcker, C. (writer) 244

Walburga, Sister M. (sister of Alfred) 51; see ill. 2
Waldmann, Fr (writer) 218, 220
Walsh, James J. (writer) 81
Fr Timothy J. (writer) 32
Dr Tom (Agricultural Institute) 186
Archbishop William 190-1

Ward, T.D., Dr 288
Warnock, E. (att-gen., Northern Ireland) 100
Washington (U.S.A.) 237
Wasmann, E. (biologist) 236
Waterford (city) 149, 152 (county) 154, 287
Waugh, Evelyn (writer) 62-5
Wayne University 90
State University 90-1
Webb, Beatrice (writer) 60
Webb, D. A. (writer) 29
Webb, Sidney (writer) 60
Weismann, August (biologist) 134
Wells, Orson (film director) 74
G. P. (writer) 276
H. G. (writer) 40, 49, 53-5, 66, 81-3, 224-69, 271, 273-83
Wellsprings of the faith (book) 171
Weltgeschichte der Steinzeit (book) 273
Werfel, Franz (writer) 34
Wessely, Dr (orientalist) 222
Westminster (archdiocese) 65, 203
Westmoreland Street (Dublin) 100, 107, 147
What are we to do with our lives (book) 277, 280
What is life? The physical aspect of the living cell (book) 76
White, Mrs (lobbyist for easy divorce) 104-5
White, W. John (T.C.D.) 28-9
Who burnt Cork city? . . . (booklet) 262
Whyte, J. H. (writer) 91
Wicklow (county) 171-2
earl of 172
Wilberforce, Bishop Samuel 236
Wild West stories 75
Williams, Professor T. Desmond 127
Williams, Tennessee (playwight) 146
Wilton (Cork) 87-8, 284-5, 287
Wirceburgenses (theologians) 130
Wissler, C. (anthropologist) 274
Wolfe Tone (Republican) 102
Wood Jones, Professor F. (anthropologist) 234, 276
Woods, Thomas (civil servant and writer) 67-8

348

Index

World Health Organisation 298
Worshipful Company of Goldsmiths (London) 249
Wutz, Fr (friend of Thérèse Neumann) 222
Wycliff (Reformer) 72

Yale (university) 298
Yeats, W. B. (poet) 73, 82, 271
York (England) 20, 22, 104

Zoology . . . (book) 251, 263